Governance and Security Issues of the European Union

Jaap de Zwaan · Martijn Lak
Abiola Makinwa · Piet Willems
Editors

Governance and Security Issues of the European Union

Challenges Ahead

ASSER PRESS

Springer

Editors
Jaap de Zwaan
Faculty of Governance,
Law and Security (BRV)
The Hague University of Applied Sciences
The Hague
The Netherlands

Abiola Makinwa
Faculty of Governance,
Law and Security (BRV)
The Hague University of Applied Sciences
The Hague
The Netherlands

Martijn Lak
Faculty of Management & Organisation
The Hague University of Applied Sciences
The Hague
The Netherlands

Piet Willems
Faculty of Governance,
Law and Security (BRV)
The Hague University of Applied Sciences
The Hague
The Netherlands

ISBN 978-94-6265-143-2 ISBN 978-94-6265-144-9 (eBook)
DOI 10.1007/978-94-6265-144-9

Library of Congress Control Number: 2016951659

Published by T.M.C. ASSER PRESS, The Hague, The Netherlands www.asserpress.nl
Produced and distributed for T.M.C. ASSER PRESS by Springer-Verlag Berlin Heidelberg

Printed on acid-free paper

This Springer imprint is published by Springer Nature
The registered company is Springer-Verlag GmbH Germany
The registered company address is: Heidelberger Platz 3, 14197 Berlin, Germany

Contents

Editors and Contributors

About the Editors

Prof. Dr. Jaap de Zwaan is Lector European Integration at The Hague University of Applied Sciences, and Emeritus Professor of the European Union Law at Erasmus University Rotterdam. He started his career as a member of the Hague bar. Thereafter he served for nearly twenty years as a member of the Diplomatic Service of the Dutch Ministry of Foreign Affairs, where he worked notably in the domain of European integration, in The Hague (Policy Department European Integration and Legal Service) and Brussels (Permanent Representation of The Netherlands to the European Union). He was also the Director of the Netherlands Institute of International Relations, Clingendael, in The Hague for almost six years.

Martijn Lak, Ph.D. (1977) is a historian and Lecturer and Researcher at the Department of European Studies of The Hague University of Applied Sciences. He studied Journalism and History at the University of Applied Sciences Utrecht, and obtained his Ph.D. in 2011. He specialises in post-war Dutch-German economic and political relations and contemporary German history. In 2015 he published his book 'Tot elkaar veroordeeld. De Nederlands-Duitse economische en politieke betrekkingen tussen 1945–1957'. He regularly publishes in national and international academic journals and is a member of the editorial board of The Journal of Slavic Military Studies.

Abiola Makinwa, Ph.D. is Senior Lecturer at The Hague University of Applied Sciences. Her book, 'Private Remedies for Corruption: Towards an International Framework' (Eleven, 2013) focuses on the role of private actors and the importance of public/private dialogue in the fight against corruption. In 2013, Makinwa was awarded an EU OLAF Hercule II Grant to research European Perspectives on Negotiated Settlements for Corruption Offences. In 2014, she was appointed as the Dutch National Reporter, together with Prof. X. Kramer of Erasmus University, to report on 'Civil Law Consequences of Corruption in International Commercial Contracts' for the 19th Congress of the International Academy of Comparative Law.

Piet Willems is Lecturer in International and European Law at The Hague University of Applied Sciences, where he focuses on project-based learning, moot court coaching and competition law. His research activities focus on regulation in the European Union. He is also a member of the Board of Directors of the Ibero-American Institute of The Hague. Previously, Piet Willems was Assistant Professor at the Department of Public International Law at Ghent University and a member of the Board of Directors at the United Nations Association Flanders Belgium (VVN). He obtained both his Master's degree and his LL.M. in European Law from Ghent University.

Contributors

Chris Aalberts, Ph.D. is Lecturer in Political Communication at Erasmus University Rotterdam and Lecturer in Research Methods at The Hague University of Applied Sciences. He is working on a book on European politics and European journalism, which is planned for the end of 2016. He is a regular contributor on the European politics for 'The Post Online', a Dutch news and opinion web site. He wrote books on European Union democracy, social media and politics, spin doctoring and right-wing political parties.

Elif Erdemoglu, Ph.D. holds her doctorate degree from the DFG Graduate School in Law and Economics at the University of Hamburg in Germany, where she obtained scholarship from the German Research Association. She holds a triple Master's degree in Economic Analysis of Law from Manchester University, Hamburg University and Bologna University. She completed her Bachelor's degree in Law at Galatasaray University, Turkey. In 2014, she was a John M. Olin Fellow in Law and Economics at Harvard Law School. Dr. Erdemoglu is currently Lecturer at The Hague University of Applied Sciences, Netherlands.

Geor Hintzen (1960) (Ph.D.) studied Chinese and Law at Leiden University, the Netherlands and has a Ph.D. in Chinese Politics (Imagining Political Science, 1998). He subsequently worked for 14 years at the Dutch Immigration and Naturalisation Service, where he established a Language Analysis Bureau and served as a senior advisor to the director of asylum matters. After serving as a researcher at the Dutch Advisory Commission for Alien Affairs, he coordinated research on governance and security at The Hague University for Applied Sciences. At present he is a senior researcher on international affairs and areas studies, covering Europe, the Middle East, and South and East Asia.

Helen Kopnina (Ph.D. Cambridge University, 2002) is a coordinator and Lecturer of Sustainable Business program, and a researcher in the fields of environmental education and environmental social sciences at The Hague University of Applied Science in the Netherlands. She also lectures on anthropology and development and environmental anthropology at the Leiden Institute of Cultural Anthropology and Development Sociology at the Leiden University. Kopnina is the author of over sixty peer-reviewed articles and (co) author and (co) editor of twelve books, including Sustainable Business: Key Issues (2014); Sustainability: Key Issues (2015); Culture and Conservation: Beyond Anthropocentrism (2015) and Handbook of Environmental Anthropology (2016).

Chris Koppe holds a Master's degree in Law and a Bachelor's degree in Arts. He worked as a lecturer/researcher in European Union Law at Erasmus University, Rotterdam and at The Hague University of Applied Sciences. He participated in the EU-28 Watch-project (Issue No. 10), the Jean Monnet Centre of Excellence of Leiden University Campus in The Hague, and still participates in the Research Group on European Integration. Before that, he took an internship at an international law firm and worked as a paralegal. Currently, he has his own consultancy firm and gives lectures in European Union Law at Utrecht University.

Margriet Krijtenburg, Ph.D. is Senior Lecturer at the Faculty of Management and Organisation/European Studies and member of the research group on European Integration of The Hague University of Applied Sciences. She is also a Visiting Professor at l'Université de Lorraine, Nancy, Département de Droit, Master Programme. She obtained her Ph.D. on 'Schuman's Europe, His Frame of Reference' from Leiden University in 2012. Margriet Krijtenburg also supervises the Annual Schuman Student Congress & Essay Competition in close co-operation with Dr. Jaap de Zwaan, the Polish Student Association and students from The Hague University of Applied Sciences. She frequently gives conferences about Schuman and his ideas about European unification in The Netherlands and abroad.

Santino Lo Bianco, Ph.D. is Lecturer at The Hague University of Applied Sciences since 2001, where he specialises in law and governance in the EU. He also delivered lectures on European politics and integration at the University of Amsterdam. Before he started teaching, he worked for six years at an autonomous institute commissioned by the Netherlands Foreign Affairs Ministry to deliver reports, studies and seminars on international and transatlantic security issues. His contributions there were mainly in the field of common foreign, security, defence and external relations policies of the EU. In 2015, Lo Bianco received his Ph.D. in social science from the VU University of Amsterdam. The subject of his Ph.D. research was the (discursive) origins of policy change in the everyday practice of decision-making in the European Union.

Stefania Marassi is lecturer in International and European Law at The Hague University of Applied Sciences, and specialises in "EU Employment Law" and "International Labour Law". She published the book "Globalization and Transnational Collective Labour Relations. International and European Framework Agreements at Company Level" in 2015. In the same year, she was invited to deliver a presentation and participate in experts meetings organised by the European Trade Union Confederation (ETUC). Stefania Marassi obtained her LL.M. *cum laude* in 'International and European Labour Law' at Tilburg University. She previously worked in different institutions, such as the Clean Clothes Campaign and the International Criminal Tribunal for the Former Yugoslavia.

Zahra Mousavi joined the Law Faculty of The Hague University of Applied Sciences in 2011, where she gives advanced seminars in International and EU Law. Ms. Mousavi received a Hijmansbeurs in 2012 to conduct a research program at the University of Amsterdam. She worked at the Iran United States Tribunal between 1998 and 2011, and has acted as legal assistant in some international ad hoc arbitrations. Earlier still and when she was in Iran, Ms. Mousavi worked for Iran's Bureau of International Legal Services, where she dealt with Iran's cases before the United Nations Compensation Commission, and was additionally involved in the distribution of compensations paid by the United States to the victims of the 1988 Aerial Incident. She is the author and co-author of a number of articles in scholarly journals, and the co-translator of a textbook regarding International Criminal Law.

Moritz Pieper, Ph.D. is Lecturer in International Relations at the University of Salford, Manchester. He has been a visiting Research Fellow at China Foreign Affairs University in Beijing, German Institute for International and Security Affairs in Brussels and the School of Oriental and African Studies in London. He holds a bachelor in European Studies from Maastricht University, a Masters in International Relations in Euro-Atlantic and Eurasian Communities from the Higher School of Economics in Moscow and a Masters and International Relations from the University of Kent where he also got his Ph.D. He has published in European Foreign Affairs Review, the European Journal of East Asian Studies and International Politics among others.

René Repasi, Ph.D. is scientific coordinator of the European Research Centre for Economic and Financial Governance (EUROCEFG) of the Universities of Leiden, Delft and Rotterdam. He studied law at the Universities of Heidelberg and Montpellier. He has been an Assistant Professor at the University of Heidelberg and senior researcher at the Institute for German and European Corporate and Economic Law. He has worked for the European Commission and at the European Court of Justice during his legal clerkship. He was also appointed as a legal expert for the European Parliament on the banking union and on the EU constitutional questions relating to economic governance. He published in several English, French and German law journals about the legal issues in the European Union.

Peter Steenwijk read History and Law at Leiden University and studied Middle Eastern Studies at the Hebrew University of Jerusalem. He has been working as a consultant for Ernst and Young and TEC. Since 2013, he is Senior Lecturer on risk management, corporate governance and compliance at The Hague University of Applied Sciences. As a researcher he is especially interested on the risk-based combat of money laundering and terrorist financing.

Ernst E. van Bemmelen van Gent graduated in law at the University of Amsterdam, the Netherlands. He received a cum-laude post-graduate degree (LL.M.) from the University of Dresden, Germany. As licensed attorney-at-law (in Dutch: advocaat), he builds on his commercial law experience in the past, and focusses on his special interest in governmental regulation of markets and corresponding compliance. Prior to becoming a lawyer, he served as assistant to Prof. Peter Hay in Dresden. Currently, he is a part-time lecturer at Utrecht University, and a part-time researcher at The Hague University of Applied Sciences. He was an initiator, designer, lecturer and program manager of the International Bachelor of Law Program of The Hague University of Applied Sciences. He was also a course manager of the Master of Arts in European Law and Policy, a combined degree, at the University of Portsmouth, UK.

Chapter 1
Introduction

Jaap de Zwaan, Martijn Lak, Abiola Makinwa and Piet Willems

Abstract This book collects a bundle of articles related to the governance and/or the security dimensions of the European Union (EU) cooperation. Europe faces serious challenges, such as the economic crisis, migration, tensions at the external borders, terrorism, and climate as well as the environment. All challenges have in common that they are related to 'security'. They thus have an impact on the stability of our continent. In order to cope with the challenges and to safeguard our basic values of peace and prosperity, the EU has to (re-)organise the governance and security infrastructures regarding its principles, procedures and policies.

Keywords Global challenges · Governance · Security · EU co-operation: principles, procedures and policies

Contents

J. de Zwaan (✉) · M. Lak · A. Makinwa · P. Willems
The Hague University of Applied Sciences, The Hague, The Netherlands
e-mail: dezwaan@law.eur.nl

M. Lak
e-mail: m.lak@hhs.nl

A. Makinwa
e-mail: a.o.makinwa@hhs.nl

P. Willems
e-mail: P.Willems@hhs.nl

J. de Zwaan et al. (eds.), *Governance and Security Issues of the European Union*, DOI 10.1007/978-94-6265-144-9_1

At present, Europe is confronted with a number of serious common and global challenges, the most important being the economic crisis, migration issues, tensions at its external borders, terrorism, as well as climate change and environmental challenges. These developments have a huge impact on the stability and security of the continent as a whole and on each individual European country.

Europe, more particularly the European Union (EU), has to organise its governance and security infrastructure in such a way that it can cope with the global threats just mentioned. In so doing, Europe has to do its utmost to have its basic values of peace and prosperity guaranteed for the time to come.

Since 2008, the economic crisis dominates the EU agenda. In the aftermath of the developments having their origin in the American financial infrastructure, the EU has been hit by respectively the banking crisis, country crises and, more recently, the euro crisis. Several Member States are still suffering from these events, with high unemployment rates, notably with regard to the younger generation. The question arises how to stimulate more opportunities for investments and how to create new economic activities and jobs, in order to develop more economic growth.

For the last three years, the European Union has had to deal with the migration problem. The massive influx of migrants has its origin in failed states and unstable regions surrounding us, in the Middle East, Asia and Africa. Thousands and thousands of people have been forced to leave their homes and countries, looking for protection and/or a better future in Europe. We have been confronted with outraging scenes of migrants drowned in the Mediterranean or smuggled to Europe after having paid high prices. The European Union clearly was not prepared to deal with these massive influxes. In fact, it was caught by surprise by these events. Although an EU Asylum and Migration system does exist, experience has demonstrated that the present policies suffer from many deficiencies and have to be improved urgently.

It is not only the migration crisis that puts the external borders of Europe under pressure. These days there are also geopolitical tensions at Europe's Eastern borders, in the Middle East and North Africa. The tensions in the East are connected particularly to the Russia-Ukraine conflict, which started in 2014 with the Russian annexation of Crimea and the violence in the Eastern Donbas region. On top of this, the turmoil in the Middle East, more particularly the ongoing conflict between Israelis and Palestinians, has not come to an end. Lastly, the so-called Arab Spring which started at the end of 2010, turned out to become a severe winter. The protests and demonstrations gave rise to conflicts and changes in government in several Mediterranean countries, with the horrifying civil war in Syria and the political instability and chaos in Libya as tragic culminating points.

The background of terrorism is certainly connected with poverty and civil unrest in unstable parts of the world. Europe, as one of the rare peaceful and stable islands on our planet, undergoes the consequences of instabilities, notably in the Middle East, Asia and Africa. Terrorist organisations like Al-Qaeda and IS (Islamic State of Iraq and the Levant) manifest themselves on a regular basis, with ruthless attacks often conducted on innocent citizens causing hundreds—not to say thousands—of casualties. Most recently, Europe has been severely shocked by the terrorist attacks in Paris on 13 November 2015 and in Brussels on 22 March 2016. These atrocities clearly have served as a wake-up call to intensify co-operation between police and intelligence services of the Member States.

Finally, the world faces the consequences of scarcity, draught, poverty and lack of natural resources, which in fact are the most global of all threats. Essentially the future of mankind, more particularly of the generations yet to come, is at stake here. The overarching topic is related to climate change and, in close connection with that phenomenon, the protection of our planet and environment. In that respect, the Paris Agreement of December 2015 is of utmost importance. During the discussions and negotiations in the run-up to that agreement, the delegations of the EU and its Member States have often played a positive and constructive role.

What all the aforementioned threats and challenges have in common is that they are all related to "security" in the widest sense. In order to deal with these issues, the EU and its Member States have to put their respective systems of "governance" in order. At the same time, the tendencies provide an impressive, but also complicated agenda for EU co-operation in the future. Clearly, choices have to be made. To put it more bluntly, the position of the EU as a credible and reliable global player is at stake here. Therefore, Member States have to make up their mind on whether to confer more responsibilities to the European level or, at least, to coordinate their policies in the aforesaid areas more structurally and more intensively.

This book collects a number of topics and themes connected to the abovementioned global themes. The initiative for writing the book originates from the Research Group European Integration of The Hague University of Applied Sciences, led by the first editor of the book, Prof. Jaap de Zwaan. Together with a group of close colleagues from the University, complemented by a number of external guest contributors, a bundle of articles has been composed, focusing on a number of topical issues and policies related to the governance and/or security dimensions of EU co-operation.

The Parts of the book deal respectively with: the values and general principles of EU co-operation; institutional aspects of EU co-operation; a number of individual policy domains; areas of European criminal law; the external relations of the EU; and the future functioning of EU co-operation as a whole.

1.1 Values and Principles

The First Part deals with the values and general principles of EU co-operation.

In Chap. 2, Martijn Lak addresses the reaction of the Netherlands and the Federal Republic of Germany to the creation of the Schuman Plan from an integration point of view. This contribution highlights the different reasons that initially motivated each state to join the early years of European Integration. Whereas the

Netherlands had essentially economic goals in mind and rejected political integration, Germany's motive to join the Schuman Plan was essentially politically driven.

Margriet Krijtenburg in Chap. 3 explores the current challenges of the European Union and discusses how Schuman would have reacted to them had he still been alive. The article digs into the personality and the Catholic background of Schuman as a driving factor explaining his search for the European Common Good, and applies his views on current topical issues.

In Chap. 4, Piet Willems focuses on the Better Regulation Agenda (BRA) of the European Commission and its significance from an institutional point of view. Basing its analysis on core institutional concepts (such as representative democracy, effectiveness, and the position of the Committee of Regions and the European Economic and Social Committee), this chapter looks into the implications of the BRA on EU policy and decision-making.

1.2 Institutional Aspects

The Second Part discusses institutional aspects of EU co-operation. As is well known, the effectiveness of EU co-operation depends on, to a large extent, the functioning of the institutions.

Santino Lo Bianco analyses the EU in Chap. 5 from the perspective of democratisation. Although the democratic character of EU policy making has positively evolved with the ever-increasing responsibilities of the European Parliament, the development of the so-called "trialogue" negotiations have restricted decision-making to a limited number of participants. Analysing democratisation from the perspective of deliberative democracy, this chapter examines to what extent this practice impedes democratic decision-making. The author argues that the practice of "trialogues" should be improved in order to effectively lead to better legislation, while ensuring that decisions taken are carefully motivated and explained to the public afterwards.

In Chap. 6, Chris Aalberts analyses the role of the media from the perspective of providing sufficient information to citizens in order for them to exert influence on the policies of European institutions. While citizens, generally speaking, lack information on European affairs, the author argues that the media fail largely to inform the public on European undertakings. On this basis, this chapter argues that the five principles formulated by Gadi Wolfsfeld—in principle mainly intended to address national political communications—may be applied to European politics as well. The author argues that all principles have a clear relationship with the lack of media coverage of EU affairs, by presenting two case studies.

In Chap. 7, Elif Erdemoglu analyses the discussion on the EU citizens' right to privacy from a law and economics perspective. Focusing on the General Data Protection Regulation (GDPR) of 27 April 2016, this chapter argues that in order to enhance the EU Digital Single Market Strategy, it is essential to increase the citizen's trust in using digital services. This could be achieved by providing the citizens with more information on the service provider's use of citizens' data. The author concludes that three improvements could be made to the GDPR: more frequent controls for issuing EU Data Protection Seal; increased independence of the Data Protection Officer; and issuance of publicly available, frequent privacy ratings.

1.3 Policy Domains

The Third Part of the book deals with individual policy domains, each of them being of fundamental importance for the EU co-operation at present and in the future.

René Repasi in Chap. 8 focuses on the Economic and Monetary Union (EMU), introduced by the Maastricht Treaty and highlights its weaknesses. In light of the Member States' spending policies following the recent economic crisis, the establishment of a European Redemption Fund (ERF) is proposed as a solution to oblige over-indebted Member States to transfer and redeem their debts within a fixed period of time. The author argues that the implementation of the ERF does not require a treaty amendment and also does not violate the "no bail-out" clause.

Chapter 9, written by Zahra Mousavi, addresses the weaknesses of the current Dublin III system in light of the Syrian mass influx migration. The author argues that none of the measures proposed so far by Member States and the EU offers a proper response to the Syrian massive migration. Noting that the EU failed to address this issue and that the current mass influx is fundamentally different from previous migrations, the author argues that the Dublin System needs to be reformed substantially.

In Chap. 10, Helen Kopnina analyses the European Union Energy Policy and the objective of the European Commission to create an Energy Union, aimed at ensuring that Europe benefits from secure, affordable and climate-friendly energy. Analysing the pro and con arguments related to the impact of transformative measures such as Circular Economy and Cradle to Cradle approach on sustainability, the author discusses the challenges posed to the European Union Energy policy. Exploring the EU's current energy policy, the chapter proposes recommendations for long-term sustainability.

In Chap. 11, Stefania Marassi centres around European framework agreements at company level (EFAs) as potential contributors to attain the employment-related objectives laid down in the EU 2020 Strategy. While analysing the EFAs concluded between the launch of the EU 2020 Strategy in March 2010 and April 2015, the author examines whether the topics touched upon by the signatory parties of these agreements align with the EU 2020 Strategy's employment-related objectives.

1.4 European Criminal Law

The Fourth Part focuses on aspects of European criminal law.

Chapter 12, written by Peter Steenwijk, focuses on money laundering, more particularly on the impact of the new Anti-Money Laundering Directive of 20 May 2015. While raising issues when it comes to over-regulation, compliance costs or privacy protection, the Directive has the merit to provide a new framework to Member States in the fight against corruption. The author argues that the mandatory application of the risk-based approach can have an impact as to how Member States will calibrate their policies and resources. The chapter proposes the adoption of a flexible anti-money laundering control model that can be used by national authorities to map, manage and evaluate their money laundering risks in accordance with the requirements of the new directive.

In Chap. 13, Ernst E. van Bemmelen van Gent focuses on the unwanted effects of criminal sanctions taken against personnel of regulated financial institutions for crimes, such as insider trading and market manipulation under Article 83(2) TFEU. Because the financial sector is increasingly faced with surveillance mechanisms giving rise to the imposition of administrative sanctions, the author argues that the EU should refrain from further harmonising national criminal law and sanctions in this area. Instead, the current framework should be used to stimulate institutions to better innovate and correct behaviours using the concept of "learning organisation." This chapter further addresses the issue of *ne bis in idem* and *nemo tenetur* when accused employees both face administrative and criminal sanctions.

Abiola Makinwa argues that effective anti-corruption enforcement is essential to achieving justice, freedom and security in the EU. In Chap. 14, she examines the spread of US-style negotiated settlements for corruption offences. She also examines the implications of the absence of an EU dimension on this best practice. The author analyses the legal scope for a possible EU regime on negotiated settlements and the compatibility of such a regime with guaranteed rights and freedoms. The author argues that introducing a European dimension on negotiated settlements will not only give Europe and its Member States an important strategic tool to realise effective anti-corruption enforcement within the EU, but also a stronger voice in shaping the growing global practice of negotiated settlements for corruption offences.

1.5 External Relations

The Fifth Part deals with a number of topics related to the external relations of the EU.

In Chap. 15, Moritz Pieper discusses the Common Foreign and Security Policy (CFSP) rules, procedures and areas of application. This chapter analyses more particularly the post-Lisbon CFSP arrangements, and shows that the current framework lacks necessary institutional consolidation. The author assesses the CFSP in light of current challenges such as the Arab Spring, the war in Syria as well as the "Ukraine crisis." It is questionable, he contends, whether the tools provided for in the Treaties and the European diplomatic machinery truly enhance the EU's external capacity to act. The author argues that the EU's credibility rests upon its ability to formulate common policies and to sustain them against third parties in order to see European foreign policy implemented beyond declaratory rhetoric.

In light of the modest achievements of the Common Foreign and Defence Policy (CFDP) since 2003, Geor Hintzen in Chap. 16 argues that a new and effective CFDP strategy has to be developed. The author contends that the CFDP has not evolved, while the world has faced dramatic changes, such as the situations in Libya, Ukraine and Syria. The recent terrorist attacks in Paris and Brussels as well as other internal challenges such as the economic crisis, shed the light on the incapacity of the EU and its Member States to act and to formulate joint, common priorities. In this perspective, this chapter proposes new elements on which an effective EU global foreign and defence strategy could be based.

In Chap. 17, Chris Koppe depicts the EU's struggle to secure its supply of natural resources. Although shaped in order to address a wide range of policies, the EU possesses only limited competences to deal with current threats and challenges regarding natural resources. In order to meet these threats and challenges, the author argues that the EU should develop an inclusive, coherent and long-term structural policy on natural resources. At the moment, however, no sufficient legal bases exist under the Treaties to shape such a policy. The author, therefore, advocates in favour of a number of treaty amendments to deal more effectively with the current threats and challenges regarding natural resources the EU is faced with.

1.6 The Future of EU Co-operation

The Sixth and final Part discusses a number of questions related to the future functioning of the EU co-operation. The focus here is on models of differentiation, flexibility and simplification.

As such, Jaap de Zwaan in Chap. 18 offers proposals on the topical issue of the evolution of the EU integration process. Supporting his analysis on the current state of play, the author argues that flexibility is a key element in the discussion regarding the deepening and continuation of the overall EU integration process in the future. In this perspective differentiation and, more specifically, the principle of enhanced co-operation, can play a major role. On the other hand, the author holds the view that while flexibility is a necessary element in the future development of the EU, a minimum set of standards must be respected by all Member States and yet-to-be acceding states. On this particularly, the question arises whether a "minimum *acquis*" should not be implemented for all applicant countries in order to allow for sufficient flexibility, and yet have a common, non-derogable set of basic rules and policies. De Zwaan also submits proposals for a new simplified treaty amendment procedure.

The editors and all other authors are extremely grateful to Mathilde Renou and Christine Mandap, both law students at The Hague University of Applied Sciences, for their precious work regarding the proofreading of all contributions to the book. Their patience and scrupulous activities have enabled the book project to proceed smoothly.

All in all, this book collects a number of contributions dealing with important and serious law and policy issues to secure a safe future for our society. In the absence of effective governance mechanisms developed at an international level, it is essentially up to regional frameworks to handle these matters and to find adequate solutions for them. The EU, with its unique structures and characteristics as to decision-making and sharing of competences and responsibilities, is well placed to play a major role in this process, to secure sustainable peace and stability, at least on the European continent.

Part I
Values and Principles

Chapter 2
The Early Years of European Integration—German and Dutch Reactions to the Schuman Plan

Martijn Lak

Abstract On 9 May 1950, Robert Schuman, the French minister of Foreign Affairs, launched his daring and—to many contemporaries—shocking plan to put the Franco-German production of coal and steel as a whole under a common High Authority. By doing so, he not only hoped to prevent war in Europe in the future, but also started the process of European integration. How did the Netherlands and the Federal Republic of Germany (FRG) react to this controversial plan and why did they decide to join the European integration process? This chapter claims that although there were a number of similarities between Bonn and The Hague, they had different reasons for joining the European integration process from the start. For the FRG, it was mainly a way to regain its sovereignty and to be seen as a normal state again. For The Netherlands, however, the reasons seem mostly to have been economic. By integrating Germany into the Western block, Europe and especially The Netherlands could profit from Germany's economic potential, while at the same time preventing the country from becoming a military threat ever again. It also explains the Dutch resistance towards more political integration. In fact, the Dutch government remained anti-supranational well into the 1950s. The Dutch European policy, especially in the early years, was driven primarily and maybe even exclusively, by economic considerations, whereas that of the Federal Republic was above all inspired by political motives.

Keywords (West) Germany · The Netherlands · Allied policy · Schuman Plan · Economic relations · Foreign policy · Supranationalism · European Coal and Steel Community · High Commission

M. Lak (✉)
Faculty of Management and Organisation, The Hague University of Applied Sciences, Room U.37, Johanna Westerdijkplein 75, 2521 EN The Hague, The Netherlands
e-mail: m.lak@hhs.nl

J. de Zwaan et al. (eds.), *Governance and Security Issues of the European Union*, DOI 10.1007/978-94-6265-144-9_2

Contents

2.1 Introduction

The European Union is going through a severe crisis. First hit by the debt crisis of 2008, it now faces a growing number of "Eurosceptics," the "Brexit," and above all a seemingly uncontrollable number of refugees desperately trying to reach and enter the Continent. This forces the EU, despite growing resistance, to further deepen the integration process, as these problems cannot be solved at a national level. For example, the EU now has a permanent fund to help member states that are in financial troubles, the so-called European Stability Mechanism.[1] Prior to 2008, this would have been unthinkable.[2] However, at the moment, national interests seem to prevail over those of the European Union as a whole.

What were the opinions of the Founding Fathers of the European integration in the first years after the Second World War? Ideas of such a process were not new in 1945. In the wake of the destruction of World War I, Louis Loucheur, a French businessman who had become minister in the French cabinet during the *Mutterkatastrophe*, suggested creating international coal and steel cartels. He did so not only for economic reasons, but most importantly to shift control of essential basic industries "from emotional nationalist warmongers to the rational, international business community."[3] This could also end the German threat to Europe.[4]

During World War II, a number of Dutch illegal newspapers advocated a new, higher, supranational institution to organise the peace after the demise of the Third Reich, that would at the same time allow Germany to retake its central position as the economic heart of Europe.[5] For example, the illegal, left-wing Protestant *Vrij Nederland—Free Netherlands*—stated on 5 July 1943, the starting day of the last great German offensive on the Eastern Front, that economic reorganisation of Europe was necessary.[6]

[1] See European Security Mechanism website 2015.

[2] de Bruijn 2013, p. 7.

[3] Klemann 2010, p. 78.

[4] de Wagt 2015.

[5] Lak 2010, p. 408.

[6] *Vrij Nederland*, 5 July 1943.

After the end of hostilities in Europe in May 1945, multiple ideas on co-operation with regard to coal and steel were going around, especially at the end of the 1940s, both from the French as well as from the Americans. In March 1949, the future first *Bundeskanzler*, Konrad Adenauer, stated in two much-discussed interviews that he did not only opt for a full-fledged union between Germany and France, but also for "*ein verschmelzen der beiden Länder in bezug auf Zölle und Wirtschaft*."[7]

However, the first specific proposal was that of the French minister of Foreign Affairs, Robert Schuman, dated 9 May 1950, almost five years to the day after the end of World War II. Although there is some discussion as to who actually initiated the plan—most historians say it was the French official Jean Monnet,[8] head of the French Planning Bureau, who wanted "to submerge Germany in international structures, thus providing the stability and prosperity in Western Europe and simultaneously ensuring France's security,"[9] while others state it was Schuman's idea from the start[10]—the plan addressed the core question after World War II: what to do with Germany? How to ensure its economic integration into Europe without it ever becoming a military threat again? European integration seemed to offer an opportunity.

Schuman proposed to put the Franco-German production of coal and steel as a whole under a common High Authority, within the framework of an organisation open to the participation of other democratic European countries. According to Schuman:

"The pooling of coal and steel production should immediately provide for the setting up of common foundations for economic development as a first step in the federation of Europe, and will change the destinies of those regions which have long been devoted to the manufacture of munitions of war, of which they have been the most constant victims. The solidarity in production thus established will make it plain that any war between France and Germany becomes not merely unthinkable, but materially impossible. By pooling basic production and by instituting a new High Authority, whose decisions will bind France, Germany and other member countries, this proposal will lead to the realisation of the first concrete foundation of a European federation indispensable to the preservation of peace."[11]

Schuman's plan took almost everyone by surprise. It came as a true shock, even in France itself,[12] as Schuman had hardly told anyone about his plan except, interestingly, Adenauer on 7 May 1950, who reacted very positively.[13]

7 "A merger of the two countries with regard to customs and economy." As quoted by Lappenküper 1994, p. 407.

8 See for example Judt 2007, p. 156; Milward 1984, p. 395.

9 Stone 2014, p. 74.

10 Krijtenburg 2012, pp. 118–119; Krijtenburg 2015, p. 148.

11 Schuman 1950.

12 Harryvan and Van der Harst 2008, p. 125.

13 Segers 2013, p. 75.

The Netherlands and West Germany participated from the start in this process of European integration, although the latter did so more enthusiastically than the former. Why did they do so? For both countries this development was something that above all just seemed to happen to them, without much planning.[14] With hindsight, the reasons to join the European integration process are clear: the developing Cold War, the need to rebuild the shattered Continent, and the material and economic advantages. This article analyses the differences and similarities between The Netherlands and West Germany in their policy towards the ideas of European integration. It starts with a sketch of the economic situation in Europe in the early post-war years and the ideas of the Allies with regard to Germany's future, so as to provide a context for the developments after World War II. As such, this article focuses on the 1945–1950 period. Secondly, it analyses the reaction of West Germany and especially The Netherlands on the announcement of the Schuman Plan.

2.2 Europe and Germany in Shambles

On 8 May 1945, people in large parts of Europe swept to the streets to celebrate feverously the Allied victory over Nazi Germany and the formal end of World War II.[15] At the same time, the Continent was in ruins and millions of its inhabitants were adrift. Inflation ran rampant, cities had been obliterated, millions of forced labourers were returning home. Europe's trade had come to a standstill and "resembled a spaghetti bowl of more than two hundred bilateral arrangements."[16] The Allied bombing campaign had inflicted extensive damage to the German infrastructure. In the last year of the war, Allied planes roaming the skies by the thousands, had bombed German roads, bridges and rails with impunity. Ninety percent of the country's rail network was either blocked by wrecked rolling stock or rendered impassable by bomb damage to the tracks.[17] The river Rhine, the most important European waterway, was "one big ruin of blown bridges, distorted steel constructions, wrecks and debris, on which all shipping has become impossible."[18] Only one bridge across the Rhine remained intact.[19] More importantly, however, was the fact that Germany, the dominant economic power in Europe since the late nineteenth century, had ceased, at least temporarily, to be an independent, sovereign nation. This slowed and severely threatened Europe's economic recovery.

[14] This point has especially been brought forward by Segers 2013, p. 10.

[15] The mood of exaltation is described very well by Buruma 2013, especially Chap. 1.

[16] Eichengreen 2007, p. 73.

[17] *Ibid.*, pp. 54–55.

[18] As quoted by Lak 2015a, b, p. 79.

[19] Judt 2007, p. 82.

The core of the German economic problem and in its wake European problem lay in the fact that the industrial area of the Ruhr was at a standstill. Although industrial damage from Allied bombing was limited, production was low because the Ruhr was isolated from the rest of Germany and Europe. The transport of vital raw materials was impossible for a long time.[20] It meant, for example, that the Ruhr could not be supplied with food and clothing.[21] The problems in infrastructure had an immense and acute impact on the economy of occupied Germany. The occupying authorities had seized most available means of transport and capacity dropped to a minimum. For example, by 1947, the number of serviceable locomotives in the Bizone—the fusion of the American and British occupation zones as of 1 January 1947—had dropped from almost 9,000 in 1936 to 6,821, or just 76%, whereas the percentage of serviceable passengers' wagons was only 59% of the 1936 figure. Moreover, there were fewer foreign ships on the Rhine and they were seldom admitted to the internal German waterways. Germany was not the only country dependent on Ruhr coal; many other parts of Europe were as well.[22] Before the war, the Ruhr—the industrial heart of Europe, but also the weapon blacksmith of the Reich—had supplied coal to a major part of Europe.[23] This meant that the problems in Germany always had immense European-wide repercussions.

2.3 The Future of Germany?

Germany's future was *the* central question in Europe after the end of hostilities in May 1945. The main problem was that the Allies that now occupied the former Third Reich differed strongly on the topic and all had a veto in their own occupation zone. This made the creation of central German institutions all but impossible, and deepened the gulf between the various zones.[24] The division of the country shattered its pre-war economic unity. As a number of Dutch and German historians have stated, the Allied trade policy was not based on economic considerations.[25] According to the Dutch economist Jozias Wemelsfelder, the general trend seemed to be to try "to keep Germany small and broken."[26] The Allies were primarily concerned with their own interests and not those of Germany, the Germans or its neighbouring countries.

20 Reichardt and Zierenberg 2009, p. 71.

21 Schlieper 1986, p. 149.

22 Abelshauser 1984, p. 7.

23 Rombeck-Jaschinski 1990, p. 11.

24 Abelshauser 2004, p. 66.

25 Wemelsfelder 1954, pp. 3–4; Kleßmann 1991, p. 46; Abelshauser 2004, p. 87.

26 *Ibid.*, Wemelsfelder 1954, p. 4.

As the Allies were unable to reach agreement on the future of Germany and the creation of joint German economic institutions, the occupation authorities only paid attention to matters relevant to their own zones. According to the Potsdam Agreement, the responsibility for the implementation of the treaty would be in the hands of the Allied Control Council (ACC), the supreme authority in occupied Germany. It should govern Germany as a united country and treat it as an economic unit.[27] In practice, it soon turned out to be incapable of functioning adequately.[28] Decisions had to be supported unanimously,[29] but any proposal could be blocked by one of the commanders of the occupation zones. They interpreted any decision and regulation according to their own insights. In fact, this was implicit in the Potsdam Agreement stating that, in principle, each military governor was the highest authority in all zonal affairs.[30] This meant that the principle according to which the German population should be treated equally in all zones and that the German economy should be treated as a unit,[31] was seriously undermined from the start.[32] The Allies reserved the right to act as they deemed necessary in their own zones.[33] These became closed areas with their own economic systems. Trade between them was complicated, to say the least, and this even worsened the poor economic situation in Germany. Countries like The Netherlands that depended on trade with Germany were faced with the negative consequences of this policy. A normal export-oriented economy could not prosper under these circumstances.[34] The economic chaos in Germany was probably the biggest stumbling block on the road towards German recovery. To sum up, Germany was described by many as a hopeless case.[35]

Moreover, the Allies displayed very different opinions on the treatment of German industry.[36] The French government wanted security. Although France was not invited to any of the major conferences about Germany's future, including Potsdam,[37] Paris advocated a policy aimed at containing and limiting German industry, and keeping it in a permanent state of weakness.[38] The Union of Soviet Socialist Republics (USSR) strove for nationalisation. It intended to dismantle German companies and remove as much industrial machinery and capital goods as

---

[27] Van Hook 2004, pp. 19, 39.

[28] Benz 2000, p. 267.

[29] Benz and Faulenbach 2002, p. 7.

[30] Schwarz 1980, p. 108.

[31] Benz 1984, p. 35.

[32] Kleßmann 1991, p. 32.

[33] Schwarz 1980, pp. 107–108.

[34] Abelshauser 2004, p. 87.

[35] Wolf 2006, p. 323.

[36] Wubs 2008, p. 172.

[37] Kiersch 1977, p. 61.

[38] Wubs 2008, p. 172.

possible to compensate for the enormous damage done to their own industry.[39] The United Kingdom followed a somewhat ambivalent policy in its zone of occupation. Germany's war potential was to be eliminated, but Whitehall also hoped to be able to obtain certain machines from Germany to further British economic recovery. At the same time, London did not oppose a peaceful German economic reconstruction. On the contrary, a wealthy Germany would be less prone to war and would be a good consumer market for British products.[40] There was an obvious reason for this. Britain was practically bankrupt and had to import food from the United States "[I]t had nothing to spare for Germany from its own domestic resources [...] Morgenthau-style deindustrialisation—*i.e.* to dismantle German industry and turn Germany into an agricultural nation so it could never again be a threat—began rapidly to fade in the light of the terrific burden that a helpless Germany represented for a Britain that was itself economically prostrate."[41] In the end the British promoted a constructive approach in their occupation zone.[42]

2.4 American Policy Towards German Industry

The United States advocated at first a harsh policy when it came to, for example, the deconcentration of German industry. Although opinions differed strongly on the post-war industrial policy in Germany, German major businesses were held accountable for their co-operation with Hitler.[43] The most radical plan was Henry Morgenthau's of 1944, which envisioned a major deindustrialisation of the Ruhr and flooding of the coal mines.[44] Most US bankers and industrialists held quite different views, however, and advocated Germany's industrial recovery.[45] During the war, Harry Hopkins, Roosevelt's chief diplomatic adviser, strongly opposed the destruction of the Ruhr area. As it was the main European supplier of coal, iron and machines for ten European nations and the best customer for seven others, disrupting this pattern would be sheer folly. "I cannot see as realistic the suggestion that such an area in the present economic condition of the world can be turned into a non-productive ghost territory."[46]

In the immediate post-war period, radicals had the upper hand in US decision-making, resulting in the splitting up of companies like *IG Farben*. This firm had

[39] Becker 1979, p. 20. See also: Lak 2014, pp. 446–447; Slaveski 2013, p. 127.

[40] Farquharson 1997, p. 334.

[41] Taylor 2011, p. 204.

[42] Wubs 2008, p. 172.

[43] Wiesen 2004, p. 43; Also Eisenberg 1996, p. 139.

[44] Wubs 2008, p. 172.

[45] *Ibid.*, p. 172.

[46] As quoted by Eisenberg 1996, p. 40.

indeed been pro-Nazi, had built a massive factory complex near Auschwitz and had produced the Zyklon B poison gas that was used in the gas chambers of Auschwitz and Treblinka.[47] It was subsequently split up into the *Bayer*, *Höchst*, *Agfa* and *BASF*-companies.[48] Likewise, the highly interwoven coal and steel industries were cut up into twenty-three independent steel producers and dozens of collieries.[49] All this reflected the US anti-trust policy, which manifested itself in the Joint Chiefs of Staff (JCS) policy directive 1067 (JCS 1067) of April 1945. One of its goals was "to prohibit all cartels and other private business arrangements and cartel-like organisations."[50] JCS 1067 provided for rigid control of political life and a strong reduction and control of the German economy. Steps towards economic recovery or to strengthen the German economy were forbidden.[51] The German industry should be dismantled. The directive "foresaw a period of punitive deprivation for the German people as not merely inevitable, but just."[52]

In practice, however, many Americans, especially those working in the military occupation authorities in Germany, resented JCS 1067. With approval of his boss, an employee of Lucius D. Clay—the commander in the US zone of occupation—referred to the directive as the work of "economic idiots."[53] The directive showed little insight in what was happening at that time: those on the ground held quite different and also more realistic views. Although on paper Great Britain and the United States sided with the USSR and France in advocating a rigid approach towards Germany, in practice it soon turned out to be otherwise. According to the Americans in the occupation zone, hundreds of thousands of Germans would starve to death if the country was forbidden to export to acquire revenues. The most practical officials considered that the main priority towards Germany should be the rapid restoration of its capacity to pay and feed itself.[54] They felt that Washington failed to recognise the seriousness of the situation, and insisted upon making amendments to JCS 1067, although it provided limited room for manoeuvre, and the local military authorities in Germany were rather free in their interpretation of it.[55] In fact, although JCS 1067 was only withdrawn officially in July 1947, the American occupation policy was constructive from day one. The chemical industry, for example, was seen as an engine for economic growth that contributed to an enhanced standard of living. Thus, it "could be instrumental in helping one of the sides—*i.e.* East or West in the developing Cold War—prevail."[56]

[47] Taylor 2011, p. 245. Also Hayes 1987, pp. 347–364 and Rees 2005, p. 62.

[48] See for example Stokes 2009.

[49] Jarausch 2006, p. 77.

[50] As quoted by Wubs 2008, p. 172.

[51] Kleßmann 1991, pp. 22–23.

[52] Taylor 2011, p. 253.

[53] Kleßmann 1991, p. 100.

[54] Taylor 2011, pp. 118–119.

[55] Ahrens 2010, p. 29.

[56] Stokes 2006, p. 67.

Moreover, curbing war potential and constraining future German industrial competition contradicted "the desire to limit costs and length of the occupation."[57]

Nevertheless, a considerable number of German firms were dismantled as a consequence of the Allied policy. This often cut up foreign investment in these firms as well, especially in the mining, steel and iron industries.[58] In 1945, fifty-five percent of all coal mining was technically, economically, or by ownership, combined with the iron industry: "Technically through the exchange of fuels and energy, economically through the harmonisation of investments and of profits and losses, organically through the combination of mines and iron factories into integrated business concerns."[59] The Allies aimed to break up these conglomerates, as many were convinced that the Ruhr industry was not only guilty of having supported the rise of National Socialism, "but also of having provided the basis for German war production and for nearly six years of warfare."[60]

In December 1945, seventy-six senior executives from major Ruhr conglomerates were arrested, among which were the directors of *Thyssen*, *Hoesch* and the *Vereinigte Stahlwerke*. Most of the senior management of *Krupp* had been rounded up in September 1945.[61] Deconcentration of the Ruhr industry and especially of its coal mining industry did, however, not only affect Germany, but also the neighbouring countries. Because of Germany's central position in Europe—geographically as well as economically—the Allied policy had consequences for the whole of Europe, not in the least to the small and middle-sized economies in the West and North-West.[62] They depended on supplies of German coal and industrial products. Therefore, deconcentration always had an international dimension. This and decartelisation were not just German problems, but had far-reaching European implications as well.[63]

After the collapse of the Third Reich, it became fundamentally important to reactivate mining in the Ruhr and to breathe new life into its industry. The economic recovery of Europe depended on it.[64] The Continent could simply not do without the products of the Ruhr industry. This applied especially to The Netherlands. In spite of all that had happened during the war, nothing could erase the fact that Germany was indispensable for The Netherlands's long-term recovery.[65] For this reason, in October 1945, the Dutch Council of Economic Affairs stated that demolition of German industry would not be in the best interests of The

---

57 *Ibid.*, pp. 46–47.

58 Harryvan and Van der Harst 2008, p. 119.

59 Diegmann 2004, p. 197.

60 *Ibid.*, p. 198.

61 Taylor 2011, pp. 307–308.

62 Klemann 2004, pp. 1–2.

63 Diegmann 2004, p. 198.

64 Kleßmann 1991, p. 110.

65 Griffiths 1984, p. 33.

Netherlands, as it would hit the country's means of existence.[66] A strong German economic recovery was seen by some as a means of strengthening Western Europe, provided this would go hand in hand with the economic integration of the community of states.[67] While Germany was down, Europe's economic recovery would fail. The problem was that this only became clear to the British and Americans much later. The policy of the Allies, and especially the Americans, had serious repercussions for Europe's recovery. This policy only changed as the Cold War developed and the Marshall Plan was introduced.[68]

During the first post-war years, Dutch policy towards Germany showed a marked ambivalence. On the one hand, The Netherlands sought to punish Germany by annexation and reparations, but on the other, The Hague continuously demanded that the Allies restore normal trade relations with Germany as soon as possible.[69] In October 1945, The Netherlands objected to plans to dismantle German factories. The Dutch Ministry of Agriculture stated that "Germany is vital to us as a trading partner, especially with regard to agriculture."[70] In numerous discussions with the Allies shortly after the war, The Netherlands emphasised the importance and bare necessity of re-establishing the Dutch-German trade relations as a stimulus for the Dutch economy.[71]

This was not because the Dutch liked the Germans, but because the recovery of the Dutch-German trade relations was a necessity. To most Dutch politicians and businessmen, one thing was crystal clear: at the basis of the relations with Germany were the economic ties, and the necessity to restore these as soon as possible. In November 1947, a report by the Ministry of Foreign Affairs stated: "When the war was won, our main goal was to prevent any new German aggression in the future [...] but this has already taken second place. It is inevitable that we help put Germany on its feet again if we do not want to go down with it."[72] Without a healthy Germany, The Netherlands's most important trading partner since the mid-nineteenth century, a Dutch economic recovery was out of the question. The emphasis shifted slowly towards the recovery of economic relations, while pleas for reparation payments, restitution of stolen goods and annexation of parts of Germany quietly moved into the background.[73]

However, the Dutch appeals with the Allies fell on deaf ears for years. Only as late as September 1949 did the Americans suddenly—and to the astonishment of

---

66 National Archives 1945.

67 Hess and Wielenga 1987, p. 352.

68 Lak 2008, p. 5.

69 See for example Lak 2015a, b, especially Chap. 2 and conclusion.

70 Nordrhein-Westfälisches Hauptstaatsarchiv Düsseldorf (HstAD) 1948.

71 Wielenga 1989, p. 226.

72 Ministry of Foreign Affairs 1947 Otto 1948.

73 For an extensive analysis in of the Dutch policy towards Germany in the first post-war years see Lak 2009, pp. 45–85 and Lak 2011.

the Dutch delegation—liberalise the German imports of Dutch products, with spectacular results. Dutch exports to Germany between 1947 and 1950 grew from 58 to 1109 million guilders, about as much as total Marshall Aid in the 1948–54 period. In practice, this meant that the extra demand from Germany resulted in an impulse of 8% of Dutch Gross Domestic Product,[74] that is around four times as much as the Marshall Aid in the 1948–1954 period, which has been estimated at two per cent,[75] making the recovery of economic relations with Germany of greater importance to the Dutch economic recovery than the Marshall Aid.[76] The liberalisation of German imports basically normalised the Dutch-German economic relations.[77]

2.5 Not a *Deus ex Machina*

However, the question how to deal with West Germany—the *Bundesrepublik* had been established on 23 May 1949—and its economic potential still hovered over Europe. How was this to be exploited to the benefit of the Continent, without Germany once again becoming a military threat? It is no coincidence that many of the plans for European economic integration as a way of ending the German menace came from France. The country had waged war against its arch enemy three times between 1870 and 1945, had been decisively beaten in two of them, and had only just survived the Great War. Both economically and demographically, Germany was potentially a far stronger nation. As coal and steel were indispensable for waging war, it seemed to be a good idea to put them under some sort of supranational authority, and to promote competition by breaking up large producers and pre-World War II cartels, most of which were found in Germany.[78] The Schuman Plan "did not emerge like a *deus ex machina*." Its contours had already been visible during the London Conference of 1948.[79] What was lacking was a precise economic formulation of such a policy "which went beyond the vague ideas of an understanding between French and German industries in a wider European framework so that it was acceptable to the Western European countries and so that it was acceptable to the United States and did not appear there as a barrier to American ideas on integration."[80]

The French ideas partially found their origins in the Marshall Plan, which had a resounding effect on the European integration. With the Americans, especially

[74] Centraal Bureau voor de Statistiek (CBS) 1970; own calculations.

[75] Fase 1997, p. 426.

[76] Lak 2011, p. 140.

[77] Lak 2015a, b, p. 161.

[78] Eichengreen and Boltho 2010, p. 279.

[79] Milward 1984, p. 164.

[80] *Ibid.*

since late 1947, now completely focused—convinced as they had become that the alliance with the Soviet Union had finally and irreparably faltered—on Germany's economic and political revival, Paris had to reformulate its policy towards Germany. No longer did or could it strive for dismantling the German potential, especially in the Ruhr and the Rhineland, which had also collided with American plans on the future of Europe.[81]

Therefore, it was suggested that France and Germany—and for that matter any other democratic European state in Western Europe that wished to join—"should pool their coal and steel industries, placing them under the international, binding control of a High Authority." The latter would contain Germany, as the High Authority would in effect preside over a new European economic balance of power. However, this was to be done in a constructive way, not by means of a humiliating military occupation. As such, "it would offer an olive branch to Germany while placating French anxieties over German recovery."[82] Moreover, the Americans would be pleased by it, since they had been pressing Schuman for some time to take such an unprecedented step, especially by the efforts of the US Minister of Foreign Affairs, Dean Acheson.[83] Above all, in the words of Tony Judt, "it would take control of the Ruhr and other vital German resources out of purely German hands."[84] That way, it would ensure France's security.

On 9 May 1950, Schuman indeed launched a bold plan for the creation of a European Coal and Steel Community, although he called it a jump into uncertainty.[85] His declaration can be seen as "Europe's moment of conception," although it was both a cry of distress as well as a cry of joy.[86] Washington warmly accepted the Schuman Plan.

The US ambassador in Paris, David Bruce, hailed it as "the most constructive thing done by the French government since the Liberation,"[87] hinting at the strong American irritation with France's early post-war policy. The British, who had not been informed beforehand, felt as having been ambushed.[88]

2.6 West Germany: A Prospect of Regained Sovereignty

How did The Netherlands and Germany respond to Schuman's bold and unexpected move? Which differences and similarities can be distinguished, how can

[81] Segers 2013, p. 77.

[82] This paragraph and its quotations are based on: Hitchcock 2010, p. 171.

[83] van Middelaar 2009, p. 203.

[84] Judt 2007, p. 156.

[85] Schwabe 2007, pp. 13–14.

[86] van Middelaar 2009, p. 204.

[87] Hitchcock 2010, p. 171.

[88] *Ibid.*, p. 171.

they be explained and why did Bonn and The Hague join the European integration from its earliest moment? Of course, no one could reasonably have anything against the prospect of harmony between France and Germany.[89] At the same time, leaders in both countries were taken completely by surprise.[90] Except for, as mentioned earlier, Adenauer, who wholeheartedly welcomed Schuman's initiative, and thanked him in a personal letter, stating: "*Ich begrüße die Gedanken als einen entscheidenden Schritt zu einer engen Verbindung Deutschlands mit Frankreich und damit zu einer neuen, auf der Grundlage friedlicher Zusammenarbeit aufgebauten Ordnung in Europa. Der Plan der französischen Regierung, den Sie mir in großen Zügen entwickelt haben, wird in der deutschen öffentlichen Meinung einen starken Widerhall finden, da zum ersten Mal nach der Katastrophe des Jahres 1945 Deutschland und Frankreich gleichberechtigt an einer gemeinsamen Aufgabe wirken sollen.*"[91]

To West Germany, Schuman's proposal was mostly interesting from a political point of view to regain (parts of) its sovereignty and independence. Adenauer interpreted the French offer mainly from this point of view. In his correspondence with French representatives, he was very polite, calling it "a fresh impetus towards constructive co-operation". In a more private setting, for example when speaking to his aides, he was much blunter, stating "*Das ist unser Durchbruch*"—this is our breakthrough. For the first time since the end of World War II, Germany would enter an international organisation on equal terms,[92] and no longer as the pariah among the nations.[93] It would also mean that the Federal Republic of Germany would be bound to the Western alliance—precisely what Adenauer had been aiming at for a number of years.[94]

Adenauer followed two clear policy goals. First, there was his policy of "Binding to the West and Integration in the West"—*Westbindung* and *Westintegration*. It was a policy directed at integration with the Western powers and in a Western block.[95] In practice, this meant integrating West Germany into the European and Atlantic organisations by concluding agreements with the Western Allies. Secondly, Adenauer strove to regain West German sovereignty and an equal place in Europe.[96] These policies were highly criticised, even within the

---

89 Davies 1998, p. 1084.

90 Segers 2015, p. 88.

91 'I welcome the ideas as an essential step towards a close collaboration with France and therewith towards a new European order, based on peaceful co-operation. The plan of the French government, as you have generally explained them, will be warmly welcomed in the German public opinion, as for the first time after the catastrophe of 1945, Germany and France will work together on a task on an equal footing. **Gez. Adenauer** 1950.

92 Judt 2007, p. 151.

93 van Middelaar 2009, p. 193.

94 Judt 2007, p. 151.

95 Kitchen 2006, p. 326.

96 Boterman 2005, p. 418.

FRG. One KPD Member of Parliament even called the *Bundeskanzler* "nothing but an American general."[97] Adenauer's great rival, the leader of the social-democrats, Kurt Schumacher, referred to him as "the Chancellor of the Allies."[98] The young Federal Republic had indeed long been little more than a protectorate of the victorious Allies.

Although the FRG was formally established on 23 May 1949, it was by no means a sovereign state. Allied influence remained enormous, as can be seen in the Occupation Statute, part of the Constitution of the *Bundesrepublik*, which came into effect on 21 September 1949. The Western Allies still controlled the foreign relations of the new West German state, and the Ruhr area. Decartelisation, the dismantling of German industry and reparation payments also remained in Allied hands. Finally, the Allies held the right to take back authority completely, should democracy in the FRG fails to materialise,[99] although at the end of 1949 Adenauer had been able to make claims for West German sovereignty and equal treatment for the first time in the advent of the so-called "*Petersberger Abkommen*" of November that same year.[100]

In fact, the Schuman Plan offered much that Adenauer strived for. He saw the European Coal and Steel Community as "*die Erfüllung seiner eigenen Hoffnungen auf eine Versöhnung zwischen Fransozen und Deutschen.*"[101] Moreover, for the first time since 1945, the stipulations that the Allied High Commission was to represent the Federal Republic in international affairs, was lifted. West Germany could now speak for itself in a central theme of its foreign policy.[102] That is why the French proposal was given full support by the Germans.[103]

The Schuman project offered the prospect of a joint control of coal and steel, and as such on the armaments-sector as well. Adenauer even hoped that the Schuman Plan would serve as an example to other sectors of the European economy, which might even result in political and military co-operation. Moreover, the Schuman Plan collided with parts of the Occupation Statute and as such offered the way to political sovereignty. Finally, with West Germany joining, it could be respected as a normal state again.[104] In short, to the Federal Republic, the Schuman Plan was of importance above all from a political point of view.

---

[97] van Clemen 2009, p. 162.

[98] Kleßmann 1991, p. 229.

[99] *Ibid.*, p. 199; Boterman 2005, p. 418.

[100] Lappenküper 1994, p. 406.

[101] "The fulfilment of its own hopes to a reconciliation between the French and the Germans." Schwabe 2007, p. 21.

[102] *Ibid.*, p. 23.

[103] van Middelaar 2009, p. 70.

[104] Lappenküper 1994, p. 443.

2.7 The Netherlands: Primacy of Commercial Considerations

Like West Germany, The Netherlands was taken completely by surprise by Schuman's announcement. Bonn and The Hague shared a number of similarities. Both were forced to shift their focus more towards the Continent after the war. This was especially true for The Netherlands, as the loss of the Dutch East Indies only augmented the importance of Germany as an economic partner.[105] At the same time, both Bonn and The Hague were more focused on their Atlantic partnership with the United States, which led to a remarkable split in their policy. After World War II, the Dutch reality became more and more continental European, especially more German, but at the same time "the Netherlands was going somewhere else. The future would be Atlantic."[106]

The Schuman Plan meant the start of the so-called "Small-European" co-operation with West Germany, but without the United Kingdom, which rejected the plan. The French proposal was received with mixed feelings. Some Dutch politicians—most notably prime minister Willem Drees—preferred intergovernmental co-operation, and were hesitant of supranational ideas.[107] The Dutch Minister of Finance, Piet Lieftinck, had doubts as well and was hesitant in transferring national sovereignty, as did his colleague of Social Affairs, A.M. Joekes.[108] Their colleague of Foreign Affairs, Dirk Uipko Stikker, made public that he did not know what to think of the French plans.[109] However, the Minister of Economic Affairs, Jan van den Brink, strongly urged the Dutch government to participate in the negotiations, with Stikker accepting the underlying conditions of the plan as a basis for these talks.[110] Sicco Mansholt, Minister of Agriculture, also strongly supported the French plan.[111] When the content of the Schuman Plan became clearer, Stikker supported it. However, the Dutch government would remain "anti-supranational" and anti-political integration well into the 1950s.[112]

The Hague was in fact taken completely by surprise by the Schuman Plan,[113] although that remained, in the words of historian Mathieu Segers, "a well-kept secret." The establishment of the European Coal and Steel Community by "the

105 Van der Linden 1985, p. 64; See also Lak 2011, p. 44.

106 Segers 2013, p. 11.

107 Brouwer 2008, p. 125.

108 Lieftinck, pp. 241–260; Salzmann 1999, pp. 240–241.

109 *Ibid.*, Salzmann 1999, p. 240; See also: Hellema 2001, p. 163.

110 Aanhangsel tot het Verslag van de Handelingen der Tweede Kamer (7 June 1950) Vel 78, 157.

111 Segers 2013, p. 80.

112 Vollaard et al. 2015, p. 19. Also: Harryvan and Van der Harst 1994, pp. 143–171.

113 Salzmann 1999, p. 240.

Six" was reduced as much as possible to a "non-event."[114] In fact, The Netherlands had few options but to join. Its economic dependence on West Germany was simply too strong.[115] The establishment of the ECSC did result in some difficult questions, above all about how much power this new supranational institution would have, for example on wages and prices. Coal prices were indeed harmonised and dual coal prizing was brought to an end, but "differential national and international rail freight rates remained in force."[116]

What bothered The Hague the most was the lack of clarity of the ECSC's power. It objected to the presumably great and undefined powers of the new High Authority.[117] Stikker and the Dutch administration saw supranationalism as problematic, and, during the negotiations, emphasised time and again its reservation towards this topic.[118] In the end, historian Bob Reinalda writes, the ECSC "created a framework for transparency and competition in the coal and steel sectors that was acceptable to the Dutch coal mines and steel industry."[119]

So why did the Netherlands—be it with reservations and sometimes hesitantly—ultimately decide to join the ECSC? One reason could be that it resembled plans developed earlier by the Dutch Minister of Foreign Affairs of the Dutch government in exile in London, Eelco Nicolaas van Kleffens. In April 1943, he wrote a note to the big powers in order to prevent a renewed German aggression in the long run. In this perspective, he suggested the establishment of an international organ for the control of the import and production by Germany of three products—iron, steel and nitrogen—that were indispensable for modern warfare.[120]

However, joining the Schuman Plan and later the ECSC was also—and perhaps above all—inspired by the economic importance of Germany to the Netherlands. As stated by the economic historian Jan Luiten van Zanden, "[e]very plan that would further the integration of Germany in Western Europe, was self-evidently accepted by the Dutch."[121] To the Netherlands, the integration of the FRG enabled "the necessary western reinforcement against the Soviet Union. In this way, German recovery could be continued without risk and the other European countries could benefit from West German economic potential."[122] The Netherlands would not consider any form of co-operation that would exclude its largest trading partner.[123] It was also clear that the Dutch European policy was driven by "the

[114] Segers 2013, p. 84.

[115] *Ibid.*, p. 77.

[116] Milward 1984, p. 408.

[117] *Ibid.*, p. 409.

[118] Reinalda 2009, p. 751.

[119] *Ibid.*, p. 751.

[120] Lak 2010, pp. 406–407.

[121] van Zanden 1997, p. 177.

[122] Wielenga 1999, p. 42.

[123] Griffiths 1990a, b, p. 10.

consistency and primacy of commercial considerations."[124] The Dutch historian Albert Kersten states that "one can draw the conclusion that the Dutch government was primarily, and maybe even exclusively, interested in economic co-operation and integration."[125]

Moreover, it should not be forgotten that a growing number of those responsible in the Dutch Ministries of Economic and Foreign Affairs believed that after the loss of the Dutch East Indies, the Dutch future lays in co-operation in Western Europe.[126] The first West German ambassador to The Netherlands, Karl Du Mont, confirmed this view, as he noted that the loss of the Dutch East Indies and the failure of the Benelux had once again confirmed that co-operation with Germany was a necessity.[127] This points to the economic importance of West Germany to The Netherlands, which seems to have caused the Dutch policy described above: "Trade was simply too important to the Dutch to allow ideology or dislike to get in their way."[128]

Integration also meant Western reinforcement against the Soviet Union. It corresponded with the Dutch wish for the economic integration of the *Bundesrepublik,* on the one hand, and security in the Atlantic treaty, on the other hand.[129] It seems likely that the economic side of the European integration and especially the integration of West Germany in this process was the most important reason for The Netherlands to strongly support the project. Bonn, with the division of Germany, focused on Western Europe more than ever before.[130] It had mostly political considerations and the quest for a renewed sovereignty at heart.

2.8 Conclusions

Why did The Netherlands and West Germany participate from the start in the process of European integration? With hindsight, the reasons to join the European integration process are clear: the Cold War, the need to rebuild to shattered continent and the material advantages.

There were a number of similarities between The Netherlands and the *Bundesrepublik*. After the war, both countries were forced to increasingly focus their attention on the Continent. This was especially true for the Netherlands, as the loss of the Dutch East Indies only augmented the importance of Germany as an economic partner. At the same time, both Bonn and The Hague were more focused

124 *Ibid.*, "Preface," p. XI.

125 Kersten 1992, p. 6. Also Kersten 1990, p. 119–138.

126 *Ibid.*, p. 138.

127 Politisches Archiv Auswärtiges Amt Berlin 1950.

128 Mallinson 2010, p. 196.

129 Hellema 2001, p. 191.

130 Klemann 2006, p. 59.

on their Atlantic partnership with the United States—especially militarily—which led to a remarkable split in their policy.

The integration of the new Federal Republic of Germany was also seen, for example by The Netherlands, as a way to make sure that the country and the Continent as a whole could profit from West Germany's economic potential, but at the same time to prevent the country from ever becoming a military threat again. Although the Schuman Plan came like a bolt from the blue, Bonn and The Hague decided—the former much more enthusiastically than the latter—to join the European integration process and the ECSC.

However, there were different reasons why The Netherlands and West Germany were part of the European integration process from the start. For the latter, it was above all an opportunity to regain its sovereignty and independence, and to be respected as a normal state again. That was essentially the core element of Konrad Adenauers *Westbindung* and *Westintegration.* For the *Bundesrepublik,* political considerations seem to have been dominant. To The Hague, however, economic reasons were the most important. It remained fundamentally the case for the upcoming years. When it came to economic integration the Dutch were keen to take this process further, but politically it was far more hesitant, mostly with regard to supranational institutions.

References

Abelshauser W (1984) Der Ruhrkohlenbergbau seit 1945. Verlag C.H. Beck, Munich

Abelshauser W (2004) Deutsche Wirtschaftsgeschichte seit 1945. Bundeszentrale für politische Bildung, Bonn

Adenauer G (1950) Offizielles Schreiben des Bundeskanzlers Adenauer an den französischen Außenminister Schuman zum Vorschlag einer gemeinschaftlichen hohen Stelle für die deutsche und französische Kohle- und Stahlproduktion. http://www.konrad-adenauer.de/dokumente/briefe/schreibenschuman1?highlight=Schuman. Accessed 30 Apr 2016

Ahrens R (2010), Von der "Säuberung" zum Generalpardon: Die Entnazifizierung der westdeutschen Wirtschaft. Jahrbuch für Wirtschaftsgeschichte – Europäische Wirtschaftseliten nach dem Zweiten Weltkrieg, 51(2):25–45

Becker J (1979) Die Deutsche Frage in der internationalen Politik 1941–1949. Grundzüge und Hauptprobleme ihrer Entwicklung. In: Becker J, Stammen T, Waldmann P (eds) Vorgeschichte der Bundesrepublik Deutschland. Zwischen Kapitulation und Grundgesetz. Fink Verlag, Munich, pp 9–59

Benz W (1984) Von der Besatzungsherrschaft zur Bundesrepublik. Stationen einer Staatsgründung. Fischer Verlag, Frankfurt am Main

Benz W (2000) Geschichte des Dritten Reiches. Bundeszentrale für politische Bildung, Munich

Benz W, Faulenbach J (2002) Deutschland 1945–1949. Bundeszentrale für politische Bildung, Bonn

Boterman F (2005) Moderne Geschiedenis van Duitsland 1800-heden. De Arbeiderspers, Amsterdam

Brouwer JW (2008), Nederlands grootste onderhandelaar. Dirk Pieter Spierenburg (1909–2001). In: Van der Zwan B, De Graaf B, Hellema D (eds) In dienst van Buitenlandse Zaken. Achttien portretten van ambtenaren en diplomaten in de twintigste eeuw. Boom, Amsterdam, pp 119–132

Buruma I (2013) Year Zero. A History of 1945. Atlantic Books, London
Centraal Bureau voor de Statistiek (CBS) (1970) Zeventig jaar statistiek in tijdreeksen 1899–1969. Staatsdrukkerij, The Hague
Davies N (1998) Europe. A history. Harper Perennial, Oxford
de Bruijn T (2013) Voorwoord. In: Van Meurs W, De Bruin R, Hoetink C, Van Leeuwen K, Van de Grift L (eds) Europa in alle staten. Zestig jaar geschiedenis van de Europese integratie. Uitgeverij Vantilt, Nijmegen, pp 7–9
de Wagt W (2015) Wij Europeanen. Bas Lubberhuizen, Amsterdam
Diegmann A (2004) American deconcentration policy in the Ruhr coal industry. In: Diefendorf JM, Frohn A, Rupieper HJ (eds) American policy and the reconstruction of West Germany, 1945–1955. Cambridge University Press, Cambridge, pp 197–215
Eichengreen B (2007) The European economy since 1945: coordinated capitalism and beyond. Princeton University Press, Princeton
Eichengreen B, Boltho A (2010) The economic impact of European integration. In: Broadberry S, O'Rourke KH (eds) The Cambridge economic history of modern Europe. Volume 2: 1870 to the Present. Cambridge University Press, Cambridge, pp 267–295
Eisenberg C (1996) Drawing the line. The American decision to divide Germany, 1944–1949. Cambridge University Press, Cambridge
European Security Mechanism website (2015) http://www.esm.europa.eu/. Accessed 27 Apr 2016
Farquharson JA (1997) A Game of Cat and Mouse? Dismantling for Reparations in the British Zone of Germany 1947–1950. Ger Hist 15(3):333–357
Fase MMG (1997) De Marshall-hulp opnieuw beschouwd. ESB 82 (4108):424–428
Griffiths RT (1984) Economic reconstruction policy in the Netherlands and its international consequences, May 1945–March 1951. European University Institute, San Domenico
Griffiths RT (1990a) Preface. In: Griffiths RT (ed) The Netherlands and the integration of Europe. NEHA, Amsterdam, pp IX–XII
Griffiths RT (1990b) The stranglehold of bilateralism. In: Griffiths RT (ed) The Netherlands and the integration of Europe 1945–1957. NEHA, Amsterdam, pp 1–26
Harryvan AG, Van der Harst J (1994) Het Nederlandse Europabeleid na het einde van de Koude Oorlog. Transaktie 23:143–171
Harryvan AG, Van der Harst J (2008) Max Kohnstamm. Leven en werk van een Europeaan. Het Spectrum, Utrecht
Hayes P (1987) Industry and Ideology—I.G. Farben and the Nazi Era. Cambridge University Press, Cambridge
Hellema D (2001) Neutraliteit & Vrijhandel. De geschiedenis van de Nederlandse buitenlandse betrekkingen. Het Spectrum, Utrecht
Hess JC, Wielenga F (1987) Die Niederlande und die Wiedervereinigung Deutschlands. Ein Beitrag zur Debatte um die "Verpassten Gelegenheiten" im Jahr 1952. Vierteljahresheft für Zeitgeschichte, 35(3):349–384
Hitchcock WI (2010) The Marshall Plan and the Creation of the West. In: Leffler MP, Westad OA (eds) The Cambridge history of the cold war. Volume I: Origins. Cambridge University Press, Cambridge, pp 154–174
Jarausch K (2006) After Hitler. Recivilizing Germans, 1945–1995. Oxford University Press, Oxford
Judt T (2007) Postwar. A history of Europe since 1945. Pimlico, London
Kersten AE (1990) Die Niederlande und die Westintegration der Bundesrepublik. Wirtschaft, Sicherheit und politische Kontrolle. In: Herbst L, Bührer W, Sowade H (eds) Vom Marshallplan zur EWG. Die Eingliederung der Bundesrepublik Deutschland in die westliche Welt. Oldenbourg Verlag, Munich, pp 119–138
Kersten AE (1992), Oorsprong en inzet van de Nederlandse Europese integratiepolitiek. In: Bloemen E. (ed) Het Benelux-effect. België, Nederland en Luxemburg en de Europese integratie, 1945–1957. NEHA, Amsterdam, pp 1–12

Kiersch G (1977) Die Französische Deutschlandpolitik 1945–1949. In: Scharf C, Schröder HJ (eds) Politische und Ökonomische Stabilisierung Westdeutschlands 1945–1949. Fünf Beiträge zur Deutschlandpolitik der westlichen Alliierten. Verlag Philip, Wiesbaden, pp 61–76

Kitchen M (2006) A history of modern Germany 1800–2000. Wiley, Oxford

Klemann HAM (2004) Point Zero. The economic problems of Western Europe in 1945. Paper presented to the ESF-Conference Post-war Economic Reconstruction, Utrecht, The Netherlands, 3–4 Sept 2004, pp 1–7

Klemann HAM (2006) Waarom bestaat Nederland eigenlijk nog? Nederland-Duitsland: Economische integratie en politieke consequenties 1860–2000 Erasmus University Rotterdam

Klemann HAM (2010) Europe without economy. Low Countries Historical Review—BMGN, 125(4):74–80

Kleßmann C (1991) Die doppelte Staatsgründung. Deutsche Geschichte 1945–1955. Bundeszentrale für politische Bildung, Bonn

Krijtenburg M (2012) Schuman's Europe. His frame of reference. Leiden University Press, Leiden

Krijtenburg M (2015) Robert Schuman's commitment to European unification. The inspiring role of his Roman Catholic faith. Philosophia Reformata 80:140–157

Lak M (2008) Na de overwinning. De Amerikanen, Britten en Russen in Duitsland na WO II. De Academische Boekengids 69:3–5

Lak M (2009) Eine Angelegenheit von fundamentaler Bedeutung. Die Wechselwirkung zwischen der ökonomischen und politische Beziehungen zwischen der Niederlanden und Deutschland, 1945–1949. In: Klemann HAM. Wielenga F (eds) Deutschland und die Niederlande. Wirtschaftsgeschichte im 19. und 20. Jahrhundert. Waxmann, Münster, pp 45–85

Lak M (2010) 'Onze welvaart valt en staat met die van Duitschland'. Opvattingen over naoorlogs Duitsland bij de Nederlandse regering in Londen en de illegale pers tijdens de Tweede Wereldoorlog. Tijdschrift voor Geschiedenis, 123(3):401–413

Lak M (2011) Because we need them… German-Dutch relations after the occupation: economic inevitability and political sovereignty, 1945–1957. Unpublished PhD-thesis, Erasmus University Rotterdam

Lak M (2014) De Tweede Wereldoorlog werd aan het Oostfront beslist. Recente geschiedschrijving over WO II in Europa. Tijdschrift voor Geschiedenis, 127(3):439–458

Lak M (2015a) The Rhine in Ruins. The consequences of World War II for the Rhine shipping between the Netherlands and Germany, 1945 to 1957. Zeitschrift für Unternehmensgeschichte/Journal of Business History, 60(1):75–96

Lak M (2015b) Tot elkaar veroordeeld. De Nederlands-Duitse economische en politieke betrekkingen tussen 1945–1957. Uitgeverij Verloren, Hilversum

Lappenküper U (1994) Der Schuman-Plan. Mühsamer Durchbruch zur deutsch-französischen Verständigung. Vierteljahresheft für Zeitgeschichte, 42(3):403–445

Lieftinck P (1950) Europese economische integratie. De Economist 98(1):241–260

Mallinson W (2010) From neutrality to commitment. Dutch foreign policy, NATO and European integration. I.B. Tauris Publishers, London

Milward AS (1984) The reconstruction of Western Europe 1945–1951. Methuen & Co. Ltd, London

Ministry of Foreign Affairs, Map 565 (912,230) Duitsland West. Geallieerden en Nederlandse politiek t.a.v. Duitsland; Rapportage Ir. L.F. Otto 1948; L.F. Otto, Commissaris-Generaal voor de Nederlandse Economische Belangen in Duitsland, enkele aantekeningen betreffende de huidige situatie in Duitsland, Nov 1947

National Archives (1945) The Hague, Ministerraad, 1823–1988, access code 2.02.05.02, inventory number 570; Council for Economic Affairs, Verslag van de vergadering gehouden op maandag, 22 Oct 1945

Nordrhein-Westfälisches Hauptstaatsarchiv Düsseldorf (HstAD) (1948), NW 397–199 Staatskanzlei; Discussion Zum Wirtschaftverhältnis Deutschland-Holland

Politisches Archiv Auswärtiges Amt Berlin, AA B 11, Bd. 434, Microfiche 434–1; letter Du Mont to Auswärtiges Amt: Aussenpolitik der Niederlande, 2 July 1950
Rees L (2005) Auschwitz. The Nazis and the "Final Solution." BBC Books, London
Reichardt S, Zierenberg M (2009) Damals nach dem Krieg. Eine Geschichte Deutschlands 1945 bis 1949. Wilhelm Goldman Verlag, Munich
Reinalda B (2009) The Netherlands, the United States, and the development of a postwar international economy. In: Krabbendam H, Van Minnen CA, Scott-Smith G (eds) Four centuries of Dutch-American relations 1609–2009. State University of New York Press, Albany, pp 741–760
Rombeck-Jaschinski U (1990) Nordrhein-Westfalen, die Ruhr und Europa. Föderalismus und Europapolitik 1945–1955. Klartext Verlag, Essen
Salzmann WH (1999) Herstel, wederopbouw en Europese samenwerking. D.P. Spierenburg en de buitenlandse economische betrekkingen van Nederland 1945–1952. Sdu Uitgevers, The Hague
Schlieper A (1986) 150 Jahre Ruhrgebiet. Ein Kapitel deutscher Wirtschaftsgeschichte. Verlag Schwann-Bagel, Düsseldorf
Schuman (1950) Declaration of Robert Schuman in Paris, 9 May 1950. http://www.robert-schuman.eu/en/declaration-of-9-may-1950. Accessed 11 May 2015
Schwabe K (2007) Die Gründung der Montanunion aus deutscher und französischer Sicht. In: Rasch M, Düwell K (eds) Anfänge und Auswirkungen der Montanunion auf Europa. Die Stahlindustrie in Politik und Wirtschaft. Klartext Verlag, Essen, pp 13–30
Schwarz HP (1980) Vom Reich zur Bundesrepublik. Deutschland im Widerstreit der außenpolitische Konzeptionen in den Jahren der Besatzungsherrschaft 1945–1949. Klett-Cotta, Stuttgart
Segers M (2013) Reis naar het continent. Nederland en de Europese integratie, 1950 tot heden. Bert Bakker, Amsterdam
Segers M (2015) Nederland en de Europese integratie. In: Pekelder J, Raben R, Segers M (eds) De wereld volgens Nederland. Nederlandse buitenlandse politiek in historisch perspectief. Boom, Amsterdam, pp 83–106
Slaveski F (2013) The Soviet occupation of Germany. Hunger, mass violence, and the struggle for peace, 1945–1947. Cambridge University Press, Cambridge
Stokes R (2006) Opting for oil. The political economy of technological change in the West German chemical industry, 1945–1961. Cambridge University Press, Cambridge
Stokes R (2009) Divide and prosper. The heirs of I.G. Farben under allied authority 1945–1951. Hexagon Press, Huddersfield
Stone D (2014) Goodbye to all that? The story of Europe since 1945. Oxford University Press, Oxford
Taylor F (2011) Exorcising Hitler. The occupation and denazification of Germany. Bloomsbury Press, New York
van Clemen S (2009) Konrad Adenauer. Een biografie. Uitgeverij Aspekt, Soesterberg
van der Linden JTJM (1985) Economische ontwikkeling en de rol van de overheid. Nederland 1945–1955. Wolters-Noordhoff, Groningen
Van Hook JC (2004) Rebuilding Germany. The creation of the social market economy, 1945–1957. Cambridge University Press, Cambridge
van Middelaar L (2009) De passage naar Europa. Geschiedenis van een begin. Historische Uitgeverij, Brussels
van Zanden JL (1997) Een klein land in de 20e eeuw. Economische geschiedenis van Nederland 1914–1995. Het Spectrum, Utrecht
Vollaard H, Van der Harst J, Voerman G (2015) Inleiding. In: H. Vollaard H, Van der Harst J, Voerman G (eds) Van aanvallen! naar verdedigen? De opstelling van Nederland ten aanzien van Europese integratie, 1945–2015. Boom Bestuurskunde, Amsterdam, pp 13–27
Vrij Nederland, 5 July 1943
Wemelsfelder J (1954) Het herstel van de Duits-Nederlandse economische betrekkingen na de Tweede Wereldoorlog. H.E. Stenfert Kroese, Leiden

Wielenga F (1989) West-Duitsland: partner uit noodzaak. Nederland en de Bondsrepubliek, 1949–1955. Het Spectrum, Utrecht

Wielenga F (1999) Van vijand tot bondgenoot. Nederland en Duitsland na 1945. Uitgeverij Boom, Amsterdam

Wiesen SJ (2004) West German industry and the challenge of the Nazi past, 1945–1955. University of North Carolina Press, North Carolina

Wolf HC (2006) Post-war Germany in the European context: domestic and external determinants of growth. In: Eichengreen B (ed) Europe's post-war recovery. Cambridge University Press, Cambridge, pp 323–352

Wubs B (2008) International business and national war interests. Unilever between Reich and Empire. Routledge, Abingdon

Chapter 3
Schuman in Times of Upheaval

Margriet Krijtenburg

> *World peace cannot be safeguarded without the making of creative efforts proportionate to the dangers which threaten it.*
> Schuman's first words of the Schuman Declaration, 9 May 1950. *See:* Krijtenburg 2012, pp. 204–207.

Abstract The European Union (EU) is struggling to survive. Its disintegration has been predicted and contradicted by ever more Europeans since the start of the financial crisis in 2008. European citizens protest and increasingly lack confidence in "Brussels." Member States also show a lack of confidence in measures proposed by the EU. The EU is internally and externally surrounded by conflicts and humanitarian problems that it needs to face and help to solve, but does not seem able to soften in a proper way. This article focuses on the original vision on European unification of the "Father of Europe," Robert Schuman, and applies it to today's society. Schuman's personality and background as a practising Catholic from the region of Alsace-Lorraine explain to a large extent the intrinsic content of his view on integration. They help to understand his sensitivity to transparency and his person-centred approach to integration which implies his stress on the subsidiarity and solidarity principles as crucial for a proper way of integration. He emphasised the need to protect regional, national and continental interests, unless these went against the national, European or universal common good. Schuman's point of view shows that the problems faced by Europe today extend well beyond the economic and financial domain. Thus, an analysis is welcomed with regards to the above-mentioned principles and concepts which laid the basis for the European project. This chapter will further add an interpretation of Schuman's way of thinking on current topics to underline the topicality of his insights.

M. Krijtenburg (✉)
The Hague University of Applied Sciences, Johanna Westerdijkplein 75,
2521 EN The Hague, The Netherlands
e-mail: G.Krijtenburg@hhs.nl

J. de Zwaan et al. (eds.), *Governance and Security Issues of the European Union*, DOI 10.1007/978-94-6265-144-9_3

Keywords Schuman · Reconciliation · Solidarity · Subsidiarity · Person · Peace · Common good · Border · Ecology · Refugee

Contents

3.1 Introduction

"There needs to be a united response to the question of migration. We cannot allow the Mediterranean to become a vast cemetery."[1] In the fall of 2014, Pope Francis addressed the European leaders in the European Parliament with these words. He thus referred to the disasters of refugees that drowned in the Mediterranean Sea while trying to flee from their countries in conflict so as to reach the promised European continent. The High Representative of the Union for Foreign Affairs, Federica Mogherini, said as much, declaring, "We have said too many times, 'never again.' Now is the time for the European Union as such to tackle these tragedies without delay."[2] Since then, the EU held several Summits on Migration so as to try to solve the ongoing migrant crisis. Hundreds of thousands of migrants have crossed European borders waiting for their final destination. Not only has the migrant problem imposed itself on the European Union, but another threat imported from outside Europe appeared in the form of terrorism. Terrorist attacks have taken place in Europe as well, and the threat of terrorism persists on a broader scale than in the past decades. This turmoil at and within European borders without a clear and consistent response to them by the EU has increased the lack of confidence among European citizens and among Member States. They have equally caused a growth of populism and nationalistic movements.

This short enumeration of threatening situations at and within the borders of the EU indicates the need for a thorough insight in and understanding of the profound cause of the problems the EU has to deal with, so as to be able to work towards the

[1] Pope Francis 2014.

[2] BBC News 15 April 2015. European External Union Action (2015).

improvement and solution with regard to the current state of affairs. This article will not explore the problems faced by the EU as such, but will show that Schuman's thoughts as the main architect of the European unification project provide surprising insights and make clear that—using his own words—the European Union will need to come up with "creative efforts proportionate to the dangers which threaten it."[3]

The first part will introduce the person of Robert Schuman for a better understanding of his vision on European unification and of the topicality of his line of thought on main concepts. The second part gives a short interpretation of Schuman's way of thinking on four current topics so as to give an idea of the applicability of his frame of reference.

Schuman can be considered the main architect[4] of the European unification project for having prepared its ground and ideas, such as the Franco-German reconciliation and the supranational aspect of the integration project. Konrad Adenauer, Chancellor of West Germany at that time, said about him: "[t]hanks to his prudence and values, he laid the foundation between our two countries and for the construction of a united and strong Europe."[5] Dean Acheson, Schuman's contemporary U.S. Secretary of State, wrote in his memoirs: "Schuman possessed a vision of a united Europe in a day and age when it was difficult to have a vision in France of any kind."[6] Schuman regarded this unique kind of integration, in which part of the national sovereignty was surrendered to a common institution that safeguarded common interests—today's European Commission—as an infringement in the history of politics that was of worldwide importance. He said so already a year before the Schuman Declaration came about during his speech at the Council of Europe in Strasbourg, on 16 May 1949. He referred to this upcoming European integration when he said, "[I am speaking about] [t]he inauguration of a new kind of politics that will probably be the strongest effort to protect our continent and to preserve the world from suicide."[7] This new kind of politics was

---

[3] Krijtenburg 2012, Schuman 1950, preface.

[4] Many think Jean Monnet is, together with his team, the protagonist of the Schuman Declaration based on the detailed description of Monnet's *Mémoires* about this period, and on Monnet's noticeable presence in European affairs. This last decade, however, there is increasing evidence that Schuman and his staff were the brains behind the Schuman Declaration. This "discovery" is based on archives that opened and facilitated the study of Schuman's speeches, writings and actions of the years before, during and after the Declaration. *See:* Krijtenburg 2012, pp. 117–123.

This acknowledgement denies the former suppositions such as mentioned in Milward 1984, p. 395. "The Schuman Plan was invented to safeguard the Monnet Plan"; Judt 2005, p. 156. "Monnet proposed to France's Foreign Minister what became known to history as the Schuman Plan." Also Segers was not yet aware of the latest investigations in this field as is evidenced in: Segers 2013. Segers's lecture 2014 in which he minimized Schuman's role to one that did not need to be given any special attention.

[5] *See:* Lejeune 2000, Chap. 21.

[6] *Ibid.*, Chap. 15.

[7] *See:* Price 2014, p. 13. Translated by the author of the article. «l'inauguration d'une nouvelle politique qui constituera probablement l'ultime tentative pour sauver notre continent et préserver le monde du suicide.»

the creative effort that was needed and was proportionate to the dangers which threatened Europe. Nowadays, a similar amount of creative effort seems to be needed to work towards a solution with regard to the current dangers threatening the EU and the world as such.

In Schuman's vision, the individual with his spiritual dimension, or transcendence, needs to be at the core of the unification process and of politics, economics, judicial and social affairs as such. He foresees the building of a society in which every person can achieve moral perfection and material welfare. This implies in conceptual and practical terms as believed and practised by Schuman, reconciliation, effective solidarity and subsidiarity as principles to be put into practice for proper unification.

3.2 Robert Schuman (1886–1963)[8]

Schuman laid the first stone of an integration project that is unique, not only in European history, but in the history of the entire world. With the Schuman Declaration on 9 May 1950 marking the birth of the European unification project, he helped to achieve the first peaceful revolution on the European continent in times of poverty, threat of war and the perceived danger of communism.[9] Never before had states freely surrendered part of their sovereignty to a supranational institution that took charge of their common interests and helped with the originated interdependence to make war among those states, "not only unthinkable, but materially impossible."[10] This Declaration brought forth the longest period of peace among the EU Member States since the Treaty of Verdun in 843.

[8] A lot of information is based on Krijtenburg's PhD dissertation *Schuman's Europe. His frame of reference* of 2012, the French translation of which, *L'Europe de Schuman. Ses Racines*, was published on 4 September 2013, on the occasion of Schuman's 50th death anniversary. Many of the references are also retrieved from the Schuman Archives of the Maison de Robert Schuman in Scy-Chazelles and the Archives of the Département de la Moselle in Metz. The original French texts of citations translated from French into English by the author will be provided in the footnotes. Other articles and books of which ideas have been used are: Brague 2002; Krijtenburg 2015a, pp 140-157; Krijtenburg 2015c; Sabine and Thorson 1973; Schuman 2005; Villarós 2006.

[9] See also: Gerbet 1962.

[10] Schuman 1950. He refers to the impossibility of war between the archenemies Germany and France as that was the main issue to be dealt with for centuries already, but the interdependence counts for all states concerned. «La solidarité de production qui sera ainsi nouée manifestera que toute guerre entre la France et L'Allemagne devient non seulement impensable, mais matériellement impossible».

3.2.1 Biography

Robert Schuman was born in Luxembourg in 1886. He had the German nationality, as his father was from Alsace-Lorraine, the north-eastern region in France that belonged to Germany after the Franco-German war of 1870–1871. Schuman settled down as a lawyer in Metz in 1911. In 1918, after the First World War, when Alsace-Lorraine returned to France, Schuman obtained the French nationality. From the moment Schuman started studying law, he had been searching for a way to obtain permanent peace on the European continent, especially between the arch-enemies France and Germany which were constantly in war precisely because of this conflictive border region, rich in coal and steel and therefore of primary importance for the production of arms. Schuman's geographical background partially explains why he looked for a solution to this endless Franco-German conflict and why he discovered the potentiality of coal and steel as means to obtain this peace.[11]

An equally important fact is that Schuman lived his Catholic faith in his personal and public life. He took seriously the Social Doctrine of the Church[12] that put man's spiritual dimension at the core of all endeavours. His *leitmotiv* was that, "we are all instruments, however imperfect, of a Providence who uses them to accomplish grand designs, which surpass us [humanly speaking]."[13] He applied this to both himself and anybody else.

As chosen representative of Alsace-Lorraine in the French Parliament right after the First World War, Schuman was asked to adapt the laws of his region to those of the central government that was led by the principles of *laïcité,* and thus, knew a strict separation of Church and State. The expression of faith was restricted to the private area. Congruent with the Social Doctrine of the Church, Schuman took the subsidiarity principle[14] into account by safeguarding the characteristics of Alsace-Lorraine, in which the *laïcité* was not introduced as it fell under the reign of Germany at that time (1905). He adapted the laws no further than the national common good required. He did so to the satisfaction of all concerned. His work became known as the *Lex Schuman,* and served as a point of reference for other regional laws that possibly had to be adapted to those of the central government.

Schuman's background encouraged him and his Catholic faith inspired him to constantly foster a policy of reconciliation with Germany from the moment he was a French parliamentarian (1919) onwards. During the Second World War, he, as an

---

[11] Krijtenburg 2012, pp. 17–24.

[12] As a side note, it might be observed that the Roman Catholic Church is the oldest and biggest international organization for social development in the world. The Papacy's opposition to ideologies and situations that endanger human dignity is acknowledged by many irrespective of their (non) faith.

[13] Roth 2008, p. 562.

[14] *See*: Leo XIII 1891. The subsidiarity principle was first explained by Thomas Aquinas (1225–1274).

escaped prisoner of war, continued to stress the need for reconciliation with Germany. When holding his Minister positions right after the Second World War, his focus on reconciliation became ever more concrete, also because of his reputation among friends and foes as a highly esteemed politician. The period between 1947 and 1950 saw the birth of the Marshall Plan, the United Nations, the North Atlantic Treaty Organisation, the Council of Europe and the Schuman Declaration. These were crucial Treaties and organisations in which his role as Prime-Minister and Minister of Foreign Affairs of France were fundamental.[15] It needs to be reminded that Jean Monnet, Head of the French Planning Committee, is often mistakenly regarded as the intellectual father of the Schuman Declaration of 1950. Monnet is one of the main Founding Fathers. He did, however, not "invent" the European unification project, but acknowledged Schuman's ideas, made them more specific and put them on paper in a few days.[16] This will become the Schuman Declaration that Schuman, Minister of Foreign Affairs at that time, launched on 9 May 1950. It has brought already more than 65 years of peace among the Member States of the EU.

In 1961, Schuman was unanimously and officially acclaimed as the "Father of Europe" by the European Parliament. Schuman died in Scy-Chazelles (Metz) in 1963.

3.3 Schuman's Europe

Schuman's life was led by his wish to give heed to his vocation and to attain peace on the European continent. For these very reasons, he integrated already the practice of concepts such as reconciliation, solidarity and subsidiarity. His drive is echoed in his observations regarding European unification. His remarks are surprising both for their topicality, their wake-up call for Europe as well as their dedication to blaze a trail. "World peace cannot be safeguarded without making the creative efforts proportionate to the dangers which threaten it."[17]

This is Schuman's device. His own creative efforts translated themselves into starting a new kind of politics so as to come to this desired peace. As mentioned before, he began a supranational kind of politics in which the person with his transcendence—which implies solidarity with deeds and a focus on the common good—plays the pivotal role in economic, political, judicial and social affairs. He thought "out of the box" for those days and possibly still. Adenauer, Chancellor of Western Germany, and Alcide De Gasperi, Prime-Minister of Italy, the two other very first Founding Fathers of the EU, were on the same wavelength. The revolutionary idea was to put a political project into practice that went beyond the

[15] Krijtenburg 2012, pp. 125-173.

[16] *Ibid.*, pp. 117–125. Reuter 1980. Gerbet 1962.

[17] Schuman 1950.

immediate national political, economic and social interests for having its focus on the common good, even beyond national borders. This had never happened before in the world history. The EU is still unique in its structure.

Schuman is convinced that with the start of a supranational project—a project that focuses on the common European interests that do not go against universal interests—, national egoism, a cause of friction, discontent and unrest, would become ever less possible. Member States surrendered part of their sovereignty to a common supranational entity because it benefited them immediately or in the shorter or longer run. This created at the same time interdependence among Member States that made war not only "unthinkable, but also impossible".[18] Schuman thus gave heed to his conviction about the need of "The inauguration of a new kind of politics that will probably be the strongest effort to protect our continent and to preserve the world from suicide."[19] With this insight, Schuman[20] became the main architect of the Schuman Declaration (1950) which started the first peaceful revolution in Europe after far more than a thousand years of conflict on the European continent.

Schuman stressed, like Adenauer and De Gasperi, the importance of the European spiritual and cultural heritage primarily composed of its Greek and Roman roots as well as Judeo-Christian spirituality. The three of them considered this heritage to be the soul and binding element of all European States, while at the same time being the DNA of the Europeans, despite citizens considering sometimes the start of the European heritage from the Enlightenment onwards, as Schuman reflected in the following statement: "Christian ideas survived in the people's subconscious and influenced men who gave up practising a dogmatic religion, but who were nevertheless inspired by its main principles. These principles have become the features of our civilisation, owing to which the 18th century rationalists proclaimed and made popular human and citizens' rights, which are essentially Christian."[21]

In his professional practice, Schuman followed conscientiously the Social Doctrine of the Church. He put the following set of thoughts into effect in line with this doctrine. Its topicality will be shortly referred to in this section and more extensively in the next section about "Schuman in today's world."

The person with his transcendence needs to be at the core of economic, political, judicial and social development. This concept of the person has as a logical

[18] *See:*Krijtenburg 2012, p. 272.

[19] Schuman at Palais des Fêtes, Strasbourg 16 May 1949. *See also:* Price 2003, p. 52. *See:* Krijtenburg 2012, p. 187.

[20] Worthwhile in this regard is that Schuman, a politician, is in a process of beatification since 2004. The last and only politician until now (2016) who was beatified was Thomas More in the 16th century. These processes usually take several years.

[21] Schuman 2010a, pp. 43–45. *See:* Krijtenburg 2012, p. 224.

consequence the output of effective solidarity[22] also beyond borders and a focus on the common good as it is clearly expressed in the *Compendium of the Social Doctrine of the Church*. This means looking for the common interests of peoples where and when needed, so as to foster or attain peace and development. "We shall have to replace all the tendencies inherited from the past with the notion of solidarity, that is to say the conviction that the real interest of all lies in acknowledging and accepting the interdependency of all. Egoism does not pay any more."[23] This implied for him that the Franco-German common interest in coal and steel—instruments of war until then—changed into instruments of peace. The European Coal and Steel Community (ECSC) has come into being so as to avoid war and obtain mutual benefit. This line of thinking is confronting the EU with the content and main motives of its procedures. It is also topical for the problems it is currently facing. More will be said in the section on Schuman in today's world.

In line with the effective solidarity principle, he introduced the concept of supra-nationality so as to safeguard the higher common European interests above the national interests and ensure the peace among the Member States and their citizens. "Our century that has witnessed the catastrophes resulting in the unending clash of nationalities and nationalisms, must attempt and succeed in reconciling nations in a supranational association."[24] This ECSC was governed by the supranational High Authority, the current European Commission, so as to make this possible. This observation offers as well input for solving current problems as it will be suggested in the next section.

Schuman wanted to break the power of cartels, also because their power had contributed largely to the arms production during the World Wars. The supranational structure of the European unification project makes this possible. Transparency also in this realm is a necessity according to Schuman. The fact that the power of cartels can monopolise not only markets, but can also direct politics and contribute to warfare is a well-known secret. The German arms industry during the Second World War provides a clear example.[25]

Based on the concept of the person with his transcendence—and solidarity—, Schuman promoted the Franco-German reconciliation policy from 1919 onwards (the year in which the Treaty of Versailles was signed, which is also popularly known as the Treaty of Revenge). Reconciliation by looking for the common interests however far apart countries, parties or persons may be, is proper to the teachings of Thomas Aquinas that Schuman had made his own. Once the common interests are found, the proactive approach to build on those interests without

[22] For Schuman "Solidarity highlights in a particular way the intrinsic social nature of the human person, the equality of all in dignity and rights and the common path of individuals and peoples towards an ever more committed unity." *Compendium of the social doctrine of the Church* 2004, No. 192.

[23] Schuman 1950.

[24] *Ibid.*

[25] From Heilbron Price D (not yet published).

wanting to beat the other party is needed. As mentioned before, the field for reconciliation in those days was hidden in the Franco-German common interests in coal and steel. The practice of solidarity as mentioned in point 1, can therefore be considered a practical output of the policy of reconciliation.

"The gathering of the nations of Europe demands the elimination of the age-old antagonism of France and Germany. The first concern of any action undertaken must involve these two countries."[26] This line of thought is highly topical considering the globalised world of today. It is necessary to find and work on common ground and interests that extend not only beyond national borders, but also beyond European and other continental borders. When following Schuman's line of thought, reconciliation will be needed in order to recognise, acknowledge and wish to share the common interests. Solidarity among the peoples will need to be the practical output. The following section will consider this aspect especially when dealing with ecology.

Schuman stressed the need of subsidiarity so as to foster and protect the development as close to the person, enterprise, region, state or continent as possible, unless this goes to the detriment of the common good. Referring to the protection of national interests unless these go against the common good on a larger scale, Schuman said, "[w]e are not, and we shall never be, given to deny our mother country; we shall never forget our duties towards it. But beyond each country, we increasingly and clearly acknowledge the existence of a common good, superior to national interest. A common good into which our countries' individual interests are merged."[27] Again, it can be concluded that this observation is topical. The development of the person in line with the common good of the community is meant to play a pivotal role in economic, political, social and judicial affairs. Only thus can human rights be safeguarded and social cohesion take place within the society. More on this in the section on Schuman in today's world.

The content of his focus on the European spirit is clear when he says, "[t]he European spirit signifies being conscious of belonging to a cultural family and to have a willingness to serve that community in the spirit of total mutuality, without any hidden motives of hegemony or the selfish exploitation of others. [...] This would safeguard the diversities and aspirations of each nation while coordinating them in the same manner as the regions are coordinated within the unity of the nation."[28] For Schuman, there was no doubt that the Eastern and Central European countries belonged to Europe as they share a large part of the same European heritage. They would need to re-join the western world again as soon as the Communist system would fall apart.[29]

His speech for the signature of Statutes for the Council of Europe in 1949, in London, highlights clearly that the work ahead was to create a rejuvenated nucleus

---

[26] Schuman 1950.

[27] Schuman 2010a, p. 30. *See:* Krijtenburg 2012, p. 217.

[28] *Ibid.*, Schuman 2010a, p. 30. *See: Ibid.*, Krijtenburg 2012, p. 66.

[29] *Ibid.,* Krijtenburg 2012, p. 69.

of Europe that could possibly welcome countries in, such as those then behind the Iron Curtain, making it whole.[30] "We must construct Europe, not in the interest of the free peoples alone but also to be able to welcome in it the peoples of the East, who freed from the repression that they have been subject to until the present, will ask us for their adhesion and for our moral support… We consider as integrating part of a living Europe all those who desire to re-join us in a reconstituted Community. We pay homage to their courage and their faithfulness as well as their suffering and their sacrifices."[31]

The European spirit puts the person and his transcendence at the core and therefore implies respect for every person, irrespective of his denomination or non-denomination, sex, race or class. The openness and welcoming attitude towards those in need and the attitude of reconciliation are logical consequences of the European spirit. Thinking of the refugee-influx and of bad practices of Europeans and non-Europeans alike, this line of thought may be called revolutionary these days. Schuman continues saying that Europe, once recovered economically,[32] was called upon to contribute to the needs of the whole world with a special care of the development of the African continent. He affirmed that: "[t]his [solidarity of] production will be offered to the world as a whole without distinction or exception, with the aim of contributing to raising living standards and to promoting peaceful achievements. With increased resources Europe will be able to pursue the achievement of one of its essential tasks, namely, the development of the African continent."[33] The Malta conference with European and African Ministers of Foreign Affairs and Heads of State that took place in November 2015 so as to work towards a solution for the migrants from Africa to enter Europe, shows, on the one hand, that Schuman's call for development of the African continent was not followed in his days and, on the other hand, that it seems to be put into practice nowadays. More will be said in the section on Schuman in today's world.

Schuman warns against interpreting effective solidarity equally to economic and technical "gluttony" and advancement, as the danger then exists that man forgets that the economy and technology are meant to serve man and not the other way round. "This whole cannot and must not remain an economic and technical enterprise: it needs a soul, the conscience of its historical affinities and of its responsibilities, in the present and in the future, and a political will at the service of the same human ideal."[34] This observation is highly topical when considering the lack of ethical demand and the aberrations a main focus on technology can

[30] Price 2014. The Statutes were signed by the Ministers of Foreign Affairs of Belgium (Spaak), Denmark (Rasmussen), France (Schuman), Irish Republic (MacBride), Italy (Sforza), Luxembourg (Bech), The Netherlands (Stikker), Norway (Lange), Sweden (Undén), the UK (Bevin).

[31] Schuman quoted by Price 1997, p. vii.

[32] Schuman refers to the Marshall Plan with its financial aid that required economic co-operation among European states so as to rebuild its continent and be able to confront communism.

[33] Schuman 1950.

[34] Schuman 2010a, 58. *See:* Krijtenburg 2012, p. 165.

bring about when it is considered to be free from the individuals and community-related interests of mankind. Cybercrime is only an example. A main focus on the economic development without taking the individuals and community-related interests into account, is (in)directly the cause of unemployment, bad functioning of politics and social unrest. The economic crises and their consequences are only an example.

Schuman foresees an integration that follows the human psychology and will therefore go step-by-step. "We are still at the start of things. We would do well to bridle our impatience. If not, we are likely to make the doubters more distrustful and what is more serious, endanger not only the experiment but also the whole idea of a united Europe".[35] Schuman's call for an integration step-by-step is topical in the sense that the person cannot digest big changes if he or she is not prepared for them. Even at moments such as today's crises, a step-by-step procedure is needed. The steps can go fast as long as they are understood. Most importantly, the people must be informed, listened to, understood, felt understood and helped with consistency to put the steps into practice as amiable as possible.

Schuman's vision and mission for Europe seem to be summarised somehow in his belief that: "[w]hat Europe wants is to uplift the rigidity of its borders. They should become the lines of contact where the material and cultural exchanges take place. They define the particular tasks, responsibilities and innovations proper to each country taking into account as well the problems all countries together—and even the continents—face and thus foster solidarity."[36] This observation highlights that Schuman's vision on European unification is closely connected to his preoccupation for the universal common good and that borders are lines of communication, not of separation.

3.4 Schuman in Today's World, an Interpretation

Four main points currently standing on the EU's agenda will be interpreted in a short, general and plausible way along Schuman's line of thought. The topics dealt with are: Ecology, Refugees, Economic Crisis and Terrorism.

3.4.1 Ecology

With a reference to today's society and the Climate Summit of Paris in 2015, it can be expected that Schuman would stress the crucial need to take care of our universal common good, our "common home." Like today's statesmen and climate

[35] Schuman's Speech at Council of Europe Strasbourg. *See:* Krijtenburg 2012, p. 69.

[36] Schuman 2010a, pp. 26–27. *See:* Krijtenburg 2012, p. 173.

experts, he would subsequently underline that the ecological system needs the world's attention as well as practical and effective protection so as to avoid natural and human disasters. Schuman would suggest anchoring the agreement on the protection of this common universal good in a supra-continental way as it concerns the well-being of the whole mankind.

Just like human beings, nature cannot also be governed primarily by (inter) national economic and political laws, and therewith be exploited insofar as to provoke both harm to itself and mankind in the short or longer run. Deforestation, desertification, pollution of air and water are only examples of what can happen and happens when the ecology is not taken into account for economic and political reasons.

The importance of taking care of nature or creation is—along Schuman's line of thought—parallel to the need of caring for the nature of mankind. Rapid changes due to economic or political reasons going against the nature of creation will also go against the nature of man. This observation is clearly echoed in the following quote that belongs to the Social Doctrine of the Church: "[t]he continued acceleration of changes affecting humanity and the planet is coupled today with a more intensified pace of life and work which might be called 'rapidification.' Although change is part of the working of complex systems, the speed with which human activity has developed contrasts with the naturally slow pace of biological evolution. Moreover, the goals of this rapid and constant change are not necessarily geared to the common good or to integral and sustainable human development. Change is something desirable, yet it becomes a source of anxiety when it causes harm to the world and to the quality of life of much of humanity."[37]

It can be assumed that Schuman would want to tackle the problem at its roots. He would call for a gathering of leaders of state and specialists in the field that are comparable to the gathering for the Declaration on Human Rights in 1948 when experts, also philosophers and theologians of all religions and denominations or non-denominations, came together to extract the fundamental human rights applicable to each human being all over the world. It would go further therefore than the Climate Summits already organised. In those meetings, the leaders—after having heard the specialists—would express the concerns of their countries on topics such as droughts, desertification, deforestation, air or water pollution as well as all the implications these provoke, such as migration, poverty and changes in lifestyles for the people concerned. Collecting this data would help to find out together—with the help of experts in the fields—how these problems can be tackled from a supra-continental perspective by burden-sharing and by adapting juridical, political, economic and social structures. Such collection could be done in such a way that nature with its natural resources will be at the core of those structures together with the person with his transcendence and effective solidarity. Supranational thinking, as a way of reasoning for the institutions of the EU, will in

[37] Pope Francis 2015.

this regard be replaced by supra-continental thinking as well as taking action with effective policies and legal obligations. Economic, political, social and judicial thinking will be geared by ecological thinking, with a pivotal role of human ecology which cannot be separated from taking care of the ecology of nature, and vice versa.[38]

This will have a huge impact in all realms of life, from individual and family life to national and continental life. Although the person with his transcendence and effective solidarity will always remain at the core and different identities will continue to exist and be fostered, the impact of structures in which nature and man are at the heart might very well bring a better sharing and wiser use of natural resources as well as an image of the world that one cannot yet portray. This is supported by another quote of the Social Doctrine of the Church in which it calls explicitly for a new social, economic and political order founded on man and his spiritual dimension, when saying: "[t]he Church (…) intends to propose to all men and women (…) an integral and solidary humanism capable of creating a new social, economic and political order, founded on the dignity and freedom of every human person, to be brought about in peace, justice and solidarity. This humanism can become a reality if individual men and women and their communities are able to cultivate moral and social virtues in themselves and spread them in society."[39]

3.4.2 Refugees

One main point on the EU agenda concerns the refugees. As Secretary General of Refugees appointed in 1940, Schuman did all he could to protect French refugees of Alsace-Lorraine from the Nazis. But when he had gone to Metz to burn information about the refugees that should not fall into the hands of the Germans, he was caught as first parliamentarian by the Gestapo and sent to prison.

Nowadays, he would, first of all, surely try to find out the real story behind the refugee problem—How and why this refugee problem originated. This goes deeper than pointing the finger at Assad, the terrorists of the Islamic State, or referring to the lack of employment or to the need to flee for environmental reasons such as drought.

---

[38] This observation is supported by Ban Ki-moon in his Address at the International Symposium on Climate Change at Pontifical Academy of Science, Vatican. According to him "Climate change is intrinsically linked to public health, food and water security, migration, peace and security. It is a moral issue of social justice, human rights and fundamental ethics. […] Science and religion are not at odds on climate change. Indeed, they are fully aligned. […] Our response has to be global, holistic and rooted in universal values. […] We need to see, with the eyes of faith … the link between the natural environment and the dignity of the human person." *Zenit*, Rome 2015.

[39] *Compendium of the Social Doctrine of the Church 2014*, No. 19.

He would also wonder and examine why the surrounding countries and European countries react as they do to this problem. In the meantime, he would stress the need to commonly tackle the registration and accommodation of the enormous influx of refugees, and not to leave this exclusively up to the countries where the migrants get ashore. He would surely applaud the set up and well-functioning of legal migration channels in order to offer the refugees a better hope of a decent living and development in the recipient countries or—if this cannot be—back in their own countries thanks to financial and practical aid from the EU and other countries and institutions, such as decided upon during the Malta Conference in November 2015.[40] On top of this need to be tackled by the EU along with other countries providing aid, there are also reasons of an economic nature which militate in favour of pardoning the debts that less developed countries might have in order to help building up upright, stable economic and political structures in those same countries.

As Schuman sees the person and his transcendence at the core of all social, economic, political and judicial affairs, social cohesion will always be a priority. His device would therefore be to welcome and integrate the refugees that enter(ed) Europe as soon as possible into the society. Interreligious dialogue[41] will be needed, precisely as a consequence of the European spiritual and cultural heritage which professes human rights as defined in the Universal Declaration of 1948. This would be a good deterrent against possible radicalisation and would contribute largely to peace and development among the citizens.

Although the circumstances were very different, the content of the following quote is worthwhile to be remembered regarding the attitude to adopt towards the refugees. "The example and the conviction will be our only means in an enterprise that will be exclusively peaceful and constructive. We will not threaten anyone when we get associated for mutual assistance; but we serve Europe at the same time as a whole by creating the nucleus of a renewed Europe, regenerated in the common hardships and aware of its eternal civilising mission."[42]

3.4.3 Economic Crisis

Putting Schuman's frame of reference on today's European economic crisis in general would imply a thorough, but prudently implemented change of today's

---

[40] *See also:* Gruyter 2015.

[41] Coexister: a French interreligious movement erected after the Charlie Hebdo attack on 7 January 2015. The movement has a large impact on the French society, won a state Prize for fostering social cohesion and has international reach-out. See Coexister 2016.

[42] Schuman Speech at the signatures of Statutes of the Council of Europe, London, 5 May 1949. [...] l'exemple et la persuasion seront nos seuls moyens dans une entreprise qui sera exclusivement pacifique et constructive. Nous ne menacerons personne en nous associant en vue d'une aide mutuelle; mais nous servons en même temps l'Europe dans son ensemble en créant le noyau d'une Europe renouvelée, régénérée dans les épreuves communes et consciente de son éternelle mission civilisatrice.

mind-set regarding the leading role of the economy in the European unification project. In Schuman's philosophy, economic integration was not the aim of European unification. It needed to serve first and foremost mankind and his social and spiritual development, while being an important means to provide peace and political unification. Just as Western Europe received financial aid after the Second World War to rebuild its economies, the European Union would need to practise more effectively and more generously its subsidiarity and solidarity principles towards its economically backward Member States. The EU would therefore need to attain transparency on what's going well or not and why. The EU should thus analyse the strong and the weak points of the economies in each of its Member States. In Schuman's view, building on the strong points and giving responsibility in those fields as well as helping out on the weak points so as to make these strong where needed would provide mutual satisfaction. These insights and help would equally contribute to the eradication of corruption, to more transparency in economic structures as well as to social cohesion beyond borders. The national economic interests would no longer prevail over the European interests. Schuman's warning not to make the unification project an economic and technological enterprise without a soul, would have been taken to heart by the European Union and its Member States.

3.4.4 Terrorism

Taking Schuman's line of thought into account, the terrorist attacks might best be "fought" through intensely fostering the process of social cohesion within the states and among the peoples. Welcoming the people that arrive(d), integrating them into our societies and fostering interreligious dialogue such as promoted by coexister, including people that do not believe, will be translating Schuman's mind-set. Focusing on the common ground as human beings will not only help to avoid radicalisation, but also to discover, respect and appreciate the richness of each other's culture and spiritual identity as well as encourage a real care for each other. It equally helps to better discern the richness of one's own culture and spiritual identity for the need to explain it to others, and thus, delve more into its content. This togetherness fosters a brotherhood of people(s).

3.4.5 In Short

Europe has been woken up in a brutal way. It now has the challenging opportunity to be the master of its fate and a key player in what will be the fate of peoples all over the world, precisely for living the scene that is making crucial history. Europe needs to fight its possible fear with the attitude of embracing its task of being supportive and caring and put effort to overcome its lack of confidence in the EU among its citizens and Member States by trying to solve together as far as possible not only the European problems, but also those extending beyond European borders. Schuman would call for a focus on caring for the universal common good and for not being afraid, but, on the contrary, for taking the initiative to serve others better beyond borders in order to thus serve ourselves better.

Schuman's words for Europe and the world today, followed by an observation of the Social Doctrine of the Church in the same line, may well be adequate closing remarks: "Europe is searching for an identity; it is aware that it has its own future in hand. It has never been so close to the goal. May God not let Europe miss the hour of its destiny, its final chance of salvation."[43] "We have to, we want to give Europe its radiance back, its strength, its independence, in other words, its secular mission as a guide and arbitrator."[44] And again: "[w]hat Europe wants is to uplift the rigidity of its borders. They should become the lines of contact where the material and cultural exchanges take place. They define the particular tasks, responsibilities and innovations proper to each country taking into account as well the problems all countries together—and even the continents—face and thus foster solidarity."[45]

Put in today's words, Schuman launches a call to consider and dare giving heed to effective solidarity beyond borders among peoples worldwide, while taking the universal common good into account as: "[…] there exists an intimate bond between solidarity and the common good, between solidarity and the universal destination of goods, between solidarity and equality among men and peoples, between solidarity and peace in the world. The term 'solidarity,' […] translates [itself] into the willingness to give oneself for the good of one's neighbour, beyond any individual or particular interest."[46]

3.5 Conclusion

The current upheaval on the European continent in a large variety of realms can be considered as a wake-up call for opening up the profound cause of the turmoil, which in the end resides in the lack of having the person and, thus, human solidarity at the core of the integration process. It now calls for the need to work towards a solution to tackle the crises.

This article endeavours to show that Schuman's frame of reference offers guidelines on the principles of subsidiarity and solidarity based on the person with his transcendence, with which to work towards a blueprint and solution for today's

[43] Schuman 2010a, pp. 143–144. *See:* Krijtenburg 2012, p. 174.

[44] *See:* Krijtenburg 2012, p. 174. Schuman quoted in: Muñoz 2008, p. 47. «Nous devons, nous voulons rendre à l'Europe son rayonnement, sa force, son indépendance, en d'autres termes la rendre à sa mission séculaire de guide et d'arbitre».

[45] Schuman 2010a pp. 26–27. Krijtenburg 2012 p. 173.

[46] *Compendium of the Social doctrine of the Church* 2004, n. 194.

problems. Schuman's frame of reference puts man with his spiritual dimension at the core of integration, in accordance with the European spiritual and cultural heritage.[47] It regards economic co-operation as a means to reach political integration, but always and only in accordance with the subsidiarity and solidarity principles, and, therefore, at the service of man and his transcendence. This applies equally to a region, a state, Europe, and other continents, which all needs to be as independent as possible, unless this goes to the detriment of the common good at a larger scale. We'are living in a global society and are therefore much more interconnected than ever before. We need thus to be even more aware of the intrinsic dignity of every human person so as to live up to the principles of subsidiarity and solidarity in all realms. To quote Schuman: "[i]f one day a state of peace, really deserving this name, will be established solid and sustainable among the peoples, then that will not depend on only political, economic and financial arrangements made by diplomats and statesmen, neither on only the judicial edifice of a coordinating real supranational organism with effective means of action, [but] that will depend as well on the profound adhesion obtained in the conscience of men because of the practice of the human rights principles."[48]

Schuman's frame of reference echoes nowadays' Social Doctrine of the Church, that Schuman himself already followed cautiously as well. This Social Doctrine offers the same guiding principles of subsidiarity and solidarity, and also puts man and his spiritual dimension at the core.

So as to end with Schuman's conviction on Europe's calling to serve humanity—and thus live solidarity—backed by Pope Francis observation in the European Parliament on 25 November 2014, for which amongst others he obtained the Charlemagne Prize 2016,[49] this conclusion finishes with: "[t]his Europe which is still split up and torn, continues to be ever more aware of its calling to become the heart of a pacific co-operation of all peoples and of all races at the service of a humanity that embraces all continents."[50] "The time has come to work together in building a Europe which revolves not around the economy, but around the sacredness of the human person, around inalienable values. [...] A Europe which cares

---

[47] The spiritual heritage Schuman speaks about finds its secular outlook in the Human Rights Declaration of 1948, see Universal Declaration of Human Rights (1948) 217 A (III) http://www.ohchr.org/EN/UDHR/Documents/UDHR_Translations/eng.pdf, accessed on 1 July 2016.

[48] In Schuman's Speech at General Assembly UNESCO 1947, *Synthèses*, pp. 271–282. 1947, translated by the author of the article. «Si un état de paix qui mérite vraiment ce nom et qui soit solide et durable doit être établi un jour entre les peuples, cela ne dépendra pas seulement des arrangements politiques, économiques et financiers conclus par les diplomates et les hommes d'État, cela ne dépendra pas seulement de l'édification juridique d'un organisme coordinateur véritablement supranational pourvu d'efficaces moyens d'action, cela dépendra aussi de l'adhésion profonde obtenue dans la conscience des hommes par des principes pratiques tels que les droits de l'homme».

[49] Der Internationale Karlspreis zu Aachen (2016).

[50] Schuman 2010b p. 30. «L'Europe qui est encore aujourd'hui divisée et déchirée, continue de prendre toujours plus conscience de sa vocation à former le cœur d'une coopération pacifique de tous les peuples et de toutes les races au service d'une humanité embrassant tous les continents».

for, defends and protects man, every man and woman. A Europe which bestrides the earth surely and securely, a precious point of reference for all humanity!"[51]

Jurists, politicians and political scientists, economists, social scientists and experts of other disciplines from different continents are invited to flesh out this world vision that goes along with Schuman's frame of reference and for which today's world is yearning for showing the profound root of and a—the?—way in which current problem areas can be changed into sources for a new economic, political and social world order that gears around human dignity, together with the principles of subsidiarity and solidarity.

References

Brague R (2002) Eccentric culture: a theory of western civilization. St. Augustine's Press, South Bend

Coexister (2016) http://coexister.fr [information also available on the website in English]

Compendium of the Social Doctrine of the Church (2004). Libreria Editrice Vaticana, Rome

Der Internationale Karlspreis zu Aachen (2016) Begründung des Direktoriums der Gesellschaft für die Verleihung des Internationalen Karlspreises zu Aachen an Seine Heiligkeit Papst Franziskus. http://www.karlspreis.de/de/aktuelles/karlspreis-2016. Accessed 1 July 2016

European External Union Action (2015) Statement of the High Representative and Vice-President Federica Mogherini on the capsizing of a migrants' boat in the Mediterranean Sea. http://eeas.europa.eu/statements-eeas/2015/150419_01_en.htm. Accessed 17 Apr 2015

Gerbet P (1962) La Genèse du Plan Schuman. Centre de recherches européennes, Lausanne

Gruyter C (2015) Illlegale migratie is maar één stukje van de puzzel. NRC Weekend, 22–23 Aug 2015, pp 12–13

Havard A (2014) Virtuous leadership. Scepter Publishers, New York

Heilbron Price D (not yet published) Manuscript on cartels before the Second World War. Document of Supreme Headquarters Allied Expeditionary Force (SHAEF), Combined Intelligence Objectives Sub-Committee, G-2 Division, APO 419. I.G. Farbenindustrie, A.G., 1943

Judt T (2005) Postwar, a history of Europe since 1945. The Penguin Press, New York

Krijtenburg M (2012) Schuman's Europe. His frame of reference. Leiden University Press, Leiden

Krijtenburg M (2013) L'Europe de Schuman. Ses Racines. Éditions des Paraignes, Metz

Krijtenburg M (2015a) Robert Schuman's commitment to European unification: the inspiring role of his Roman Catholic faith. In: Philosophia Reformata, vol 80, no 1. Brill Publishers, Leiden, pp 140–157

Krijtenburg M (2015b) Robert Schuman, principal architect of the European Union. In: Research papers Market, Culture & Ethics Pontificia Università della Santa Croce, Rome

Krijtenburg M (2015c) Schuman's referentiekader voor de EU van nu. In: Europa, méér dan een economische eenheid. Centrum voor de Sociale Leer van de Kerk, Vogelenzang, pp 15–35

Krijtenburg M (2016a) Schuman, yesterday and today. The Hague University of Applied Sciences, The Hague

Krijtenburg M (2016b) Schuman, hier et aujourd'hui. Éditions des Paraignes, Metz

Lejeune R (2000) Père de l'Europe. Fayard, Paris

Maritain J (1968) Humanisme intégral, Aubier edn. Montaigne, Paris

[51] Pope Francis 2014.

Milward AS (1984) The reconstruction of Western Europe 1945-1951. Methuen & Co. Ltd, London

Muñoz A (2008) L'engagement européen de Robert Schuman. Robert Schuman et les Pères de l'Europe. Peter Lang, Brussels, pp 39–57

Pennera C (1985) Robert Schuman: la jeunesse et les débuts politiques d'un grand Européen de 1886 à 1924. Pierron, Sarreguemine

Poidevin R (1988) Robert Schuman. Beauchesne, Paris

Pope Francis (2014) Speech at the European Parliament, Strasbourg, Nov 2014

Pope Francis (2015) Encyclical Letter Laudato si. Libreria Editrice Vaticana, Rome

Pope Leo XIII (1879) Encyclical letter Aeterni Patris. Libreria Editrice Vaticana, Rome

Pope Leo XIII (1891) Encyclical letter Rerum Novarum. Libreria Editrice Vaticana, Rome

Pope Pius XI (1931) Encyclical letter Quadragesimo Anno. Libreria Editrice Vaticana, Rome

Price D (1997) New cold war or common European home? Bron Communications, Brussels

Price D (2003) Schuman or Monnet? Bron Communications, Brussels

Price D (2014) Jalonneur. Schuman, Jalonneur de la Paix Mondiale. Bron Communications, Brussels

Ratzinger J (2006) Values in times of upheaval. Ignatius Press, San Francisco

Reuter P (1980) La naissance de l'Europe communautaire. Jean Monnet Foundation, Lausanne

Rhonheimer M (2009). Rialp, Madrid

Roth F (2008) Robert Schuman. Fayard, Paris

Sabine GH, Thorson TL (1973) A history of political theory. Dryden Press, 4th edn, Hinsdale, IL

Schuman R (1950) La déclaration de Schuman du 9 Mai 1950. http://europa.eu/about-eu/basic-information/symbols/europe-day/schuman-declaration/index_fr.htm. Accessed 16 June 2016

Schuman R (2005) Pour l'Europe. Les Éditions Nagel, 4th edn, Geneva

Schuman R (2010a) For Europe. Les Éditions Nagel, Geneva

Schuman R (2010b) Pour l'unité de l'Europe. In: Du Pater Europae aux Pères de l'Europe. Silvana Editoriale, Milan, pp 24–32, 58–60

Segers M (2013) Reis naar het continent. Nederland en de Europese integratie, 1950 tot heden. Bert Bakker, Amsterdam

Segers M (2014) Lecture on "De totstandkoming van de EU in duizend en een verhalen", Pro-Demos, The Hague

The Navarre Bible: New Testament (2001). Scepter Publishers, New York

Villarós G (2006) La spiritualité de Robert Schuman. In: de Guibert F-X (ed) Robert Schuman, homme d'état, citoyen du Ciel, Office d'Édition Impression Librairie, Paris, pp. 103–120

Zenit, Rome (2015) UN Secretary General Ban Ki-moon's Address at International Symposium on Climate Change. https://zenit.org/articles/un-secretary-general-ban-ki-moon-s-address-at-international-symposium-on-climate-change/. Accessed 1 July 2016

Chapter 4
Better Regulation in the EU—A Process and Debate at the Core of Regional Integration

Piet Willems

Abstract This chapter assesses whether the European Commission has respected the limitations that follow from the European Union's institutional design and the notion of mutual sincere co-operation, when launching and implementing its Better Regulation Agenda (BRA). The analysis focuses on three different concepts that are key to the Union's institutional design: the concept of representative democracy, the principle of effectiveness and the privileged position of both the Committee of the Regions and the European Economic and Social Committee. This selection is based on an analysis of the different critiques on the BRA by other European institutions as well as civil society actors. The focus is on the legal implications for the European Commission when implementing the BRA as well as on the possibility of enforcement of these concepts in case of transgressions. At the same time the chapter provides an insight into the historic antecedents of the BRA and places this topic within the overall principles and dynamics of region integration within Europe. Particular emphasis is paid to the role of inter-institutional agreements.

Keywords European Union · Better Regulation Agenda · Better Law-Making · Inter-institutional agreements · Effectiveness · Representative democracy · Mutual sincere cooperation · Committee of the Regions · European Economic and Social Committee · Institutional design

P. Willems (✉)
The Hague University for Applied Science, Johanna Westerdijkplein 75, 2521 EN The Hague, The Netherlands
e-mail: P.Willems@hhs.nl

J. de Zwaan et al. (eds.), *Governance and Security Issues of the European Union*, DOI 10.1007/978-94-6265-144-9_4

Contents

4.1 Introduction

Nearly fifteen years after the adoption of the Laeken Declaration[1] by the European Council and the launch of a White Paper on European governance by the European Commission[2] the European Union is still struggling to redefine its regulatory processes to support, rather than to undermine, the legitimacy of the Union.[3]

This chapter will focus on the institutional and conceptual limits that shape the political and institutional efforts to better EU regulation. The immediate cause for this chapter is the critique on the most recent attempt to further the quality of the EU's regulatory cycle, namely the launch of the Better Regulation Agenda (BRA)[4] by the European Commission in May 2015.[5] The BRA is a comprehensive set of initiatives, or "reforms" as the BRA labels them,[6] that should help the EU overcome or at least effectively tackle some of the challenges outlined in the Laeken Declaration.

The Laeken Declaration identified three key areas to bring about more democracy, transparency and efficiency in the European Union: (1) the role of national parliaments, (2) the increase of the democratic legitimacy and transparency of the present institutions and (3) the efficiency of decision-making and the workings of the institutions.[7] All three areas were discussed at length prior to the introduction

[1] European Council, Laeken Declaration 2001.

[2] European Commission 2001.

[3] Schmidt 2013, pp. 2–22.

[4] European Commission 2015a.

[5] For an initial assessment that reflects some of the initial reactions to the launch, *see* Renda 2015.

[6] European Commission, Press release 2015.

[7] European Council, Laeken Declaration 2001.

of the BRA, most notably in the European Convention[8] and the subsequent Intergovernmental Conferences. This resulted in the introduction of several amendments or reforms to the Union's design by the Lisbon Treaty.[9]

As for the role of the national parliaments this process, which ended with the Treaty of Lisbon, resulted in a fundamental upgrade of their role and involvement in the EU's regulatory cycle.[10] The impact on the two other key areas identified in the Laeken Declaration is less tangible. The Treaty of Lisbon merely introduced some new concepts like *representative democracy*[11] and *effectiveness*,[12] but failed to clarify how these concepts relate to the already complex institutional design of the European Union.

The launch of the BRA provides for a unique opportunity to assess the impact of these new concepts in the European Union's design and particularly on the institutional and conceptual limits and obligations of the different European institutions involved.

In an attempt to provide constructive input into the debate surrounding the BRA, this chapter aims at evaluating whether the European Commission has overstretched its mandate by launching the BRA or by the position it is taking in the negotiations of a new inter-institutional agreement on Better Regulation.[13] The evaluation will specifically look into three characteristics of the regulatory process as defined by the Treaty on the European Union (TEU) and the Treaty on the functioning of the European Union (TFEU): (1) the principle of mutual sincere cooperation within the context of a representative democracy (Article 13(2) TEU *juncto* Article 10 TEU),[14] (2) the principle of effectiveness (Article 13(1) TEU)[15] and (3) the privileged position of the Union's advisory bodies (Article 13(4) TEU).[16] This selection is based on a review of the main institutional criticisms on the BRA.[17]

[8] Treaty establishing a Constitution for Europe (Draft Constitutional Treaty), 18 July 2003, CONV 850/03.

[9] Treaty of Lisbon amending the Treaty on European Union and the Treaty establishing the European Community, opened for signature on 13 December 2007 O.J. C 306 (entered into force on 1 December 2009).

[10] Consolidated Version of the Treaty on European Union, opened for signature [2007] O.J. C 326 (entered into force on 1 December 2009) as amended on October 10, 2012 (Hereafter "TEU"), Article 12 and for a detailed description see Olivetti 2013, pp. 467–526.

[11] *Ibid.*, TEU Article 11.

[12] *Ibid.*, TEU Article 13.

[13] European Commission 2015b, later the Commission issued a revised version see below n 61.

[14] TEU above n 10, Articles 13(2) and 10.

[15] *Ibid.*, TEU Article 13(1).

[16] *Ibid.*, TEU Article 13(4).

[17] This review is based in part on a review of scholarly comments, but mostly on publicly accessible documents issued by political groups within the European Parliament as well as the official reactions by the Committee of the Regions and the European Economic and Social Committee.

Before analysing the specific items mentioned above, it is necessary to contextualise the launch of the BRA. The second section of this chapter will highlight some of the intrinsic challenges that are associated with the furthering of one or more dimensions of the process of regional integration. The third section will then examine earlier efforts to advance Better Regulation and the associated challenges and shortcomings, which led to the BRA. Building on these two sections, the fourth section will then proceed with the specific evaluation as outlined before.

4.2 Better Regulation and the Structural Challenges of Regional Integration

The European motto "Unity in Diversity" probably best describes the structural and fundamental challenges that any process of regional integration faces.[18] The enormous diversity amongst EU citizens and their representatives makes it challenging to achieve any common ground that is strong enough to spark true and widely supported enthusiasm for any plan or project to advance European regional integration.[19] This is no different in the case of BRA. On the contrary, it highlights substantial differences amongst Member States as well as political groups, since regulation is often at the very core of how one engages with issues of governance and public authority.

To create an environment of trust for these different interests to meet and to foster a strong and stable dynamic for the integration process, the founding fathers and all those who have followed have crafted a predictable and reliable institutional design built on limited and attributed competences.[20] The consequence of this choice is that the legitimacy of any change depends on either remaining within predefined institutional limits or the willingness of the Member States to take the regional integration one step further.[21]

Even if there is a willingness to take the regional integration process one step further, then still such initiatives may be confronted with some of the fundamental challenges of regional integration within the European Union. The subsequent subsections will deal with two of these challenges: the diversity of interests and the rigidity of the institutional design respectively.

[18] The European motto is one of the symbols of the European Union, for more information and translations see: European Union website 2016.

[19] Historic examples of difficulties to come to a common ground on the next step for regional integration include, but are not limited to: Schengen, the Euro, a European military capacity.

[20] As Jean Monnet said: "Nothing is possible without men, nothing is lasting without institutions." Monnet 1978, pp. 304–305.

[21] The integration of defence cooperation into the Treaties and the need prior to that to organize the defence co-operation in the WEU as a parallel structure are clear historical examples.

4.2.1 *Diverging Interests: Quality of Regulation Lies in the Eyes of the Beholder*

Like any other regulatory entity, the European institutions are scrutinised on their ability to achieve certain goals and results for their addressees, without creating an excessive administrative or financial burden.[22] It is virtually impossible to perfectly balance all the demands of these addressees, and this is the conundrum that the EU institutions face.

At the political level the critique on Better Regulation is not only coming from Euro sceptics, who continue to argue that the regulatory process creates a vast amount of red tape.[23] In fact, those who actively support further regional integration have also expressed concerns over the economic focus[24] of many of the Better Regulation initiatives and argue that the efforts simply fall short of the true ambitions of the European project.[25]

The analysis conducted on the position taken by the different political groups in reaction to the launch of the BRA confirms this view.[26] All political groups expressed substantial criticism or disappointment, irrespective of their overall endorsement of the BRA. Markus Pieper, from the European People's Party, the largest political group in the European Parliament, stated that the Regulatory Scrutiny Board—one of the BRA initiatives—was "only a good starting point, which must be improved."[27] Jutta Steinruck, from the Progressive Alliance of Socialists and Democrats, the second-largest political group in the European Parliament, heavily criticised certain aspects of the revised procedures for the Regulatory Fitness program (REFIT)[28] and stated: "We are opposed to such a proposal. The autonomous social dialogue, and the central role of the social partners in European social policy, must not be questioned.".[29] The reaction by other groups such as the Greens/European Free Alliance was even sharper, the latter argued that the BRA is "a coup against EU democratic process".[30]

Also in society at large one can hear similar almost irreconcilable expectations about the BRA. This contributes to the overall dissatisfaction with both the

[22] One such example could be the creation of a Better Regulation Delivery Office in the United Kingdom, for more information, see Better Regulation Delivery Office 2016.

[23] For a comment on the UK's most recent cut red tape initiative, see De Sousa 2013.

[24] European Commission 2015c.

[25] The reactions to the withdrawal of the circular economy proposal are a good example. For a more detailed discussion, see Crisp 2014.

[26] The full overview of this analysis of the different position could unfortunately not be included in the present format.

[27] Epp Group in the European Parliament 2015.

[28] For more information on REFIT see European Commission Better Regulation 2015.

[29] Hélin-Villes 2015.

[30] The Greens European Free Alliance in the European Parliament 2015.

process as well as the outcome. A good example is the critique by civil society organisations on the inability of the Union to deliver on its social or environmental goals.[31] At same time effort to do so could in turn be subject to criticism by representatives of small and medium-sized enterprises for generating excessive administrative burden.[32] The type of media coverage and the level of ill-informed statements by national politicians complicates matters even further.

All in all, the European institutions have long understood that handling this diversity will always be a particular challenge in an ever-changing and interconnected world. Compelled by the need for public support for the European project as well as their responsibility to ensure the consistency, effectiveness and continuity of its policies and actions,[33] the European institutions will continue to be faced with the challenges of finding this difficult and inherently dynamic balance.

Against this background, the present European Commission should be commended for launching such a major reform project as well as for putting it at the core of its political agenda.

4.2.2 Strict Institutional Design: Legitimacy Requires Due Respect for the Institutional Design of the European Union

In striving to buttress the legitimacy of the European Union by effectively balancing these interests, the European institutions are confronted with the limits of the EU's institutional and conceptual design as laid down in the Treaties. These limitations are reflected in two of the main organisational principles of the Union, namely the principle of conferral and the principle of procedural autonomy.

The principle of conferral was introduced in Article 4 of the Treaty of Rome and was inserted to ensure that the institutions[34] will not act beyond the mandate explicitly conferred upon them. In its vertical dimension as reflected in Article 5 TEU, the principle of conferral safeguards the Member States from legal action taken by EU entities.[35] In its horizontal dimension enshrined in Article 13(2) TEU, it safeguards EU institutions from each other's actions.[36] The principle of conferral may be enforced by the Court of Justice of the European Union (CJEU) that

---

[31] Van den Abeele 2015.

[32] See for example: Hendrickx 2012; equally interesting: Better Europe 2015.

[33] TEU, above n 10, Article 13(1).

[34] TEU above n 10, Article 13(1) TEU contains a limitative list of seven European institutions: the European Parliament, the European Council, the Council, the European Commission, the Court of Justice of the European Union, the European Central Bank, the Court of Auditors.

[35] For an overview of the CJEU cases on the basis of Article 5 TEU see InfoCuria 2016a.

[36] For an overview of the CJEU cases on the basis of Article 13(2) TEU see: InfoCuria 2016b.

can ensure that these relationships are respected by assessing whether the institution under consideration had a sufficient legal basis for its actions.

The principle of procedural autonomy entails that each of the entities can adopt its own rules and procedures in its endeavour to diligently execute its mandate.[37]

The combined result of these principles is that the European institutions often prefer to test the limits of their competences rather than triggering a debate on the necessity of changes in their respective mandates, since these types of changes can only be brought about by amending the Treaties. The past two decades have taught us that doing so is not an option to be taken lightly.[38] The debate surrounding treaty amendment often exposes widely diverging views on the EU's structure, its goals and competences, and can lead to periods of institutional dead-lock.

The alternative—testing the limits of their respective competences—is not desirable either as it most likely will trigger both public and institutional contestation. In turn, this may feed a perception of contempt by the European institutions for the very principles that underpin their legitimacy and that of the European Union.

4.3 Better Regulation, an Introduction

4.3.1 The Historic Antecedents to the BRA

Over the past two and a half decades, the European institutions have identified and tried to remedy part of the internal deficiencies in the regulatory cycle.[39] In doing so, they have also drawn on parallel developments in other international organisations like the Organisation for Economic Co-operation and Development.[40]

Originally, the focus of the Better Regulation efforts was on the quality of legislation and the following series of initiatives were taken in that respect:[41]

---

[37] Consolidated Version of the Treaty on the Functioning of the European Union, opened for signature [2007] O.J. C 326 (entered into force on 1 December 2009) as amended on October 10, 2012 (Hereafter "TFEU"). To give just a few examples of how the principle of procedural autonomy is reflected in the TFEU: Article 232 TFEU for the European Parliament; Article 235(3) TFEU for the European Council; Article 240(3) for the Council and Article 249(1) TFEU for the Commission.

[38] Especially the impact of referenda as part of the ratification process has proven to be challenging.

[39] For a comprehensive overview of the key documents in relation to Better Regulation see: European Commission Better Regulation 2016.

[40] For an overview of the relevant OECD initiatives see OECD 2016.

[41] For a more complete overview see European Commission Legal Service 2016.

- 1993 Council Resolution on the quality of drafting of Community legislation;[42]
- 1997 Declaration 39 on the quality of the drafting of Community legislation annexed to the Treaty of Amsterdam;[43]
- 1998 Interinstitutional Agreement on common guidelines for the quality of drafting of Community legislation.[44]

Soon after, following the adoption to the Lisbon strategy by the European Council in March 2000, the focus of the Better Regulation efforts shifted to simplifying and improving the regulatory environment. Some of the milestones of this phase are as follows:

- 2000 establishment of a high-level advisory group, also known as the Mandelkern group;[45]
- 2001 White paper on European governance[46] and subsequent documents;[47]
- 2003 Interinstitutional Agreement on better law-making.[48]

Following this broader approach, different specific programs and action plans were developed. The most important ones would be SMART Regulation and REFIT. SMART Regulation focuses on reducing the economic impact of red tape on small and medium-sized enterprises, while REFIT simplifies the existing *acquis* primarily by using the recasting technique whereby old legislation is repealed or replaced.[49]

4.3.2 Lessons to Be Drawn from the Historic Antecedents to the BRA

An evaluation of these early initiatives brings three structural problems to light. First, the challenge of diverging interest is amplified in the case of Better Regulation. The interests at stake are not limited to diverging views on the purpose or goal of Better Regulation or the focus that should be applied in light of societal priorities. In the case of Better Regulation, the self-interest of the institutions

[42] Council Resolution (1993), The quality of drafting of Community legislation O.J. C 166 17/06/1993 P. 0001–0001.

[43] Amsterdam Intergovernmental Conference 1997.

[44] Interinstitutional Agreement on common guidelines for the quality of drafting of Community legislation, opened for signature (1998) entered into force on 22 December 1998 O.J. C 73.

[45] Ponzano 2001.

[46] European Commission 2001.

[47] For an overview of the subsequent documents see European Commission Legal Service (2016).

[48] Interinstitutional Agreement on better law-making opened for signature (2003) O.J. C 321/01 *31/12/2003 P. 0001–0005* (entered into force on 16 December 2003).

[49] Interinstitutional Agreement on a more structured use of the recasting technique for legal acts, opened for signature (2001) O.J. C 77 (entered into force on 29 March 2003).

involved accounts for an additional layer of complexity, resulting in even more wheeling and dealing in the decision-making process[50] on Better Regulation.

Second, the creation of a better regulatory environment is fundamentally at odds with the strict institutional design set out by the principles of conferral and procedural autonomy. Better regulation is a horizontal policy that affects all the institutions. Therefore, it requires the institutions to engage in active and structural coordination, rather than respecting each institution's distinct mandate.

The third problem is the use of Inter-Institutional Agreements (IIAs). The necessity to organise institutional coordination was not envisaged in the Treaties and would effectively intertwine the functioning of the different institutions involved to such an extent that they could be considered to have agreed to curtail their own procedural autonomy. Despite this lacuna in the institution design, the different European institutions did rely on IIAs to formalise the agreements on coordination amongst themselves. This is also the case for Better Regulation, where the institutions resorted to the use of IIAs in almost every phase of the development of the better regulatory policy. This despite the fact that up until the Lisbon Treaty, IIAs lacked a legal basis in the Treaties. They nevertheless are reported to be used to the extent that they even alter the institutional design of the European Union. As recently as 2010, the legal service of the General Secretariat of the Council issued a legal opinion in relation to the draft of a new IIA between the European Parliament and the European Commission. This document concluded that this particular IIA aims, on several points, to modify the balance between the institutions as established by the Treaties, since it allocates powers to the European Parliament that are not conferred upon it by the Treaties.[51]

The combination of the presence of institutional self-interest and the preference to rely on an instrument that has previously been used in a manner that falls short of the fullest respect for the institutional design, warrants the necessary vigilance in approaching the BRA.[52]

4.3.3 The Better Regulation Agenda (BRA)

The latest phase in this horizontal policy area coincides with the instatement of the Juncker Commission.[53] The President of the Commission has put "Better Regulation" at the top of the political agenda of the Commission.[54] Together with the mantra "Big on big things and small on small things," the Commission

[50] This issue is most often referred to by using the maxim "A camel is a horse designed by a committee," reportedly coined by Sir Alec Issigonis the designer of the Mini car.

[51] Council of the European Union 2010.

[52] A large number of civil society organization have set up a platform to actively monitor the implementation of the BRA, for more info see Better Regulation Watchdog 2016.

[53] European Commission Press Release 2014.

[54] Juncker 2014b.

President believes that investing in Better Regulation is necessary to increase both the legitimacy of the European project and the public support for it.[55] This priority is reflected both in the revised structure of the Commission and its internal decision-making procedures. For the first time, the Commission has appointed a Vice-President, who has a veto over all legislative proposals.[56]

Another potential driver for the initiation of the BRA might also stem from the need to align the EU's regulatory process to the regulatory chapter in the negotiations of the Transatlantic Trade and Investment Partnership (TTIP) with the United States of America. Several scholars have referred to this obligation.[57] At this point, however, it is very difficult to comment any further on this given the confidentiality of the negotiations.

During the launch in May 2015, Frans Timmermans, the first Vice-President of the Commission, introduced a package of initiatives, now commonly referred to as the Better Regulation Agenda or BRA.[58] The package aims at bringing about change in four main areas: (1) quality of regulation; (2) revision of the existing legislation; (3) stakeholder participation; and (4) public consultation and feedback.

The appointment of a Regulatory Scrutiny Board empowered by the Commission to independently review the Commission's own legislative initiatives is a clear example of the Commission's dedication to quality of regulation and the control thereof.

The package confirms the pre-existing efforts to reduce the administrative burden of the existing legislation, through the Regulatory Fitness and Performance Programme (REFIT). It strengthens these efforts by creating the REFIT Platform that structurally seeks the input of stakeholders like representatives of business, civil society and social partners.

Most impressively, the Commission decided to embrace public consultation in the context of all impact assessments and evaluations it organises.

Most initiatives and documents clearly fall within the procedural autonomy of the Commission, for example:

- the launch of the website "Lighten the Load—Have your Say!" to provide citizens with a platform to make suggestions in order to reduce the regulatory burden;[59]
- the publication of a set of guidelines and toolboxes to guarantee the consistent implementation of the BRA by all Commission officials;
- the conversion of the former Impact Assessment Board to the more independent Regulatory Scrutiny Board.

---

[55] Juncker 2014a.

[56] Juncker 2014b.

[57] Alemanno 2015, pp. 625–640.

[58] At the time of the launch the BRA was presented as part of a Better Regulation Package containing an additional eight documents. For an overview, see Better Regulation 2016.

[59] European Commission Website 2016.

However, the package also contained a proposal for a new inter-institutional agreement,[60] since the Commission—despite its monopoly on legislative initiative—would face huge difficulties delivering on its steep promises and ambitions without the co-operation of the Council and the European Parliament.

The initial proposal raised serious concerns with the European Parliament as to the level of control the Commission envisaged over both the legislative agenda and process. The most notable example was the requirement for a mandatory impact assessment of any amendment made by the Parliament that the Commission deemed to be a substantive change to its original legislative proposal. These concerns have been taken up during high-level political negotiations between the European Commission, the European Parliament and the European Council.

A revised proposal was released by the Commission in December 2015[61] and a final version was adopted in April 2016.[62] Both seem to accommodate for most of the Parliament's concerns, but also highlight that part of the discussion simply revolves around semantics.[63] That the institutions—despite their joint statement—[64] are not in full agreement yet, is further illustrated by the fact that the Constitutional Affairs Committee of the Parliament is considering a unilateral motion on the interpretation and implementation of the new inter-institutional agreement.[65]

4.4 BRA and Its Compatibility with the EU's Institutional Design

4.4.1 BRA, Representative Democracy and Mutual Sincere Cooperation

One of the main criticisms of the BRA expressed by both the Parliament and different societal actors is the unprecedented degree of control the Commission wants to exercise over the legislative process through an extensive use of its right of initiative. A high-level control by a non-democratically elected institution seems to be at odds with the concept of representative democracy. This criticism therefore

---

[60] European Commission 2015b above n 13.

[61] European Parliament, Council of the European Union, the European Commission (2015) Provisional text of the proposed interinstitutional agreement on Better Regulation. http://ec.europa.eu/smartregulation/better_regulation/documents/20151215_iia_on_better_law_making_en.pdf. Accessed 12 June 2016.

[62] Interinstitutional agreement between the European Parliament, the Council of the European Union and the European Commission on better law-making (2016) http://ec.europa.eu/smart-regulation/better_regulation/documents/iia_blm_final_en.pdf, accessed on June 12, 2016.

[63] The title of the revised proposal and the final version now refers to better law-making rather than Better Regulation.

[64] European Commission, European Parliament 2016.

[65] For more information, see European Parliament Legislative Observatory 2016.

triggers the question whether Article 10 TEU—that recognises the representative democracy as one of the fundamental characteristics of the European Union—has any counterbalancing effect and could therefore affect the scope and content of an inter-institutional agreement on this point.

The criticism is not merely theoretical, since the jurisprudence of the CJEU seems to endorse a high level of control on the regulatory process by the Commission. In Case C-409/13, initiated by the Council, the CJEU endorsed the Commission's view—although conditionally—that its right to initiative extended to the right to withdraw any legislative proposal.[66] In addition, in Joined Cases T-424/14 and T-425/14, the CJEU was asked by a civil society organisation to express itself on the Commission's obligations when deciding to put a legislative proposal forward. The CJEU confirmed that the Commission has only a limited obligation to motivate its decision not to pursue legislative initiative or to provide transparency and access to documents it relied on for that decision.[67]

Both cases seem to indicate absolute control and discretion by the Commission to start the legislative process. This seems to be fundamentally at odds with the notion of a representative democracy as known by most EU citizens in their respective national jurisdictions, where direct democratic accountability is a natural corollary to the right of initiative.

It is clear from these cases that the term "representative democracy" as mentioned in Article 10 TEU does not in itself have the necessary counterbalancing effect, nor does it truly possess that potential. Not only has its exact meaning and legal effect not been determined by the CJEU yet, but the concept of "representative democracy" additionally only features under the general and introductory heading "provisions on democratic principles."

Even if a clear definition would be available, it would not automatically trump the other choices made in the overall institutional design, which has clearly exempted certain institutions from the concept of "representative democracy." The Treaties do not put a lot of expectations on either the European Commission or the European Central Bank in as far as their representative democratic character is concerned, let alone their functioning or democratic accountability.

EU citizens could potentially rely on one of the many different articulations of the same principle. Article 10(3) TEU *in fine* contains the only articulation with an operational dimension: "Decisions shall be taken as openly and as closely as possible to the citizen." This provision would surely not trigger direct effect. Therefore, citizens would only be able to rely on this provision if the Commission opted to use the concept itself as a guiding principle in exercising its procedural autonomy. It can thus be concluded that this provision would not have a

66 CJEU, *Council of the European Union v European Commission*, Judgment, 14 April 2015 (Case C-409/13), not yet published. For an accessible digest, Crisp 2015.

67 CJEU, *ClientEarth v European Commission*, judgment joined cases T-424/14 and T-425/14, judgment of 13 November 2015, not yet published. To foster full understanding of the potential impact of these cases and especially on transparency, please read: Leino 2016.

counterbalancing effect. A simple reference in the White paper on European Governance does not suffice to come to a different conclusion.[68]

Alternatively, the Parliament could seek to rely on two closely related concepts essentially created by the CJEU, namely mutual sincere co-operation and institutional balance. The CJEU has used both concepts to determine whether the different institutions respected both the letter and the spirit of different rules dealing with the division of competences as well as different aspects of coordination and communication between the institutions.[69] Both concepts have found their way into the Treaties, especially the principle of mutual sincere co-operation expressed in Article 13(2) TEU. This explicit articulation may somewhat restrict the CJEU to express itself on a potentially wider scope of application for the concept of representative democracy, as there is a significant overlap with the combined notions of mutual sincere co-operation and institutional balance.[70] This effectively renders the notion of representative democracy to be non-enforceable.

Even if representative democracy were enforceable, it would be of no use prior to the adoption of a final inter-institutional agreement, since resort to the CJEU is simply not available for general policy documents or draft inter-institutional agreements.

The respect for and implementation of this notion as well as the intention of its drafters will therefore completely depend on the inter-institutional debate.

Although maintaining a large degree of discretion, the new inter-institutional agreement seems to create some room to influence the Commission's right of initiative through the formalisation of discussion and debate on the annual and multiannual work programs.[71] Practice will have to show to what extent the formal requirement compelling the presidents of the three institutions to sign off on the different work plan will sufficiently guarantee that the Commission's right of initiative is properly embedded within a representative democracy as envisaged in Article 10 TEU.[72]

4.4.2 Better Regulation and Effectiveness

If Article 10 TEU does not provide for any guidance, the principle of effectiveness as enshrined in Article 13(1) TEU may well be of use. The article requires the institutions to safeguard the effectiveness of the Union's policies. In the case of Better Regulation—a horizontal policy—this concept presents itself most prominently in the debate surrounding impact assessments.

---

68 European Commission 2001.

69 Chevallier-Govers 2013, pp. 557–564.

70 *Ibid.*

71 Interinstitutional agreement on better law-making, above n 62, paras. 4–11.

72 *Ibid.* para 7.

One of the criticisms on the BRA shared both by the European Parliament and societal actors relates to the attempts by the Commission to standardise impact assessments and enforce its own methodology of conducting such assessments on the other institutions.[73]

Impact assessments are studies that help to assess the added value of a particular legislative proposal. Only a few Member States have long used impact assessments in their own legislative processes. Their best practices have shaped the Commission's position.[74] Under this influence, the Commission has favoured economic cost-benefit analyses as the methodological basis for its impact assessment. This has been widely criticised since some of the key principles or goals of the European Union—like the principle of subsidiarity or the goal to protect the environment—cannot be translated into quantifiable data as easily as the impact of a particular proposal on the economy or the economic actors involved.[75]

When analysing the difference between the initial proposal for a new inter-institutional agreement and the final text, it seems that the inter-institutional negotiations leading up to the revision have been successful in keeping the ambitions of the Commission in check. The revised text no longer allows the Commission to set the threshold for the obligation for the European Parliament to conduct an impact assessment, but recognises the Parliament's discretion to do so.[76] The final text of the IIA curtails the Commission's initial ambitions even further by recognising the freedom of the Parliament to conduct its own impact assessment,[77] provided that the European Parliament agrees to use the outcome of the impact assessments conducted by the Commission as its starting point.[78]

One could applaud this evolution and consider it to be a manifestation of due respect by the European Commission for the European Parliament's procedural autonomy. At the same time, one could also qualify it as a demonstration of the European institutions' inability to come to a truly coordinated approach on impact assessments with severe adverse effects on both the duration and transparency of the legislative process. All of this whilst the text of Article 13(1) TEU puts effectiveness at the core of the Union's institutional design.

This prompts questions in relation to the currently legal standing and interpretation of the concept of effectiveness under Article 13(1) TEU as well as how this could impact the institutions' margins for negotiations in concluding an inter-institutional agreement.

Like the concept of representative democracy, the concept of effectiveness is not likely to have direct effect. This renders the concept non-actionable, especially for citizens and other non-privileged actors before the CJEU.

---

[73] European Commission 2015b.

[74] This refers mostly to the Netherlands and the United Kingdom.

[75] Vogel 2010 pp. 7–52.

[76] Interinstitutional agreement on better law-making, above n 62, para 15.

[77] *Ibid.* para 17.

[78] *Ibid.* para 15.

By comparing the different language versions of the TEU, it can further be argued that there was even no common understanding amongst the Member States when incorporating this concept into the institutional design of the Union. The French and German version of the TEU for example mention *efficacité* and *effizienz* respectively. These terms refer to the concept of efficiency, similar to the wording used in the Laeken Declaration, rather than to the concept of effectiveness. This disparity effectively deprives the concept from any clear legal meaning and makes it a difficult to use it as a guiding criterion in inter-institutional negotiations. This is further evidenced by the reintroduction of the concept of "the cost of non-Europe" in the final text of the new IIA,[79] as an additional reference standard to assess the relevance or necessity of any legislative proposal.

In conclusion, the concepts of efficiency and effectiveness are not perceived to have any limiting effect on the inter-institutional debate.

4.4.3 Better Regulation and the Union's Advisory Bodies

A much less heard criticism is the impact the BRA will have on the two institutionally recognised advisory bodies: the European Economic and Social Committee (EESC) and the Committee of the Regions (CoR). The BRA seems to ignore the existence of either advisory body. The best illustration of this is that none of the drafts nor the final version of the inter-institutional agreements make any references to the advisory bodies at all. This is despite their prominent place in the institutional design,[80] which recognises their independent and representative character as well as the obligation for the European Commission, the European Parliament and the European Council to consult with the EESC and the CoR.

This raises the question whether the Treaties' institutional design does bring about any obligations or limitations for the Commission and the European Parliament in their interaction with either the EESC or the CoR, especially when it comes to the negotiation of a new inter-institutional agreement on Better Regulation.

In their reactions to the launch of the BRA, both bodies are quite clear. In October 2015,[81] the CoR issued an opinion that states that the BRA can never replace the function of the treaty-based advisory bodies. One month before that,[82] the EESC took a similar position in its separate opinion, again emphasising that the impact assessments and foreseen advisory entities (e.g. REFIT platform or Regulatory Scrutiny Board) should not undermine the institutional privileges

[79] *Ibid.* para 10.

[80] TEU, above n 10, Article 13(4), above n 37, TFEU, Articles 300–307.

[81] Committee of the Regions (2015).

[82] European Economic and Social Committee 2015.

granted by the Treaties to both the EESC and CoR. Both bodies further demanded to be explicitly mentioned in the final text of the inter-institutional agreement.

The balanced and constructive nature of these opinions makes that these positions cannot be reduced to statements of politically self-interested or potentially marginalised bodies. The EESC and CoR acknowledge the importance of taking new initiatives in the policy area of Better Regulation. They both welcome the Commission's use of its procedural autonomy to embed independent and professional expertise into the Commission own pre-legislative procedures. They support the Commission in doing so by providing constructive criticism, for example on the composition and functioning of the Regulatory Scrutiny Board, or in the case of the CoR, by offering its own expertise in the area of impact assessments to the Commission.[83]

In their motivation, they do not rely on the overall institutional design, but focus on the specific legal provisions that outline their role or on qualitative arguments that relate to concerns over the representative character of the new consultative mechanisms. They even concentrate on the way these mechanisms could further disadvantage citizens over organised interest groups both in relation to access to and transparency of the Union's legislative process.

For the EESC, there simply was no other alternative than to emphasise these qualitative elements, since it could not make a case on the basis of elements of the institutional design. This chapter already outlined that concepts like representative democracy are non-actionable and even if they were, the EESC would probably struggle to establish the necessary standing before the CJEU to force any of the other institutions into compliance. The EESC can also not rely on the principle of mutual sincere cooperation, since the scope of its application has been limited to only some of the institutions mentioned in Article 13(1) TEU.[84] Thus, the EESC's demand to be incorporated in the inter-institutional agreement cannot rely on the provisions that relate to the institutional design in the Treaties. It would, however, be courteous of both the European Commission and the European Parliament to indicate that the provisions of the inter-institutional agreement will be without prejudice to the position and role of the advisory bodies in Article 13(4) TEU. Yet, they are under no such obligation.

All of this while the EESC, especially in recent years, has capitalised on its unique composition and network to promote Better Regulation, and remains ideally placed to organise and facilitate consultations among high representative actors of the civil society.[85]

The CoR is potentially in a different situation as it has been successful in its efforts to enhance its status and privileges within the institutional design of the

[83] This was confirmed by Mr. Michael Latsch (Unit on Stakeholder Consultations at the European Commission Secretariat-General) during a conference on Better Regulation organized by Maastricht University Campus Brussel on December 3, 2016.

[84] Chevallier-Govers 2013, pp. 560–564.

[85] For a comprehensive overview of the EESC's past actions and initiatives, see European Economic and Social Committee 2016.

EU. Its efforts during the European Convention were widely commented on, especially when it came to acquiring standing before the CJEU.[86] With the adoption of the Lisbon Treaty, the CoR has now been granted standing before the CJEU, be it limited to its own prerogatives.[87]

The CoR has not yet brought a case before the CJEU on the basis of these provisions. The success of such a legal action would be questionable, especially if the inter-institutional agreement would in effect be without prejudice to the CoR's prerogatives, but would simply not be integrated into any of the BRA initiatives.

The chance that the CoR will resort to legal action will therefore depend on the actual implementation of the IIA and other BRA initiatives, but is not excluded.

Taking this into account, the European Commission and the European Parliament are advised to at least indicate that the BRA does not intend to disrespect the place of the consultative bodies as part of Union's institutional design.

4.5 Conclusion

This chapter intended to evaluate if the European Commission has overstretched its mandate by launching the BRA or by the position it has taken in the negotiations on a new inter-institutional agreement on Better Regulation. In order to make this evaluation the Commission's actions were assessed on their compatibility with: (1) the concept of representative democracy and the principle of mutual sincere co-operation, (2) the principle of effectiveness and (3) the privileged position of the EESC and the Committee of the Regions.

The chapter first contextualises the BRA and its different historic antecedents as part of the overall process of regional integration. It further recognises the importance of the Commission's initiative to take the Better Regulation agenda forward and outlines the complexities of such an undertaking, especially in view of the inherent need to coordinate and co-operate the actions of different European institutions to do so.

The substantive analysis showed that apart from mutual sincere cooperation, none of the concepts and principles have been given a meaning or definition in the latest intergovernmental conferences that is specific enough to constitute a counterbalancing legal obligation to the established principles of conferral and procedural autonomy for any of the Commission's actions to qualify as a violation of EU Law.

The absence in the BRA of a clear link with the consultative bodies is the only aspect that could give rise to a partially different conclusion. Since the adoption of the Lisbon Treaty the Committee of the Regions has been granted legal standing before the CJEU to protect its prerogatives. Given the absence of any reference to either of the consultative bodies in the final text of the interinstitutional agreement

[86] Committee of the Regions, Press Release 2009.

[87] TFEU, above n 37, Article 263.

on better law-making, the chance that the Committee of the Regions would bring a case to the CJEU would largely depend on future institutional practice in consulting the EESC and the Committee of the Regions.

The European Commission appears to be fully aware of the large discretion offered by the absence of a fully defined institutional design, and has attempted to exploit this by trying to maximise its control over the other institutions through a new inter-institutional agreement.

If it were not for the counterbalancing effect of the perpetual political dialogue that exists between the European Commission and the European Parliament, the launch of the BRA could have fundamentally impacted the Union's institutional design.

The outcome of the negotiations on a new inter-institutional agreement on better law-making confirm this counterbalancing effect, but also shows that this comes with a price. For example, in the case of impact assessments a total control by the European Commission over the European Parliament on this topic seems to have been avoided through negotiations, which, however, resulted in a situation where there will be hardly any coordination on the issue. In the past, it was precisely the very lack of coordination that contributed to the fact that fifteen years after the Laeken Declaration, the Union was still only taking incremental steps to deliver on the promise to bring about more democracy, transparency and efficiency in the European Union.

When the next revision of the institutional design of the Union takes places, the participants to the intergovernmental conference may want to draw from this analysis and make sure that the principles and concepts they introduce are more accurately defined for them to have any effect. This in turn would help enhance the clarity of the institutional design in the quest to increase and secure the European Union's democratic legitimacy.

Acknowledgments In addition to the fruitful interaction with many of the co-authors, the author recognizes the efforts of his research assistants: Mathilde Renou, Rastislav Betko and Lukas Vician, who were extremely helpful in the initial research for this book chapter as well as Stefania Marassi and William Worster for their review of this chapter.

References

Alemanno A (2015) The Regulatory Cooperation Chapter of the Transatlantic Trade and Investment Partnership: institutional structures and democratic consequences. J Int Econ Law 18(3):625–640

Amsterdam Intergovernmental Conference (1997) Declaration on the Quality of the Drafting of Community Legislation O.J. C 340

Better Europe (2015) Better Regulation Agenda https://www.businesseurope.eu/topic/better-regulation-agenda-0. Accessed 12 June 2016

Better Regulation Delivery Office (2016) Better Regulation Delivery Office became part of regulatory delivery in March 2016. https://www.gov.uk/government/organisations/better-regulation-delivery-office. Accessed 12 June 2016

Better Regulation Watchdog (2016) Making better regulation—better for all. http://www.betterregwatch.eu/. Accessed on 12 June 2016

Chevallier-Govers (2013) Article 13 [The Institutions]. In: Blanke H-J, Mangiameli S (eds) The Treaty on European Union (TEU): A commentary. Springer, Heidelberg, pp 557–564

Committee of the Regions (2015) Opinion on EU agenda on better regulation, 0.J. C 423/08

Committee of the Regions, press release (2009). http://europa.eu/rapid/press-release_COR-09-113_en.htm. Accessed 12 June 2016

Council (1993) Council Resolution of 8 June 1993, The Quality of Drafting of Community Legislation, 1993 O.J. C 166

Council of the European Union (2010) Item Note on Framework Agreement on Relations Between the European Parliament and the Commission. http://register.consilium.europa.eu/doc/srv?l=EN&f=ST%2015018%202010%20INIT. Accessed 12 June 2016

Crisp J (2014) Circular economy package to be ditched and re-tabled. http://www.euractiv.com/section/sustainable-dev/news/circular-economy-package-to-be-ditched-and-re-tabled/. Accessed 12 June 2016

Crisp J (2015) Judges limit Commission's power to retract EU laws. http://www.euractiv.com/sections/eu-priorities-2020/judges-limit-commissions-power-retract-eu-laws-314129. Accessed 12 June 2016

De Sousa C (2013) Cut the EU red tape. http://bruegel.org/2013/10/cut-the-eu-red-tape/. Accessed 12 June 2016

EPP Group in the European Parliament (2015) Better Regulation Package "potentially a breakthrough". http://www.eppgroup.eu/press-release/Better-regulation-package-%22potentially-a-breakthrough%22. Accessed 12 June 2016

European Commission (2001) White paper of 12 October 2001, "European Governance," COM (2001) 428 final

European Commission (2015a) Communication of 19 May 2015, "Better Regulation for Better Results—An EU Agenda," COM (2015) 215 final

European Commission (2015b) Communication of 19 May 2015, "Proposal for an Interinstitutional Agreement on Better Regulation", COM (2015) 216 final

European Commission (2015c) Communication of 16 December 2015, "Commission Work Programme 2015," COM (2014) 910 final

European Commission Better Regulation (2015) "REFIT–making EU law lighter, simpler and less costly". http://ec.europa.eu/smart-regulation/refit/index_en.htm. Accessed 12 June 2016

European Commission Better Regulation (2016). http://ec.europa.eu/smart-regulation/better_regulation/key_docs_en.htm. Accessed 12 June 2016

European Commission, European Parliament (2016) Statement of the European Parliament and of the Commission on the occasion of the adoption of the Interinstitutional Agreement on Better Law-Making. http://ec.europa.eu/smart-regulation/better_regulation/documents/iia_on_better_law-making_statement_all_lls_en.pdf. Accessed 12 June 2016

European Commission Legal Service (2016) Helping to improve the quality of drafting of EU legislation. http://ec.europa.eu/dgs/legal_service/legal_reviser_en.htm. Accessed 12 June 2016

European Commission Press Release (2014), Juncker Commission takes office. http://europa.eu/rapid/press-release_IP-14-1237_en.htm?locale=en. Accessed 12 June 2016

European Commission Press release (2015) "Better Regulation Agenda: enhancing transparency and scrutiny for better EU law-making". http://europa.eu/rapid/press-release_IP-15-4988_en.htm. Accessed 12 June 2016

European Commission website (2016) Lighten the load—have your say. http://ec.europa.eu/priorities/democratic-change/better-regulation/feedback/index_en.htm. Accessed 12 June 2016

European Council (2001) Laeken Declaration on the future of the European Union, 14–15 Dec 2001

European Economic and Social Committee (2015). Opinion on Better Regulation for Better Results—An EU Agenda, O.J. C 383

European Economic and Social Committee (2016) Opinion on Better Regulation for Better Results—An EU Agenda, O.J. C 13/28, for a comprehensive overview of the EESC's past actions and initiatives

European Parliament, Council of the European Union, the European Commission (2015) Provisional text of the proposed Interinstitutional Agreement on Better Regulation. http://ec.europa.eu/smart-regulation/better_regulation/documents/20151215_iia_on_better_law_making_en.pdf. Accessed 12 June 2016

European Parliament Legislative Observatory (2016). http://www.europarl.europa.eu/oeil/popups/ficheprocedure.do?lang=&reference=2016/2018(INI). Accessed 12 June 2016

European Union website (2016) "European Motos". http://europa.eu/about-eu/basic-information/symbols/motto/index_en.htm. Accessed 12 June 2016

Hélin-Villes S (2015) "The Commission must respect the autonomy of social partners," S&Ds warn. http://www.socialistsanddemocrats.eu/newsroom/commission-must-respect-autonomy-social-partners-sds-warn. Accessed 12 June 2016

Hendrickx L (2012) UEAPME position on the Report from the Commission to the Council and the European Parliament "Minimizing regulatory burden for SMEs—adapting EU regulation to the needs of microenterprises". http://www.ueapme.com/IMG/pdf/111221_pp_report_micros.pdf. Accessed 12 June 2016

InfoCuria (2016a) Case-law of the Court of Justice. http://curia.europa.eu/juris/documents.jsf?pro=&lgrec=en&nat=or&oqp=&dates=&lg=&language=en&jur=C%2CT%2CF&cit=TRT%252CC%252CCJ%252CR%252C2008M%252C%252C%252C%252C%252C%252C5%252C%252C%252C%252C%252Ctrue%252Cfalse%252Cfalse&td=%3BALL&pcs=Oor&avg=&page=1&mat=or&jge=&for=&cid=132776. Accessed 12 June 2016

InfoCuria (2016b) Case-law of the Court of Justice. http://curia.europa.eu/juris/documents.jsf?pro=&lgrec=en&nat=or&oqp=&dates=&lg=&language=en&jur=C%2CT%2CF&cit=TRT%252CC%252CCJ%252CR%252C2008M%252C%252C%252C%252C%252C%252C13%252C2%252C%252C%252C%252Ctrue%252Cfalse%252Cfalse&td=%3BALL&pcs=Oor&avg=&page=1&mat=or&jge=&for=&cid=133074. Accessed 12 June 2016

Juncker J (2014a) Political guidelines for the next European Commission. http://ec.europa.eu/priorities/sites/beta-political/files/juncker-political-guidelines_en.pdf. Accessed 12 June 2016

Juncker J (2014b) Mission letter to Frans Timmermans. https://ec.europa.eu/commission/sites/cwt/files/commissioner_mission_letters/timmermans_en.pdf. Accessed 12 June 2016

Leino P (2016) On knowledge as power: transparency of EU law-making procedures. http://eulawanalysis.blogspot.nl/2016/01/on-knowledge-as-power-transparency-of.html. Accessed 12 June 2016

Monnet (1978) Memoirs, London, Collins

OECD (2016) Regulatory Policy. http://www.oecd.org/gov/regulatory-policy/#d.en.194409. Accessed 12 June 2016

Olivetti M (2013) Article 12 [The role of national parliaments]. In: Blanke H-J, Mangiameli S (eds) The treaty on European Union (TEU): A commentary. Springer, Heidelberg, pp 467–526

Ponzano P (ed) (2001) Mandelkern Group on Better Regulation Final Report. http://ec.europa.eu/smart-regulation/better_regulation/documents/mandelkern_report.pdf. Accessed 12 June 2016

Renda A (2015) Too good to be true? A quick assessment of the European Commission's new Better Regulation Package, CEPS Special Report, no 108. http://www.ceps.eu/system/files/SR108AR_BetterRegulation.pdf. Accessed 12 June 2016

Schmidt VA (2013) Democracy and Legitimacy in the European Union Revisited: Input, Output and "Throughput". Polit Stud 61:2–22

The Greens European Free Alliance in the European Parliament (2015) "Better Regulation shackling legislators would be a coup against EU democratic process". http://www.greens-efa.eu/better-regulation-14014.html. Accessed 12 June 2016

Van den Abeele E (2015) "Better Regulation" a bureaucratic simplification with a political agenda. ETUI, Brussel

Vogel L (2010) Making lies sound truthful: applying the standard cost model to European health and safety law. In: Vogel L, Van den Abeele E (2010) Better Regulation: A critical assessment. ETUI, Brussels, pp 7–52

Part II
Institutional Aspects

Chapter 5
Informal Decision-Making in the EU: Assessing Trialogues in the Light of Deliberative Democracy

Santino Lo Bianco

Abstract With the adoption of the Lisbon Treaty, the process of democratisation in the European Union (EU) seems to have made further progress. The number of policy areas that is subject to what now is called the ordinary legislative procedure has increased. As a consequence, the involvement of the European Parliament as a co-legislator alongside the Council has expanded. However, the practice of co-decision-making that has taken shape between the co-legislators in the EU over the last fifteen years appears to run counter to the traditional precepts of democracy. The legislating partners in the EU (the European Parliament, the Council, and the Commission) found themselves increasingly involved in the practice of reaching first-reading agreements in the context of so-called informal "trialogue" negotiations where discussions are held in seclusion and where access to discussion is restricted to a limited number of discussants. This chapter examines whether and to what extent this practice actually conflicts with the idea of democratic decision-making. In doing so, it considers the question mainly from the deliberative democracy perspective. That is, rather than focusing on the institutional aspects of democratic decision-making (the liberal democracy perspective), this chapter examines "trialogue" negotiations in the light of public will formation through communicative process. It thereby focuses on aspects of (public) justification and accountability under conditions of pluralism as criteria for assessing democratic legitimacy in the practice of "trialogue" decision-making in the EU. Even though shortcomings have been identified in light of these notions, they should, however, not lead to the conclusion that the practice of reaching agreements in "trialogue" setting should be abandoned. Rather, deliberation behind closed doors among a limited number of discussants has even a better chance to efficiently lead to better quality legislation in the EU, as long as a variety of positions advanced in these

S. Lo Bianco (✉)
Faculty Public Management, Law and Safety, The Hague University of Applied Sciences, Johanna Westerdijkplein 75, 2521, EN, The Hague, The Netherlands
e-mail: S.LoBianco@hhs.nl

J. de Zwaan et al. (eds.), *Governance and Security Issues of the European Union*, DOI 10.1007/978-94-6265-144-9_5

discussions mirrors the diversity of interests in society and the choices made can be carefully motivated to the public afterwards.

Keywords EU decision making · Democracy · Trialogues · Interinstitutional · Democratic legitimacy · Deliberative democracy theory · Liberal democracy theory

Contents

5.1 Introduction

Since its introduction in the 1992 Maastricht Treaty, the co-decision procedure—today also known as the "ordinary legislative procedure"[1]—steadily developed into a key component of legislation and decision-making in the EU. Since its introduction in 1992, its scope of application has constantly been broadened. It started with only 15 policy areas. Following the modifications of respectively the Amsterdam, Nice and Lisbon Treaties, co-decision now covers a total of 83 policy areas. Its substance boils down to the basic understanding that alongside the Council—as the representative of the member states—the European Parliament and the Commission also have a key role in the decision-making process. The procedure can only start when the Commission drafts and issues a legislative proposal, and it can only come to a successful end if both the Council and the Parliament accept each other's amendments to the proposal. For the Parliament, this means that it co-legislates on an equal footing with the Council. At face value, it can thus be stated that with these developments the process of democratisation in the EU has made further progress.

However, over the last fifteen years a practice took shape which appears to run counter to the precepts of democracy. The legislating partners in the EU (the European Parliament, the Council, and the Commission) found themselves increasingly involved in a practice of reaching informal first-reading agreements in the context of so-called "trialogues." In this setting, the Parliament and the Council, together with the Commission, have developed a practice of frequent,

[1] For the sake of convenience, this chapter refers to "co-decision", although since the Lisbon Treaty the appropriate name for the procedure nowadays is "ordinary legislative procedure."

highly informal exchanges in closed settings between a limited group of delegates in order to sort out differences and to build mutual trust and understanding on various legislative files.

This chapter examines whether and to what extent this practice actually conflicts with the idea of democratic decision-making. In doing so, it considers the question from a perspective that is different from the traditional view on the functioning of democracy. That is, rather than focusing on the institutional aspects of interest aggregation or voting procedures (the liberal democracy perspective), it examines "trialogue" negotiations in the light of the process of public will formation (the deliberative democracy perspective). The focus is primarily on aspects of communicative process that leads debate to a democratically legitimate adoption of a public decision or policy. In that light, questions of (public) justification and accountability under conditions of pluralism are addressed.

This chapter first starts with an overview of the developments that gave rise to the growing practice of reaching early agreements in the informal trialogue setting. Second, this chapter shifts the attention to the relevance of deliberative democracy theory for assessing the democratic quality of decision-making in the EU. Third, this chapter presents an assessment of the trialogue process and reaching early agreements in light of the deliberative democracy perspective. The assessment has been made on the basis of findings revealed in deliberative democracy research and a number of interviews held with EU and national officials who were directly or indirectly involved in trialogue discussions.

5.2 The Origins of Trialogues and Their Rise

The co-decision (or ordinary legislative) procedure nowadays consists of up to three readings.[2] To briefly summarise, a first-reading agreement between the Parliament and the Council is reached if the latter approves the amendments added to the proposal text by the latter. If not, the Council adopts a position which shall be shared with the Parliament and the act moves to the second reading stage. If during this stage, the Parliament adds amendments to the Council's position and the Council does not approve them, the procedure moves to the final, third reading stage. During this stage, the Parliament and the Council bring together an equal number of representatives in a joint Conciliation Committee—to be joined by delegates from the Commission who are expected to mediate between the two co-legislators. If the co-legislating partners cannot reach an agreement at this stage, the legislative process comes to an end without an outcome.

There are many aspects to the practices, terms and formal rules in each of the three reading stages.[3] What is relevant in the context of this study is that there are

[2] Before the changes introduced by the Amsterdam Treaty, there were two readings.

[3] For a comprehensive overview see Corbett et al. 2007.

no specific formal rules and no time limits during the first reading stage. Furthermore, the Parliament can adopt its position at first reading by a simple majority. The second reading stage is more formal in that there is a time limit (three to four months) and that there are strict admissibility criteria for the Parliament to adopt the draft text (among other things, there must be an absolute majority). The time limit during the third reading is even stricter: the co-legislating partners will have to come to an understanding within six to eight weeks. Throughout the procedure, the Council always acts on the basis of a qualified majority, in response to the Parliament's position.

In the 1990s, there was frequent recourse to conciliation committees.[4] The Parliament and the Council had to settle their divergences through conciliation in 66 out of the 165 completed co-decision procedures (40%).[5] The procedures were quite lengthy. The settlement through conciliation required on average 27 months, while reaching an understanding without recourse to conciliation took on average 21 months. In conjunction with the unease about lengthy procedures, there was a concern that the extension of the co-decision procedure to more policy fields would lead to a further increase of the workload and a further prolongation of the legislative process. It is against this backdrop that a modality was included in the Amsterdam Treaty that would allow the co-legislating institutions to conclude an agreement at a still earlier stage. In a separate declaration attached to the Amsterdam Treaty, the co-legislating partners pledged "to make every effort to ensure that the co-decision procedure operates as expeditiously as possible."[6]

As a result, a mode of inter-institutional co-operation took shape that is still being practiced up until today. This so-called "fast-track" practice implies that an agreement between the institutions can be reached at an early stage, even before a joint compromise text has been subjected to a formal debate and a subsequent vote respectively in the Parliament and the Council.[7] In addition to the possibility of reaching these so-called "first-reading agreements," this "fast-track" procedure may also consist of a conclusion of an "early second-reading agreement." In the latter case, inter-institutional negotiations are successfully concluded after the Parliament has formally adopted its first-reading position but before the Council has formally adopted its common position.[8]

Indeed, the conditions in the first reading stage—or the early stage of second reading—promote quite a favourable and expeditious decision-making environment. There is no time-limit or formal rules that constrain the exchanges between

---

[4] Costa et al. 2011.

[5] European Parliament 1999.

[6] Declaration No 34 annexed to the Final Act of the Intergovernmental Conference which adopted the Treaty of Amsterdam Amending the Treaty on European Union, The Treaties Establishing the European Communities and Related Acts, opened for signature (1997) entered into force on 1 May 1999, OJ C 340/1.

[7] See Bressanelli et al. 2014.

[8] De Ruiter and Neuhold 2009.

the Parliament and the Council. Under these circumstances, the Parliament and the Council, together with the Commission, are able to develop a practice of frequent, highly informal exchanges in closed settings between a limited group of delegates in order to sort out differences, and build mutual trust and understanding on various legislative files.[9] Their meetings, referred to as "trialogues," usually involve secluded discussions on technical details, but also on political subjects.[10] Usually, it is the rapporteur and her/his assistants—and occasionally also the chairman of the parliamentary committee responsible for the legislative file—who act on behalf of the Parliament. The Council is always represented by the member state holding the Presidency, with a team consisting of officials from the member state's government, diplomats from the member state's permanent representation, and officials from the Council Secretariat. On occasion, the Presidency team is headed by the responsible minister. The Commission delegates vary from the responsible director general or senior official to the desk officer who is responsible for the file under discussion. On occasion, the Commission team is headed by the responsible Commissioner.

The number of early agreements—and the preparatory trialogues leading up to them—has increased dramatically in the last fifteen years (see Fig. 5.1). Compared to the Parliament's fifth legislature (1999–2004), the share of first-reading agreements almost tripled in the period 2009 to 2014 (from 29 to 85%), while the share of the second-reading and third-reading agreements combined has decreased from 46% in the period 1999–2004 to only 7% in 2009–2014. Agreements following from early second reading—which, similarly to first-reading agreements, are also the outcome of informal trialogue discussions—has decreased, but not as significantly as the decrease of the number of agreements following (the strictly regulated) second and third readings.

It has to be noted that the workload for the co-legislating institutions has certainly not diminished. Over the period 1999–2014, the number of co-decision proposals increased from 432 to 584.[11] The number of adopted proposals rose from 403 to 488 (see Fig. 5.2). This means that the share of failed co-decision procedures has increased significantly, from 29 to 96. In terms of the average length of the co-decision procedure, the time it took to reach first-reading agreements was eleven months in the period 1999–2004. It took longer in the period 2009–2014: seventeen months. The Parliament ascribes this trend to the fact that they "include more and more controversial files which need time to be negotiated".[12] Overall, the duration of the co-decision procedure has, however, diminished, from 22 to 19 months.[13]

---

[9] Costa et al. 2011, Stie 2013.

[10] See e.g. Bressanelli et al. 2014, Dobbels and Neuhold 2011.

[11] European Parliament 2014.

[12] European Parliament 1999, p. 13.

[13] European Parliament 2014, p. 10.

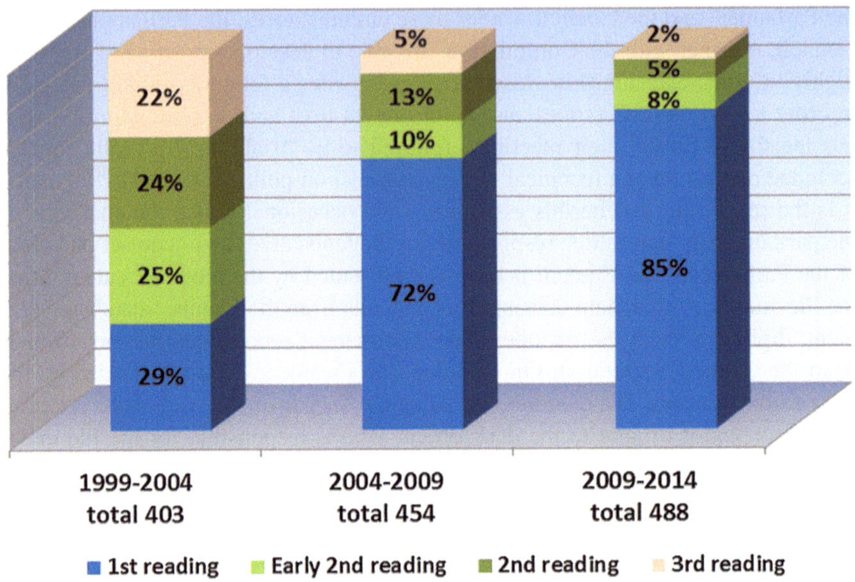

Fig. 5.1 Percentage of co-decision files adopted at 1st, early 2nd, 2nd or 3rd reading per legislature since 1999–2004. *Source* European Parliament (2014) Activity Report on Codecision and Consultation 2009–2014, Brussels

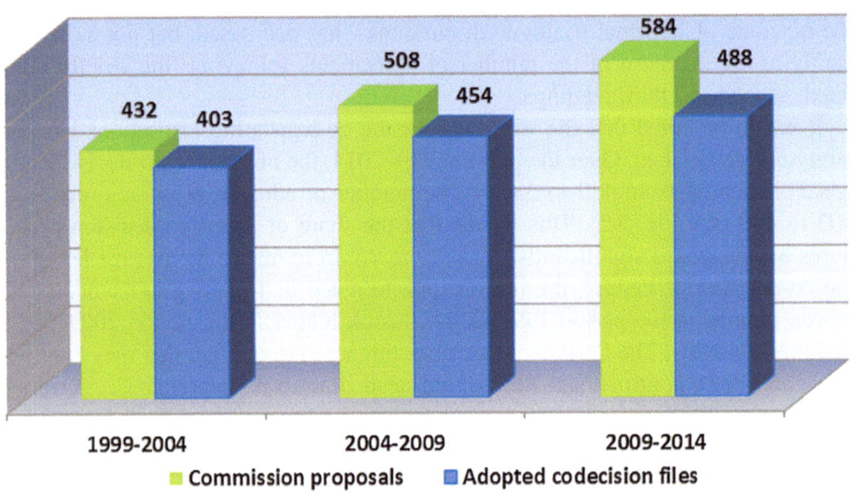

Fig. 5.2 Number of Commission proposals and adopted co-decision files per legislative term between 1999 and 2014, based on the date of adoption. *Source* European Parliament (2014) Activity Report on Codecision and Consultation 2009–2014, Brussels

For all the practical reasons that may appear to justify the practice of informal, fast track legislation, there is a shared concern that the practice of trialogue and early agreements has an adverse effect on the process of democratisation in the EU. A recent expression of this concern is the urgent letter that the European Ombudsman, Emily O'Reilly, sent to the Parliament, the Council and the Commission on 26 May 2015. In this letter, she announced an investigation of the practice of trialogues and early agreements.[14] Acknowledging that "[t]rialogues are where deals are done that affect every EU citizen [and] are an established feature of how the EU adopts laws," the Ombudsman expressed serious concern about the "lack of transparency, ethical issues such as conflicts of interest and problems with citizens participation in EU decision-making."[15] These concerns need to be taken seriously, considering that democratisation in the EU is regarded as a highly problematic issue and that the problem of "democratic deficit" continues to exist.

However, to express concern that the EU's "fast-track" practice would endanger democracy is taking sophistry a bit too far. After all, closed, small-group settings are by no means typical of EU decision-making only. Conventional wisdom tells us that *in camera* discussions among a limited group of people can be found in any democratic system. Findings even show that the importance of full transparency and full access to the legitimacy of decision-making is generally overrated.[16] Moreover, it has been found that they can have an adverse effect on the quality and (long-term) legitimacy of decisions taken in democratic communities.[17]

More importantly, it would be an oversimplification to dismiss the practice of trialogue meetings and ensuing early agreements in the EU as unacceptable. Firstly, the EU is a dense environment with a huge variety of interests and issues that is continuously changing, both in formal and informal ways. Secondly, it would be a misconception to consider the EU able to live up to the standards of democracy as it has taken shape at nation-state level. The informal "fast-track" practice is to be considered in a setting where the very basic structures of policy and decision-making are in a continuous state of flux. There is some truth in what De Ruiter and Neuhold say about the co-decision procedure: "[since] the Maastricht Treaty, the procedure has been transformed considerably—both constitutionally and informally—leading some to coin it as a laboratory for innovation and change."[18] Even more to the point is the remark that "[t]he proliferation of trialogues is a feature of an evolving legislative system."[19] Considering the EU's evolving nature, a more appropriate question would then be what constitutes the

---

[14] Letters to the European Commission, the European Council, and the European Parliament, opening the European Ombudsman's own-initiative inquiry OI/8/2015/FOR concerning transparency of trialogues, 26 May 2015.

[15] Ombudsman, press release 2015.

[16] See De Fine Licht et al. 2011, Naurin 2007.

[17] Chambers 2004, pp. 389–410, see also Elster 1995, pp. 237–257.

[18] De Ruiter and Neuhold 2009, p. 2.

[19] Kardasheva 2012, p. 21.

moment of democratic authorisation in a political-administrative entity of which the basic structures are still not settled. In order to address this question, we need to go beyond the conventional perspective on democracy.

5.3 Why the Deliberative Democracy Perspective?

Whilst there seems to be agreement among scholars that informal and insulated processes of decision-making are likely to be at variance with any concept of democracy, public accountability and transparency, there is a divergence of views on what actually provides the basis for democratic legitimacy. This applies especially to the EU, which is an entity unlike any form of (nation) state organisation. While there is the widely shared view that the EU suffers from a democratic deficit, it still remains open to question whether the EU lacks any form of democratic legitimacy. The notion of a democratic deficit may be helpful in identifying which elements of the EU's decision-making capacity fail to live up to the conventional standards of democracy, but it certainly would be more useful—and far more challenging—to ask oneself what keeps the EU running despite the shortcomings identified in light of the conventional wisdom on democracy. In other words, it would be worthy to study the matter beyond the traditional perspective that has been modelled in light of the historical development of the nation-state. Eriksen and Fossum have a valid point in stating that "we cannot simply equate democracy at the national level with legitimacy."[20]

Conventional wisdom on democracy is still largely premised upon the vote-centric perspective of decision-making, as it took shape in the modern (nation) state, introduced in the major work of Joseph Schumpeter, *Capitalism, Socialism and Democracy*, in 1947.[21] At the heart of this vote-centric thinking, commonly referred to as the liberal democracy theory, is the basic idea that participation in collective decision-making through voting is the moment of democratic authorisation and legitimation. In short, democracy boils down to the representation and aggregation of given—hence fixed—preferences and interests of the voter. It is a liberal individualist understanding of democracy, in that individual preferences and interests are the inviolable point of departure for a process of representation and aggregation. Each individual interest is supposed to have a fair and equal chance to compete for a share in the collective decision-making. Moreover, it is an economic understanding of democracy in that both voters and politicians are engaged in a competition for, and trading in, attention and a share in the collective decision-making.[22]

---

[20] Eriksen and Fossum 1999, p. 8.

[21] For a discussion see Chambers 2003, Dahlberg 2004, Dryzek 2009, Janssen and Kies 2004, Tinnevelt 2003.

[22] Tinnevelt 2003, pp. 4–5.

Proponents of the liberal democracy theory place a high value on the act of voting and the rules and procedures that come with it. In order to ensure a legitimate basis for any government to make decisions, policies and choices, the interests, preferences and values of all who are affected by government action will have to be expressed through a fair and effective aggregation or voting mechanism.

The main criticism levelled at the liberal-democracy perspective is that it is focused on the formal aggregative event alone.[23] There is an overly strong emphasis on the aggregation of interests, which confines the notion of legitimacy only to that moment of popular consent following from the formalised voting procedure. This criticism is voiced by scholars who argue that the communicative process preceding the formal aggregative procedure is equally—if not more—important. Their approach is "talk-centric".[24] Proponents of this approach, also known as the deliberative democracy theory, emphasise that rather than the mere consent through aggregation or voting, it is the process of deliberation—or accountability—prior to the voting that gives substance to the notion of legitimacy. John Dryzek, one of the main proponents of deliberative democracy reasoning, stressed that: "accountability is key to the generation of broad deliberative legitimacy for collective outcomes."[25] Deliberation, or accountability, implies that, prior to the voting, citizens/voters and politicians/representatives are engaged in a mutual dialogue of public opinion formation enabling them to form, state, exchange and modify their opinions or arguments. Instead of focusing on a priori given (fixed) interests, theorists of the deliberative democracy perspective emphasise the malleability of opinion and interest. It is through communicative interaction that preferences and values of individuals are formed and likely to shift or change.[26]

The shift of analytical focus towards the legitimising effect of the preceding communicative process is relevant for a number of reasons. It has for instance been pointed out that the deliberative democracy theory has proven its value in explaining and evaluating the communicative gap between politics and society, also in relation to national politics.[27] The deliberative line of reasoning is especially valuable in relation to the EU, considering the complex and sometimes lengthy chains of representation, the lack of a clearly defined governmental core and the various levels of governance—including the supranational, as well as inter-governmental and transnational levels.[28] In light of the talk-centric perspective, aspects of EU policy and decision-making have actually been found to come significantly closer to meeting democratic legitimacy standards than if they were examined in light of the vote-centric view.[29]

---

[23] *See* Chambers 2003, Eriksen and Fossum, Kohler-Koch and Rittberger 2007.

[24] *Ibid.*, Chambers 2003.

[25] Dryzek 2009, p. 1386.

[26] Tinnevelt 2003, p. 4.

[27] *See* Dryzek 2009, Graham 2009.

[28] For discussion see Risse-Kappen 1996.

[29] Eriksen and Fossum 1999, Kohler-Koch and Rittberger 2007, Stie 2013.

Moreover, the uniqueness of the EU also resides in it being an entity that is in a continuous state of flux and the destination of which is far from clear. A vote-centric perspective, with its primary focus on the *actual* participation in a decision-making process, is likely to direct most of the attention to the deficiencies of (only) an instance in the (historical) process of institution building. As has been pointed out earlier, its focus is on the aggregation of (given!) preferences and interests, and not on their alteration. As Eriksen and Fossum have so aptly put, from a vote-centric perspective one "sees the development of international political institutions as incomprehensible, and an expression of obvious normative deficiencies, rather than a means to rectify persistent ills and normative challenges."[30] The talk-centric line of thinking, with its focus on the communicative process of public opinion (or will) formation, is, on the other hand, more able to shift analytical focus beyond the procedural shortcomings—which basically are mere snapshots of a long-term process of institution building—and bring to light some of the most dynamic aspects of an evolving entity, the EU, which after all (still) continues to be supported by all 28 democracies.

Much of the work in the deliberative democracy field is devoted to the specification of standards that indicate the context or conditions of conversation—mainly in the sense of the communicative action theory developed by Jürgen Habermas.[31] It is, as Chambers explained, still about a set of "predominantly procedural" standards, since the elaboration of a deliberative theory about the status of substantive proposals always remains a risky undertaking.[32] Considered in that light, both the liberal and the deliberative approaches have much in common when it comes to the basic requirements of a democratic order (e.g. openness, equality, public scrutiny, or accountability). However, the latter approach directs attention—away from the more quantitative aspects of the formal voting event—to the qualitative elements of communication preceding the formal voting event (e.g. no restrictions on access to debate, free and open discussions, exchange of valid/reasoned arguments, individual autonomy during discussion, etc.).

Relevant here are two key criteria of a deliberative event that leads debate to a democratically legitimate adoption of a public decision or policy. First, in an ideal deliberative debate all possible viewpoints of the parties or community members affected by the decision or policy are raised during the debate. This, as it mostly happens in pluralist (mass) democracy, requires a selection of delegates that is representative of the diversity of society. In the case of the (present-day) EU, the capacity to reproduce pluralism has two implications. At one level, the pluralism of the EU's legislative process mirrors the diversity of national interests. At another, interest representation in the EU is also taking form in terms of ideological division. In particular, during the Prodi and Barroso Commissions of the last

30 *Ibid.*, Eriksen and Fossum 1999, p. 20.

31 Habermas 1984. *See also* Graham 2009, Janssen and Kies 2004, Jensen 2003.

32 Chambers 2004, pp. 316–317.

two decades a unified centre-right majority took shape inside and across the three (legislating) EU institutions.[33]

This key aspect of public will formation, hereinafter referred to as *deliberative pluralism*, implies in more operationalised terms that, ideally, the position of all political parties across the spectrum of political and issue-specific interests are represented in the debate. It also means, for instance, that there is a hierarchy between the popularly elected representatives and the unelected officials or technical experts.[34] Those who actively participate and, in doing so, shape the public will are the legitimate delegates who represent the more particular or group interests of their respective rank and file. Deliberative pluralism does not necessarily mean that all who wish to participate in the discussions can have access. Deliberation behind closed doors, away from the public eye, can even be conducive to the adoption of democratically legitimate decisions or policy, as long as the arguments raised and the positions defended "reproduce the pluralism of the public in the private."[35]

The second key requirement of deliberative democratic debate—or process of public will formation—is that discussants engage in an exchange of reasoned arguments in a free and open dialogue. More specifically, the decision-makers ideally commit themselves to a mutual *account-giving* of their respective positions, which induces them to (re)think, articulate and reason their preferences, values and interests and also to render the positions and counter-positions in the discussion accessible to public scrutiny.[36] This assessment criterion—hereinafter: *deliberative accountability*—thus implies that in the drafting and adopting of decisions and policies, positions need to be justified not only towards their opponents in the debate, but also to the outside world that is affected by the decision or policy. The salutary effect of going public is evident. The decision-makers are forced to account for their negotiated claim, policy proposal or legislative measure with reason and argument. The audience, at which the claim, proposal or measure is directed, has the chance to have its objections heard, its questions answered, and to challenge the validity of the justification.[37]

Deliberative accountability does not necessarily mean that the deliberations preceding the adoption of a decision or policy always need to be conducted in an exposed setting, within the glare of the media and public eye. On the contrary, as Chambers points out, effective deliberations have more chance to lead to better quality legislation if discussions take place in an insulated, *in camera*, setting. In such a setting, positions and preferences are more likely to be reconsidered, more

---

[33] Hix 2008.

[34] Stie 2013.

[35] Chambers 2004, p. 390.

[36] Chambers 2004; Dahlberg 2004, Dryzek 2009.

[37] Chambers 2003, Dryzek 2009.

carefully articulated, well-reasoned and fully examined, whilst under the glare of publicity, decision makers are more prone to resort to general, ill-founded appeals, demagoguery, and rhetoric.[38] Chambers is well aware of the difficult trade-off between democratic legitimacy (the public needs to be informed and heard) and epistemic legitimacy (*i.e.* high quality deliberation and fuller consideration of public policy). She argues that insulated processes of decision-making are in principle democratically legitimate as long as their necessity can be accounted for in the public and as long as the positions and outcomes can be examined and scrutinised in an open and accessible manner. De Fine Licht et al. have detected that it is rather the capacity to provide the public with the insight into the reasoning behind the decision, than the exposure of discussion itself.[39] According to these findings, legitimacy can still be secured and/or improved if decisions which are taken behind closed doors can be carefully motivated afterwards. Rather than the exposure of discussions, its deliberative accountability is thus more critical (*i.e.* the capacity to demonstrate reasonability to the public). Seen in this light, public choices and decisions, even though often highly technical in nature, are (made) accessible to the public if they make sense to public opinion and can be publicly explained. As Dryzek explained, "a much bigger obstacle to deliberative capacity may be when elites cultivate a form of language unavailable to the masses as a way of bolstering their standing and power."[40]

5.4 A Deliberative Democracy Assessment of the Trialogue Process

It needs to be stressed that the practice of trialogue and early agreement in the EU grew out of the need to ensure that the two co-legislating partners, the Parliament and the Council, would eventually succeed in a last-ditch attempt—that is: in the conciliation procedure—to get an agreement. The trialogue practice was drawn from the experience with the preparatory talks in the run-up to conciliation procedures in the period before the Amsterdam Treaty.[41] Yet, contrary to the formal setting of the conciliation procedure, the actual practice of trialogue talks is—and still remains—of an unsettled and tentative nature, and is constantly subject to

[38] Chambers 2004, pp. 398–405.

[39] De Fine Licht et al. 2011.

[40] Dryzek 2009, p. 1395.

[41] De Ruiter and Neuhold 2009, Kardasheva 2012.

change.[42] Informal trialogue meetings and developing early agreements are "a kind of working method in which we have to find progress on the [legislative] file," as a former assistant to a Member of the European Parliament (MEP) of the Alliance of Liberals and Democrats for Europe (ALDE) explained.[43]

In the light of deliberative democracy theory, one of the challenges for the three institutions—in this unsettled process—is to strike a balance between, on the one hand, the need to have "repeated interactions" among a limited number of representatives[44]—which would help to foster common understanding—and, on the other hand, to have a representative selection of delegates that ensures due consideration of all relevant viewpoints and interests. It thus requires a trade-off between the need for a practicable number of representatives facilitating expedient decision-making and a selection of representatives that mirrors the diversity of societal interests in the EU. More pertinent than the size of trialogue meetings is thus the question whether and to what extent deliberative pluralism is actually at work in the trialogue process.

From an institutional point of view, there is reason to believe that there is a fair amount of pluralism in the trialogue practice in that national interests are represented through the involvement of the Council, the Community interest through that of the Commission, and the citizen interests through the Parliament. Moreover, there are rules on representation in both the Parliament and the Council. The Council mandates the Presidency to negotiate on its behalf, on the basis of a qualified majority of national delegations in the Council. Less clear are the rules on the representation of the Parliament in this regard. As a rule, it is the rapporteur of the committee responsible for the legislative file who is mandated by the committee and acts on behalf of the Parliament. Often, the shadow rapporteurs (who monitor the process on behalf of the political groups other than that of the rapporteur), the committee chairs and political group leaders are also involved.

On closer examination, however, deliberative pluralism appears to be problematic. As far as the Parliament is concerned, one of the main—and recurrent—findings in deliberationist research is that the Parliament is overrepresented in the inter-institutional negotiations by the leaders of only the majority political groups. Kardasheva noted that whilst in 28% of the cases (in the period 1999–2007), in particular the most controversial ones, majority party leaders had an incisive role in reaching early agreements thereby "largely undermining the work of the

[42] Indeed, a number of attempts have been made, either internally or at the inter-institutional level, to formalize the trialogue process, including the interinstitutional Joint Declaration on Practical Arrangements for the Co-decision Procedure (adopted by the European Parliament, the Council and the Commission on 30 June 2007) and the Parliament's Code of Conduct for Negotiating Co-decision Files (adopted by the Parliament's Working Party on Parliamentary Reform at its meeting on 23 April 2008). There is a widely held view that these attempts fail to capture the trialogue process in clear and unambiguous rules (see for instance Costa et al. 2011, pp. 35–37; De Ruiter and Neuhold 2009, pp. 9–14).

[43] Interview, 4 June 2012.

[44] Kardasheva 2012, p. 6, Lo Bianco 2015, pp. 305–307.

rapporteur and overriding the position reached in the EP drafting committees."[45] According to Costa, Dehousse and Trakalová, the co-decision procedure is in the "stranglehold" of the three largest political groups (*i.e.* Party of European Socialists [PES], European People's Party [PPE] and ALDE), not only because about 80% of the co-decision files are assigned to a rapporteur of either of these three groups. Also because the likelihood of an (informal) early agreement is higher when a MEP of either of these three groups is in charge of a legislative file.[46] Overall, there is the shared view that informal exchanges and trialogues allow majority party leaders in the Parliament to directly negotiate with Council delegates, at the expense of the smaller political groups.

As for the Council, it has been pointed out that because of the informal nature of trialogues, the Member State's delegation holding the six-month office of Presidency has far more leverage in decision-making than the other national delegations.[47] In this light a Commission official, who attended various meetings in the Council and trialogue level in the field of Justice and Home Affairs, noted that when the focus of the discussions gravitates from internal discussions in the Council to negotiations at inter-institutional level, "the power shifts a lot to the Presidency."[48] In this regard, reference has been made—to the criticism that has been levelled in the Council structures regarding the wide margin of discretion that the Presidency usually affords itself in its dealings with Parliament delegates.[49]

Equally serious is the problem that the Presidency (*i.e.* the Member State's delegation holding the office) sometimes tends to directly approach the majority leaders, sidestepping the rapporteur and his/her mandate (whenever a MEP of smaller political group is appointed as rapporteur). This was also observed in relation to a case where the Presidency, driven by a sense of priority and urgency, pushed for an informal fast-track procedure in order to ensure that a result was achieved in the shortest possible period of time.[50]

Also problematic, in light of deliberative pluralism, is that much of the work done in trialogue meetings is delivered by non-elected officials, in particular on the Council's side. While on the Parliament's side the discussions are regularly attended by (popularly elected) MEPs, in many cases the Council is represented by (unelected) expert officials and diplomats coming from the Council Secretariat, national permanent representations and national governments holding the Presidency. Relevant here is the consideration that the trialogue meetings are not limited to discussions on technical subjects. While trialogues were initially meant to iron out the differences on technical details, they have become more a venue of

---

[45] Kardasheva 2012, p. 17; see also De Ruiter and Neuhold 2009.

[46] Costa et al. 2011, p. 33.

[47] Stie 2013, p. 14.

[48] Interview, 5 May 2011.

[49] Costa et al. 2011, p. 34.

[50] See Lo Bianco 2015, see also De Ruiter and Neuhold 2009.

debate on the most sensitive *dossiers*.[51] This shift from technical or administrative files to the politically more sensitive *dossiers* has certainly not led the Council to send elected politicians to trialogue meetings on a more regular basis.[52]

Closely related to the shortcomings identified in light of the pluralist requirement, there is also the question whether the public or the outside world is able to ascertain whether all positions have been voiced or taken into consideration during a trialogue discussion. It refers to what can be identified in light of the notion of deliberative accountability. As opposed to the third formal reading stage, where a joint explanatory statement is required in the conciliation procedure, there is no public record of the trialogue discussions (except for internal documents distributed in the Parliament, Council and Commission circles). Moreover, the reporting back of trialogue discussions in the Council and the Parliament is certainly not without problems. As for the Parliament, it has been found that even though the rapporteur is accountable to both the committee that is responsible for the legislative file and the plenary, agenda constraints and heavy work-load prevent MEPs from engaging in "informed interactive debates" which would allow them to have their objections heard and questions answered.[53] As for both institutions, reference has been made to the "take-it-or-leave-it" style of the rapporteur and the Presidency when they report back the outcome of the trialogue negotiations in their respective institutions.[54] Rather than a starting point for internal debate and account-giving in the respective co-legislating institutions, the outcomes of trialogues are often presented as "take-it-or-leave-it" deals.

It is not only difficult for the most informed MEPs and delegates in the Council to identify politically salient issues and to articulate counterclaims, it is also—if not more—difficult for the outside world to understand trialogue outcomes and to hold the delegates accountable for their action in the informal trialogue process. For trialogue to become more in line with the standards of deliberative accountability, trialogues outcomes need to be rendered public, stripped of their technical terminology, and presented as clearly identifiable alternatives for public discussion and opinion shaping.

5.5 Conclusion

Considering that the steadily growing practice of informal decision-making between the co-legislating institutions of the EU is of an unsettled and tentative nature, it would be an oversimplification to dismiss out of hand the practice of conducting trialogue discussions and concluding early agreements as incompatible

51 Costa et al. 2011; Fuglsang and Olsen 2009, Stie 2013.

52 Lo Bianco 2015, Stie 2013.

53 Lo Bianco 2015, pp. 277, 389.

54 *Ibid*., p. 202, Stie 2013, p. 15.

with (any notion of) democracy. Rather than using a notion of democratic legitimacy that is confined to the formal voting procedure, a broader perspective that takes on board the more dynamic elements of democratisation would do more justice to the continuously evolving decision-making system of the EU. According to this perspective, democratic authorisation and legitimation is considered to already take shape through the preceding communicative process of public deliberation where preferences, values or opinions are freely and openly exchanged and formed.

The shift of analytical focus towards the legitimising effect of the preceding communicative process entails an assessment of decision-making according to two key recurrent notions in deliberative democracy research: pluralism and accountability (in the sense of account-giving or exchange of valid justifications). In light of these notions, several shortcomings have been identified in the EU's decision-making framework (structural over-representation by majority party leaders; lack of effective scrutiny over the action of the representatives; disproportionate share of non-elected officials in the discussions; and lack of accessibility to the discussions in terms of both openness and comprehensibility).

These shortcomings should, however, not lead to the conclusion that the practice of "fast-track" agreement-reaching in EU decision-making should be abandoned. Firstly, secluded *in camera* discussions between a limited group of representatives leading to decisions that affect our daily lives simply occur in any democratic order, and not just in the EU. Secondly, for decisions or policies to be publicly legitimate, discussions do not necessarily need to be conducted in an exposed setting, under the glare of publicity. One of the key reasons explaining the introduction of the trialogue process in the EU, was the need to cope with exposure to a multitude of interests, parties and issues of various sorts (national, regional, sectoral, etc.) in a densely institutionalised decision-making environment. Deliberation behind closed doors among a limited number of discussants has even a better chance to efficiently lead to better quality legislation, as long as the choices made can be carefully motivated to the public afterwards.

If the EU is to address the shortcomings of the "fast-track" practice identified in this chapter, it would need to consider ways to safeguard pluralism in debate which mirrors the diversity of interests and to turn the trialogue discussions and their outcomes into a solid basis for post hoc public account-giving. This implies the sending of mainly elected politicians to the trialogue discussions (especially on the politically more sensitive dossiers), the inclusion of representatives (or positions) of minorities in the trialogue discussions and the disclosure of records of trialogue discussions. Such steps would not only raise the legitimacy of the fast-track practice in the EU, they would also help to address the long-standing issue concerning the communicative gap between the EU and the citizen. In motivating carefully afterwards the decisions, the parties of the trialogue discussions are more likely to be induced to provide an account that is stripped of its technical terminology and presented as clearly identifiable choices for public discussion and opinion shaping. Such initiatives would do more justice to the unsettled and tentative nature of trialogue practice. They would certainly do more justice to the transformative nature of the EU.

References

Bressanelli E et al (2014) The informal politics of co-decision: introducing a new data set on early agreements in the European Union. Robert Schuman Centre for Advanced Studies, working paper no. 64

Corbett R et al (2007) The European Parliament. John Harper Publishing, London

Costa O et al (2011) Co-decision and early agreements: an improvement or a subversion of the legislative procedure? Notre Europe, study no. 84

Chambers S (2003) Deliberative democratic theory. Annu Rev Polit Sci 6:307–326

Chambers S (2004) Behind closed doors: publicity, secrecy, and the quality of deliberation. J Polit Philos 12:389–410

Dahlberg L (2004) The Habermasian public sphere: a specification of the idealised conditions of democratic communication. Stud Soc Polit Thought 10:2–18

De Fine Licht J et al (2011) Does transparency generate legitimacy? An experimental study of procedure acceptance of open and closed-door decision-making. University of Gothenburg, the Quality of Government Institute, QoG Working Paper Series 8

De Ruiter R, Neuhold C (2009) 'Deals between the Council and the European Parliament behind closed doors? The choice for agreeing early in the co-decision procedure.' Draft Paper University Twente and Maastricht University

Dobbels M, Neuhold C (2011) The roles bureaucrats play. The input of European Parliament (EP) administrators into co-decision. A case study approach. Maastricht University, EGPA conference paper

Dryzek J (2009) Democratization as deliberative capacity building. Comp Polit Stud 11:1379–1402

Elster J (1995) Strategic uses of argument. In: Kenneth J et al (eds) Barriers to conflict resolution. Norton, New York, pp 237–257

Eriksen E, Fossum J (1999) Democracy in the European Union: integration through deliberation? Routledge, Abingdon

European Parliament (1999) 'Activity report 1993–1999. From the entry into force of the Treaty of Maastricht to the entry into force of the Treaty of Amsterdam'. http://www.europarl.europa.eu/code/information/activity_reports/activity_report_1993_99_en.pdf. Accessed 4 July 2016

European Parliament (2009) Activity Report on Codecision and Consultation 2004–2009, Brussels. http://www.europarl.europa.eu/code/information/activity_reports/activity_report_2004_2009_en.pdf. Accessed 4 July 2016

European Parliament (2014) Activity Report on Codecision and Consultation 2009–2014, Brussels, 2014. http://www.europarl.europa.eu/code/information/activity_reports/activity_report_2009_2014_en.pdf. Accessed 4 July 2016

Fuglsang N, Olsen K (2009) Staying in the loop. The Commission's role in first reading agreements. EPIN working papers 25

Habermas J (1984) The Theory of Communicative Action. Volume I, Reason and the Rationalisation of Society. McCarthy T (trans), Beacon Press, Boston

Graham T (2009) What's wife swap got to do with it? Talking politics in the net-based public sphere. University of Amsterdam (dissertation)

Hix S (2008) What's wrong with the Europe Union and how to fix it. Polity Press, Cambridge

Janssen D, Kies R (2004) Online forums and deliberative democracy: hypotheses, variables and methodologies. Paper Conference on Empirical Approaches to Deliberative Politics, European University Institute, Florence

Jensen J (2003) Public spheres on the internet: anarchic or government-sponsored—a comparison. Scand Polit Stud 4:349–374

Kardasheva K (2012) Trilogues in the EU legislature. King's College London, Department of European and International Studies, research paper

Kohler-Koch B, Rittberger B (2007) Debating the democratic legitimacy of the European Union. Rowman & Littlefield Publishers, Plymouth, The United Kingdom
Lo Bianco S (2015) Tectonic shifts of European integration, identifying deliberation and change in the everyday practice of decision-making in EU's Justice and Home Affairs. Eleven International Publishing, The Hague
Naurin D (2007) Deliberation behind closed doors: transparency and lobbying in the European Union. ECPR Press, Colchester, The United Kingdom
Risse-Kappen Th (1996) Exploring the nature of the beast: international relations theory and comparative policy analysis meet the European Union. J Common Market Stud 1:53–80
Stie A (2013) Legislative politics in the EU—also a matter of democracy? Paper presented at the 4th International Conference on Democracy as Idea and Practice. University of Oslo
Tinnevelt R (2003) Representatie en deliberatieve democratie. Oikos, Politiek, Milieu, Cultuur 24/1. http://www.oikos.be/archief-oikos/jaargang-2003/oikos-24-1-2003/192-24-04-tinnevelt-representatieve-en-deliberatieve-democr/file. Accessed 13 March 2015

Chapter 6
The Five Principles of European Political Communication

Chris Aalberts

Abstract Over the last few years, there is an increasing awareness that the European Union (EU) should become more democratic. For a democratic EU, it is essential that citizens can exert influence on the policies of European institutions and have sufficient information about the EU. However, media largely fail to bring enough political news about European affairs. This chapter will analyse the main principles of political communication on the EU, based on the work of Gadi Wolfsfeld: *Making sense of media and politics.* Two cases are analysed to see whether the principles of Wolfsfeld, which are formulated for national politics, also hold for European politics. The research question is: what are the main principles that apply to political communication on the EU? This analysis focuses on two case studies that vary in the amount of coverage that they received: the Value Added Tax Mini One-Stop Shop rules (VATMOSS) and the Transatlantic Trade and Investment Partnership (TTIP). The analysis shows that the five principles of Wolfsfeld on national political communication should be reformulated for political communication on the EU. While all reformulated principles have a clear relation with the relative lack of coverage of the EU, we can wonder whether the media fulfil their role to inform the public satisfactorily.

Keywords EU-journalism · Public sphere · Political communication · EU-coverage · TTIP · VATMOSS

Contents

C. Aalberts (✉)
Erasmus University Rotterdam, Rotterdam, The Netherlands
e-mail: info@chrisaalberts.nl

J. de Zwaan et al. (eds.), *Governance and Security Issues of the European Union*, DOI 10.1007/978-94-6265-144-9_6

6.1 Introduction

The recent years have witnessed increasing discussions on the democratic character of the European Union (EU). Two major developments show that there are attempts to make the EU more democratic. First, in recent decades, the power of the European Parliament has expanded with each treaty amendment. The Parliament was once only an advisory body, but is now the only directly elected EU institution with decision-making power over most policies.[1] Second, the election of the President of the European Commission has been democratised. Whereas government leaders used to designate this post in the past, the President is now appointed from the largest political group in the European Parliament since the 2014 elections. Still, despite these efforts to democratise the EU, there is more discussion than ever about democracy in the EU, for example in the call of Dutch citizens for a referendum on the association treaty between the EU and Ukraine and the plans of several Non-International Organisations (NGOs) to launch referenda on Free Trade Agreements, respectively the Comprehensive Economic and Trade Agreement (CETA) and the Transatlantic Trade and Investment Partnership (TTIP).

For a democratic EU, it is important that citizens can exert influence on the policy of European institutions. In order to do so, citizens must have sufficient information. When citizens are provided with enough information on European politics, they become aware of which politicians in which institutions make relevant decisions, and who is responsible for certain policies.[2] By evaluating the choices of their politicians, citizens may make a reasoned choice in the European elections. In the case of the EU, this applies both at the European and national level. Citizens need to be adequately informed about EU-decisions made on both scales. Political communication is therefore essential. In this field, the relationship between citizens, media and politics is studied.

Media play an essential role in informing citizens about European politics. In recent decades, citizens have become increasingly inactive in politics. Their main activity is to vote in elections. When there are no elections, they are hardly active, for example in political parties. Citizens have become floating voters and do not

[1] For example: Hix 2005.

[2] Delli Carpini and Keeter 1996.

feel engaged with certain political parties anymore. Moreover, their confidence in those parties is decreasing.[3] Politicians have to take these developments on the electoral market into account. Electoral fluctuations are greater than ever. In addition, citizens find European politics much less interesting than national politics. This is clear from the turnout in European elections, which is lower than in almost all other elections. European politicians have therefore difficulty to interest citizens in their activities and gain their trust.[4]

Journalists are the main purveyors of political information. In theory, they bring independent and impartial news as objectively as possible. Journalists present themselves as watchdogs of democracy. Over the past few years, this role became under pressure. The rise of the Internet has led to the availability of a massive number of free information on various subjects. The willingness of citizens to pay for journalism is therefore greatly diminished. As a result, newspapers are in decline, independent titles disappear and editorial rooms are merged.[5] Moreover, the speed of news has increased dramatically. In addition, there is more emphasis on news that is attractive to people such as scandals and human interest, for example, and less on technical issues such as European affairs. In this environment, news about the EU appears relatively unattractive for editors, because citizens express little interest in it. For example, not enough scandals take place in Brussels to make it appealing. For this reason, many media ignore news related to European affairs, and focus only on major European events such as summits, elections, the Euro Crisis and the Refugee Crisis.[6]

Politicians feel the burden of both trends and this is particularly true at the European level. It is difficult for them to build a stable electorate. Politicians need enough attention from the media to create such a bond with their voters. However, journalism largely fails in this regard. The main solution available to politicians is to communicate with voters themselves and no longer through journalistic outlets. An increasing number of communication consultants is employed in political parties, and politicians have become massive social media users. Social media are increasingly seen as an alternative way to reach voters.[7] These problems for politicians are present at all political levels, but are even greater on the European plane.

In this chapter, I describe the relationship between citizens, journalists and European politicians. I look at the five key principles of political communication based on the book *Making Sense of media and politics* of Gadi Wolfsfeld, which is an original synthesis of the research available in this field.[8] In this article, I look at

---

[3] De Beus 2001.

[4] Aalberts 2014.

[5] For example: Landman et al. 2015.

[6] Aalberts 2014.

[7] Aalberts and Kreijveld 2011.

[8] All references in this chapter on Wolfsfeld come from the following work: Wolfsfeld 2011.

two case studies to see whether these principles also apply in the context of the EU. The research question therefore is: what are the main principles that apply to political communication on the EU?

6.2 Five Principles

Wolfsfeld formulates five principles in the field of political communication. Although he does not make it explicit, he formulates these principles on the basis of political communication at the national level. After all, this is the level where most political communication takes place. In this section, I describe these principles in general.

The first principle is that political power can usually be translated into power over the news media. The politicians who have most power in the political arena, also have most power over the media. This applies both to access to the media and to the way politicians are presented. The prime minister or a minister has many chances to be in the media or even to choose in which media he wants to show up. These politicians also have many chances to have an influence on the coverage. This is hardly the case for Members of the Parliament (MPs), especially those who have no great reputation and who have a relatively unimportant portfolio. They are rarely asked for interviews, and when they are asked, they have little bargaining power to adjust their image to their advantage.

The second principle is that media and politicians have a particular power relationship. When politicians lose control over the political environment, they also lose control over the media. This is especially true for politicians in power, who generally have some control, especially in comparison to relatively unknown politicians. If these politicians run into the political problems, they also run into problems with the media. Politicians are confronted with negative stories that take on a life of their own. In these situations, politicians are no longer seen as sources of authority.

The third principle is that news is never neutral and that it cannot be neutral. In order to make news, journalists need to be present at sites where the news takes place. Journalists cannot be everywhere and therefore news cannot come from everywhere. Journalists assume that the public finds events in some places more important than elsewhere, so they accumulate in these specific places. The selection of news is never neutral and so is the presentation of news. A story can be told from very diverse angles and therefore choices are needed. There is always framing involved and a story is written from a particular perspective, such as from an economic or moral context. Other angles remain out of sight.

The fourth principle is that the media try to tell good stories. Citizens must become fascinated by media stories and this means that there is a preference for specific types of stories and perspectives. For example, media prefers a mix of information and entertainment to information per se, in order to attract a larger audience. Media also prefers scandals, human-interest and follow-up stories, because these are attractive for the audience as well. In this regard, there are differences between media groups, but these preferences are widely present among journalists and editors.

The fifth and final principle is that the main media effects go unnoticed and are not intentional. Citizens can change their political opinions or gain knowledge because of media coverage, but these effects are relatively small. Much knowledge that is gained through the media is inaccurate and citizens do not always change their opinions in the direction that is desired by the messenger. Agenda setting is, however, a very important effect. Citizens find that certain topics are important because they are in the news, but still, the media do not determine what they think of these issues. Framing is another powerful phenomenon. Citizens often view political themes from the same angles offered in the media. These effects are certainly not intentional.

6.3 Methodology

In this chapter, an exploratory analysis is presented on two case studies of European policy and how it was covered in the Dutch media. These two examples are confronted with the five principles of political communication of Wolfsfeld.

In case studies, the criteria for inclusion of cases are essential. The cases should differ enough from each other in order to make a meaningful comparison between them. From existing research on media coverage of the EU a clear criterion emerges: the lack of coverage of European politics and the emphasis in the media on major political events and major political themes.[9] Relatively "small" European issues rarely make the news unless they are part of a scandal or they are remarkable for another reason. Larger issues such as the accession of new countries, new treaties or elections do, however, get relatively much attention from the media. This distinction is applied in this chapter. A topic that was largely ignored by the media is compared with a topic that received much media coverage.

VATMOSS was almost completely ignored by the media. This policy proposal on Value Added Taxes (VAT) harmonisation is representative of the majority of European policies that are rarely covered in newspapers, on television or on web sites. This theme is probably not noticed by citizens because it is not covered at all. Politicians who work on this proposal do not experience pressure from the media or from the public to take certain decisions. At the same time, politicians have trouble explaining to citizens how this case would translate in their everyday life. Because citizens lack background knowledge, they do not ask questions on this issue and are mostly unaffected by the measures taken. In this example, few Dutch politicians are involved and so the media miss appealing names that could tell the story of VATMOSS.

---

[9] Aalberts 2014.

The analysis covers a second theme that received extensive media coverage, the TTIP. This treaty is reported on elaborately and there are many Dutch politicians who are willing to make statements on this matter. For a longer period, the media ignored the TTIP, but later it did become a recurring theme. Both national and European politicians are regularly asked to comment on the TTIP and it even became relevant for the electorate. The TTIP is thus a relative exception in European politics, because Dutch politicians can be held accountable for their positions and can be criticised on these opinions in the media.

In this chapter, I look at these policies first: what is the essence of these policies, what are the main discussions and who has formal authority to make decisions in these cases? In addition, I analyse the media coverage on these policies: which claims are made on these topics in the media and who makes these claims? What can we conclude about the principles of political communication at a European level, based on these two cases?

6.4 VATMOSS

VATMOSS is the name of a VAT harmonisation for digital products. MOSS is the abbreviation for Mini One Stop Shop, the online system that suppliers can use to pay the VAT on their services. VATMOSS is part of an on-going project to harmonise taxes in the EU Member States. In the past, suppliers of digital products paid VAT in their own Member State. As an example, a Dutch supplier of e-books has always used the Dutch VAT rate, regardless of where the customer buying the e-books was located.

This is undesirable from the perspective of an integrated European market. In the example given above, the e-books buyer may establish his company in a Member State with a lower VAT rate in order to sell his e-books at a lower price. As a result, the government of the Member State where he was originally established receives less tax money. Since there is not one European VAT rate, but there are open borders, this problem cannot be solved. Therefore, a different form of harmonisation was devised. For digital products, the VAT rate of the country where the customer is located is used, not the VAT rate of the country where the supplier is located. This creates a level playing field within the EU. Whether the supplier of e-books—or other digital products—is based in the Netherlands or elsewhere does not matter, it is essential to know where the buyer is located. If the supplier is located in Germany, the German VAT rate applies, regardless of whether the supplier is located in Germany, the Netherlands or Croatia, and regardless of whether the buyer also has German nationality.

For citizens and journalists, it is essential that they understand how these decisions have been made so they can evaluate the work of their politicians. The process is as follows. First, the Council of Ministers voted on VATMOSS. Although the European Parliament does not have a formal role, it does give an advice. Second, the decision in the Council of Ministers is then evaluated by national parliaments. If one of the ministers in the Council makes a decision that national MPs disagree with, there can be a debate at the national level. In the Netherlands, the parliament is officially informed on proposed decisions in the Council of Ministers. Finally, MPs can request a debate or ask questions on the basis of this information. In practice, however, there is usually no debate about these proposed decisions. This was also the case with VATMOSS.

The amount of public information about VATMOSS is extremely limited. Although many databases are available with information on the European policy process, they contain very little information on this matter. The databases on the European Parliament and the Dutch parliament contain no information on the decision-making related to VATMOSS. For the Dutch parliament, this indicates that there never was a debate. In the European Parliament, it seems that no resolutions were adopted. There is no vote available online.

The media ignored VATMOSS almost completely. When VATMOSS was adopted, there was no coverage. There was only some international attention when the harmonisation was introduced on January 1, 2015. This happened because suppliers started complaining about the increased administrative burden. Only when parliamentary questions were asked by the Labour Party ("PvdA") and the Socialist Party ("SP"), there was a minimal amount of media attention. Specialised media at EU level did not cover VATMOSS either. As a result, VATMOSS is still largely unknown by many. Only suppliers of digital products are aware of these harmonisation rules, because they are directly affected. A petition was launched against the harmonisation, but this did not make any difference. In terms of public attention, VATMOSS seems a representative example of many detailed European policies.

6.5 TTIP

"TTIP" is the name of the new trade agreement between the EU and the United States of America (USA). At the time of writing of this chapter there were still negotiations pertaining to this treaty, and the outcome and timeframe of the negotiations were unknown. The trade agreement TTIP is not unique, because the EU negotiates many more trade agreements with other countries. The TTIP is only unique in the sense that the USA is a potentially huge market.

The TTIP delivers three important political discussions. The first is about removing trade barriers between the EU and the USA. According to proponents, this would be good for companies because they will have access to hundreds of millions of consumers. Estimates of the economic impact, however, vary. According to critics, the economic benefit of the TTIP is very uncertain. The second debate focuses on the legal standards in the areas of labour, human rights, environmental and food safety. These standards vary between the EU and the USA and will be harmonised by the TTIP. For proponents, this is a way to achieve better global standards. For opponents, such harmonisation is dangerous because it can lower European standards. The now famous "chloric chicken" which is allowed in the USA would also be allowed into the EU where it is currently prohibited. The third debate is about the Investor-State Dispute Settlement (ISDS) mechanism whereby investors who feel disadvantaged by national policies of a certain country can bring a claim to an arbitration court in order to challenge such national policies. This procedure can reduce countries in their policy space and lead to the payment of massive fines. Critics call this is a threat to democracy.[10]

The TTIP is a good example of a complex topic that can be discussed from various perspectives. At the moment, the European Commission conducts the negotiations with the USA on behalf of the Member States. When an agreement is reached, the European Parliament will vote on the TTIP, just as the Council. It is still unclear whether national parliaments will be requested to approve of the TTIP. This depends on the contents of the final treaty.

The exact content of the treaty is not yet public, because the negotiations have not been concluded. Until that time, the formal information about the TTIP is limited. The European Commission publishes part of the information on the negotiations and gives confidential briefings to the International Trade Committee of the European Parliament. Members of the European Parliament (MEPs) are not allowed to speak with the media or with their supporters about these briefings. Still, there is more transparency than there was in other negotiation processes for trade agreements. The European Commission publishes more documents than they would normally do, but citizens or journalists cannot get a complete picture of the negotiations or of the positions taken by various politicians in this process. This also applies to the elected MEPs.

Yet journalists often report on the TTIP. The negotiations initially generated little publicity, but this has changed over the past years. Several news and current affairs programs have repeatedly paid attention to the TTIP. Sometimes, this even took the form of entertainment. The most striking example was the program *Sunday with Lubach* [Zondag met Lubach, CA] where presenter Arjen Lubach commented on the TTIP and ISDS in a humorous way. Other media have since then picked up the theme. In interviews, both national and European politicians make statements about the trade agreement.

Although the TTIP is still a theme that is not very important to many citizens, this applies to all other European themes that are prominently covered in the media. The notoriety of the TTIP has at least dramatically increased. There is considerable social resistance against the treaty. A petition against the TTIP was signed more than two million times and a public consultation yielded 150,000 responses. There have also been demonstrations against the TTIP in several European cities. This turned this agreement into an iconic European theme.

[10] For example: GroenLinks 2014.

6.6 European Principles

We have seen that there are five principles of political communication but that they appear to be based primarily on national politics. In this chapter, I explore these principles in a European context, based on VATMOSS and the TTIP. Below, the five principles of Wolfsfeld are discussed and reformulated from a European perspective.

6.6.1 Principle 1

According to Wolfsfeld, the first principle of political communication is: "Political power can usually be translated into power over the news media." To test whether this principle also applies in the EU, we must first see where the political power lies in the EU. This shows an immediate problem. It is often not immediately clear where the power lies in the EU, because power is shared and this varies per theme.[11] According to Wolfsfeld's principle, the power over the media should then differ for each policy area.

We see that the political power lies with the Member States to achieve a VAT harmonisation. The national parliaments make the final decision. The primacy is with the Council of Ministers. However, the Dutch government does not get any media attention with its position on this VAT harmonisation. There has been attention for VATMOSS in the Dutch parliament years after the measures were already implemented. Some MPs asked questions about the administrative burden for suppliers of digital products. The Dutch Lower House is in theory decisive, but that role is very limited in practice. The media coverage of these parliamentary questions is nil.

During the TTIP negotiations, the political power lies primarily with the European institutions—the European Commission, the European Parliament and the Council. It is not immediately clear who takes on which task. Although the European Commission determines the progress of the negotiations, this does not translate into media power, because there is no public access to these negotiations. At a later stage, the European Parliament and the Council of Ministers will play a decisive role. We see that some politicians are already making statements about the TTIP, although their role lies in the future. Dutch Minister Ploumen made statements about the treaty, just as Marietje Schaake, a Dutch MEP from the Alliance of Liberals and Democrats for Europe group (ALDE-group), who is a member of the International Trade Committee. The other Dutch MEP in that committee—Anne-Marie Mineur from United Left—has the same formal role as Schaake, but she is almost never in the news. The Dutch Labour Party MEP,

[11] For example: Hix 2005.

Agnes Jongerius, sits as a deputy in this committee and is much more prominent in the news on the TTIP than Mineur. Media attention seems to be a function of the media profile of these MEPs. Mineur is a relatively new MEP, while Schaake has six years of experience in the European Parliament and is often quoted in the media on diverse subjects. Jongerius can boast a reputation as the former President of the main Dutch trade union.

Politicians make statements about European policy issues at different times and in different roles. A majority of these statements never get into the media. Who has a formal say in these policy areas does not play a role in whether these statements are covered. In all these cases, political power is not necessarily translated into media power. Just as political power is distributed in the EU, this also applies to the media power of the politicians who have a say on EU issues. In practice, distributed media power means that a majority of the EU-politicians lack real media power. In the case of European issues, the media have a preference for politicians who were already well known.

The first principle of European political communication can therefore be reformulated as: “In EU-affairs, well-known politicians get media attention, regardless of their political power.”

6.6.2 Principle 2

The second principle of Wolfsfeld reads: “When the authorities lose control over the political environment, they also lose control over the news.” Political control primarily means that politicians bring a particular dossier to a successful conclusion, a law, a vote or a successful election. Control over the media is about whether media coverage is in line with the wishes of the politicians covered and whether the media become an obstacle to their daily work.

With regard to VATMOSS, there was no question of a loss of political control. There were also no problems with the media coverage for the simple reason that the media did not pay attention to this issue anyway. So there was political control, but a lack of publicity and this was probably not what politicians wanted. Some positive coverage was probably desirable. At the same time, this lack of attention was not problematic.

As for the TTIP, there was also no question of a loss of political control. The media control is limited. Opponents of TTIP try to bring negative stories about the trade agreement. An example is the story that democracy is undermined by the ISDS arbitration mechanism. Another example is that an earlier trade treaty with the USA—the North American Free Trade Agreement (NAFTA) with Mexico and Canada—has led to increased poverty in Mexico and not to prosperity. Thus, this would also be the case with the TTIP. The entertainment show of Arjen Lubach could be understood in the same way. It can stir up the fear that the TTIP undermines product standards because the “chloric chicken” could be permitted in the Netherlands in the future. If these criticisms are increasing in the media and spark concerns for citizens, this can result in politicians losing control over the TTIP. It then becomes difficult for proponents to agree with the trade agreement. This issue remains a sword of Damocles hanging over the negotiations.

Political control appears not to be a major problem in the EU. The EU institutions function according to agreed rules, and there are few media who cover these processes. There will not be many journalists who will find out irregularities in the legal and administrative procedures, especially because of the general lack of journalists and their lack of time. However, the EU has little control over the media, because they generally ignore the EU. All EU institutions have a relatively weak position in the media. They are not very influential in how they will be covered. In the case of the EU, we see that lack of control over the media can lead to a loss of political control. If media pick up controversial issues, a lack of political control is likely to be the result. This is reflected in the various quarrels that shook the Dutch delegations in the European Parliament between 2009 and 2014. It also applies to the reports that the Dutch web log *GeenStijl* made in 2013 on MEPs who violated the declaration rules.

The second principle of European reporting should keep in mind that European politicians rarely appear in the media and that adverse publicity can be a source of political problems. The second principle could be formulated as: "Negative EU-coverage leads to inadequate political control."

6.6.3 Principle 3

Wolfsfeld formulates as a third principle: "There is no such thing as objective journalism (nor can there be)." To test this principle, we must consider which approaches journalists use and which choices they make. This principle is so broad that it applies to all reports as journalists always make choices and choose specific angles.

Publicity on the VATMOSS-dossier appeared only at a very late stage, namely long after the new rules were adopted. Shortly after the introduction of the VAT-harmonisation, parliamentary questions were asked. It was very clear that objectivity in media coverage did not exist. VATMOSS was framed in a one-sided way, suppliers suffered from the high administrative burden of the new rules. The media were not looking for alternative frames and used only the frames that were offered to them by politicians. In theory, the media could figure out how the decision about VATMOSS was made and which politicians had played a role in this process, but they did not. It was decided to follow the frame of the MPs and there were no alternative perspectives added.

Also in the case of the TTIP there is no objectivity, as politicians or civil society organisations select the stories around the new treaty on the basis of a specific angle that is put forward. This selection is certainly in favour of the TTIP-opponents, because it is relatively easy to make "a good story", for example that democracy is in danger and that scary products will appear on the Dutch market.

Furthermore, the media coverage over the TTIP is pragmatic. Journalists do not check what the contribution of every stakeholder is to the negotiations, but they reproduce the frames that are on offer.

The lack of objectivity that Wolfsfeld articulates in his third principle of political communication is very clear in the case of the EU. We see this in the fact that journalists do little research into subjects with a European dimension. This "lazy approach" means that many issues ahead are seen as complex and not covered at all because of a lacking interest of the audience. If there are issues to be addressed, there is little journalistic research into the actual operations of those involved in the decision-making. Instead, journalists often use frames that were put forward by politicians or civil society organisations and do not attempt to come up with alternative frames.

The third principle of Wolfsfeld can readily be endorsed since the selection and framing of European news is not objective. Yet we can also define this principle more sharply: "Journalistic framing of European issues follows the agenda of politicians and civil society."

6.6.4 Principle 4

Wolfsfeld's fourth principle states: "The media are dedicated more than anything else to telling a good story." According to Wolfsfeld, these are especially stories that cater to the interests of the public such as human interest, contests, serials and scandals. Are these stories told about the EU too?

In the case of VATMOSS, it is difficult for the media to tell a good story. Negotiations revolved around an abstract, complicated subject and, therefore, the media opted to ignore it. These negotiations were about purely technical proposals whose impact was unclear, and it was difficult to give them a human face or to frame them as a conflict, probably because the negotiations took place behind closed doors. Perhaps there were conflicts about VATMOSS, but this was not visible to the outside world. Only after the harmonisation took place, a good story could be told: VATMOSS could be framed as unnecessary bureaucracy for entrepreneurs.

In the case of the TTIP, this principle is even more visible, because there has been much more media attention. The media have indeed concentrated on good stories. Journalists chose angles that are clear and easy to explain to citizens. The best example is the "chloric chicken" that would flood the Dutch market. Another example is that ISDS is a threat to democracy because companies will get more power than anyone else. The TTIP can also be presented with conflicting frames: left versus right, America versus Europe, and market versus state.

The media have a general tendency to tell good stories on diverse subjects, such as the EU. In practice, this is difficult to achieve. In theory, many themes could be framed as conflicting, because there are political differences within the EU institutions. However, as negotiations take place behind closed doors and conflicts are hidden, these frames are practically impossible to broadcast. In addition, telling good stories is difficult, because there are few well-known EU politicians, which makes it difficult to use personalisation. Continued stories are an option, but often only because negotiations take a long period of time. However, this type of narrative appears to be relatively uninteresting as long as conflicts are hidden. Therefore, we see a preference for stories that can evoke anger, fear or wonder. The EU can certainly call upon emotions—and this is consistent with the aim of media to tell engaging stories—but this is the only angle constituting a real option where EU stories would be attractive.

The fourth principle of Wolfsfeld applies to European coverage as media want to tell engaging stories. The problem is, however, that there are not so many of these stories available. The only way to make the EU appealing is to evoke these emotions. A better formulation of the fourth principle would therefore be: "The media mostly tell stories about the EU that can evoke emotions."

6.6.5 Principle 5

The final principle of Wolfsfeld is: "The most important effects of the news media on citizens tend to be unintentional and unnoticed." Although it is difficult to accurately measure the impact of media, we may look at how the audience responds to policy proposals, and whether that is in line with the kind of responses that the politicians or institutions wanted to get.

VATMOSS provides a good illustration of the effects of a lack of EU coverage. These effects are both accidental and relatively unnoticed. Suppliers of digital products heard of the tax harmonisation at the moment of the introduction of these new rules. The media never informed them about the upcoming measures. This was nobody's intention, but still this was the result of the lack of coverage. The effect may be that the EU looks unreliable because measures "were suddenly taken."

The TTIP shows that coverage of European issues can certainly have consequences that are not intentional. The unintended effects are easy to guess. The TTIP can easily serve as a story, which proves that all kinds of prejudices and negative images of the EU are correct. Through the TTIP: the EU would gain power; the TTIP would threaten sovereignty; the EU would make rules that do not correspond to the preferences of the population; and the EU would be an anti-democratic force only concerned with the economy and not with human rights or the environment. The TTIP provides examples of these negative images, and because these images are repeated in many subjects, this could lead to unnoticed effects too.

The media can place EU issues on the public agenda and the media also play a role in framing effects.[12] Citizens do not change their views on Europe after one

[12] De Vreese 2003.

report, but in the longer term they do learn when Europe is important and what important frameworks are to understand Europe. However, in many European policy areas, it is not the media coverage that affects public opinion, but the lack of coverage. An important principle seems to be that the lack of media attention has unintended and unintentional effects. Often, there is "surprise" in the Dutch media about European decisions or new European rules. This is not really surprising, because there is a lengthy negotiation process that precedes the introduction of these rules. Still, citizens are surprised, because the media never reported on these negotiations.

Wolfsfeld's fifth principle of political communication also applies to European coverage since coverage has unintentional and unnoticed effects. Yet, it is more accurate to turn the proposition the other way around: "The lack of coverage of EU affairs has non-intentional and unnoticed effects."

6.7 Conclusion

To make the EU more democratic, there must be sufficient information for citizens to inform themselves and make informed decisions in European elections. The interaction between citizens, media and politics is the subject of the research area of political communication. In this chapter, we looked at the principles of political communication at the EU level. Two cases were analysed to see whether political communication at the EU level differs from that at national level. There appears to be significant similarities and differences.

In national politics, the first principle of political communication is that political power also produces power over the media. This principle does certainly not predict political communication in the EU. Power is spread over the European institutions and hence the power also spreads over the media. In practice this means that EU institutions do not have much power over the media. It's not the power of politicians at EU level that determines their power over the media. It is mainly a question of whether they are already well known. The first principle can be reformulated as: "In EU-affairs, well-known politicians get media attention, regardless of their political power."

The second principle in political communication is that when politicians lose political control, they also lose their control over the media. In the case of the EU, politicians have usually political control, because procedures are simply monitored, and there is relatively little public interest. There is no watchdog, because the media largely ignore EU issues. The principle is therefore reformulated as: "Negative EU-coverage leads to inadequate political control."

The third principle states that objective news do not exist. This principle is so general that it applies to all political levels. The news selection and the framing of political issues are not objective, but a matter of journalistic preferences. The media often have little interest in EU-issues. When the media cover EU issues, they often choose frames that are offered by politicians or civil society organisations. The third principle can therefore be reformulated as: "Journalistic framing of European issues follows the agenda of politicians and civil society."

The fourth principle states that the media especially tell good stories. This principle is correct in a European context too. However, in the case of the EU, it is difficult for the media to do so, and, therefore, they often choose to ignore the EU. Telling engaging stories is difficult, because there are hardly any famous people in Europe, and there are few visible conflicts. The main way to render EU issues attractive is to evoke emotions. The fourth principle in the EU context could thus be: "The media mostly tell stories about the EU that can evoke emotions."

The fifth principle is that the main media effects are not intentional and remain unnoticed. This also applies to European news, but ignores that underreporting has unintentional and unnoticed effects too. The latter is more important than the effects of real coverage, because of the limited EU coverage in general. The formulation may therefore better be: "The lack of coverage of the EU has non-intentional and unnoticed effects."

All in all, EU affairs coverage can be summarised by the fact that there is often little news in Brussels, and that this has a major impact on all aspects of political communication: a selection of other politicians who may speak in the media; the neglect of the actual power to let the most powerful tell about their decisions and opinions; journalists taking over frames that are delivered by politicians and civil society; and the emphasis on emotion in the absence of conflict and appealing personalities. Whether this media coverage is a good contribution to democracy within the EU will continue to be a point of discussion.

References

Aalberts C (2014) Kunnen burgers Europa van koers laten veranderen? Eburon, Delft

Aalberts C, Kreijveld M (2011) Veel gekwetter, weinig wol: de inzet van sociale media door overheid, politiek en burgers. SDU, The Hague

De Beus J (2001) Een primaat van politiek. Vossiuspers UvA, Amsterdam

Delli Carpini MX, Keeter S (1996) What Americans know about politics and why it matters. Yale University Press, New Haven

De Vreese CH (2003) Framing Europe: television news and European integration. Aksant, Amsterdam

GroenLinks (2014) Vijf bezwaren tegen het handelsakkoord met de VS. https://groenlinks.nl/nieuws/vijf-bezwaren-tegen-het-vrijhandelsakkoord-met-de-vs. Accessed 9 May 2016

Hix S (2005) The political system of the European Union. Palgrave, Houndmills

Landman L, Kik Q, Hermans L, Hietbrink N (2015) Gelukkig zijn hier geen journalisten: nieuwsvoorziening in de regio 2014. Uitgeverij AMB, Diemen

Wolfsfeld G (2011) Making sense of media and politics: five principles of political communication. Routledge, New York

Chapter 7
A Law and Economics Approach to the New EU Privacy Regulation: Analysing the European General Data Protection Regulation

Elif Erdemoglu

Abstract The discussion on the regulation on citizens' right to privacy grows parallel to the widespread usage and collection of Big Data. This chapter analyses from a law and economics perspective the discussion on the European Union (EU) citizens' rights to privacy with regards to collection, retention, analysis and transfer of personal data in light of the EU General Data Protection Regulation (GDPR). The GDPR is drafted in coherence with the EU Digital Market Strategy, which aims to create the correct incentives for digital networks and services to flourish by providing trustworthy infrastructure supported by the right regulations. A significant part of achieving this aim would require the EU citizens to trust in using digital services. The GDPR is designed to increase the citizens' trust to use online and digital services by obliging the service providers to comply with the GDPR. This chapter analyses two key compliance requirements of the GDPR through the economic analysis lens and proposes possible changes to the GDPR in line with the Digital Single Market Strategy of the EU. The scope of this chapter's analysis is limited to how to cure information asymmetries between the citizens and the data collectors in order to increase the citizens' trust in using digital services given the fast-changing and delicate legal issues arising from collecting the personal data of the EU citizens. This chapter concludes by suggesting three improvements to the GDPR; more frequent controls for issuing the EU Data Protection Seal, increased independence of the Data Protection Controller and issuance of publicly available, frequent privacy ratings.

Keywords General Data Protection Regulation · GDPR · Digital Single Market Strategy · Right to privacy · EU data protection · EU citizens' privacy rights · Economics of privacy

---

E. Erdemoglu (✉)
The Hague University of Applied Sciences, The Hague, The Netherlands
e-mail: e.erdemoglu@hhs.nl

J. de Zwaan et al. (eds.), *Governance and Security Issues of the European Union*, DOI 10.1007/978-94-6265-144-9_7

Contents

7.1 Introduction

Citizens' private information is ubiquitous in today's digital society. The citizens are not fully aware of which private information is being collected, when this information is collected and which information can be retrieved by processing this private information. This information asymmetry makes it possible to infringe citizens' fundamental rights without the knowledge of the citizens. The new European General Data Protection Regulation (GDPR), which was published in the Official Journal of the EU in May 2016, introduces better protection of citizens' rights to privacy as compared to the previous European Data Protection Directive of 1995. This chapter examines the strengths and deficiencies of the new data protection regulation from a law and economics perspective in order to give recommendations for an improved regulatory framework. The GDPR is drafted in coherence with the EU Digital Market Strategy[1] that aims to create the correct incentives for digital networks and services to flourish by providing trustworthy infrastructure supported by the right regulations. A significant part of achieving this aim would require the EU citizens to trust in using digital services. The GDPR is designed to increase the citizens' trust to use online and digital services by obliging the service providers to comply with the General Data Protection Regulation. By designing the GDPR, the EU is taking an active role in regulating the collection, retention and analysis of the Big Data in a manner that is expected to have extraterritorial effects and lead the international discussion on the regulation of the Big Data. This is why it is of fundamental value for enhancing the EU Digital Market Strategy to point out the weakness of the GDPR and suggesting improvements for increasing citizens' trust to use digital services.

Big Data can be very broadly defined as very large amounts of data brought together using a variety of algorithms in order to improve the ability of accurate future-guessing. In simpler words, analysing Big Data that is based on personal data of citizens can increase a state's potential possibility to catch a criminal or a company's potential possibility to satisfy more consumers. Thanks to Big Data, the state would have more information on criminals' previous activities and

[1] European Commission 2015a.

correctly guess where they would be located in the next couple of days following the crime. More importantly, relying on Big Data, the state can even know before a crime has been committed, at the planning stage, that there is a high probability of occurrence of a crime and prevent the offence.[2] The usage of Big Data for companies is aimed at reaching to a similar objective of accurate future-guessing. A company can accurately estimate the future needs of an existing or a potential customer by analysing the individuals previously collected data. Depending on the outcomes of the analysed information, the company may start producing new products addressing these needs, may start targeted-advertising of products that the customer theoretically would be interested in, or may decrease product prices according to the "forecasted" reserve prices of the customers.

Emphasising the importance of protection of EU citizens' right to privacy, the discussion focuses on the potential negative consequences of collecting and analysing citizens' data. While discussing the optimum regulation for protecting citizens' data, it is essential to understand that the same group of collected data can be used in various manners that might lead to negative or positive consequences for the individual and for the society. Positive consequences of analysing citizens' data can lead to examples such as preventing criminal activities or providing consumers with new products that are better suited to their needs. On the negative side, Big Data analysis can potentially be used to suppress citizens' rights that oppose governments or can be used to manipulate the consumer behaviour such as increasing the product prices according to "forecasted" reserve prices of the customers.

The discussion on the regulation of Big Data starts with the question of what data should be collected and what usage purposes should be permitted by law. The discussion on Big Data analysis is strongly integrated to the discussion on privacy regulation because even where there are positive outcomes of Big Data analysis, the citizens still pay the price of giving up on their privacy. Citizens face trade-offs when it comes to requesting protection of their privacy. If the citizens benefit from an extended right to privacy,[3] this could constitute an obstacle to prevention of crime or on customers need-oriented products shaped by future-guessing. These trade-offs can be grouped as *security vs. privacy* or *comfort vs. privacy*.

---

[2] Geographic information systems (GIS) that collect and analyse geographic data is used extensively in crime mapping in order to accurately guess future criminal activity. For more information, see Spencer and Ratcliffe 2013. Global positioning systems (GPS) integrated on individuals' cell phones enhance the use of GIS technologies by allowing guesses on locating of an individual with an accuracy of one-centimetre. For more information, see Harries 1999, see Caplan et al. 2011.

[3] For a discussion on the economic value of right to privacy see Posner 1981, 1983. The author bases his economic analysis on the assumption that people who do not have anything to hide would not benefit from an extended right to privacy. Similarly, in 2009, the CEO of Google Eric Schmidt replied to questions on how Google respects and manages individuals' privacy by publicly stating 'If you have something that you don't want anyone to know, maybe you shouldn't be doing it in the first place' Esguerra 2009. For arguments against Posner see Solove 2007.

EU citizens are confronted with the relevant trade-offs, but they do not exist solely due to European Institutions. Foreign governments and multinational companies are also important actors in the privacy regulation debate as they are also parties to these trade-offs. Moreover, current privacy trends in the EU data protection regulation tend to set the bar also for the international debate on how to regulate individuals' privacy.[4] This is why, this chapter is using economic analysis with the aim to explain these trade-offs from a functional perspective through analysing the policy implications for EU citizens in order to suggest improvements to the regulatory framework regarding individuals' data protection and right to privacy.

The first sub-chapter provides information on the background of the discussion regarding the GDPR in order to highlight that the EU Data Protection Regulation has extraterritorial influence and shapes the privacy rights discussion internationally. The main case used in this chapter shows the mistrust between the citizens and the data collector company. The second sub-chapter provides an economic analysis on the right to privacy and on the GDPR in order to address thoroughly the deficiencies of the GDPR in regards to information asymmetries between the citizens and the companies. The information asymmetry is understood as the cause of the mistrust between the citizens and the companies that the Digital Single Market Strategy of the EU is aimed at curing. The last sub-chapter focuses on the predefined deficiencies and suggests solutions to cure this information asymmetry so that the citizens' trust could be improved. This improvement is expected to enhance the Digital Single Market Strategy, which aims to create the correct incentives for digital networks and services to flourish by providing trustworthy infrastructure supported by the right regulations.

7.2 Background of Discussion on EU Data Protection Regulation

The right to privacy can be understood as a fundamental right or as a contractual right. The difference between how the right to privacy is understood and treated by the EU and the United States of America (USA; US) became the central topic of a recent discussion on whether the US government or US companies should have access to the EU citizens' personal data.

Article 8 of the Charter of Fundamental Rights[5] defines privacy as a fundamental right while within the US jurisdiction the right to privacy could be opted out in a

[4] Bradford 2012, p. 23.

[5] Charter of Fundamental Rights of the European Union (2000) C 364/01, entered into force on December 1, 2009.

contract.[6] Defining citizens' rights in relation to their personal data as a fundamental right or as a contractual right, has implications as to how this data can be used.

The difference between how right to privacy is understood and treated by the EU and the US became the central topic of a recent discussion on whether the US government or US companies should have access to the EU citizens' personal data. On October 6, 2015, the Court of Justice of the European Union (CJEU) declared invalid the Safe Harbour Decision[7] regarding citizens' private data transfer between the US and the EU. The CJEU justified this decision on the following ground. According to the Safe Harbour agreement between the EU and the US, the transfer of citizens' private data collected by the EU-based institutions could only be permitted in relation to a country that shows an adequate level of protection of personal data.[8] In this decision, the CJEU stresses the importance of preserving personal data from the perspective of the citizens by emphasising that any legislation relating to personal data should allow citizens an option to have access to or to request removal of one's collected data.[9]

It is important that the CJEU addresses citizens' concerns about the collection and transfer of their personal data. In addition to the new EU regulation, the General Data Protection Regulation,[10] The Safe Harbour decision shows that new suggestions for an international regulatory framework must be structured by taking into account these concerns. The US government also made an effort to enhance protecting personal privacy by passing the Freedom Act[11] on June 2, 2015. The Freedom Act is the first reform of US surveillance practice since the Patriot Act,[12] which came into effect after 9/11. The Patriot Act was designed to protect citizens' security, but favoured security over privacy when the *security vs. privacy* discussion was addressed with regards to collecting and analysing individuals' data.

One of the key issues in protecting citizens' right to privacy is the fact that citizens are not fully informed on what type of data is collected concerning them by companies and by governments. Citizens are also not fully informed on how their

---

[6] United States jurisdiction is an example for defining right to privacy as a contractual right in Bradford 2012, p. 22., for comparison on how approaches to privacy differs between the EU and the US, see Schwartz 2013.

[7] CJEU, *Maximillian Schrems v. Data Protection Commissioner, joined party: Digital Rights Ireland Ltd*, Judgement, 6 October 2015, Case C-362/14, [hereinafter "*Digital Rights Ireland*" case]. Safe Harbour scheme included principles that would allow the United States an "adequate level of protection in line with the EU regulations" to collect, retain, and process EU citizens' private data.

[8] *Ibid.*

[9] Court of Justice of the European Union 2015.

[10] European Commission 2012a.

[11] Public Law 114–23, 2 June 2015, Uniting and Strengthening America by Fulfilling Rights and Ensuring Effective Discipline Over Monitoring Act of 2015.

[12] Public Law 107–56, 26 October 2001, Uniting and Strengthening America by Providing Appropriate Tools Required to Intercept and Obstruct Terrorism Act of 2001.

data can be used. This suggests that there are information asymmetries between the *data controller*[13] and the *data subject* that might result in infringement of the right to privacy. The *data subject* individuals distrust the companies or the government's ability not to infringe their privacy. This leads to EU citizens not trusting companies or governments in relation to their data. A recent survey conducted by the European commission show that 67% of the respondents report that they are concerned about having no control over the information they provide online.[14] Due to this concern, the citizens refrain from sharing their data. The European Council refers to this refrainment by declaring that GDPR aims to provide individuals with control over their data, "given the importance of creating the trust that will allow the digital economy to develop across the internal market."[15] Moreover, the GDPR proposal recognises that citizens' hesitation and mistrust to online services are obstacles for the EU Digital Single Market Strategy.[16] This trust is difficult to establish due to the fact that the data subject individuals do not know for which purposes their data is collected.[17] In order to enhance the EU Digital Single Market Strategy, it is important to incentivise the citizens to share their data online. To create this incentive, it is necessary to cure the information asymmetries between the citizens and the companies so that citizens can trust that companies will respect their privacy once their data is collected.

Another way to win citizens' trust is to provide the citizens with more individual control on the private data upon collection. EU citizens have prior experience with this type of individual control as they have the right-to-be-forgotten.[18] This right could be explained with an example as follows; citizens have the right to request removal of certain links from a Google search of their name if this content is inappropriate and infringes their right to privacy. Critics over the right-to-be-forgotten centred around the fact that removal of certain search results might cause harm to the public. GDPR provides control over personal data in a similar way as allowing the data subjects to request removal of personal data. For the purposes of this chapter, it is understood that even if citizens have the right to ask for the removal of their data, they cannot be sure whether this data will ever be used again. Even with a control right over their data under the EU regulation, citizens

[13] Regulation (EU) 2016/679 of the European Parliament and of the Council of 27 April 2016 on the Protection of Natural Persons with Regard to the Processing of Personal Data and on the Free Movement of Such Data, and Repealing Directive 95/46/EC [hereinafter "General Data Protection Regulation"]. The institutions that collect and administer individuals' data are referred to as "data controllers" in Article 4. See also, European Commission 2015c.

[14] European Commission 2015b, shows the results of a survey on EU citizens' trust in digital environments.

[15] GDPR above n 13.

[16] European Commission 2012 app. 1–2.

[17] Acquisti et al. (forthcoming).

[18] CJEU, *Google Spain SL, Google Inc. v. Agencia Espanola de Proteccion de Datos (AEPD), Mario Costeja Gonzalez [hereinafter "Google Spain"]*, Judgement, 13 May 2014, Case C-131/12.

remain as the less informed party in comparison to the companies, which collect and retain the data. This is why, the analysis of this chapter focuses on the problems caused by the information asymmetries between the citizens and the companies.

The CJEU's decision on the Safe Harbour agreement highlights the importance of this information asymmetry, and explained in its reasoning why the agreement on the free transfer of citizens' private data between the US and the EU was unconstitutional. Given the importance of winning the citizens' trust with regard to online services, it would be one of the expected elements of a future policy proposal to integrate tools of private access for the *data owner* individuals. However, this expectation would inevitably raise more questions to be answered that could be sampled in a non-exhaustive manner as follows. Can the individual also control the previously collected personal data following the path opened by the right-to-be-forgotten?[19] What kind of information should be classified as inappropriate for individual control? Even if private access or limited control rights are to be given to the data owner individual over his collected data, what kind of enforcement mechanism can guarantee that the data collecting institutions or firms are not going to abuse this regulation by keeping a copy of each collected data for themselves?

The case that led to the CJEU Safe Harbour decision started with an EU citizen's dissatisfaction with the safety of his personal data. Mr. Schrems, who was an Austrian law student, followed the news of the US National Security Agency (NSA) surveillance as revealed in the declarations of a US citizen, Mr. Edward Snowden. Mr. Snowden's declarations questioning the extent to which the US government could access citizens' data lead Mr. Schrems to enquire what type of his own personal data was collected and actively stored by US social media networks, such as Facebook. Mr. Schrems requested for his data and he was provided with hundreds of pages gathering his personal data collected by Facebook between 2008 and 2012.[20] Forbes reports that the type of information kept was a "file that was over 1200 pages long, including everyone he had ever friended and defriended, every event he had ever been invited to (and how he responded), a history of every 'poke' he had ever received, a record of who else signed onto Facebook on the same computers as him, email addresses that he hadn't provided for himself (but that must have been culled from his friends' contact lists) and all of his past messages and chats, including some with the notation 'deleted'."[21] Mr. Schrems had knowledge on the EU privacy laws and given that Facebook had a European headquarters in Ireland, he started an online campaign called Europe vs. Facebook stating that Facebook's collection and retention of private data was against European privacy regulations. At the time of the claim, the regulation in question was mainly the EU Directive on Data Protection of 1995.

[19] *Ibid.*

[20] Vermeulen and Gutwirth 2013.

[21] Hill 2012.

Mr. Schrems realised that he was probably not provided with full information, such as his face recognition data. Facebook argued that because their unique face recognition technology is merged with this data, it is protected by law as a "trade secret" and that the company cannot be forced to disclose this data.

The first claim of Mr. Schrems stating that Facebook's data retention was a violation of his fundamental right to privacy was submitted to the Irish Data Commissioner's officer, who rejected the claim.[22] The case was then brought to the Irish High Court who referred the situation to the CJEU which held that the "adequate level of privacy protection" required by the EU was not provided by the US, and, therefore, the agreement allowing free transfer of citizens' data is invalid.

In December 2015, Mr. Schrems announced from his website[23] that he had filed complaints with the Data Protection Authority of Ireland, Belgium and Hamburg, Germany, holding that the data collection of EU citizens by Facebook should be controlled and stopped based on the essence of the CJEU decision according to which data in question was not subject to Safe Harbour agreements, but collected under user contracts.

The European GDPR was already being prepared before the developments regarding the Safe Harbour decision. The GDPR limits the use of European citizens' data by institutions and treats individuals' right to privacy as a fundamental right. The GDPR follows the path opened by the CJEU decision on "the right-to-be-forgotten."[24]

The decision over the right-to-be-forgotten was not the first occurrence where Europe has focused on protecting citizens' right to privacy. Previous regulatory work on protecting EU citizens' data includes the 1995 EU Data Protection Directive,[25] the Framework decision of 2008[26] with its amendments, Article 16 of the Lisbon treaty, the European Parliament resolution on Stockholm Programme,[27] and the Europe 2020 strategy. These instruments highlight the Digital Agenda for Europe.[28] The GDPR seeks to harmonise the fragmented data protection framework within the EU, by clarifying the legal uncertainty due to different applications of this protection and also to change the public perception on the risks of online activity.[29]

---

[22] *Digital Rights Ireland* case, above n 7.

[23] Schrems 2015.

[24] Google Spain case, above n 18.

[25] Data Protection Directive, Directive 95/46/EC of the European Parliament and of the Council of 24 October 1995 on the Protection of Individuals with Regard to the Processing of Personal Data and on the Free Movement of Such Data.

[26] European Council Framework Decision, 2008/977/JHA of 27 November 2008 on the Protection of Personal Data Processed in the Framework of Police and Judicial Cooperation in Criminal Matters.

[27] European Parliament Resolution of 25 November 2009 on the Communication from the Commission to the European Parliament and the Council: An Area of Freedom, Security and Justice Serving the Citizen, Stockholm Programme.

[28] European Commission 2010.

[29] European Commission 2012.

In the recent discussion on the unconstitutionality of the Safe Harbour agreement, when the CJEU communicated that the US data protection laws do not provide an adequate level of protection, the suggestion to provide more user control over collected data was already included as a standard in the GDPR Proposal.[30]

Although the GDPR protects and favours the citizens' right to privacy to a great extent, an economic analysis of the key aspects of the GDPR such as giving the individual control over personal data should be helpful in making recommendations on a future regulatory framework. The average EU citizens cannot be expected to know in what ways data is collected, and what outcomes can be obtained by processing their data. Given the information asymmetry between citizens and data processing companies, this chapter suggests that it is necessary to make amendments to the GDPR in order to make sure that the citizens' best interests were protected.

7.3 The Economic Analysis of General Data Protection Regulation

As stated in the first sub-chapter, the General Data Protection Regulation implements more individual control mechanisms as well as more compliance requirements for collecting European Union citizens' data. This section addresses the role of information asymmetries in privacy regulation by analysing the information gap between the *data controller* and the *data subject,* and focusing on whether the individuals' regulated control over their private data is an adequate solution to protect the right to privacy. The GDPR's stated objective is to facilitate the European Single Digital Market Strategy through increasing the citizens' trust in online tools. The economic analysis of GDPR will be used to detect the deficiencies that might pose an obstacle to reach this stated objective.

The analysis takes its foundation from the fact that technology and information security is a sector that requires specific and rather complicated knowledge. The characteristic of this sector makes the *data collector* significantly more informed than the *data subject* individuals when it comes to using their data. The economic analysis of the GDPR is based on the literature on information economics.

The focus of the data reform was also announced when it was suggested by the European Commission as "more user control and cut costs for businesses."[31] More control from the user's side might not be the most appropriate way to facilitate the citizens' trust in sharing voluntarily their private data with external parties, since

[30] *Ibid.*

[31] European Commission 2012b.

citizens are not as informed as the firms on what results can be achieved by processing their data.[32]

The GDPR proposal starts with an explanatory memorandum where the 1995 EU Directive's two main objectives are presented as (1) protecting the fundamental right to data protection, and (2) enabling the free movement of such data within the Member States. The Framework Decision of 2008[33] is also mentioned in this explanatory memorandum with regards to judicial and police co-operation on the processing of personal data. To stress the importance of personal data protection, the GDPR makes an initial reference in this explanatory section to the vitality of the use of the digital environment, by defining the importance of consumers' trust[34] to online products and services as the "key element" for economic advancement. It is mentioned that the "lack of trust" results in the blocking of the adoption of new online services or products by a larger group of consumers, and, therefore, becomes an obstacle for technological developments. The EU Digital Single Market Strategy aims to create a reliable digital environment for the citizens in order to enhance the use of online services.

In order to reach the wished-for outcome of citizens increased trust in disclosing their private data in digital venues, economic analysis addressing to cure information asymmetries could be helpful. Nobel Prize winner on economics of information, George Akerlof, describes in his seminal paper[35] the unwanted outcomes of information asymmetry with economic models by taking examples from the second-hand cars market. In short, he explains that the buyer of a second-hand car does not know the defects of the car whereas the seller is fully informed on these defects. This could lead to a market failure, as the buyer would not wish to pay a reasonable amount for the car's true value because the buyer would assume that the second-hand car is not worth its announced value as it might be in much worse condition than it is promised to be by the seller. This would lead eventually to buyers' less willingness to pay, and there would be only a buying offer that equates a much lower price than the actual value of the car. This is why the seller would not be willing to sell, and the second-hand cars market would not function. This market failure is caused by the mistrust of the buyer since the buyer was aware that the seller has more information on the car.

---

32 Acquisti and Grossklags 2005. 'Further evidence of simplified mental models comes from comments that expanded respondents' answers. For example, some commented that if a transaction with the merchant was secure, nobody else would be able to see data about the transaction. However, the security of a transaction does not imply its privacy. Yet, security and privacy seem to be synonyms in simplified mental models of certain individuals." On the use of metadata and US surveillance practices see Schneider 2015.

33 European Union, Council Framework Decision 2008/977/JHA of 27 November 2008 on the Protection of Personal Data Processed in the Framework of Police and Judicial Cooperation in Criminal Matters, 30 December 2008.

34 For an analysis of consumer law within the European Framework see Helberger et al. 2013.

35 Akerlof 1970.

The link between the analysis of the GDPR and the second-hand cars market begins here. The GDPR gives more control to citizens on disclosing or deleting their own data in order to win their trust in online technologies so that the EU Digital Market Strategy can be successful. However, just like the second-hand car buyer, the *data subject* individual (the EU citizen) knows that the *data controller* company (*i.e.*, the website) has more information on what can be done with the citizens' data. This is why, if the sole key approach of the GDPR to respect citizens' fundamental right to privacy is to put them in control of their data, the regulation can fall short of reaching the objective of convincing citizens to disclose more private data while using digital services, because the citizens acknowledge their weaker position in having the information on what their data is used for.

The GDPR explains its basis by referring to Article 16 of the TFEU and Article 8 of the Charter of Fundamental Rights.[36] Article 16(1) of the TFEU and Article 8(1) of the Charter uses the exact wording "Everyone has the right to the protection of personal data concerning them."[37] Article 8(2) of the Charter continues by stating that the personal data of individuals should be processed "fairly for specified purposes." It is not clear what "fairly" would mean in this article. However, it is important to note that the GDPR uses its explanatory memorandum section to clarify the economic importance of a better personal data protection regulation. Therefore, it might be difficult to argue whether processing personal data with the sole purpose of generating more economic profits could be seen as an "unfair" use of the personal data. The fair usage of personal data for specified purposes is conditioned in the Article 8(2) of the Charter, either on the consent of the individual or "other legitimate basis laid down by law." The article makes it clear that the individuals' personal data can be collected and processed without their consent. Already justifying the condition of "consent" in order to collect and process individuals' personal data would be difficult given that the average individual's knowledge is very limited when it comes to what can be done with what type of personal data. This is also why the GDPR's main focus on "putting individuals in control of their own data"[38] proves to be problematic to win the citizens' trust in data controllers.

A recent empirical study[39] looked into the awareness level of consumers regarding how their digital data is used. The survey study was conducted on 900 individuals across five countries—namely the United States, the United Kingdom, Germany, India and China. The results of this study show that only a very small percentage of consumers know what kind of data is collected by the websites they visited. For example, the study observes that 86% of the individuals did not know that websites collect the personal website visiting history of the consumers, while

[36] GDPR above n.13.

[37] Article 8(1) of the Charter uses the words "him or her" instead of "them" based on the English version of the official document.

[38] European Commission 2012, p. 2.

[39] Morey et al. 2015.

only 75% of the survey participants knew that the websites they visit collect their location information. Other findings in this research show that even if the consumers do not know what kind of information is collected and retained, they do know that there is digital surveillance, and 97% of the survey participants declared that they are concerned about the potential misuse of their data by states or companies.

7.3.1 Signalling

The GDPR brings in two novelties that can be used to cure the potential market failure due to information asymmetries: the EU Data Protection Seal, and the assignation of a mandatory Data Protection Officer. The GDPR aims to use the Data Protection Seal and the Data Protection Officer in order to guarantee that the citizens can differentiate privacy respecting companies from those that do not respect citizens' privacy. These mechanisms would allow the citizens to be informed of which companies to trust, and incentivise them not to refrain from using online services. In response to Akerlof's paper,[40] Nobel Prize winners, Spence[41] and Stiglitz,[42] offered two possible solutions: signalling and screening. The Data Protection Seal will be explained in relation to signalling while the role of the Data Protection Officer will be explained in relation to screening.

Spence's signalling theory[43] is first described in his paper regarding the information asymmetries in the employee selection. However, in order to explain the link with the GDPR clearly, an example on what signalling theory would look like in the previous scenario of the second-hand cars market will be introduced. The buyer would have more trust and willingness to pay for a second-hand car if the seller could signal that the second-hand car in question is a good quality car. The seller could signal the quality of the car also via signalling that he, himself, is a reliable seller that would never misinform a customer about the quality of a second-hand car. If the seller could signal his respectability, via an award from the city municipality that would read "Most Trustworthy Seller of the City," for example, the buyer would trust this signal, and would trust in doing business with this seller. The mistrust of the citizen to data collector firms is born because the citizens cannot trust for which purposes the firms will use their private information. If the firms could signal to the citizens that they can be trusted for not infringing the right to privacy and for using the private data only as promised for the sake of the relevant purpose of the transaction, then the individuals can be encouraged to disclose their private data in a way that would enhance the EU Digital Single Market.

[40] Akerlof 1970.

[41] Spence 1973.

[42] Stiglitz 1975.

[43] Spence 1973, pp. 355–374.

A focus point in signalling is the quality of the signal because it determines whether the signal is credible. For example, if the award "Most Trustworthy Seller of the City" is issued by the municipality, it might have a better signal value than if it was issued by an automobile company. Better signal value equates to winning more trust. The GDPR foresees an important signalling mechanism for firms that would like to win the trust of the citizens, the EU Data Protection Seal. A firm can be more convincing for the citizens for sharing their data with this firm and for not infringing their privacy rights if the firm can show that it has the EU Data Protection Seal. For this reason, it is essential that the GDPR or the relevant Directives on the protection seal, should clarify strict requirements for obtaining this seal. The policy suggestion in Sect. 7.4 will highlight how to improve the signal quality of the EU Data Protection Seal.

7.3.2 Screening

Stiglitz argues that a screening mechanism[44] that allows the less informed party to better understand the value of the product can also cure the unwanted outcomes of information asymmetries. Again, to use our example of the second-hand cars market, screening could be understood as some mechanism that would force the second-hand car seller to disclose the correct information, such as bad and good qualities of each car he is selling, so that the buyer could choose the car for which he is willing to pay a certain amount. The fact that each company controlling data will be mandated to designate a Data Protection Officer under Article 37 of the GDPR can be one way of enabling screening. The Data Protection Officers will report breaches of data and this is how the citizens might be able to screen firms that are not subject to data breaches from those that are providing weaker-data protection. This would give a more concrete meaning to users control[45] over their private data as described in the GDPR.

---

[44] Stiglitz 1975.

[45] More examples on how the GDPR enables more user control can be seen on Article 8(2). The Article continues by emphasizing the right of the individuals over their personal data by defining a right to "access" to and to "rectify" data. The Charter provides the individuals with limited rights over their data. Accessing or rectifying the collected data over oneself does not stop institutions to reuse this data. The GDPR introduces a broader protection by introducing individuals' right to "delete" their previously collected personal data in para 30 of the introductory section of the GDPR. In the press release regarding the GDPR, it is stated that individuals can request their personal data to be deleted unless there is no "legitimate ground for retention" of this data. Defining the "legitimate ground" is still ambiguous, such as the "fair" processing of personal data. Another important aspect of para 30 is that it provides a clear definition on the precondition for requesting personal data to be deleted. The precondition is that the data collected about an individual has to be "inaccurate" for the individual to legally request its deletion. Even if it is an improvement in comparison to Article 8(2) of the Charter, once again the European regulation remains silent on the reuse of the previously collected data by institutions after its deletion.

In other words, citizens would be outsourcing the screening function to Data Protection Officers and using them as a screening device. The latter should be functioning accurately in order to provide a solution for the information asymmetries that could lead to a market failure, where the citizens would be reluctant to disclose their personal data while using digital services, because they would not be able to differentiate between trustworthy and not-trustworthy firms. As explained before, information asymmetries in data protection arise from the complexity and the specificity of the sector-based knowledge. Another sector where the information asymmetry is a key problem due to the complexity and the specificity of the sector-based knowledge is finance. Thus, the role of the Data Protection Officer could be understood as being similar to that of an auditor. This similarity brings us to the policy suggestion made in the next chapter: independency of Data Protection Officers in order to avoid moral hazard problems.

The GDPR proposal concludes the explanatory memorandum by pinpointing its aim at supporting the "development of the digital economy within the internal market," and to allow individuals to be in control of their data. By reading through each article of the GDPR, it is easy to see how it aims to create "consumer trust" whilst using the digital services in line with the enhancement of the online services goal of the EU Digital Single Market Strategy. With a critical eye on the GDPR, the safety assurance could be understood as strategies to incentivise the consumers to disclose more in order to develop better digital services and infrastructure. However, without establishing the institutions that would support citizens' trust in good protection of their right to privacy, the consumers might not be convinced that the GDPR provides the required protection of privacy. In fact, the EU Digital Single Market strategy[46] states clearly that one of the pillars of this strategy is to maximise the growth potential of European Digital Economy via investing more in Big Data technologies. This aim can only be reached—by providing better signalling and screening mechanisms that would win citizens' trust, and, therefore, incentivise them to use online services.

7.4 Recommendations for Possible Future Steps for GDPR

Neither the new regulation nor the policy suggestion put the required emphasis on curing the information asymmetries between the *data controller* and the *data subject*. Thus, it is important to design amendments of the GDPR that would address this weakness as it could potentially stop it from reaching the objective of contributing to the growth of the European Digital Single Market. Given the information asymmetries and the cyber-security risks regarding the collected data, the prevailing suggestion would be to limit the scope of the permission to collect citizens' private data to a well-selected, trustworthy group of firms. The quality of

[46] European Commission 2015a.

the selection process should be limited by increasing the signal value of European Data Protection Seal, and by increasing the citizens' screening capacity in relation to the improvements in the independence of the Data Protection Officers.

The current technology does not only authorise the collection of data, but it also allows the collected data to be used several times after its collection for different purposes. This point is also relevant for the discussion on the Safe Harbour agreement given that the CJEU declaration on the unconstitutionality of this agreement does not ban US corporations or institutions to stop using the previously collected data. Therefore, limiting the collection of the data is the first step that would save the EU from the negative consequences of misusing of collected data.

The first recommendation on improving the GDPR for addressing information asymmetries between the citizens and the firms concerns the EU Data Protection Seal. Providing compliance through a system of certification on Data Protection is one of the novelties to be brought by the GDPR. Article 39 offers to create a safe environment for the consumer via the EU Data Protection Seal. It is important to understand that the technical requirements for issuance of this certificate would require expert knowledge given the fast-changing characteristics of the information technologies. This is why, it would be problematic to decide on a number of years according to which this Seal could be valid for.

The GDPR suggests that the EU Data Protection Seal could be valid for three years. However, it is almost impossible to foresee what encryption requirements have to be implemented by firms to keep their information systems secure enough for obtaining the EU Data Protection Seal for the upcoming three years. Recent developments show that the quantum computer technology—which invalidates any actively used encryption system—is so advanced that scientists from NASA and Google already declared that the prototypes of these computers are functioning correctly.[47] The European Commission has also a recent research project call where quantum cryptography is given as an example for innovative trends in cybersecurity.[48] Quantum computers have the function to solve very complex algorithms in a very short amount of time, and, therefore, it is unrealistic to ignore that encryption systems that are perceived safe today, can stay safe for three long years. Even though shorter control periods on suitability for the EU Data Protection Seal would create additional transaction costs for the society, bearing the consequences of the weak data protection regulation and the risks associated with it could be costlier in the long run. Thus, it is necessary to implement stricter requirements for receiving this seal in order to protect the signal quality of the EU Data Protection Seal to convince the citizens that the sealed firms are secure.

The second recommendation on improving the GDPR for addressing information asymmetries is regarding the position and role of Data Protection Officers. To enable better screening by the citizens in order to decide which firms are more reliable with managing their private data, a couple of changes shall be made on the

---

47 See NASA (n.d.) and Schulz 2015.

48 European Commission 2016.

role of the Data Protection Officers. Similar to the role of auditors or credit rating agencies in financial sectors, the Data Protection Officers might not be responsible only for reporting breaches, but they might give "*privacy ratings*" for companies that are publicly available.[49] These ratings would be based on a compliance percentage to the GDPR, and it would provide additional incentives for firms to comply and for citizens to trust in disclosing private data for digital transactions. The privacy ratings can only be credible if the moral hazard issues are eliminated. If the Data Protection Officer is hired by the firm and is authorised to grade its own employer, the credibility of the rating would be lower. This is why, the GDPR should consider making amendments in order to make Data Protection Officers independent. This could be provided both by delegating the Data Protection Officer choice and assignment to the National Data Protection Authorities or by creating independent data protection firms, similar to auditing firms, and by only authorising the employees of these firms to provide "*privacy ratings*."

As a final remark, although this paper discussed the weaknesses of the GDPR, it is very important to underline the novelty brought by the GDPR on the international scene via providing better protection and respect for EU citizens' right of privacy. It is essential to stress that these rights granted to the European citizens are still significantly more generous than the privacy rights afforded to the US citizens. The GDPR will be applicable to multinational and foreign firms as long as they are processing EU citizens' data, and this extraterritoriality of the GDPR also equates to the European Union setting the tone of the privacy discussions internationally.

7.5 Conclusion

The EU introduced the General Data Protection Regulation in order to better protect the citizens' fundamental right to privacy so that the citizens can trust sharing their private data with firms in order to enhance the EU Digital Single Market Strategy. The GDPR allows citizens to be more in control of their data, both while sharing it and after sharing it with firms. Enabling citizens' control might not be enough to achieve the objective of increasing the citizens' trust in digital transactions as citizens might realise that they are not as informed as the firms on the methods according to which their private data could be used. The GDPR does not address this information asymmetry directly, and possible changes suggested in this chapter—such as increasing issuance frequency of the EU Data Protection Seal, establishing independency of Data Protection Officers and allowing them to

[49] Data Protection Officers can also prepare privacy reports or data protection reports as an integrated part of the financial reports in order to enhance their companies' reputation regarding their privacy respecting practices. Similar to environmental reporting, privacy reporting as an integrated part of the financial reports would allow privacy respecting practices of companies to become publicly observable to the third parties.

provide publicly available frequent privacy ratings—can be used for advancing towards the EU Digital Single Market Strategy.

References

Acquisti A, Grossklags J (2005) Privacy and rationality in individual decision-making. IEEE Secur Priv 1:26–33

Acquisti A, Taylor C, Wagman L (forthcoming) The economics of privacy. J Econ Lit:6

Akerlof G (1970) The market for lemons: Qualitative uncertainty and the market mechanism. Q J Econ 84:488–500

Bradford A (2012) The Brussels effect. Nw UL Rev 107:23

Caplan J, Kennedy L, Miller J (2011) Risk terrain modelling: brokering criminological theory and GIS methods for crime forecasting. Justice Q 28(2):360–381

Court of Justice of the European Union, 2014 ECLI:EU:C:2014:317, Judgment of 13 May 2014 in Case C-131/12, Google Spain SL, Google Inc. v. Agencia Espanola de Proteccion de Datos (AEPD), Mario Costeja Gonzalez

Court of Justice of the European Union, 2015 ECLI:EU:C:2015:650, Judgment of 6 October 2015, Case C-362/14, Maximillian Schrems v. Data Protection Commissioner, joined party: Digital Rights Ireland Ltd

Court of Justice of the European Union (2015) Press Release, No. 117/15, Luxembourg, 6 Oct 2015. http://curia.europa.eu/jcms/upload/docs/application/pdf/2015-10/cp150117en.pdf. Accessed on May 31, 2016

Esguerra R (2009) Google CEO Eric Schmidt dismisses the importance of privacy, Electronic Frontier Foundation official website, December 10, https://www.eff.org/deeplinks/2009/12/google-ceo-eric-schmidt-dismisses-privacy. Accessed 10 Nov 2016

European Commission (2010) Communication, "Europe 2020: a strategy for smart, sustainable and inclusive growth". COM (2010) 2020

European Commission (2012a) Communication, "Proposal for a regulation of the European Parliament and of the Council on the protection of individuals with regard to the processing of personal data and on the free movement of such data (General Data Protection Regulation)", COM (2012), 2012/0011 (COD)

European Commission, Press Release (2012b) IP/12/46, "Commission proposes a comprehensive reform of data protection rules to increase users" Control of their data and to cut costs for businesses', http://europa.eu/rapid/press-release_IP-12-46_en.htm?locale=en. Accessed 15 Oct 2015

European Commission (2015a) Communication, "Commission to the European Parliament, the Council, the European Economic and Social Committee and the Committee of the Regions: A Digital Single Market Strategy for Europe", COM (2015) 192

European Commission (2015b) Eurobarometer 431. http://ec.europa.eu/public_opinion/archives/ebs/ebs_431_sum_en.pdf. Accessed 31 May 2016

European Commission (2015c) Official website. Who can collect and process personal data? http://ec.europa.eu/justice/data-protection/data-collection/index_en.htm. Accessed 12 Nov 2015

European Commission (2016) Horizon 2020 Call on EU Cooperation and International Dialogues in Cybersecurity and Privacy Research and Innovation. http://ec.europa.eu/research/participants/portal/desktop/en/opportunities/h2020/topics/2422-ds-05-2016.html. Accessed 31 May 2016

Harries K (1999) The integration of GIS and GPS in mapping crime: principle and practice. U.S. Department of Justice, Washington

Helberger N, Guibault L, Loos M, Mak C, Pessers L and Sloot B (2013) Digital consumers and the law: towards a cohesive European framework (No. 28). Kluwer Law International, Alphen aan den Rijn

Hill K (2012) Max Schrems: the Austrian thorn in Facebook's side. http://www.forbes.com/sites/kashmirhill/2012/02/07/the-austrian-thorn-in-facebooks-side/#2715e4857a0b1d8384d06b30. Accessed 3 Feb 2016

Morey T, Forbath T, Schoop A (2015) Customer data: designing for transparency and trust. Harvard Bus Rev https://hbr.org/2015/05/customer-data-designing-for-transparency-and-trust. Accessed 20 Mar 2016

NASA (n.d.) QuAIL: Quantum computers. http://www.nas.nasa.gov/quantum/quantumcomp.html. Accessed 12 Nov 2015

Posner R (1981) The economics of privacy. Am Econ Rev 71(2):405–409

Posner R (1983) The economics of justice. Harvard University Press, Cambridge

Schneider B (2015) Data and Goliath: the hidden battles to collect your data and control your world. WW Norton & Company, New York City, New York

Schrems M (2015) Data Protection Authorities in Ireland, Belgium and Germany requested to review and suspend Facebook's data transfers over US spy programs. http://www.europe-v-facebook.org/prism2_en.pdf. Accessed 5 Apr 2016

Schulz T (2015) Rechner-revolution: Google und NASA präsentieren Quantencomputer. Spiegel Online. http://www.spiegel.de/netzwelt/web/google-und-nasa-praesentieren-ihren-quanten-computer-a-1066838.html. Accessed 12 Oct 2015

Schwartz P (2013) The EU-US privacy collision: a turn to institutions and procedures. Harvard Law Rev 126:1

Solove D (2007) "I've got nothing to hide" and other misunderstandings of privacy. San Diego Law Rev 44:745

Spence M (1973) Job market signalling. Q J Econ 87:355–374

Spencer C, Ratcliffe J (2013) GIS and crime mapping. Wiley, Hoboken

Stiglitz J (1975) The theory of screening, education, and the distribution of income. Am Econ Rev 65:283–300

Vermeulen M, Gutwirth S (2013) Empowering social network site users through creating new rights: analysing the right to be forgotten and the right to data portability in the EU. User Empowerment in a Social Media Culture, EMSOC, Belgium

Part III
Policy Domains

Chapter 8
The EU Economic Governance Framework and the Issue of Debt

René Repasi

Abstract The Maastricht Treaty introduced the Economic and Monetary Union (EMU) based on a supranational pillar covering the monetary policy and on an intergovernmental pillar covering the coordination of entirely national economic and fiscal policies. This construction relies on the assumption that the disappearance of monetary policy measures to remedy excessive government deficits would discipline Member States' spending policies. In addition, the European level should only guarantee that Member States do not enter into excessive deficits and debts. The recent economic crisis unveiled the weaknesses of the Maastricht EMU construction and its underlying assumptions. Some Member States piled up debt in such an excessive manner that they were not able anymore to refinance themselves on the private markets. Reforms of the EMU's economic governance framework made in the aftermath of the peak of the crisis tightened the margin of public spending without addressing the issue of reducing excessive debt within the tightened limits of the reformed framework. In this context, the idea of establishing a European Redemption Fund (ERF) was put forward, into which all government debts amounting to above 60% of Gross Domestic Product (GDP) would be transferred, and where participating Member States would be obliged to redeem the transferred debt over a fixed period of time. This idea can be realised within the existing Treaty boundaries and would not violate the so-called "no bail-out" clause. It would put overindebted Member States in a position to comply effectively with the reformed economic governance framework.

R. Repasi (✉)
Erasmus School of Law, Erasmus University Rotterdam, European Research Centre for Economic and Financial Governance (EURO-CEFG) of the Universities of Leiden, Delft and Rotterdam, Burgemeester Oudlaan 50, 3000 DR Rotterdam, The Netherlands
e-mail: repasi@law.eur.nl

J. de Zwaan et al. (eds.), *Governance and Security Issues of the European Union*, DOI 10.1007/978-94-6265-144-9_8

Keywords Economic governance · Economic and Monetary Union · European Redemption Fund · Debt · Excessive deficit procedure · Eurobonds · Fiscal compact · Economic crisis

Contents

8.1 Introduction

Europe is in a state of permanent crisis. Since the outbreak of the economic and financial crisis in 2008, the European Union operates in "crisis modus.' The tools for managing the economic crisis can be found in Title VIII of the Treaty on the Functioning of the European Union (TFEU) on "Economic and Monetary Policy." Essentially, the crisis revolves around the declining refinancing of Member States' expenditure.[1] By that, government debt, as well as its origins and its management in the future, forms the core of the challenges for the European Union. The origins of the excessive debt in some Member States are linked to the existing economic governance framework as it was apparently not able to prevent it. Based on this consideration, the question arises whether this framework is able to manage debt in the future, and which reforms are necessary for enhancing its effectiveness. This chapter will analyse the role of debt in the existing economic governance framework in Sect. 8.2. Section 8.3 will explore ways to manage government debt in the future within the Treaty boundaries.

[1] For a comprehensive understanding of the economic and financial crisis, one has, of course, also to look at the reasons for increasing expenditure of Member States such as the reasons for the reputed necessity to save ailing credit institutions.

8.2 The Role of Debt in the Existing Economic Governance Framework

8.2.1 The Asymmetric Economic and Monetary Union in the Maastricht Treaty

The Maastricht Treaty established "an economic and monetary union"[2] in which "Member States shall regard their economic policies as a matter of common concern and shall coordinate them within the Council."[3] It installed "a European System of Central Banks"[4] whose "primary objective [...] shall be to maintain price stability"[5] (and which shall "define and implement the monetary policy of the Community."[6] This basic construction of EMU remained untouched during the subsequent Treaty reforms and can hence be found in this state in the Lisbon Treaty.

The basic construction of EMU is characterised by its asymmetry. Whilst the Monetary Union is a supranational union, the Economic Union remains for the most part an intergovernmental construct. This asymmetry follows from the kind of competences the European Union (EU) has for implementing policies in the respective union and from the kind of mechanisms the Union can use in order to achieve compliance. A supranational union is defined by the existence of exclusive or shared Union competences.[7] Adopting legally binding acts on these competences takes precedence over conflicting national law and includes the obligation for the Member States to implement Union law into national law. An intergovernmental "union" is characterised by the existence of mere coordination competences.[8] In fields covered by these competences, national law remains unaffected by Union action. Monetary policy is, according to Article 3(1)(c) TFEU, an exclusive Union competence, where Member States are not allowed to act unilaterally anymore. Economic policies can, according to Article 5(1) TFEU, only be coordinated so that Member States remain, in principle, legally free to pursue own economic and fiscal policies.

In order to achieve compliance of Member States with Union action, one can distinguish five means to ensure compliance: *First*, there can be private enforcement. Private action builds up pressure on the non-compliant Member State, and

---

[2] Treaty establishing the European Community, OJ 1992 C 224, entered into force on 1 November 1993 [hereinafter "EC Treaty"], Article 2.

[3] *Ibid.*, Article 103(1).

[4] *Ibid.*, Article 4a.

[5] *Ibid.*, Article 105(1).

[6] *Ibid.*, Article 105(2).

[7] Consolidated version of the Treaty on the Functioning of the European Union, OJ 2016 C 202/47, entered into force on 1 December 2009 [hereinafter "TFEU"], Articles 3 and 4.

[8] *Ibid.*, Articles 5 and 6.

pushes the latter to modify its economic and fiscal policy decisions. *Second*, there can be public enforcement. Within public enforcement, one may distinguish several degrees of intensity. The least intense means of enforcement is "naming and shaming." A publication of non-compliance creates public pressure on the non-compliant Member State to align its economic and fiscal policies with the commonly set policy goals. There can be, *third*, sanctions for non-compliance, and, *fourth*, incentives for compliance. *Fifth*—and this is the most intense means to ensure compliance—European policy decisions substitute national economic and fiscal policy decisions. Non-compliance is then "sanctioned" by substitution. The latter compliance mechanism is characteristic of a supranational union, whilst an intergovernmental "union" can be identified by the absence of such a mechanism. Within the Monetary Union, national central banks and the European Central Bank (ECB) form the "European System of Central Banks" (ESCB).[9] According to Article 14 of the Statute of the ESCB and of the ECB,[10] national central banks are legally bound by the decisions taken by the Governing Council of the ECB within its mandate. By that, ECB Governing Council decisions replace national central bank decisions.

When it comes to the Economic Union, Article 121(1) TFEU only requires that "Member States shall regard their economic policies as a matter of common concern and shall coordinate them within the Council." Guidelines adopted by the Council may therefore only set policy goals and benchmarks for national economic and fiscal policies, but cannot replace national decisions that are inconsistent with the Union guidelines. National policies have to be aligned with those policy goals without any legally binding enforcement mechanism. They should be disciplined by the markets based on the assumption that, as long as the position of a Member State on the financial markets is the same as of any other private institution, markets will indicate—in the form of decreasing or increasing interest rates on government bonds—whether a national economic and fiscal policy is sustainable and convincing. Therefore, the Treaties provide for the so-called "no bail-out" clause,[11] according to which neither the Union nor the Member States shall be liable for or assume the commitments of other Member States. The provisions also bar central banks from purchasing government bonds on primary markets,[12] and prevent any kind of privileged access by central governments to financial institutions.[13]

Based on these considerations, one can classify the current choice of the Treaties to achieve compliance within the Economic Union, as a combination of private enforcement and "naming and shaming." As already mentioned, higher interest rates on government bonds should make Member States modify their national policy choices. This "private enforcement" can be reinforced or

---

[9] *Ibid.*, Article 282(1).

[10] Protocol (No. 4) on the Statute of the European System of Central Banks and of the European Central Bank, 2016 C 202/230.

[11] TFEU, above n 7, Article 125.

[12] *Ibid.*, Article 123.

[13] *Ibid.*, Article 124.

even triggered by the Council under the multilateral surveillance procedure in Article 121(4) TFEU. Where non-compliance of a Member State's national policies with the Union economic policy guidelines is established, and where the Member State concerned persistently refuses to remedy the state of non-compliance, the Council can make this situation and its recommendations public. Further means to achieve compliance are, however, not foreseen under the Treaties.

8.2.2 The Role of Debt

Yet, the EMU legal framework draws one red line for Member States' freedom to conduct their economic and fiscal policies by setting certain budgetary goals that should not be exceeded. This red line is based on the assumption that national economic and fiscal policies of one Member State can only harm other Member States if the budgetary consequences of these economic and fiscal policies lead to a default risk of the Member State in question, which could entail the necessity for a bailout by the other Member States.[14] Therefore the debt situation of the Member States should remain underneath a certain threshold that guarantees that a Member State can refinance its expenditure, which surpasses the revenue generated from own resources such as taxes, on the financial markets at low interest rates. Article 126(1) TFEU implements this assumption by requiring that "Member States shall avoid excessive deficits." An excessive deficit is thereby assumed if either the ratio of the planned or actual government deficit to GDP exceeds 3% or the ratio of government debt to GDP exceeds 60%.[15] The choice of both reference values is considered "arbitrary"[16] and was only reflecting the budgetary situations of the Member States at the time of the negotiations of the Maastricht Treaty. This can be demonstrated by looking closer at the explanation for the introduction of the reference value of 3% of GDP for the tolerated deficit: If, on the basis of a given debt of 60% of GDP, one assumes that nominal GDP increases annually by 5%, a deficit of 3% would not result into any increase of government debt.[17] The fact that since the entry into force of the Maastricht Treaty in 1992, the Member States that form today's Euro area had, on average, only five times a nominal growth of more than 5% of GDP,[18] already shows these reference values could not be suitable to prevent excessive deficits.

---

[14] De Grauwe 2016, p. 148.

[15] Cf. Article 126(2) TFEU in conjunction with Article 1 of Protocol (No. 12) on the Excessive Deficit Procedure.

[16] De Grauwe 2016, p. 148.

[17] This is based on the following simple calculation: deficit $d = $ annual growth $g \times$ government debt D: $5\% \times 60\% = 3\%$, cf. De Grauwe 2016, p. 148.

[18] This was in 1992, 1994, 2000, 2006 and 2007, cf. OECD 2016.

The arbitrariness of the chosen reference values led soon to the adoption of the so-called Stability and Growth Pact (SGP),[19] which consisted of two Council regulations that aim at preventing a government deficit to become excessive[20] and at correcting an excessive government deficit.[21] The former implements its purpose by "lowering" the tolerated annual government deficit to "close to balance or in surplus." This "lowered deficit" was called "medium-term objective" (MTO) and Member States, whose budgets were not in line with this objective, had to present an "adjustment path" towards this objective in so-called "stability programmes" or, for non-Euro Area Member States, in "convergence programmes." Those programmes were monitored by the Commission and the Council under the multilateral surveillance procedure. When reforming the SGP in 2005,[22] the legislator specified the MTO so that it had to be "within a defined range between −1% of GDP and balance or surplus, in cyclically adjusted terms, net of one-off and temporary measures".[23] From an economic perspective, lowering the tolerated annual government deficit from 3 to 1% in the form of the MTO was only consequent given the lower nominal growth in the EU.

Yet both the limit for government deficit and the limit for government debt are already under the budgetary surveillance procedure under Article 126 TFEU, and are not as strict as they appear to be at first sight. A transgression of the reference values is only considered an excessive government deficit if a Member State cannot rely on certain "mitigating" factors. A transgression of the 3-per-cent-criterion with regard to the annual deficit is exempted if either "the ratio has declined substantially and continuously" in the past or the excess was "only exceptional and temporary and the ratio remains close to the reference value." The excess is considered to be exceptional if it results "from an unusual event outside the control of the Member State concerned and which has a major impact on the financial position of the general government, or when resulting from a severe economic downturn".[24] A government debt of more than 60% of GDP is negligible if "the ratio is

[19] European Council (1997) Resolution on the Stability and Growth Pact, 17 June 1997, OJ 1997 C 236/1.

[20] Council Regulation (EC) (1997) No. 1466/97 on the strengthening of the surveillance of budgetary positions and the surveillance and coordination of economic policies, OJ 1997 L 209/1 amended by Council Regulation (EC) (2005) No. 1055/2005, OJ 2005 L 174/1 and by Regulation (EU) (2011) No. 1175/2011, OJ 2011 L 306/12.

[21] Council Regulation (EC) (1997) No. 1467/97 on speeding up and clarifying the implementation of the excessive deficit procedure, OJ 1997 L 209/6 amended by Council Regulation (EC) (2011) No. 1056/2005, OJ 2005 L 174/5 and by Council Regulation (EU) No. 1177/2011, OJ 2011 L 306/33.

[22] Council Regulation (EC) (2005) No. 1055/2005 amending Regulation (EC) (1997) No. 1466/97 on the strengthening of the surveillance of budgetary positions and the surveillance and coordination of economic policies, OJ 2005 L 174/1.

[23] Regulation (EC) No. 1055/2005, above n 20, Article 1(1) introducing Regulation (EC) No. 1466/97, Article 2a.

[24] Regulation (EC) No. 1467/97, above n 21 Article 2(1).

sufficiently diminishing and approaching the reference value at a satisfactory pace." It is worth mentioning that until the adoption of the reformed SGP with the so-called "six-pack" legislation[25] in 2011 the Commission and the Council did not initiate one excessive deficit procedure because of a transgression of the debt criterion.[26]

Beyond these mitigating factors, in case one or both reference values is exceeded, the Commission has, when preparing its report on the existence of an excessive deficit, to "take into account whether the government deficit exceeds government investment expenditure and take into account all other relevant factors, including the medium-term economic and budgetary position of the Member State."[27] If despite all mitigating factors the Commission considers the presence of an excessive deficit, the Council has still formally to establish its existence by a decision. Before adopting this decision, the Council has to consider, "any observations which the Member State concerned may wish to make."[28] In doing so, the Council is not bound by the considerations of the Commission and may, in particular on the basis of a different assessment of the relevant economic data, come to a different conclusion, and reject to establish the existence of an excessive deficit. The Council has, hence, a broad political discretion.[29] The same applies, in case the Council establishes the existence of an excessive deficit, to subsequent Council recommendations outlining policy measures to remedy the situation. Since, finally, Article 126(10) TFEU excludes the infringement procedure at the ECJ, the Commission is also not allowed to prosecute Member States with judicial means.

In sum, a system of economic and fiscal policy coordination, which ensures compliance mainly by inducing self-determined states to modify their policy choices through the increase or decrease of the costs of refinancing these choices on private markets, must focus on the control of Member States' debt, in particular with regard to states that are unified in a monetary union. If markets for whatever reason do not trigger necessary policy choices of states and their debt level increases continuously, the risk of state bankruptcy and, by that, of assisting

[25] The "Six Pack" consists of five regulations and one directive: Regulation (EU) No. 1173/2011 on the effective enforcement of budgetary surveillance in the euro area, OJ 2011 L 306/1; Regulation (EU) No. 1174/2011 on enforcement measures to correct excessive macroeconomic imbalances in the euro area, OJ 2011 L 306/8; Regulation (EU) No. 1175/2011 amending Council Regulation (EU) No. 1466/97 on the strengthening of the surveillance of budgetary positions and the surveillance and coordination of economic policies, OJ 2011 L 306/12; Regulation (EU) No. 1176/2011 on the prevention and correction of macroeconomic imbalances, OJ 2011 L 306/25; Council Regulation (EU) No. 1177/2011 amending Regulation (EC) No. 1467/97 on speeding up and clarifying the implementation of the excessive deficit procedure, OJ 2011 L 306/33; Council Directive 2011/85/EU on requirements for budgetary frameworks of the Member States, OJ 2011 L 306/41.

[26] Ohler 2010, p. 340.

[27] TFEU, above n 7, Article 126(3).

[28] *Ibid.* Article 126(6).

[29] ECJ, *Commission v Council, Judgement, 2004,* Case C-27/04, ECR I-6649, para 80.

failing states financially by the higher level or other states increases simultaneously. The usual last resort in such a situation to devaluate the own currency in order to reduce government debt denominated in own currency is excluded for states that are part of a monetary union. Based on these considerations, it becomes clear that debt and the control of debt is crucial in an asymmetric Economic and Monetary Union. Against this background, one may cast serious doubts whether a surveillance procedure such as the one introduced by the Maastricht Treaty and specified by the SGP is suited to meet the challenge of an effective debt control. These doubts refer to the very foundations of the debt control assuming that no debt issues would raise as long as the annual government deficit remains below 3% of GDP and the government debt remains below 60% of GDP, foundations which induce pro-cyclical spending. The doubts refer, furthermore, to the decision-making procedure, which puts the Member States in the Council in the driver's seat of the debt control procedure although it is them that accumulate the debt. The financial and economic crisis that broke out in 2008 revealed ultimately the shortcomings of both the asymmetric EMU and the erroneous debt control.

8.2.3 The Reformed Economic Governance Framework After the Economic Crisis

The debt control in place did not achieve its goal to keep government debt underneath the 60% threshold. Before the outbreak of the crisis, in 2006 and in 2007, the consolidated government debt of only 18 out of 27 EU Member States or only 9 out of 17 Euro area Member States met the debt criterion.[30] After the outbreak of the crisis government debt rocketed upwards so that several Member States were not even able to refinance their expenditure on the financial markets anymore.

In order to address and to overcome shortcomings in the debt control, the Union legislator and the Member States introduced several modifications. The debt level is now already important for the prevention of an excessive deficit. Member States faced with a debt level exceeding 60% of GDP or with pronounced risks of overall debt sustainability have to provide in their stability or convergence programmes for an annual improvement of the cyclically adjusted budget balance, net of one-off and other temporary measures of more than 0.5% of GDP.[31] Furthermore, the reformed corrective arm of the SGP clarified that an excessive deficit procedure may also be initiated if only the debt criterion is not met.[32] When

[30] Eurostat (2016), Government consolidated gross debt 1999–2015.

[31] Regulation (EC) No. 1466/97, above n 20, Article 5(1)(2) as amended by Regulation (EU) No. 1175/2011.

[32] Regulation (EC) No. 1467/97, above n 21, Article 1(1) and Article 2(4)(1) as amended by Regulation (EU) No. 1177/2011.

assessing whether an excessive government deficit because of the transgression of the debt criterion exists, the ratio of the government debt exceeding 60% of GDP is now only considered as "sufficiently diminishing" under Article 126(2) TFEU if "the differential with respect to the reference value has decreased over the previous three years at an average rate of one twentieth per year as a benchmark."[33] In addition to these modifications to the SGP, 25 Member States concluded the Treaty on Stability, Coordination and Governance in the Economic and Monetary Union (TSCG).[34] This international Treaty supplements the existing primary and secondary EU law without modifying it.[35] It requires from the Contracting Parties to introduce a debt brake rule into their national law "of binding force and permanent character, preferably constitutional."[36] Under this rule, an automatic correction mechanism shall be triggered in the event of a significant observed deviation from the MTO or the adjustment path towards it, whereby the MTO is defined with a lower limit of 0.5% of GDP.[37] Only where the ratio of the government debt is "significantly below 60%," the country-specific MTO can be of at most 1% of GDP.

The role of the Commission was strengthened in the face of the Council by introducing the reversed qualified majority voting.[38] Briefly, this voting procedure foresees that a Commission recommendation is deemed to be adopted by the Council unless the latter decides by a qualified majority to reject the recommendation within 10 days of the Commission's adoption thereof or otherwise to adopt an amended decision. According to Article 7 TSCG "the Contracting Parties whose currency is the euro commit to support the proposals or recommendations submitted by the Commission where it considers that a Member State [...] is in breach of the deficit criterion in the framework of an excessive deficit procedure," unless "it is established among the Contracting Parties [...] that a qualified majority of them [...] is opposed to the decision proposed or recommended." Surprisingly, the reverse qualified majority voting only applies to Council decisions or recommendations relating to the deficit criterion and not to the debt criterion.

In sum, the reformed economic governance framework adopted after the outbreak of the economic crisis in 2008 defined the criteria for the existence of an excessive deficit in a more precise and strict manner and enhanced the importance

---

[33] *Ibid.*, Article 2(1a).

[34] Treaty on Stability, Coordination and Governance in the Economic and Monetary Union [hereinafter "TSCG"], opened for signature (2012), entered into force on 1 January 2013 http://www.consilium.europa.eu/european-council/pdf/Treaty-on-Stability-Coordination-and-Governance-TSCG, accessed on May 23, 2016.

[35] See for more details Repasi 2013, p. 45.

[36] TSCG, above n 34, Article 3(2).

[37] *Ibid.*, Article 3(1)(b) and (e).

[38] Critical on the legality of the introduction of the reversed qualified majority voting: Ruffert 2011, p. 1800 et seq. with further references.

of the debt criterion. The reforms try to overcome the shortcomings of the market-induced enforcement mechanism under the existing framework by placing the emphasis on legal enforcement based on national law and initiated by national institutions. The predominant role of the Council is supposed to be reduced by the introduction of the necessity to organise a qualified majority against Commission proposals and recommendations instead of organising a blocking minority in order to reject these proposals and recommendations.

Stepping back from the details of the reformed economic governance framework, one has to come to conclusion that these reforms of the asymmetric EMU were rather of cosmetic than of substantive nature. The reforms did not mitigate the risk of a sovereign default of those Member States whose budgets got into troubled waters in the aftermath of the economic and financial crisis. The requirement to reduce the annual government deficit is, in practice, impossible to meet for a state whose economy is in a state of heavy recession or even depression. Public spending in times of decreasing private consumption and investments is needed in order to keep the national economy running and to maintain the working capacity of state institutions without the state being able to reduce government debt. In times, in which five Member States have a government debt of more than 100% of GDP[39] and further 7 Member States have a government debt of more than 80% of GDP[40] and in which between 2009 and 2014 only 4 out of 28 EU Member States managed to reduce their government debt for more than only one year,[41] it appears detached from reality to believe that the annual government deficit could be in balance and even in surplus and is used in order to reduce government debt. At the same time, refinancing government debt, provided that the Member State concerned has still access to private financial markets, entails for Member States with a high ratio of government debt to GDP additional expenses, which have to be covered by the annual government deficit.

All things considered, beyond the reforms already made, one has to face the challenge of how to reduce the existing high levels of government debt of the Member States and of how to avoid that Member States pile up government debt in an excessive manner again in the future.

---

[39] Data for the year 2015: Belgium (106.0%), Greece (176.9%), Italy (132.7%), Cyprus (108.9%) and Portugal (129.0%), cf. Eurostat (2016), Government consolidated gross debt 1999–2015.

[40] Data for the year 2015: Ireland (93.8%), Spain (99.2%), France (95.8%), Croatia (86.7%), Austria (86.2%), Slovenia (83.2%) and the United Kingdom (89.2%), cf. Eurostat (2016), Government consolidated gross debt 1999–2015.

[41] Denmark, Germany, Ireland and Hungary, cf. Eurostat (2016), Government consolidated gross debt 1999–2015.

8.3 Managing Government Debt Within the Treaty Boundaries[42]

As a preliminary remark, it is worth mentioning that the basic asymmetric construction of the EMU cannot be changed outside a formal Treaty change procedure. This sets the limits for secondary law such as the "Six Pack" or the "Two Pack"[43] legislation as well as for international treaties concluded by a subset of Member States such as the TSCG and the Treaty establishing the European Stability Mechanism (ESM-Treaty). The ECJ confirmed this view in its "Pringle" decision on the compatibility of the ESM-Treaty with EU law when it concluded that the ESM-Treaty could enter into force even before the formal introduction of the third paragraph of Article 136 into the TFEU, which stated that the Euro area Member States might establish a stability mechanism.[44] Independently of this "Treaty change," the ESM-Treaty had to comply with the EU Treaties in order to be lawful.

In the following, it will first be discussed how to solve, within the Treaty boundaries, the issue of the existing government debt that is, in parts, too high to ever steer a Member State's budget into calmer waters, in which the current economic governance framework can be applied effectively (Sect. 3.1). In this context, in particular the idea of a European Redemption Fund will be addressed. After having discussed the issue of existing government debt, the management of future debt of Member States will be addressed (Sect. 3.2). Here the prospect of success of automatic correction mechanisms and of the debt brake, as foreseen by the TSCG, will be considered before turning to a short assessment of the possibility to issue common debt at EU level in form of "Eurobonds."

[42] This section partly reproduces Repasi (2016). This study was commissioned, overseen and published by the European Parliament's Policy Department for Citizens' Rights and Constitutional Affairs in the framework of a project IP/C/AFCO/IC/2015-080 at the request of the Parliament's Committee on Constitutional Affairs. It is available at EP website www.europal.europa/studies free of charge.

[43] The "Two Pack" consists of two regulations: Regulation (EU) No. 472/2013 on the strengthening of economic and budgetary surveillance of Member States in the euro area experiencing or threatened with serious difficulties with respect to their financial stability, OJ 2013, L 140/1, and Regulation (EU) No. 473/2013 on common provisions for monitoring and assessing draft budgetary plans and ensuring the correction of excessive deficits of the Member States in the euro area, OJ 2013, L 140/11.

[44] ECJ, *Thomas Pringle v Government of Ireland, Ireland and The Attorney General* Judgment 2012, Case C-370/12 [Hereinafter "*Pringle*"] ECLI:EU:C:2012:756, para 185.

8.3.1 The Fate of the Existing Government Debt: The European Redemption Fund

In 2012, the German Council of Economic Experts ("Sachverständigenrat") proposed in its annual report a solution on how to deal with the excessive past government debt of the Member States. It recommended the establishment of a European Redemption Fund (ERF) following the sample of the German "Redemption Fund for Inherited Liabilities" ("Erblastentilgungsfonds"), which was created in 1995 in order to pay off debts incurred by the former German Democratic Republic.[45] The ERF proposal consists of several elements:[46] Government debt, which amounts above the reference value of 60% of GDP, would be transferred to a common redemption fund subject to joint and several liability. During a "roll in" phase of around five years the transferral of government debt is made by a purchase of bonds with a maturity of more than two years of participating Member States on the primary market.[47] The debts remain exclusively with the participating countries. A consolidation path has to be laid down for each Member State in a legally binding way, which would require from the Member State to redeem autonomously the transferred debt over a period of 20 to 25 years.

After the "roll in" phase, a Member State's outstanding debt level would comprise (1) debts for which it is individually liable amounting to 60% of GDP, and (2) debts that, at the time of the transfer, exceed the reference value of 60% of GDP, which are transferred to the ERF. The transferring Member States bear the primary liability and the ERF a secondary liability. The joint liability during the repayment phase means that bonds would be issued by the ERF with a high rating in order to stabilise the European financial system until the national bond markets regain sufficient functionality. Participation is subject to strict conditionality. If a Member State does not meet its political reform commitments, which are supposed to lead to consolidation and growth, the "roll in" would be discontinued and the Member State in question would be fully exposed once again to the financial markets. Finally, in order to cover the eventuality that an individual participating Member State is called on to pay up under its joint and several liability, its risk would have to be limited by agreeing a burden-sharing scheme amongst the participating Member States.

In September 2013, the European Commission established an expert group chaired by the former member of the ECB Executive Board Gertrude Tumpel-Gugerell whose mission was to analyse possible merits, risks, requirements and obstacles of partial substitution of national issuance of debt through joint issuance in the form of a redemption fund and eurobills (hereinafter: "Expert Group"). The

[45] See Gesetz über die Errichtung eines Erblastentilgungsfonds (1993), Bundesgesetzblatt 1993, vol I, pp. 944, 984.

[46] German Council of Economic Experts 2011, p. 107.

[47] Schorkopf 2012, p. 9.

report of the Expert Group dealt with legal issues relating to the establishment of an ERF and came to the conclusion that it could not to be introduced under the existing Treaties.[48] This conclusion was based on two arguments. First, the ERF would violate Article 125 TFEU, even read in the light of the ECJ's decision in the "Pringle" case.[49] Second, Article 352(1) TFEU would not suffice as a legal base within the existing Treaties. A Treaty change is required.[50] Both arguments will be critically assessed in the following.

8.3.1.1 Violation of Article 125 TFEU

According to Article 125(1) TFEU, neither the Union nor a Member State is "liable for [...] the commitments" of another Member State or "assume[s] [those] commitments." The wording of Article 125(1) TFEU suggests that any legal construction which leads to an automatic payment of the full amount of financial commitments of one Member State by the other Member States or the Union, such as a guarantee structure based on joint and several liability, violates per se Article 125(1) TFEU.

Yet, in its *Pringle* judgement, the ECJ specified the content of this provision. According to the Court, Article 125 TFEU is not intended to prohibit either the Union or the Member States from granting *any* form of financial assistance whatsoever to another Member State. The Court relies on the purpose of Article 125 TFEU, which is to ensure that Member States remain subject to the logic of the market when they enter into debt. Markets prompt them to maintain budgetary discipline. Compliance with such discipline contributes at Union level to the attainment of a higher objective, namely maintaining the financial stability of the monetary union. The Court therefore concludes that "Article 125 TFEU [...] prohibits the Union and the Member States from granting financial assistance as a result of which the incentive of the recipient Member State to conduct a sound budgetary policy is diminished. However, Article 125 TFEU does not prohibit the granting of financial assistance by one or more Member States to a Member State, which remains responsible for its commitments to its creditors provided that the conditions attached to such assistance are such as to prompt that Member State to implement a sound budgetary policy."[51] This leads to the assumption that financial assistance, which meets the two following criteria, does not violate Article 125(1) TFEU. Financial assistance must be indispensable for the safeguarding of the financial stability of the euro area as a whole and must be subject to strict conditions.

When applying these two conditions to the establishment of a redemption fund, one comes to the conclusion that it would not violate Article 125(1) TFEU.

---

[48] Expert Group 2014, pp. 57–66.

[49] *Ibid.*, p. 58 et seq.

[50] *Ibid.*, p. 64 at para 250.

[51] *Pringle*, above n 44, para 136 et seq.

The financial and economic crisis revealed that overindebted government budgets lead to significant crises of the financial stability within the monetary union. Reducing debt to the level that can be tolerated under the Maastricht criteria is therefore indispensable for the safeguarding of the financial stability of the euro area. Furthermore, participation in the redemption fund is, as shown above, subject to strict conditionality.

This strict application of the two conditions ignores, however, the purpose of Article 125(1) TFEU. If one reduces the legality test of financial assistance programmes under Article 125(1) TFEU to the fulfilment of these two criteria, any financial assistance programme could pass it. The purpose of Article 125(1) TFEU, which is that Member States remain subject to the logic of the market that coordinates their economic, fiscal and budgetary policies, would be completely ignored.[52] Therefore, the ECJ also required in the *Pringle* judgement that the Member State, which receives financial assistance, "will remain responsible to its creditors for its financial commitments".[53] It appears now that the legality test for a redemption fund fails to meet this understanding of the purpose of Article 125(1) TFEU. Government debt of more than 60% of the GDP of the participating Member State is taken over by the ERF. The ERF is backed by a joint and several guarantee of the participating Member States. Member States will rather be pulled out of the market than remain subject to market logic. This was the main argument, on which the Expert Group based its assumption that Article 125(1) TFEU would be violated by the establishment of an ERF.

Against this understanding, one may now refer to the concrete assessment of the ECJ in the *Pringle* case of the several instruments of the ESM. Under Articles 17 and 18 of the ESM-Treaty, the ESM may purchase bonds issued by an ESM Member State on the primary market. The ECJ compared such purchases to the granting of a loan under Articles 15 and 16 of the ESM-Treaty.[54] According to the ECJ, granting a loan does not imply "that the ESM will assume the debts of the recipient Member State. On the contrary, such assistance amounts to the creation of a new debt, owed to the ESM by that recipient Member State, which remains responsible for its commitments to its creditors in respect of its existing debts."[55] The Court emphasised that "any financial assistance granted on the basis of Articles 14 to 16 thereof must be repaid to the ESM by the recipient Member State."[56] In light of these considerations, the purchase of government bonds covering the government debt above 60% of GDP by the ERF would not violate Article 125(1) TFEU. The Member State in question remains responsible for its commitments. These commitments are now not anymore vis-à-vis a private financial market operator but vis-à-vis the ERF.

52 Expert Group 2014, p. 60.

53 *Pringle*, above n 44, para 138.

54 *Ibid.*, para 140.

55 *Ibid.*, para 139.

56 *Ibid.*, para 139.

This leads to the final question whether the joint and several liability of the participating Member States for the ERF is to be considered a violation of Article 125(1) TFEU. The wording of Article 125(1) TFEU refers to "the commitments of central governments, regional, local or other public authorities, other bodies governed by public law, or public undertakings of any Member State" when defining which commitments are covered by it. The wording does not refer to commitments of the EU or other international entities. Commitments of a European redemption fund therefore seem not to be covered by Article 125(1) TFEU and, thus, a joint and several liability of Member States participating in the ERF is not violating Article 125(1) TFEU.[57] Yet, one may argue, as the Expert Group did, that such an understanding of Article 125(1) TFEU would undermine its effectiveness as Member States could escape their obligations under this article by simply establishing an international fund.[58] Even if Article 125(1) TFEU could be applied to commitments of the ERF, a joint and several liability would not conflict with it.

In the *Pringle* case, the ECJ examined the legality of Article 25(2) ESM-Treaty, which dealt with a situation in which an ESM member fails to meet the required payment under a capital call under the ESM-Treaty. In such a situation, under Article 25(2) ESM-Treaty, "a revised increased capital call shall be made to all ESM Members with a view to ensuring that the ESM receives the total amount of paid-in capital needed." This situation can be understood as some sort of joint and several liability of the other ESM members in case of the inability to pay by one of the ESM members. The ECJ upheld this provision by referring to the fact that "under that same provision, the defaulting ESM Member State remains bound to pay its part of the capital. Accordingly, the other ESM Members do not act as guarantors of the debt of the defaulting ESM Member."[59] This means that as long as every Member State participating in the ERF remains bound to its consolidation path—even in the event of a default—a temporary additional financial assistance of the other participating Member States to the ERF would be in line with Article 125(1) TFEU. This shows that, according to the ECJ, a legally binding internal burden sharing between the participating Member States is sufficient in order to consider a liability of participating Member States, which goes beyond its predefined share, to be a financial commitment, which is not in violation of Article 125(1) TFEU.

8.3.1.2 Legal Basis

The second line of arguments against a legally possible establishment of an ERF under the existing Treaties relates to the legal basis.[60] A possible legal basis is

[57] Nettesheim 2013, p. 607.

[58] Expert Group 2014, p. 59.

[59] *Pringle*, above n 44, para 145.

[60] Expert Group 2014, p. 63.

Article 352(1) TFEU. According to this article, the Council, acting unanimously on a proposal from the Commission and after obtaining the consent of the European Parliament, may adopt measures if Union action should prove necessary to attain one of the objectives set out in the Treaties provided that there are no specific competences in the Treaties. The objective can be found in Article 3(4) TEU, referring to the establishment of an economic and monetary union whose currency is the euro, which includes the safeguarding of the financial stability of the euro area as a necessary condition for the functioning of the EMU. This objective is met with regard to the ERF since it guarantees a reduction of government debt down to the Maastricht criterion of 60% of GDP and stabilises, by this means, Member States' national budgets. Based on these arguments, the ESM could have been established on the basis of Article 352(1) TFEU, which was not excluded by the ECJ in the *Pringle* case.[61]

Yet, a legal act based on Article 352(1) TFEU may not modify Primary law. Otherwise, it would undermine the Treaty change procedure foreseen by Article 48 TEU. Based on these observations, one may argue against the use of Article 352(1) TFEU for the establishment of an ERF. The use of this provision would undermine Member States' budgetary sovereignty, as protected by Article 311 TFEU.[62] One may, indeed, establish a principle, according to which Union legal acts may not request any payments from Member States' budgets outside their contributions to the Union budget. Whilst this is not completely true, since Article 311(2) allows for "other revenue" including payments from Member States' budgets without being an own resource, payments to the ERF could be established at least as a new "own resource" of the Union, in accordance with Article 311(3) TFEU. It is therefore true to argue that a legal act based on Article 352(1) TFEU may not circumvent Article 311(3) TFEU and its reference to an approval of the introduction of a new category of own resources by the Member States in accordance with their respective constitutional requirements.[63] However, this argument is not against the establishment of an ERF within the existing Treaties, but in favour of it.

8.3.1.3 Conclusion

The ERF, as proposed by the German Council of Economic Experts, could legally be established within the existing Treaties on the basis of Article 352(1) TFEU,

[61] *Pringle* above n 44, para 67. It should be noted that the ECJ examined the legality of the ESM before the entry into force of Decision 2011/199, which introduced Article 136(3) in the TFEU. Since this did not harm the legality of the ESM (para 185), neither an international Treaty such as the ESM-Treaty nor a Union act based on Article 352(1) TFEU would have been in violation of the Treaties. The reasoning of the ECJ with regard to the ESM-Treaty would have to be applied in the same manner to a Union legal act.

[62] Expert Group 2014, p. 63.

[63] *Ibid.*

supplemented by a new category of own resources covering the payments of the participating Member States to the ERF on the basis of Article 311(3) TFEU. A redemption fund is not violating Article 125(1) TFEU if the Member States remain responsible for their commitments to their creditors. The ERF would purchase during the "roll in" phase bonds issued by the participating Member States. This purchase is similar to the purchase of bonds under Article 17 of the ESM-Treaty. The purchase creates a new debt, owed to the redemption fund by the recipient Member State. Participation in the ERF is subject to strict conditionality whose purpose is to prompt the implementation of a sound budgetary policy of participating Member States. Finally, there has to be a legally binding burden sharing between the participating Member States, which is not conditional upon the ability of the Member States to pay.

8.3.2 *Future Refinancing of Eurozone Member States*

After having discussed the issue of existing government debt, the question arises how to control the level of future debt issued by the Member States. An effective reduction of past debt is rendered widely meaningless if Member States can afterwards pile up again new debts, which lays the ground for future debt crises. In the reformed economic governance framework, the TSCG requires that issuing excessive new debt is to be controlled by automatic correction mechanisms and a debt brake in national law.

An interim evaluation of this instrument does, however, not turn out positively. Although all Contracting Parties of the TSCG that were obliged to implement both the balanced budget rule and automatic correction mechanisms[64] had included these rules into their national law, only three of the Contracting Parties are forecast to meet the criterion of a lower limit of the structural deficit of 0.5% of GDP in 2015.[65] The comparison of the forecast structural balance two years after the entry into force of the TSCG with the state of its implementation demonstrates that the mere adoption of national rules does not result into the desired outcome to reduce the government deficit. The German Council of Economic Experts already observed in its annual report 2012/2013 that in the past (prior to the TSCG) "the introduction of such fiscal rules was accompanied by a political willingness to consolidate government budgets, whereas their introduction by way of the Fiscal

[64] TSCG, above n 34, Article 14(5); according to Article 14(5), these obligations only enter into force for Contracting Parties that are not part of the Euro area "as from the day when the decision abrogating that derogation or exemption takes effect, unless the Contracting Party concerned declares its intention to be bound at an earlier date by all or part of the provisions in Titles III and IV of this Treaty." Such declaration was made by Denmark and Romania. On the implementation, see Burret and Schnellenbach 2013; Bova et al. 2015.

[65] These are Germany, Greece and Luxemburg, cf. Commission, European Economic Forecast, Autumn 2014.

Compact was largely driven by political pressure, since the euro-area states cannot apply for ESM support unless they ratify the Fiscal Compact. It remains to be seen whether the introduction of national fiscal rules under such circumstances will have a similarly positive impact on budget consolidation."[66] In short, the lack of political willingness to consolidate public spending cannot be replaced by simply adopting a national debt brake rule. Furthermore, if, for economic reasons, a Member State is not capable of complying with EU rules, this incapacity will not be overcome by merely implementing the TSCG rules into national law. Therefore, one has to conclude that neither the automatic correction mechanism nor the debt brake rule in the TSCG provides for sufficient legal certainty to prevent another piling up of debt of Member States in the future.

This leads to the discussion whether the common issuance of debt by the EU or at least by the Euro Area Member States could be an effective instrument to control the future level of government debt.[67] Consequence of a common issuance of debt would namely be that participating Member States would not be entitled anymore to issue debt themselves.[68] Debt issuance is, however, only an instrument to refinance public expenditure. It does not define expenditure. Member States are, under the current asymmetric legal framework, still free in pursuing a certain economic policy, which entails certain expenditure. If national expenditure goes beyond what commonly issued debt is willing or able to refinance, the Union will face similar challenges regarding the control of a non-compliant Member State as under the existing reformed economic governance framework. This last thought reveals the 'moral hazard' issue inherent to the common issuance of debt. This 'moral hazard' does not only challenge the political persuasiveness of an introduction of 'Eurobonds' but also points at the main legal impediment for their introduction. As mentioned above, the so-called 'no bail-out' clause in Article 125(1) TFEU requires that the conditions attached to any financial assistance from the Union or the Member States have to be such as to prompt the recipient Member State to implement a sound budgetary policy. In other words, common issuance of debt requires the neutralisation of the 'moral hazard' attached to it. Since this 'moral hazard' derives from Member States' autonomy to define their economic and fiscal policies within a largely still intergovernmental Economic Union, it can only be overcome by 'symmetrising' EMU. The latter as well as the alternative deletion of the 'no bail-out' clause in Article 125(1) TFEU require a Treaty change. By that, very briefly,[69] fully fledged 'Eurobonds' can only be introduced after such a Treaty change.

---

[66] German Council of Economic Experts 2012, para 180.

[67] De Haan et al. 2012, p. 323.

[68] For the sake of completeness, it has to be noted that not all the models proposed under the name of "Eurobonds" provide for a total replacement of national government bonds, cf. Claessens et al. 2012.

[69] In detail on legal options for introducing Eurobonds: Mayer and Heidfeld 2012, p. 422.

8.4 Conclusion

An effective debt control is crucial for an asymmetric Economic and Monetary Union, where Member States are free in conducting their economic and fiscal policies, but bound to the monetary policy decisions taken at European level. Market-induced enforcement of European economic policy coordination failed. Since symmetrising EMU cannot be achieved without Treaty change, existing government debt should be transferred into a redemption fund in order to put Member States into a budgetary situation, in which the reformed economic governance framework could have a chance to work effectively. This can be realised without Treaty change. A sustainable solution aims, however, not at controlling debt, but at controlling the national expenditure in a democratically legitimate manner.

References

Bova E, Kinda T, Muthoora P, Toscani F (2015) Fiscal rules at glance. Update of IMF Working Paper 12/273, April 2015

Burret HT, Schnellenbach J (2013) Implementation of the Fiscal Compact in the Euro Area Member States. German Council of Economic Experts, Working Paper 08/2013 (partly updated 2014), Wiesbaden

Claessens S, Mody A, Vallée S (2012) Paths to Eurobonds. IMF Working Paper 12/172

De Grauwe P (2016) Economics of Monetary Union. Oxford University Press, Oxford

De Haan J, Gilbert N, Hessel J, Verkaartet S (2012) Beyond the Fiscal Compact: How Well-Designed Eurobonds May Discipline Governments. Zeitschrift für Staats- und Europawissenschaften 3:323–337

Expert Group on Debt Redemption Fund and Eurobills (2014) Final Report, Brussels

German Council of Economic Experts (2011) Assume responsibility for Europe. Annual Report 2011/12, Wiesbaden

German Council of Economic Experts (2012) Stable architecture for Europe—need for action in Germany. Annual Report 2012/2013, Wiesbaden

Mayer FC, Heidfeld C (2012) Verfassungs- und europarechtliche Aspekte der Einführung von Eurobonds. Neue Juristische Wochenschrift 7:421–427

Nettesheim M (2013) Der Schuldentilgungsfonds: Rechtliche Rahmenbedingungen eines umstrittenen Instruments zur Eurorettung. In: Breuer M et al (eds) Der Staat im Recht. Festschrift für Eckart Klein. Duncker & Humblot, Berlin, pp 603–618

OECD (2016) OECD Economic Outlook: Statistics and Projections. https://data.oecd.org/gdp/nominal-gdp-forecast.htm. Accessed on 23 May 2016

Ohler C (2010) Die zweite Reform des Stabilitäts- und Wachstumspaktes. Zeitschrift für Gesetzgebung 4:330–345

Repasi R (2013) Völkerrechtliche Freiräume für EU-Mitgliedstaaten. Europarecht 1:45–74

Repasi R (2016) Implementation of the Lisbon Treaty—improving functioning of the EU: Economic and Monetary Policy. Study for the European Parliament, Brussels 2016

Ruffert M (2011) The European debt crisis and European Union law. CMLR 48:1777–1805

Schorkopf F (2012) Verfassungsrechtliche Grenzen und Möglichkeiten für eine Umsetzung des Schuldentilgungspaktes des Sachverständigenrates. Expertise commissioned by the German Council of Economic Experts, Wiesbaden

Chapter 9
Time to Shift Towards Shared-Burden Responsibility: A Review of the Syrian Mass Influx Migration

Zahra Mousavi

Abstract The Dublin III Regulation sets the mechanisms and standards that a Member State must adopt, when it comes to reviewing a submitted application for international protection by a third-country national or a stateless person. It requires that an asylum seeker register in the first country in which he enters and remains for the final decision. In the absence of any request for the application of the Mass Influx Directive, this Regulation was applied differently in the Syrian crisis by the States concerned. The end result, however, was that the Syrian migrants in most Member States were considered as refugees, and if they failed to satisfy the set criteria, they were regarded as illegal migrants. The same disparity existed in the Member States' reactions to some other issues, such as return. None of the measures that Member States and the European Union (EU) have adopted so far seems to offer a proper response to the present massive migration influx. It may be suggested that in the face of a major crisis, the EU has failed to rise up to the challenge, except with regard to some financial aids. This Chapter seeks to review some of these measures and to suggest: (i) that the issues currently faced by Member States are fundamentally different from those for which the earlier measures were adopted; and (ii) that because of that difference, the Dublin system may not be a very appropriate instrument for dealing with this situation as well as other similar circumstances, such as the African and Asian mass influxes. The Commission needs to revert to the issue of mass influx, and to find a reliable solution enhancing shared responsibility and solidarity.

Keywords Mass influx migration · Protection of displaced people · Mass Influx Directive · Reform of the Common European Asylum System · The EU-Turkey Agreement · Shared responsibility · Syria

Z. Mousavi (✉)
The Hague University of Applied Sciences, The Hague, The Netherlands
e-mail: Z.Mousavi@hhs.nl

J. de Zwaan et al. (eds.), *Governance and Security Issues of the European Union*, DOI 10.1007/978-94-6265-144-9_9

Contents

9.1 Introduction

The massive migration influx from Syria, which is the result mainly of prolonged armed conflict in that country, constitutes an extraordinary and unprecedented situation. What makes a noticeable difference between the Syrian refugees and other refugees in recent years is the fact that the formers are not individual males seeking better choices in life, but families normally composed of men, women, children, and infants. Perhaps more importantly, they do not represent isolated cases of insignificant numbers, but vast numbers of persons similarly affected by tragedies of war and religious hatred. The Dublin III Regulation (sometimes to be referred to as "The Dublin III") has proved not to be an effective solution to the present massive influx of migrants from Syria.

This Chapter seeks to review some of the measures adopted collectively by the EU or individually by the Member States in reaction to this unprecedented migration influx from Syria, and to suggest on that basis: (i) *that* the issues and problems currently faced by the Member States are fundamentally different from those for which the earlier measures were adopted; and (ii) *that* because of that difference, the Dublin Regulation may not be an appropriate instrument for dealing with the present influx, or indeed with any other similar situation in the future, such as a probable migration influx from African countries. The Chapter will further address the problems that are likely to arise if derogatory measures from the Dublin III system or discriminatory choices are adopted by the Member States. The Chapter concludes by offering some recommendations for the European Commission as alternative solutions to the application of the Dublin III Regulation, and invites the EU to reconsider the existing potential competences under the Treaty of Lisbon[1] and the Treaty on the Functioning of the European Union (TFEU)[2] for common immigration and asylum policies.

As for the work plan, the present introduction will be followed by a short account in Sect. 9.2 of the Syrian mass influx, with reference to the Kosovo forced migration as the first mass influx after the Second World War. In Sect. 9.3, the Mass Influx Directive and its relevance to the current situation will be reviewed. The pertinent question in relation to this Directive—which is commonly regarded as the creative perception of the EU Commission after the Kosovan mass influx—is whether or not the Directive was applied in the Libyan crisis of 2011 and in the Tunisia forced migration of the same year. Section 9.4 will look into the Dublin III Regulation with a short historical review of the Dublin system. The Section will further address the individual measures of the Member States, and the EU-Turkey Joint Action Plan and Agreement. The EU co-operation with a third country, here Turkey, will be followed by a summary on how full protection of the mass influx migrants will be undermined by this agreement. Section 9.4 will continue to discuss vertical and horizontal policies of the EU, as well as the recent Communication from the Commission to the European Parliament and the Council. The final Section of the Chapter will offer some suggestions for tackling the current and future mass influxes in a more sustainable and appropriate way. It will be submitted that the EU can achieve these goals by establishing a workable method of shared-burden responsibility, and by re-conceptualising the mass influx migrants.

9.2 The Syrian Mass Influx

It may be said with some justification that migration influx is not a new phenomenon for the European Union, as demonstrated by the Kosovar Albanian case. A profound difference between the present Syrian influx and the purportedly similar ones in the past may be readily observed, fore and foremost, by the sheer numbers involved in each of the two cases. In Kosovo, as noted in Security Council Resolution dated 23 September 1998,[3] over 230,000 people had been displaced from their homes due to "the excessive and indiscriminate use of force by Serbian security forces and the Yugoslavia Army." According to estimations, over 800,000

[1] Treaty of Lisbon amending the Treaty on European Union and the Treaty establishing the European Community, opened for signature on 13 December 2007 OJ C 306 (entered into force on 1 December 2009).

[2] Consolidated Version of the Treaty on the Functioning of the European Union, opened for signature [2007] OJ C 326 (entered into force on 1 December 2009) as amended on October 10, 2012 (Hereafter TFEU).

[3] UN Security Council, Resolution 1199 (1998) The Situation in Kosovo, adopted by the Security Council at its 3930th meeting on 23 September 1998, S/RES/1199 (1998).

Kosovar Albanians were forcibly displaced.[4] By contrast, in the Syrian case, the figure often suggested for the displaced refugees is about 4,185,302.[5] What can be safely said, at any rate, is that no such figure was in the thoughts of those who drafted or later signed and ratified the Dublin Regulation. Before turning to the issue of whether or not the Dublin III Regulation can adequately deal with situations like this, a few words must be said about the reaction of the European Commission in 2001, when it realised after the Kosovo refugee crisis that the cases of mass influx required special attention.

9.3 The Mass Influx Directive[6]

In a situation like the one now existing in Syria, one would immediately think of the application of the Council Directive 2001/55/EC on "minimum standard for giving protection in the event of a mass influx of displaced persons," expecting that the Member States would receive the displaced Syrians without prejudging any individual's entitlement refugee status under the Refugee Convention.[7] In other words, the gravity of the situation would create the expectation that those affected would be granted, by the Member States, at least certain temporary measures of protection and treatment other than the Dublin Regulation or the Qualification Directives.[8] Under both the Refugee Convention and the Dublin system, a person is either subject to refugee status[9] or to protection and non-refoulement.

The purpose of the Mass Influx Directive is to establish, "minimum standards for giving temporary protection in the event of a mass influx of displaced persons

[4] Mitra 2001, p. 3; see also ICTY, *Prosecutor v. Vlastimir Đorđević*, Judgement, 23 February 2011, Case No. IT-05-87/1-T, para 1.

[5] The figure includes refugees, asylum-seekers, disaster displaced, internally displaced persons (IDPs), returnees (refugees and IDPs), stateless persons, and others of concern to the UNHCR by origins. See UN High Commissioner for Refugees 2015. Between April 2011 and January 2016, a total number of 935,008 asylum applications have been submitted in European countries, for further information see UN High Commissioner for Refugees 2016.

[6] Council Directive 2001/55/EC of 20 July 2001 on Minimum Standards for Giving Temporary Protection in the Event of Mass Influx of Displaced Persons and on Measures Promoting a Balance of Efforts Between Member States in Receiving Such Persons and Bearing the Consequences Thereof, 7 August 2001, [hereinafter the "Mass Influx Directive"] OJ L.212/12–212/23.

[7] Ball 2014, pp. 116–117; Convention Relating to the Status of Refugees, opened for signature (1951), UNTS 189:137, entry into force on 22 April 1954.

[8] Directive 2011/95/EU of the European Parliament and of the Council of 13 December 2011 on Standards for the Qualification of Third-Country Nationals or Stateless Persons as Beneficiaries of International Protection, for a Uniform Status for Refugees or for Persons Eligible for Subsidiary Protection, and for the Content of the Protection Granted (recast), 20 December 2011, OJ L. 337/9–337/26.

[9] Refugee Convention, above n 7, Article 1(A).

from third countries who are unable to return to their country of origin and to promote a balance of effort between [the] Member States in receiving and bearing the consequences of receiving such persons."[10] The key elements and requirements of this provision are clear enough. In particular, the term "mass influx" is authoritatively defined, in the context of the Directive, as "arrival in the Community of a large number of displaced persons, who come from a specific country or geographical area, whether their arrival in the Community was spontaneous or aided, for example through an evacuation programme."[11]

It should be noted that the Directive refers to the people who are entitled to protection as "displaced persons from third countries." This is meant to establish a distinction between such people, and the refugees as defined in Article 1(A(2)) of the Refugee Convention.[12] Now, despite the existence and clarity of this provision, the Mass Influx Directive has never been applied in practice. It must be examined, therefore, whether this is due to the fact that in reality no mass influx has occurred or, in the event where there has been any such occurrence, why the Directive has not been implemented. The reason for the non-implementation of the Directive will be examined, by reviewing the recent Libyan and Tunisian crises in 2012.

9.3.1 The Libyan and Tunisian Inordinate Influxes

Before the Syrian crisis, there were three cases that could, with some reservations, be considered as mass influxes: the Kosovo crisis of 1997–1998, the Libyan crisis of 2011, and the Tunisian displacement of 2011—the last two of which being the outcomes of the Arab Spring.[13] It was, in fact, the Kosovo case that lead to the rat-

[10] Mass Influx Directive, above n 6, Article 1.

[11] Mass Influx Directive, above n 6, Article 2(d). The Refugee Convention was amended by the New York Protocol of 31 January 1967, as a result of which geographical and temporal restrictions were removed from the Convention. Protocol Relating to the Status of Refugees opened for signature (1967), UNTS 606:267, entry into force on 4 October 1967. See also the UNHCR comment on the Directive, it provides: "What constitutes a 'mass or large-scale influx' cannot be defined in absolute terms, but must be defined in relation to the resources of the receiving country. The expression should be understood as referring to a significant number of arrivals in a country, over a short period of time, of persons from the same home country who have been displaced under circumstances indicating that members of the group would qualify for international protection, and for whom, due to their numbers, individual refugee status determination is procedurally impractical." UN High Commissioner for Refugees 2003, pp. 5–6.

[12] Refugee Convention, Article 1(A(2)) provides: "… owing to well-founded fear of being persecuted for reasons of race, religion, nationality, membership of a particular social group or political opinion, is outside the country of his nationality and is unable or, owing to such fear, is unwilling to avail himself of the protection of that country; or who, not having a nationality and being outside the country of his former habitual residence as a result of such events, is unable or, owing to such fear, is unwilling to return to it.".

[13] For further information, see Marchetti 2012; and Nita 2013.

ification of the Directive at regional level, and to legislation at national level. It may therefore be justifiably asked why the Directive was not resorted to in other similar cases.

The number of migrants, who, at the end of 2011, originated from Libya and landed in Lampedusa was reported to be around 25,935 persons. The overall number of migrants who reached Italy from Tunisia and Libya was said to be about 62,000 people,[14] while the total number of displaced people fleeing Libya was estimated at 796,916 during the Libyan crisis.[15] In the case of the Tunisian displacement, a distinction must be made between the migration taking place due to the civil war, and the Libyan displacement made through Tunisia. In comparison to the second case, the figure for the first situation was more modest. Finally, the number of displaced Tunisians, who, by the end of December 2011, reached Italy was put at 28,000.[16] With these figures in mind, we can proceed to briefly review the regional and national reactions towards these inordinate influxes.

Before taking any other steps, Italy and Malta called for the application of the Mass Influx Directive. The then Foreign Minister of Italy, Franco Frattini, found it necessary to "invoke a European law clearly establishing the adoption of an extraordinary plan with any sudden influx of refugees towards one or more Member States, which includes the distribution of the refugees among [the] Members within the temporary timeframe necessary to repatriate those who are not refugees, as in the case of the Tunisians, who are simply economic immigrants."[17] Simon Busuttil, Maltese Member of the European Parliament, also stated that, "EU law already provides for a solidarity mechanism that can be triggered in the event of a mass influx of displaced persons. We call upon the Commission to activate it."[18] The Member States and the European Commission, however, argued that the situation did not in reality amount to a mass influx, and could not meet the conditions set for the application of the mass influx.

The similarity of numbers aside, these cases were different from the Kosovo civil war and its consequences. Tunisian migrants were basically "economic migrants," in contrast to migrants from Libya who could potentially be considered as refugees. People who left Libya included third country nationals, the Libyan nationals, asylum seekers who were transited to Libya, individuals who could not meet refugee or protection criteria, as well as people with specific needs including unaccompanied children, women at risk, and victims of trafficking. In other words, Tunisians who needed provisional protection could be sent back home after the crisis, while the Libyan migrants had a different status.[19]

---

[14] See IOM 2011, p. 22.

[15] *Ibid.*, p. 2.

[16] Heller et al. 2011, p. 14.

[17] Farnesina 2011.

[18] Times of Malta.com 2011.

[19] Nita 2013, p. 2.

A vast number of migrants left Libya for the neighbouring countries or for their country of origin. This was an important factor explaining why such a massive number of persons—who did not necessarily appear on the EU borders—were not considered as being part of a mass influx. It must be further remembered that international aid and attention accorded to these cases were quite relevant. The North Atlantic Treaty Organisation (NATO), the United Nations High Commissioner for Refugees (UNHCR) and other Non-International Organisations (NGOs) launched humanitarian evacuation programs. This meant that the EU only helped the involved Member States through financial means, provision of accommodations and resettlement necessities. Considering the apparent reluctance displayed by the Commission and by the Member States for burden-sharing and collective responsibility, this can be at least seen in line with the stated aim of the Directive, that is to say, the "balance of efforts."[20] Italy had to act individually. As for the Tunisian crisis, Italy granted protection to eligible people. On 5 April 2012, Prime Minister Berlusconi stated that "citizens from the countries of North African, who entered into the country from 1 January 2011 to midnight on 5 April 2011" were eligible "for the issuance of a six months-residence permits for humanitarian reasons."[21] The mentioned consolidated text permits the non-EU nationals to apply for the temporary protection measures in case of conflicts, natural disasters, etc., in a non-EU Member State. It is noteworthy that in the Kosovo crisis, a similar decree was issued by Italy. Tunisian nationals, whose applications were approved, would receive a residence permit for humanitarian reasons valid for six months. The residence permit entitled the holder to move within the EU. The same day, Italy signed a bilateral agreement with Tunis for coastal border control as well as for acceptance of return/repatriation measures for undocumented Tunisians arriving after the 5th of April 2011. As for the Libyan case, however, the migrants were treated differently. Their asylum applications were reviewed and the eligible applicants received reception.[22]

Looking at those approaches in general and disregarding their less significant characteristics, the conclusion that may be drawn is that the EU was indeed in a position to apply the Mass Influx Directive. As it happened, however, not only the Commission and other Member States adopted a different approach, but Italy itself opted for a different treatment. In other words, the displacement of such a massive number of migrants running from the Libyan civil war was not considered as a mass influx. Before looking into the Directive in relation to the Syrian crisis, it may be appropriate to have a few words about the Dublin system. This will help to find out why the Dublin system may not be well-suited to a mass influx situation, and hence it should not be applied in the Syrian crisis or in any future mass influx crisis.

[20] *Ibid.*, p. 4; and Hatton 2011.

[21] EMN 2011, p. 48.

[22] Marchetti 2012, pp. 2–4, and pp. 13–14.

9.4 The Dublin III Regulation[23]

The Dublin III Regulation aims at setting standards and mechanisms to be applied by a Member State in reviewing a submitted application for international protection by a third-country national, or by a stateless person. The Dublin II Regulation,[24] established by the Dublin Convention, was signed on 15 June 1990 by 12 Member States,[25] and entered into force on the 1st of September of 1997.[26] It replaced the Dublin Convention in all Member States, except in Denmark, who opted-out of implementing the Regulation until 2006.[27] The Dublin III Regulation,

---

[23] Council of the European Union, Regulation (EU) No. 604/2013 of the European Parliament and of the Council of 26 June 2013 Establishing the Criteria and Mechanisms for Determining the Member State Responsible for Examining an Application for International Protection Lodged in One of the Member States by a Third-Country National or a Stateless Person (Recast), 29 June 2013, OJ L. 180/31–180/59.

[24] Council of the European Union, Council Regulation (EC) No. 343/2003 of 18 February 2003 Establishing the Criteria and Mechanisms for Determining the Member State Responsible for Examining an Asylum Application Lodged in One of the Member States by a Third-Country National, 18 February 2003, OJ L. 50/1–50/10.

[25] Belgium, Denmark, France, Germany, Greece, Ireland, Italy, Luxembourg, the Netherlands, Portugal, Spain, and the United Kingdom.

[26] Convention Determining the State Responsible for Examining Applications for Asylum Lodged in One of the Member States of the European Communities, opened for signature (1990), OJ C 254, entered into force on 01/09/2990 the Convention. It became enforceable for Austria and Sweden as 1 October 1997, and for Finland as 1 January 1998. Norway and Iceland concluded agreement on 19 January 2001 with the EC and applied the Convention in their territories. See Agreement between the European Community and the Republic of Iceland and the Kingdom of Norway Concerning the Criteria and Mechanisms for Establishing the State Responsible for Examining a Request for Asylum Lodged in a Member State or in Iceland or Norway, entry into force: 1 April 2001, L93/40.

[27] Denmark requested to join the 2001 Agreement between the EU, Iceland and Norway. See Protocol to the Agreement between the European Community and the Republic of Iceland and the Kingdom of Norway Concerning the Criteria and Mechanisms for Establishing the State Responsible for Examining a Request for Asylum Lodged in a Member State or in Iceland or Norway, 29 June 2005, L 57/16, entry into force: 1 May 2006.

Denmark and Switzerland joined the Dublin II Regulation under a separate agreement. See Agreement between the European Community and the Kingdom of Denmark on the Criteria and Mechanisms for Establishing the State Responsible for Examining a Request for Asylum Lodged in Denmark or any other Member State of the European Union and Eurodac for the Comparison of Fingerprints for the Effective Application of the Dublin Convention, 10 March 2005, entry into force: 1 April 2006, OJ L66/38; and Agreement between the European Community and the Swiss Confederation concerning the Criteria and Mechanisms for Establishing the State Responsible for Examining a Request for Asylum Lodged in a Member State or in Switzerland, 26 October 2004, entry into force: 1 March 2008, OJ L53/5.

Switzerland concluded a Protocol with the EU and the Regulation became enforceable on 1 March 2008 for Lichtenstein. See Protocol between the European Community, the Swiss Confederation and the Principality of Liechtenstein to the Agreement between the European Community and the Swiss Confederation Concerning the Criteria and Mechanisms for Establishing the State Responsible for Examining a Request for Asylum in a Member State or in Switzerland, 28 February 2008, OJ L.83.

which was established on 26 Jun 2013 and came into force on 19 July 2013, modifies the Dublin system and applies to the Member States, to the exception of Denmark.

By allocating responsibility for asylum-seeking process to a Member State as well as setting criteria for the hierarchy of responsibility of the Member State, the Dublin system is designed to prevent asylum shopping. This, of course, is the result of establishing a mechanism under Article 73k(a) of the Amsterdam Treaty, through which the "criteria and mechanisms for determining which Member State is responsible for considering an application for asylum in one of the Member States" would be adopted by the Council in accordance with the Refugee Convention and the Protocol of 31 January 1967 relating to the status of refugees and other relevant treaties.[28] In order to achieve that aim, the Dublin III Regulation requires that the asylum seekers register in the first country in which they enter and remain for the final decision—a requirement to be observed by all Member States. Indeed, the finger printing, an integral part of the registration mechanism, is a clear device for the prevention of asylum shopping.[29]

By contrast, in cases of mass influx, migrants are expected to reside in the host country only until the end of the conflict and, for that reason, they should not be constrained by the conditions set for the refugees, nor should they be expected to integrate into the system—they just need some protection. For these special circumstances, migrants should be given the opportunity to join their families and friends who have already moved to any of the Member States. This would not only be helpful to the migrants, but also to the Member States, who would in that case carry less responsibility for providing services to the migrants.

9.4.1 Reactions of the Member States to the Syrian Mass Influx

Since nearly six years, the Syrians became involved in a savage civil war and suffered its tragic consequences. As a result of the announcement by Bashar al-Assad according to which he was unable to protect his people, the number of migrants fleeing from Syria reached its peak last year. In response to the current asylum influx—the roots of which will be dealt with briefly—Germany decided on 24 August 2015 to suspend the Dublin III Regulation for the Syrian refugees, and to process the applications directly. The Czech Republic also breached the Dublin III

[28] Treaty of Amsterdam Amending the Treaty on European Union, the Treaties Establishing the European Communities and Certain Related Acts, opened for signature (1997), OJ C 340/1, entered into force on 1 May 1999; see also Kaunert and Leonard 2012, p. 1401.

[29] The *Dublin system* includes rules on jurisdiction for examination and processing of asylum seekers. The *Dublin II Regulation* introduces a conflict prevention mechanism, See Articles 9–10. Moreover, Article 15 of the Dublin II Regulation exceptionally permits a Member State to request permission for examination of refugee status under circumstances.

Regulation with its Decision dated 2 September 2015, allowing the Syrian refugees: (i) to apply there even though they may have already applied in another Member States; or (ii) to leave the country for asylum seeking in another Member State. The EU was about to introduce a quota system that was already denied by Hungary, Poland and Slovakia.

All these divergences seem to be justified by the European Agenda on Migration,[30] which was introduced and adopted on 13 May 2015. The Agenda aims at better managing the issue of migration in all its aspects by evolving some tailor-made political guidelines. First, in order to prevent human tragedies, the Member States are supposed to take immediate actions. Second, for a medium/long-term solution, a strategic approach is introduced. This includes an implementation package based on Article 78(3) of the TFEU.

Due to the application of the Dublin system, many Syrian migrants avoided registration in the first Member State, and continued to move to the territory of the second—and sometimes to the third—Member States. They had, of course, their own reasons for doing so, including: a desire to have a better chance for obtaining asylum in countries with less restrict conditions; avoiding the difficulties of life in detention centres; not having access to facilities such as accommodation or translation services before registration; and the like. No wonder that migrants regarded Bulgaria, Hungary, Italy, Greece, Serbia, and Croatia as transit territories in which they did not wish to stay, and made Austria and Germany as their target countries. At the same time, the former countries also encouraged this attitude. Thus, it is reported for example, that Italy did not finger print or register the migrants. The UNCHR repeatedly criticised the EU for the inefficacy of the Dublin system, and for not providing legal access to the refugees. This is mainly an outcome of the Dublin system which does not recognise any categories of refugees except those that can be linked to one of the specified grounds.

With a view to setting a speedy asylum system, some countries such as Germany discarded this requirement. In fact, Germany not only followed the hierarchy responsibility for the Syrian asylum requests, but suspended the Dublin system.[31] This reveals that, in line with the Libyan case, Germany regarded the influx as requiring a protection system for which the Dublin Regulation ought not to be applied. In contrast, Cyprus offered no protection at all. However, this open-door policy of Germany is unlikely to continue for long. Criminal and terrorist attacks, such as the sexual harassment in Cologne on the New Year's Eve and the killing of ten Germans in Istanbul by the Syrian suicide bombers, are bound to raise doubts as to the capability or willingness of potential migrants to integrate, as well as the ability of Germany on controlling the situation.

Later in November 2015, Germany announced that Syrian migrants fleeing civil war would not be granted asylum or refugee status. They could only enter for one

[30] European Parliament 2015.

[31] On 21 August 2015 the German Federal Office for Migration and Refugees (BAMF) issued "Internal Instructions Suspending the Dublin Procedure in Respect of Syrian Nationals", see AIDA 2015.

year and enjoy subsidiary protection. The possible privilege of family reunion was also denied. This, and a further proposal to set "transit one" for processing the refugees on the border with Austria, were not agreed upon. Instead, the government decided to continue providing refugee status for a minimum of three years to the Syrian migrants, entitling them to family reunion and welfare benefits. Introducing Identity cards for refugees, deporting refused and illegal migrants, and prosecuting criminal migrants were some of the more important additional policies introduced by Germany with regard to the migration system.[32] In 2016, Germany called upon the Member States to contribute to the distribution of refugees, and to share financial support provided to third countries such as Turkey.

9.4.2 The EU-Turkey Joint Action Plan and Agreement[33]

The concept of safe third state was for the first time used in Denmark in 1986. In 1993, Germany under its reformed constitution made a readmission agreement with Poland to send the asylum seekers to Poland, and Poland to return them to Lithuania.[34] This was seemingly the first time that the concept was used in a large-scale migration crisis. In the current crisis, Turkey is considered as a safe third state.

The EU-Turkey Joint Action Plan was signed on 15 October 2015. It was designed to prevent migrants from travelling to the EU in return for payment to Turkey of 3 billion euros in cash, as well as some incentives on visas and renewal talks on joining the EU. Under the Plan, Turkey is to give the Syrians work permits in its land, and reduce the pressure of illegal migration to the EU. More than 2.2 million Syrians have sought refuge in Turkey due to the civil war, now in its 6th year. The Syrian children were agreed to be provided with education facilities by the EU funds. And while the unemployment rate in Turkey is about 10 %, hundreds of thousands of the Syrians are engaged in working illegally for low wages. Under a new legislation, refugees may apply for work six months after the registration. Refugees under temporary protection can work within the refugee community, e.g., as doctors and teachers in camps.[35]

The EU and Turkey further reached an agreement on 8 March 2016, which came into effect on 20 March 2016.[36] Under this Agreement, illegal migrants crossing Turkey to Greece as of 20 March 2016 will be returned. The EU resettles one Syrian refugee for every returned Syrian to Turkey, and Turkey undertakes to

---

32 Traynor 2015.

33 For the text of the joint Action Plan see European Commission 2015a*; and for the European Commission Fact Sheet, see European Commission* 2015b.

34 Mouzourakis 2014, pp. 9–10.

35 Gurses et al. 2016.

36 The EU-Turkey Agreement Factsheet is available at: http://europa.eu/rapid/press-release_MEMO-16-963_en.htm. Accessed 20 May 2016.

prevent land and sea illegal migration. A voluntary Humanitarian Admission Scheme will be activated when migration is reduced, or illegal migration is halted. The Agreement, if it is enforced properly, should be able to shut down the flow of migrants from the Balkans. In return for its undertakings, Turkey will receive 6 billion Euros under the Facility for Refugees' scheme over three years. Financial support will also be provided to Greece, while additional financial aids will be forthcoming in the course of processing the details. As in the earlier Agreement, visa liberalisation will be provided for the nationals of Turkey as from 1 June 2016. Moreover, the Turkey's accession talk will be restarted.

As to the statistics released, the number of Syrian settled refugees in 2015 in Turkey is said to be 3 million, while the number of Syrian asylum seekers in the EU is reported to have reached about 363,000.[37] The resettlement from Turkey started on 1 April 2016. As to the migrants located in Greece, it was decided that 6000 relocations should be processed in April, and at least 2000 relocations by mid-May 2016.[38] The Commission is in charge of the coordination and organisation of the Agreement, and would work together with the Member States and agencies. One of the remarkable points of this Agreement is its consideration of the UNHCR as a key actor, an incentive for monitoring the resettlement process.

9.4.2.1 The EU-Turkey Agreement: A Tool for Continuation of the Dublin III System, and a Limiting Tool for Full Protection of Mass Influx Migrants

As explained, under the Factsheet of the EU-Turkey Agreement, the admissibility of an asylum request continues to be reviewed under the Dublin System and Procedure Directive.[39] Articles 3 and 5 of the Directive provide that if a person is "already recognised as a refugee," or if he "enjoys sufficient protection," or resides in a third country that can guarantee effective access to protection, his application would not be admissible. In other words, having Turkey as a safe third country removes the possibility of migration with the exceptions of the limited numbers of the one-for-one deal.

Moreover, Article 18(1)(a)–(d) of the Dublin III Regulation, as reflected in the Qualification Directive, sets the conditions under which a Member State is responsible for "taking charge" and "taking back" responsibility. "Taking charge" applies in the case of reunion of the family of an applicant located in different Member States, while "taking back" relates to illegal residence in the territory of the Member States. In other words, sending back the asylum seekers to Turkey, or making Turkey as the place of application prevents any future asylum claim.

[37] Rankin 2016.

[38] See the EU-Turkey Agreement Factsheet, *above* note 36.

[39] Council of the European Union, Directive 2013/32/EU of the European Parliament and of the Council of 26 June 2013 on Common Procedures for Granting and Withdrawing International Protection (Recast), 29 June 2013, OJ L. 180/60-180/95180/60-180/95.

The Dublin III Regulation in the current situation of externalisation of borders is not, therefore, a suitable method for mass influx protection. Besides, the Dublin system permits the UK to avoid any possibility of shared-burden responsibility, and limits its contribution to the cases in which migrants are entered its borders.

9.4.3 Vertical and Horizontal Policies: Modest Success in Confronting Illegal Migration, but not in Handling the Mass Influx Crisis

Under the EU system, the externalisation and safety-focused approaches are applied to prevent illegal migration. These two approaches further lead the EU and the Member States to expand the vertical and horizontal venue-shopping strategies. The EU co-operation with the non-Member States, like Turkey, and the controversial alleged Malta-Italy Agreement are some examples of the venue-shopping. Neither the Refugee Convention, nor the Dublin system prevents the EU from adopting such strategies to combat illegal migration. But these strategies must be in compliance with the obligations of the Member States. Otherwise, they would violate migrants' human rights, with the externalisation of the borders and return of migrants to a third country, for examples.[40]

As suggested earlier, the national policies and methods followed by the Member States were neither consistent nor sustainable. More relevant to the point under discussion, the individual responsibility of the Member States, based on the hierarchy of criteria and on commonly agreed standards, was not regarded as suitable for the current influx, simply because the Member States either suspended the Dublin system, or left the involved Member States alone. It may, therefore, be suggested that the system does not offer a fair process of protection.

In its efforts to find a solution in which a balance between migration and security would be maintained, the EU decided to shift its large-scale migration policy beyond the territorial border of the EU, and to include non-Member States and international actors in the controlling systems of illegal migrations. It is too soon to see how the EU would monitor the transnational migration process. In the meantime, however, there are issues of concern that need to be focused upon, including the issue of whether and to what extent the venue-shopping policy can be considered legal, and if so, would benefit the mass influx migrants? Another relevant question is whether the migrants would be afforded any degrees of guarantees under this policy, or how this policy would affect the idea of disregarding the mass influx migrants and treating them as normal migrants? A final issue concerns how non-accessing migrants on the borders of the Member States would impact the duty of protection?

---

[40] Podkul et al. 2015, p. 10.

9.4.4 *The EU Commission's Options for a Better Functioning of the Dublin System*[41]

The most recent proposals from the Commission, with the title of "Towards a Reform of the Common European Asylum System and Enhancing Legal Avenues to Europe," recognises the weaknesses of the asylum system in dealing with the migration crisis.[42] It further admits that the Dublin Regulation "establishes the criteria and mechanism for which Member State is responsible for examining the application for international protection," but that it is "not designed to ensure a sustainable sharing of responsibility for asylum applicants across the EU." In other words, the Commission realises that the asylum system, which is a plan of actions for the Member States individually, may not offer an appropriate and workable formula for dealing with mass influx migrations, which calls for the active involvement of the whole community.[43] The Commission identifies five shortcomings with priority for improvement. Of these, only the first—namely, the priority of "establishing a sustainable and fair system determining the Member States responsible for asylum seekers"—relates to the subject of the present Chapter. For this priority, the Commission suggests two options, about which a few words must be said in the following sections.

9.4.4.1 Option 1: Supplementing the Present System with a Correct Fairness Mechanism

The Commission proposes that the first criterion—responsibility of the Member State—should be supplemented with a "corrective fairness mechanism." This first requirement encompasses, for example, the relocation of the asylum seeker when a Member State is confronting large-scale immigrants. This adjustment provides more chance for the applicant to be granted international protection.[44]

9.4.4.2 Option 2: A New System for Allocating Asylum Applications in the EU Based on a Distribution Key

The responsibility will be allocated on the basis of distribution, rather than being linked to the Member State of the first application or irregular entry. The difference between this option and the first one is that in this case, the applicants will be directly allocated. The option transfers responsibility from the national level to the

---

41 European Parliament and Council European Parliament and Council 2016.

42 *Ibid.*, p. 3.

43 *Ibid.*, pp. 3–4.

44 *Ibid.*, pp. 7–8.

EU, which in turn leads to the establishment of a "centralised decision-making process."[45]

9.4.4.3 Commendable Observation, but not an Effective Solution

The fact that the Commission has addressed the issue—and proceeded to identify and prioritise the problems—is to be appreciated. As regards the first option, if the proposed adjustment is that the set asylum system should be deviated from in the instances of large-scale migration, then the only difference between the proposal and the current situation is that under the former it would fall on the EU to take steps in favour of the Member State and the migrants. This may indeed be a workable mid-term solution, but hardly a sustainable solution.

The second option—which seems more sustainable and far-reaching—reveals the Commission's attempt to use all the available means to shift—with certain limitations—from national level to the EU. This may be viewed as a noteworthy reform in the structure of the EU regarding the asylum systems within the EU. As stated earlier, the option constitutes a long-term reform, which should be undertaken sooner rather than later.

Although the issues addressed by the Commission are quite interrelated, it is respectfully suggested here that the Commission needs to focus on the issue of mass influx migration in a package distinct from the reform of the asylum policy package. Otherwise—and in case the issue of mass influx is not dealt with separately—the problems of derogation and discrimination against the refugees as opposed to mass influx migrants will continue to exist. Furthermore, none of these suggestions show that the problem of migrants in a crisis—which could be under Refugee conditions considered as illegal—has been identified and solved. In short, the proposed reforms are unlikely to offer a proper solution if they are to be based on the retention of the Dublin structure and the inclusion of the mass influx migrants in the normal refugee system albeit with derogatory mechanism.

9.5 Concluding Remarks and Suggestions

The Libyan crisis was a case through which the EU could have demonstrated unity and solidarity by taking a common approach towards the migrants, instead of leaving the burden of confronting the problem to be shouldered by the individual Member States. Alternatively—and assuming that the Member States understandably lacked common interest in dealing with an issue that affected only a limited number of them—the EU could have considered this unfortunate occasion—as it did in the Kosovo crisis—as a powerful reminder that crises of that nature are not illusory, and that preparation for facing them was a necessity.

[45] *Ibid.*, pp. 8–9.

Such preparation could include, for example, the drawing of a clear distinction between the normal flow of refugee cases, and an inordinately large-scale influx of migration—each requiring its own specific responses. Such a distinction was needed, as suggested before, simply because not all migrants who were massively displaced from their land fell into the category of refugees. Failure to do so resulted, however, in the making of an unnecessary discriminatory distinction between those who reached the territory from the sea or from the land—the former were granted refugee status, while the latter cases were reviewed and checked to see whether they met the conditions set by the Directives and by the Member States. These shortcomings, amongst others, readily revealed that the Dublin system was far from being perfect, and capable of resulting in unacceptable injustices. Had the EU seized on the occasion to rectify its inadequacies on time, the Member States would not have had to wait for months and years to try different solutions in confronting the Syrian crisis.

The Syrian crisis was expected to be confronted as a mass influx for which the Directive was to be applied. This time, however, the earlier experience was disregarded, and neither the Member States nor the Commission proposed the application of the Mass Influx Directive. Apparently, the political interests of the Member States prevailed over the common interests, making the application of the Directive irrelevant, precisely at a time for which it was designed.

It makes no doubt that the Dublin III Regulation was not, due to its previously demonstrated deficiencies, an appropriate tool for dealing with the Syrian type of problem, or for establishing a workable method of shared-burden responsibility. As explained before, the Dublin system, which echoes the Refugee Convention, was devised to deal with the issue of potential refugees, and hence its application in the Syrian case, which represents a totally different problem and requires wholly different responses, was quite unjustified. It proved unfair, and it differed from one Member State to another. This pattern of inconsistent and discriminatory behaviour was additionally unsatisfactory from the human rights perspective, mistreating as it did a desperate population who is caught up between the brutalities of a civil war and the atrocities of terrorist groups, with limited or no safe option.

It is true, of course, that part of the problem is due to the EU's difficulty in finding the right balance between, on the one hand, the EU's legitimate concerns for security, significantly increased after terrorist attacks, and the crisis management, on the other hand. Still, it remains a fact that all the solutions favoured or adopted so far have focused on the Dublin system. It is suggested here, however, that it is time for the EU to reconsider the issue of mass influx for what it is, that is to say, an issue quite different from the issue of normal refugees, for which the obligations of the Member States can be guaranteed in a safe third country. Such distinction is particularly important in light of the expected mass influxes from African countries and Asia. It must not be forgotten, of course, that Turkey is also in the process of negotiations for Membership of the EU and, if it does join, it will not be a third country anymore.

The EU appropriately established a supranational monitoring system in the EU-Turkey Agreement. It is expected that the UNHCR and other institutions express their concerns as to what extent externalisation and security approaches could guarantee protection of categorised and uncategorized mass influx migrants.

The EU needs to formulate a medium/long-term solution in order to avoid breaching the common asylum system, and to avoid taking any unfair decision against migrants in crisis and refugees. Such mechanism must naturally first and foremost reflect a workable solution, taking note particularly of the deficiencies in the existing Mass Influx Directive; deficiencies that contributed to the neglect of the Directive in the present mass influx.

In order to achieve that objective, the EU must take a prominent role, rather than allowing the Member States, as it has done in the present influx, to repeatedly ignore the principle of solidarity and fair sharing responsibility—a principle upheld by Article 80 of the TFEU. The EU should, furthermore, apply the powers under Article 78(2(c)) of the TFEU to adopt measures for a common system of temporary protection comprising, *inter alia*, "displaced persons in the event of a massive inflow." The suggestion is that by resorting to this Article, the EU should re-conceptualise the mass influx migrants once again, as it did in the Mass Influx Directive, because these groups of people are in need of temporary protection. They do not have to and cannot necessarily be covered by the same common asylum system applied for the refugees or the people in need of protection in general.

References

AIDA (2015) Verfahrensregelung zur Aussetzung des Dublinverfahrens für syrische Staatsangehörige. Az. 411 - 93605/Syrien/2015 www.asylumineurope.org/news/24-08-2015/germany-halt-dublin-procedures-syrians. Accessed on 20 May 2016

Ball R (2014) The legitimacy of the European Union through legal rationality: free movement of third country nationals. Routledge Taylor and Francis Group, London

EMN (2011) Italy Annual Policy Report 2011. http://ec.europa.eu/dgs/home-affairs/what-we-do/networks/european_migration_network/reports/docs/annual-policy/2011/it_20121017_apr2011_en_version_finalrevised_en.pdf. Accessed on 20 May 2016

European Commission (2015a) Priority migration towards a European agenda on migration. http://ec.europa.eu/priorities/migration_en. Accessed 20 May 2016

European Commission (2015b) Fact sheet. See http://europa.eu/rapid/press-release_MEMO-15-5860_en.htm. Accessed 20 May 2016

European Parliament (2015) Communication from the Commission to the European Parliament, the Council, the European Economic and Social Committee and the Committee of the Regions. A European Agenda on Migration, 13 May 2015, COM (2015) 240

European Parliament and Council (2016) Communication from the Commission to the European Parliament and the Council towards a reform of the Common European asylum and enhancing legal avenues to Europe, 06 April 2016, COM (2016) 197

Farnesina (2011) Press release, "Immigration emergency: the EU must adopt a refugee distribution plan", says Frattini. Ministry of Foreign Affairs of Italy. www.esteri.it/mae/en/sala_stampa/archivionotizie/approfondimenti/2011/03/20110330_emergenza_immigrazione.html. Accessed on 20 May 2016

Gurses E et al (2016) Turkey plans to introduce work permits for Syrian refugees, minister Says. Reuters, 11 January 2016. http://mobile.reuters.com/article/idUSKCN0UP0QP20160111?feedType=RSS&feedName=worldNews. Accessed 20 May 2016

Hatton TJ (2011) Refugees from North Africa: a case for co-operation? VOX CEPR's policy portal. www.voxeu.org/article/refugees-north-africa-case-cooperation. Accessed on 20 May 2016

Heller C et al (2011) Forensic Oceanography: Report on the "left-to-die boat." Part of EU Research Council Project. Centre for Research Architecture, Goldsmiths, University of London, Report, p. 14. www.fidh.org/IMG/pdf/fo-report.pdf. Accessed on 20 May 2016

International Organization for Migration (2011) IOM Report, humanitarian response to the Libyan crisis (February–December 2011). https://publications.iom.int/system/files/pdf/final_mena_10_months_compressed.pdf. Accessed on 20 May 2016

Kaunert C, Leonard S (2012) The development of the EU Asylum Policy: venue-shopping in perspective. J Eur Public Policy 19(9):1396–1413

Marchetti C (2012) Framing emergency. Italian response to 2011 (forced migrations from Tunisia and Libya). Conference paper. www.academia.edu/2309681/Framing_emergency._Italian_response_to_2011_forced_migrations_from_Tunisia_and_Libya. Accessed on 20 May 2016

Mitra S (2001) Kosovo: economic and social reforms for peace and reconciliation. World Bank, Technical Paper No. 509. www-wds.worldbank.org/external/default/WDSContentServer/WDSP/IB/2001/12/01/000094946_01111704003347/Rendered/PDF/multi0page.pdf. Accessed 20 May 2016

Mouzourakis M (2014) We need to talk about Dublin: responsibility under the Dublin system as a blockage to asylum burden-sharing in the European Union. Refugee Studies Centre, Oxford Department of International Development, University of Oxford. Working Paper Series No. 105, pp 9–10. www.rsc.ox.ac.uk/publications/we-need-to-talk-about-dublin. Accessed 20 May 2016

Nita S (2013) Regional responses to forced migration: the case of Libya, MPC RR 2013/03. Robert Schuman Centre for Advanced Studies, San Domenico di Fiesole (FI): European University Institute. www.migrationpolicycentre.eu/docs/ASN2013-03.pdf. Accessed 20 May 2016

Podkul J et al (2015) Interdiction, border externalisation, and the protection of the human rights of migrants. Working Paper, for the thematic hearing on: human rights and the interdiction of persons eligible for international protection, p. 10. www.law.georgetown.edu/academics/centers-institutes/human-rights-institute/our-work/projects/upload/WRC-HRI-Border-Externalization_Oct-2015.pdf. Accessed 20 May 2016

Rankin J (2016) Turkey and the EU agree outline of "one in, one out" deal over Syria refugee crisis, the Guardian, 8 March 2016. www.theguardian.com/world/2016/mar/08/european-leaders-agree-outlines-of-refugee-deal-with-turkey. Accessed 20 May 2016

Times of Malta.com (2011) Busuttil calls on European Commission to activate solidarity mechanism, Times of Malta. www.timesofmalta.com/articles/view/20110329/local/busuttil-calls-on-european-commission-to-activate-solidarity-mechanism.357253. Accessed on 20 May 2016

Traynor I (2015) Confusion as Germany announces curbs on Syrian refugees, the Guardian, 6 November 2015. www.theguardian.com/world/2015/nov/06/germany-imposes-surprise-curbs-on-syrian-refugees. Accessed on 20 May 2016

UN High Commissioner for Refugees (2003) Annotated comments on Council Directive 2001/55/EC of 20 July 2001 on minimum standards for giving temporary protection in the event of a mass influx of displaced persons on measures promoting balance of efforts between Member States in receiving such persons and bearing the consequences thereof. www.unhcr.org/436620152.html. Accessed on 20 May 2016

UN High Commissioner for Refugees (2015) Refugee Statistics. UNHCR, Research, www.statisticbrain.com/refugee-statistics/. Accessed on 20 May 2016

UN High Commissioner for Refugees (2016) Europe: Syrian asylum applications from April 2011 to March 2016. http://data.unhcr.org/syrianrefugees/asylum.php. Accessed on 20 May 2016

Chapter 10
Energy Policy in the European Union: Renewable Energy and the Risks of Subversion

Helen Kopnina

Abstract The European energy policy has a significant influence on the way in which environmental and energy policies are framed and implemented, not only in member states but globally. One of the important challenges of the European energy policy is climate change. Presently, the European Commission (EC) seeks to create an Energy Union, aimed at ensuring that Europe has secure, affordable and climate-friendly energy. In order to achieve this, some propose a compromise involving efficiency in use of fossil fuel and inclusion of different types of energy in the energy mix, while others are in favour of more transformative measures engendered by the Circular Economy (CE) and Cradle to Cradle (C2C) approaches to energy. Conventional and C2C/CE approaches to sustainability in general and energy in particular are not always compatible, as C2C/CE requires radical transformation rather than promoting compromise. This chapter will focus on various types of renewable energy in the context of the European sustainability challenges and explore the EU's energy policy, providing recommendations for the long-term sustainability.

Keywords Climate change · Circular Economy (CE) · Cradle to Cradle (C2C) · Energy Union · European Union · Renewable energy · Solar energy · Wind energy

H. Kopnina (✉)
The Hague University of Applied Sciences, The Hague, The Netherlands
e-mail: h.kopnina@hhs.nl; h.n.kopnina@fsw.leidenuniv.nl

J. de Zwaan et al. (eds.), *Governance and Security Issues of the European Union*, DOI 10.1007/978-94-6265-144-9_10

Contents

10.1 Introduction

European Union's (EU) environmental law and governance are the cornerstones of global efforts to protect the environment through the use of renewable energy for the citizens of the European Member States. Although the EU was founded as the European Coal and Steel community shortly after World War II and has been involved in legislation in the area of energy policy from the beginning, the introduction of an integrated European energy policy incorporating sustainability regulation is relatively new (ECa[1]). Sustainability in the energy sector often focuses on the topics of self-sufficiency and efficiency.[2] The comprehensive European energy policy that includes sustainability concerns was approved at the meeting of the European Council, but only in 2005.

Presently, the European Commission (EC) shows new ambitions seeking to create an Energy Union. Climate change caused by carbon emissions resulting from fossil fuel use looms large in European policy agendas. Climate change threats include the increase in climate refugees due to worsening conditions in countries most vulnerable to draughts and floods, and economic damages due to extreme weather conditions.[3]

Both at the level of the European Environment Agency (EEA) as well as specialised departments and agencies concerned with energy, the debate centres on the questions of what type and which proportion (energy mix) of the alternative sources of energy needs to be used to meet emissions' targets. According to the International Energy Agency,[4] renewable energy is derived from natural processes that are replenished at a higher rate than they are consumed. Renewable energy is

---

[1] 'Energy'. https://ec.europa.eu/energy. Accessed 17 May 2016.

[2] Knill and Liefferink 2012.

[3] Kopnina and Blewitt 2014.

[4] IEA 2015.

represented by solar, wind, geothermal, hydropower, bioenergy from biomass, and ocean power, and more contentiously, nuclear power.

While some European policy-makers propose eco-efficiency (meaning doing more with less—thus *reducing* the use of fossil fuel energy) or a mix of strategies (combining both reduced fossil fuels *and* renewable energy) as discussed in the publications of the EC, others are in favour of stricter and transformative measures. These transformative measures include the so-called circular economy (CE) (ECc[5]) and Cradle to Cradle (C2C) (ECd[6]). approaches to production in general and to energy in particular. The C2C/CE approaches propose a "closed loop" system that uses only energy sources that are *infinitely reusable*—namely sun, wind, and tidal energy. Conventional and C2C/CE approaches are not always compatible. While the conventional model proposes compromise, the latter strategies require complete transformation to fully regenerative energy.

Basically, the main difference between the conventional energy mix and C2C/CE approaches is that while the former seeks reduction of harmful fuels, the latter approach attempts to eliminate them altogether, avoiding a compromise in which some forms of energy which are not sustainable in the long term are allowed to complement true renewables. The case in point is the EU's prioritisation of biofuels as a source of supposedly renewable energy. Considering that biofuel is derived from tree plantations that were planted in places where the old biodiverse forest stood, which took tens of years to grow to maturity, how sustainable is this form of green energy?[7] The use of wood as a renewable energy source was termed "Environmental lunacy in Europe" in *The Economist.*[8] The European Environment Agency has admitted that the assumption "that biomass combustion would be inherently carbon neutral … is not correct … as it ignores the fact that using land to produce plants for energy typically means that this land is not producing plants for other purposes, including carbon otherwise sequestered."[9] In fact, biofuels represent a typical example of unsustainable linear production. At the time of writing, the EC was aiming to present a new CE strategy in order "to transform Europe into a more competitive resource-efficient economy" (ECe[10]). Still, at the time of writing, the EU seems to proceed with its renewable energy policy stimulating production of biofuels.

This chapter will focus on various types of renewable energy in the context of the European sustainability challenges. It will explore the EU's reliance on biofuels and other questionable "alternatives," and provide recommendations for

[5] Circular economy strategy. http://ec.europa.eu/environment/circular-economy/index_en.htm. Accessed 17 May 2016.

[6] 'Eco-innovation'. http://ec.europa.eu/environment/ecoap/about-eco-innovation/good-practices/eu/575_en.htm. Accessed 17 May 2016.

[7] Kopnina and Shoreman-Ouimet 2015.

[8] The Economist 2013.

[9] The Economist 2013.

[10] Circular economy strategy, above n 5.

renewable energy policy targeted at the long-term sustainability. Below, the discussion of climate change and different types of renewables will be followed by the exploration of wind and solar energy. The final section will address the EU's present energy policy in relation to the C2C/CE and draw recommendations for long-term sustainability, in Europe and beyond.

10.2 Climate Change

Soon after the 1973 oil crisis, most Europeans' per capita energy consumption peaked, and subsequent economic growth was achieved by increasing energy intensity.[11] In the past decades, the EU was importing about 80% of its oil and 60% of its gas, making it the world's leading importer of these fossil fuels.[12] Increased consumption of fossil fuels resulted in emissions of greenhouse gases (GHG) and particularly Carbon dioxide (CO_2) that most scientists agree cause climate change and air pollution.

It was recognised that without drastic measures tackling dependency on fossil fuels, mitigating climate change would be impossible. The first major policy response to climate change was developed under the Kyoto Protocol[13] in 1987 and was followed by initiatives developed in the consequent climate change conferences. The curbing of emissions globally has become a matter of international environmental politics. Scientists of the International Panel for Climate Change[14] have established that it is still possible to limit GHG emissions to avoid the 2°C warming threshold. Scenarios from international agencies indicate that renewable energy, and particularly solar and wind, could supply between 10 and 31% of electricity worldwide by 2050.[15]

However, at present, the policy response based on mitigation mechanisms including carbon trading and clean development mechanism have been characterised as a large failure, with global emissions actually rising to 30–40% after the signing of the Kyoto Protocol.[16] By the turn of the millennium, and the five-year means of global surface air temperature increased by 0.5°C.[17]

Some positive news has come from the EU which, about a decade ago, became one of the pioneers of action aimed at mitigating emissions. The climate and energy package developed by the EU is a set of binding legislation which aims to

---

11 Ross 2013.

12 IPCC 2014.

13 IPCC 2014.

14 IPCC 2011.

15 Barthelmie and Pryor 2014, pp. 684–688; Diesendorf 2014.

16 IPCC 2014.

17 IPCC 2011.

ensure the targets for 2020. Known as the "20-20-20" targets, they set three key objectives for 2020, including a 20% reduction in EU emissions from 1990 levels; raising the share of EU energy consumption produced from renewable resources to 20%; and a 20% improvement in the EU's energy efficiency (ECf[18]).

Greater attention to alternative energy also reflects broad European support for ecological modernisation,[19] as well as grass-roots concerns. In June 2015, for instance, the Dutch court ordered state to reduce emissions by 25% within five years to protect its citizens from climate change in the world's first civil climate liability suit.[20] Partially in response to grass-roots pressures, the EU attempts to increase renewable sources from 55 to 75% of energy by 2050.[21] Yet, the Paris Agreement[22] on addressing climate change established in December 2015 leaves the EU some room for interpretation (ECf[23]). At the time of writing this chapter, it looks like European energy policy is continuing to embrace biofuels.[24] This is highly problematic, as will be explained below.

10.3 Renewable Energy

The organic matter that makes up plants is known as biomass. Biomass is derived from organic material such as trees, plants, and agricultural and urban waste. It can be used for heating, electricity generation, transport fuels, and chemicals (ECg[25]). Another source of biomass energy is mixed waste incineration, or "Waste to Energy," or "energy recovery" is widely used within the EU.

There are severe side-effects of most of those supposedly "green" energy sources.[26] All types of bio-generated energy involve burning of plants or algae matter from "fuel forests", which compete with agricultural land for production of food.[27] Plantations used for biofuel production have taken increasingly larger proportion of originally biologically diverse habitats. Biofuels generate CO_2 when

[18] 'A Global Deal for Climate'. http://ec.europa.eu/clima/policies/package/index_en.htm. Accessed 13 June 2015.

[19] Schelly 2015, pp. 55–69.

[20] Neslen 2011.

[21] Lewis 2015.

[22] 'Paris Agreement'. http://ec.europa.eu/clima/policies/international/negotiations/future/index_en.htm. Accessed 17 May 2016.

[23] *Ibid.*

[24] Van Renssen 2016.

[25] 'Biomass'. http://ec.europa.eu/energy/en/topics/renewable-energy/biomass. Accessed 17 May 2016.

[26] Steer and Hanson 2015.

[27] Walsh 2014.

burned, but also the process that involves planting crops for generation of biofuels, fertilising, harvesting, processing, and distribution emits significant amounts of CO_2.[28] Biofuels also require continuous supply of wood, some of which cannot be replenished for over a hundred years.[29]

Burning garbage to generate energy may seem "green", but it is only one step removed from the "cradle—to-grave" model in which valuable materials are lost.[30] In reality, "Waste to Energy" contributes to environmental degradation, literally wasting valuable resources by exacerbating raw material shortages and intensifying the loss of CO_2-capturing topsoil. It also prevents effective recycling due to competition for high-caloric recyclable content. The "Waste to Energy" paradigm fails to consider the high nutrient value of waste or the hazardous impacts of burning them for cheap fuel. Through incineration, we are throwing away exhaustible raw materials, along with the energy needed to mine natural resources and manufacture them into consumable products. With this approach, not only do we lose valuable nutrients, we also create an aggressive disincentive for materials' reuse.[31]

Although nuclear energy is considered clean energy, its inclusion in the renewable energy list is a subject of major debate because of nuclear waste,[32] and also because it has been proven unsafe. After the Fukushima nuclear accident in 2011, Germany has permanently shut down eight of its 17 reactors.[33]

Hydro energy is captured through the use of hydroelectric technology, or by damming. The hydropower generated by the dams cause disruption of natural systems, affecting river environments, fisheries and land. The dam itself blocks fish migrations, which in some cases completely separate spawning habitats from rearing habitats. The dam also traps sediments, which are critical for maintaining physical processes and habitats downstream (International Rivers).[34]

Thus, most of these "renewables" are either unsafe, or follow a "cradle-to-grave" trajectory[35] and do not satisfy the long-term aims of sustainable development. As opposed to the "European environmental lunacy" with regard to biofuels, wind and solar energy have been proposed as the most safe, clean, and sustainable energy, especially if side effects, environmental and health risks, are taken into account.[36]

---

28 Steer and Hanson 2015.

29 The Economist 2013.

30 McDonough and Braungart 2002.

31 Braungart 2013.

32 Johnson 2009.

33 Breidthardt 2011.

34 'Environmental Impact of Dams'. http://www.internationalrivers.org/environmental-impacts-of-dams. Accessed 13 June 2015.

35 McDonough and Braungart 2002.

36 Costa et al. 2008, pp. 1725–1744; Barthelmie and Pryor 2014, pp. 684–688; Diesendorf 2014.

10.4 Better Alternatives

Other energy sources that could fit within C2C/CE framework are geothermal and tidal energy. Geothermal energy, using hot water or steam reservoirs deep in the earth, taps the Earth's internal heat for electricity production (NREL[37]). Tidal stream systems utilise the kinetic energy from water currents to turn turbines (Tidal energy EUa[38]). Studies suggest that one third of the UK's total electricity needs could be met by tidal power alone (Tidal energy EUb[39]). In addition to tidal energy, there is the energy of the ocean's waves, which are driven by both the tides and the winds (Renewable Energy World[40]).

According to C2C/CE, together with solar power, wind power represents one of the most promising sources of renewable energy. The quantity of energy generated by the sun and wind is potentially limitless, and aside from harnessing, storage and transfer technology, it is cost-free.[41] The solar and wind power are also without dangers of toxic waste, as in the case of nuclear energy.[42] They are omnipresent, clean, and modular for installations of any size, and its application continues to expand as it becomes more technologically advanced and cost competitive.[43] Unlike some renewables, such as biomass and waste, burning of which actually leads to reduction of overall biomass, the sunlight and wind does not involve depletion of resources, aside from its capture and storage devices.[44] Wind and solar power does not use material resources that can be exhausted, as in the case of biomass or waste; or include potentially hazardous by-products, as in the case of nuclear energy.[45]

While wind power has not been price-competitive until recently, many of the newer technologies for harvesting, storing, and transferring wind energy have enabled greater market competitiveness. With the benefit of economies of scale, wind power has been able to realise substantial decreases in per unit cost of electricity, and provide hope for an environmentally benign generation of global energy.[46] Thus, proponents of long-term sustainability have argued against compromises in

---

37 'Geothermal energy basics'. http://www.nrel.gov/learning/re_geothermal.html. Accessed 17 May 2016.

38 'Tidal energy stream systems'. http://www.tidalenergy.eu/tidal_stream_systems.html. Accessed 17 May 2016.

39 'Tidal energy'. http://www.tidalenergy.eu/. Accessed 17 May 2016.

40 'Renewable Energy News & Information'. http://www.renewableenergyworld.com. Accessed 17 May 2016.

41 Kopnina and Blewitt 2014.

42 McDonough and Braungart 2002.

43 Kopnina and Blewitt 2014; Kopnina and Shoreman-Ouimet 2015.

44 Washington 2015.

45 Barthelmie and Pryor 2014, pp. 684–688; Diesendorf 2014.

46 *Ibid.*

energy mix and for strict reliance on wind and solar energy.[47] Below we will focus on solar and wind energy and relate it to European energy policy.

10.5 Wind Power

Wind power is known for hundreds of years for its use in windmills. Today, the windmill's modern equivalent, a wind turbine, uses wind energy to generate electricity.[48] In The Netherlands, windmills were present before the fourteenth century, with wind power applied to a wide range of industrial processes, including paper and cement production, and wood sawing.[49] In the seventeenth century, the windmills were also used to help drain lakes and marches in the Rhine River Delta, and also used widely in Southern Europe.[50] The iconic image of a delusional knight fighting mills from Miguel de Cervantes' novel *Don Quixote,* written between 1605 and 1615, still dominates public imagination.

At present, wind power can be stored either as electricity in batteries, heat in such media as molten salt, or as hydrogen, compressed air, or pumped storage, so that power is available on demand.[51] Improvement in the design of a battery energy storage system (BESS) has been crucial in attenuating the effects of unsteady power input from wind farms.[52] The design of newer batteries determines the capacity of the BESS to ensure constant dispatched power to the connected grid, while the voltage level is kept constant.[53] The significant enlargement of the grid system, linking a large number of geographically dispersed wind parks has helped to transfer power over great distances. This type of highly interconnected grid system could emulate the requirements of current energy supply systems.[54]

The challenge of integrating wind power into established electric power grids is described in the report *Technology Roadmap: Wind Energy,* by the International Energy Agency (IEA 2013[55]). The *Roadmap* estimates that wind energy could account for up to 18% of the world's electricity by 2050, compared with 2.6% today. Yet, continuous obstacles hamper the successful spread of wind energy.

---

[47] Daly 1991; Washington 2015.

[48] Manwell et al. 2010.

[49] Kaldellis and Zafirakis 2011, pp. 1887–1901.

[50] Costa et al. 2008, pp. 1725–1744.

[51] Armand and Tarascon 2008, pp. 52–657.

[52] Divya and Østergaard 2009, pp. 511–520.

[53] Teleke et al. 2010, pp. 787–794.

[54] Sathyajith 2006.

[55] Technology Roadmap: Wind Energy—2013 edition. https://www.iea.org/publications/freepublications/publication/Wind_2013_Roadmap.pdf. Accessed 17 May 2016.

One of the principal arguments against the expanded deployment of wind energy is that its costs still exceed those of conventional energy sources such as coal, oil, natural gas and nuclear power.[56] This means that wind power needs to be subsidised in the form of preferential feed-in tariffs (FITs). An integral part of the solution is the willingness of conventional power companies to buy excess power from disseminated wind power sources at a reasonable price.[57] In the UK, the Government's Department for Energy and Climate Change (DECC) introduced FITs as the electricity part of Clean Energy Cashback in 2010.[58] The UK Government's FITs schemes provided an opportunity for consumers to get money from their energy supplier if they installed an electricity-generating technology from a wind turbine.[59] Consumers are paid for the electricity they generate for themselves, saving money on self-generated electricity, and for any surplus electricity that they exported to the grid.[60] According to the European Wind Energy Association (EWEA), onshore wind is cheaper than coal, gas or nuclear energy when the costs of "external" factors like air quality, human toxicity and climate change are taken into account.

What is also helpful are international and national subsidies, in the form of direct cash transfers to producers, consumers, or related bodies, as well as indirect support mechanisms, such as tax exemptions, price controls, trade restrictions, and limits to market access. Without a phasing out of fossil fuel subsidies, clean energy sources like wind power can hardly compete and it may be impossible to reach the international climate targets, set by the Paris agreement in 2015.[61]

Yet another issue is complaints by local land owners or citizens living in proximity to windmills about the noise pollution, "horizon pollution", vibrations, or other larger and smaller objections.[62] Often times these complaints are successfully used by fossil fuel lobbies and others with interest to discredit wind power. The same lobbies often argue that fossil fuel industries provide jobs and economic prosperity and thus re-assert their dominant position within public awareness and civil society spheres.[63] Such political use of public concerns tends to underplay the long-term negative effects of fossil fuel energy or other forms of energy.[64]

---

56 Breton and Moe 2009, pp. 646–654.

57 Mendonça 2009.

58 Seyfang et al. 2013, pp. 977–989.

59 Walker 2012, pp. 383–388.

60 Energy Saving Trust 2015, UK. scheme http://www.energysavingtrust.org.uk/domestic/content/feed-tariff-scheme. Accessed 1 May 2016.

61 Rhodes 2016, pp. 97–104.

62 Visser 2016.

63 Levy and Egan 2003, pp. 803–829.

64 Michaelowa 2000, pp. 277–292.

Despite public complaints in some localities, public opinion surveys about wind power shows that wind energy enjoys stable levels of public support.[65] Renewable energy actually maintains and creates new jobs, and the public perceives multiple benefits offered by wind power.[66] Representative occupations in demand of wind technologies include environmental engineers, iron and steel workers, millwrights, sheet metal workers, construction equipment operators, industrial truck drivers, and industrial production managers.[67]

Still, public concern is also indicative of the fact that the design of wind turbines still needs to be improved.[68] Offshore farms with less visual impact have been gaining popularity, as they are further removed from inhabited areas and are steadier than wind turbines on land. Yet, construction and maintenance costs of offshore turbines are considerably higher than that of land wind turbines, as they have to withstand greater force of currents and corrosion. Other risks to the use of wind power include climatic change. The increased frequency and severity of regional droughts, wind storms and flooding may threaten the structural integrity of installed wind farms and electrical transmission grids.

10.6 Solar Power

The most significant feature of solar energy is its potential to be one of the world's most hopeful suppliers of sustainable energy.[69] The first solar photovoltaic (PV) cells were made in the 1880s. The photovoltaic effect was "popularised" by the German scientist Heinrich Hertz.[70] In late nineteenth century various "solar cells" patents were awarded to Russian and American chemists, physicists and electrical engineers.[71] In 1905, Albert Einstein published a paper explaining the photoelectric effect on a quantum basis.[72]

Generating solar power involves the conversion of sunlight into electrical charge, either directly using the method of converting the sunlight into electricity through PV, or indirectly using concentrated solar power (CSP). CSP requires generally as much space as "flat panel" PV when it comes to major installations. Small CSP applications, PV or Concentrator photovoltaics (CP) technology are becoming more prominent in Europe. Like PV, CP is also a photovoltaic process

65 Firestone and Kempton 2007, pp. 1584–1598; Firestone et al. 2009, pp. 183–202.

66 Bell et al. 2005, pp. 460–477.

67 Blanco and Rodrigues 2009, pp. 2847–2857; Cleary and Kopicki 2009.

68 Visser 2016.

69 Delucchi and Jacobson 2011, pp. 1154–1169.

70 Guarnieri 2015, pp. 1–14.

71 Sandstede et al. 2010.

72 Pais 1982.

but like CSP, it is being fuelled by direct radiation.[73] This system is capable of converting almost twice the incident sunlight into electricity as compared to conventional silicon-based systems, helping spread the technology within Europe (Cordis[74]). There are three requirements for building commercial CSP plants: suitable land area, well-established transmission lines, and a steady financing. CSP requires large tracts of relatively flat land for transmission needing permits, crossing multiple jurisdictions and political regulations. Neither of the first two requirements can be secured without a long-term investment of capital. Solar power was initially considered to be a relatively expensive and marginal source of electrical energy where grid power is inconvenient, unreasonably expensive to connect, or simply unavailable.

PV was initially used to power small and medium-sized electronic devices, while using CSP plants allowed producers to generate electricity in the absence of sunshine.[75] As CSP still requires a high level of clear-sky solar radiation, it is best situated in "sunnier" geographical areas. CSP technologies often use lenses to focus a large area of sunlight into beams.[76]

Technological as well as political developments that have stimulated the production of solar energy have helped to expand solar power's world-wide popularity. The cost of solar power fell due to increasing economies of scale. Research and development helped to further bring down the cost of CSP, to build new plants to decrease costs, improving production and construction methods, cultivating a trained workforce, and developing a competitive supply chain.[77] At present, solar technology could potentially generate enough clean, renewable energy to provide a global supply of energy, provided three factors are in ample supply: land, sunlight, and legal permits.[78]

The question of land and sun is becoming easier to solve, due to improving technologies that allow energy to be extracted from even cloudy areas, and fewer territories to be used with more efficient output. One of the relatively new areas of exploration has been biomimicry, or technology imitating nature. Using the observation of the structure of sunflowers, researchers have come up with a design drastically reducing the amount of land required to build a CSP plant by rearranging the sun-capturing mirrors in a pattern similar to a sunflower, increasing the amount of sunlight its mirrors collect.[79] Other recent developments included the Sunseeker solar airplane, designed by the Solar Flight (Solar Flight[80]). The battery capacity

[73] Blair et al. 2008.

[74] 'Cordis'. http://cordis.europa.eu/news/rcn/132388_en.html. Accessed 1 May 2016.

[75] Pfenninger et al. 2014, pp. 689–692.

[76] Boyde 2012.

[77] Nemet 2006, pp. 3218–3232.

[78] Diesendorf 2014.

[79] London 2012.

[80] 'Solar Flight'. http://www.solar-flight.com. Accessed 17 May 2016

to store solar energy has been rapidly improving.[81] Yet, while the solar industry is flourishing, and rapidly becoming a part of everyday life, there are still some considerable obstacles associated with its global use.

Recent changes in solar incentive policies in Europe prompted solar panel makers to build huge factories anticipating a continuous surge in demand in the global market, churning out solar panels to keep their factories running and workers employed. Yet, the global demand did not keep pace, partially due to competition from other types of energy providers.[82] There are also significant political and ideological barriers to the use of solar power. Solar energy was often left on the back burner whenever fossil fuels were more affordable or geopolitics favourable. Powerful fossil fuel and transportation lobbies argue that due to weaning from fossil fuels, national competitiveness and many jobs will be lost.[83]

Yet, these arguments appear highly biased. In fact, the use of solar power is likely to maintain existing and add new jobs. Representative occupations in demand of solar technologies include electrical engineers, electricians, industrial machinery mechanics, welders, metal fabricators, electrical equipment assemblers, construction equipment operators, labourers, and construction managers.[84] What is more, the end gain of adopting solar power could not be just measured in employment and money, but in long-term social and environmental sustainability.

More generally, perhaps the most important barriers to transition from fossil fuels to solar are political, with industrial power lobbies and political elites often unwilling to undertake the necessary measures to transit from fossil to renewable energy.[85] Within the EU political transition to a more centralised form of energy policy is still contested by national laws defending its own policy.[86] Thus, international competition in production of PV's and CSR, as well as different countries' regulations and protective policies, can work counter-productively to the wider applicability of solar power. Yet, the plummeting prices for solar panels can also be beneficial to both the solar power developers and consumers.

10.7 The Current European Energy Policy

The EU is particularly well-positioned to embrace wind and solar energy, thanks to its assertive policy of developing renewable energies. Yet, the EU is a long way from embracing transition to wind and solar energy. Prior to the Treaty of Lisbon

[81] Divya and Østergaard 2009, pp. 511–520; Teleke et al. 2010, pp. 787–794.

[82] Wang 2012.

[83] Adger et al. 2009, 93:335–354.

[84] Cleary and Kopicki 2009.

[85] Washington 2015.

[86] Braun 2011, p. 14.

in 2007, EU energy legislation was based on the EU's authority in the area of the common market and environment. The EU Treaty of Lisbon involved member countries' solidarity in matters of energy supply and changes to the energy policy. In practice, energy regulation remains at national Member State level, and progress in policy at a European level requires voluntary co-operation.[87]

In Austria, Finland, Sweden and Latvia, renewable energy made up more than one third of energy consumption in 2013, while Britain, Luxembourg, Malta and the Netherlands got fewer than 5% from green sources.[88] Presently, EU's wind energy generation is focusing on offshore development.[89] In terms of solar power, PVs continued its growth trend, with Italy as one of the top markets, with 9.3 GW connected, followed by Germany (7.5 GW), France (1.7 GW) and the United Kingdom (784 MW). PV is now a significant part of Europe's electricity mix, producing 2% of the demand in the EU and roughly 4% of peak demand (EPIA 2016[90]).

However, a large proportion of European renewable energy is still derived from biomass, which in 2016 accounted to about two thirds of all renewable energy in the EU. EC praises biomass as the means to "diversify Europe's energy supply, create growth and jobs, and lower greenhouse gas emissions" (ECg[91]). In the process, American and Canadian forests are being plundered to make pellets for export to Europe.[92] Environmental campaigners are calling for limits on how much energy can come from biomass along the lines of a cap already being negotiated for biofuels, arguing that the EU energy policy ignores the side-effects of using biomass[93] as specified above.

New rules to prevent cultivation of biofuels on agricultural land displace food production to previously non-agricultural land such as grasslands (ECh[94]). Yet, the effects of this include the loss of biodiversity, deforestation and the actual net increase of emissions[95] in Europe and beyond.

[87] *Ibid.*

[88] Lewis 2015.

[89] González and Lacal-Arántegui 2016, pp. 588–560.

[90] 'Global market outlook photovoltaics'. http://www.epia.org/news/publications/global-market-outlook-for-photovoltaics-until-2016. Accessed 17 May 2016.

[91] 'Biomass'. http://ec.europa.eu/energy/en/topics/renewable-energy/biomass. Accessed 17 May 2016.

[92] The Economist 2013.

[93] Lewis 2015.

[94] 'Biofuels'. http://ec.europa.eu/energy/en/topics/renewable-energy/biofuels. Accessed 17 May 2016.

[95] Walsh 2014; Steer and Hanson 2015.

10.8 The Business of Subversion?

Such compromises as biofuels in what is considered to be "green" or "renewable" energy, have considerable effects on the broader question of sustainability. Critics have stated that unlimited economic growth is physically impossible, and that by implication the energy generation that is not truly renewable will not sustain our society in the long term.[96] Non-renewables such as petroleum are limited in terms of the total amount available on earth, while renewables are limited in terms of their rate of use, although they are practically unlimited in terms of the total amount eventually harvested over time. By stricter definition, the only truly renewable sources of energy are sun and wind.

While the intermittent nature of wind and solar power is used as a reason for continued reliance on less ecologically benign renewables to compensate for the fluctuating shortfall, technologies for generating and storing wind and solar power have been rapidly improving, and prices have decreased. The real reason for the continual reliance on either fossil fuels or biomass might be industrial pressure groups and short-term thinking of elected officials. The risk of subversion stems from the oxymoronic goal of wanting to maintain economic growth and simultaneously maintaining sustainability of finite natural resources used for the production of energy.

Yet another danger area is the subversion of the C2C/CE framework itself, serving economic growth above considerations of environmental sustainability. The European Commission's Roadmap to CE seems to be narrowly focused on economic growth:

This initiative is meant as a direct contribution to the objectives pursued to give a new boost for Jobs, Growth and Investment and placed within the wider context of the Commission's commitment towards sustainable development. Moreover, eco-industries and eco-innovation currently supply a third of the global market for green technologies, worth a trillion euro and expected to double by 2020. This initiative aims to reinforce this trend, thus contributing to green growth and to other EU priorities such as the work towards developing a Forward-Looking Climate Change Policy (ECi[97]).

The same accent on growth is seen in the roadmap to C2C:

The idea that there is no such thing as waste, only raw materials yet to be put to good use, underpins the cradle-to-cradle (C2C) concept. The EU 2020 strategy calls for smart, sustainable and inclusive economic growth (ECk[98]).

[96] Daly 1991; Washington 2015.

[97] European Commission 2015a.

[98] 'Eco-innovation at the heart of European policies'. http://ec.europa.eu/environment/ecoap/about-eco-innovation/good-practices/eu/575_en.htm. Accessed 17 May 2016.

Also, the terminology used by the EC when describing CE, include recycling (which is not the same as infinite reuse), and "using resources more efficiently will also bring new growth and job opportunities" (ECl[99]) suggests the business-as-usual scenario, rather than the no-compromise radical transformation.

10.9 Recommendations

If the EU is to overcome the catastrophic environmental collapse predicted by the report of the *Limits to Growth*,[100] transformation based on C2C/CE principles needs to be considered, without resort to short-term "alternative" energy sources such as biofuels. In the words of Ross,[101] looking back to the period of oil embargo is a helpful reminder that strict standards can work; that government research support can yield spectacular payoffs; and that political leaders can take decisive, bipartisan action on global environmental problems. This also implies a chance to address European dependency on (politically unstable) countries that provide fossil fuels. While this sounds austere, the solar society was anticipated with optimism by the American inventor Thomas A. Edison many years ago: "I'd put my money on the sun and solar energy. What a source of power! I hope we don't have to wait until oil and coal run out before we tackle that".

Presently, we may hope that the EU will follow this advice. There are reasons for optimism. According to Randall,[102] the price of solar power will continue to fall, until it becomes the cheapest form of power in a rapidly expanding number of national markets. Increasing technical advances lead to the best affordability of wind[103] and solar power.[104]

Recently, political and corporate leaders in the EU have realised that adaptation processes may require certain sacrifices in terms of economic gains. Moving toward a more integrated European energy policy, *A Framework Strategy for a Resilient Energy Union*, adopted in February 2015,[105] outlined a number of important areas of action. These include new legislation to redesign and overhaul the electricity market, ensuring more transparency in gas contracts, substantially developing regional co-operation, and increased EU funding for energy efficiency

[99] Circular Economy, see above n 5.

[100] Meadows et al. 1972.

[101] Ross 2013.

[102] Randall 2015).

[103] Neslen 2011.

[104] Norwood Norwood et al. 2014.

[105] European Commission 2015b.

or a new renewable energy package. Hopefully, the new legislation will focus on sun and wind energy. The EU has a great potential to avoid the energy mix that represents a concession to short term thinking that only sustains unsustainability, and to lead the way towards a true transformation toward the C2C and CE, in energy and production.

References

Adger WN, Dessai S, Goulden M, Hulme M, Lorenzoni I, Neslen DR, Naess LO, Wolf J, Wreford A (2009) Are there social limits to adaptation to climate change? Clim Change 93:335–354

Armand M, Tarascon JM (2008) Building better batteries. Nature 451(7179):652–657

Barthelmie RJ, Pryor SC (2014) Potential contribution of wind energy to climate change mitigation. Nat Clim Change 684–688

Bell D, Gray T, Haggett C (2005) The "social gap" in wind farm siting decisions: explanations and policy responses. Environ Politics 14(4):460–477

Blair N, Mehos M, Christensen C, Cameron C (2008) Modelling photovoltaic and concentrating solar power trough performance, cost, and financing with the solar advisor model. Solar 2008, American Solar Energy Society

Blanco MI, Rodrigues G (2009) Direct employment in the wind energy sector: An EU study. Energy Policy 37(8):2847–2857

Boyde M (2012) Concentrating solar power: prospects and challenges. Environmental Health Policy Institute. http://www.psr.org/environment-and-health/environmental-health-policy-institute/responses/concentrating-solar-power.html. Accessed 17 May 2016

Braun JF (2011) EU energy policy under the treaty of Lisbon rules: between a new policy and business as usual. EPIN working papers, p 14

Braungart M (2013) Cradle to cradle: transitioning from waste incineration to beneficial materials. http://catalystreview.net/2010/02/cradle-to-cradle-transitioning-from-waste-incineration-to-beneficial-materials/. Accessed 17 May 2016

Breidthardt A (2011) German govt wants nuclear exit by 2022 at latest. Reuters. http://uk.reuters.com/article/2011/05/30/us-germany-nuclear-idUKTRE74Q2P120110530. Accessed 17 May 2016

Breton SP, Moe G (2009) Status, plans and technologies for offshore wind turbines in Europe and North America. Renewable Energy 34(3):646–654

Cleary J, Kopicki A (2009) Preparing the workforce for a "green jobs" economy. John J. Heldrich Center for Workforce Development, Rutgers

Costa A, Crespo A, Navarro J, Lizcano G, Madsen H, Feitosa E (2008) A review on the young history of the wind power short-term prediction. Renew Sustain Energy Rev 12(6):1725–1744

Daly H (1991) Steady state economics. Island Press, Washington

Delucchi MA, Jacobson MZ (2011) Providing all global energy with wind, water, and solar power, Part I: technologies, energy resources, quantities and areas of infrastructure, and materials. Energy Policy 39:1154–1169

Diesendorf M (2014) Sustainable energy solutions for climate change. Earthscan, London

Divya KC, Østergaard J (2009) Battery energy storage technology for power systems—an overview. Electr Power Syst Res 79(4):511–520

European Commission (2015a) Circular Economy Strategy, April 2015. http://ec.europa.eu/smart-regulation/impact/planned_ia/docs/2015_env_065_env+_032_circular_economy_en.pdf. Accessed 17 May 2016

European Commission (2015b) Communication of 25 February 2015, Framework Strategy for a resilient energy union with a forward-looking climate change policy, COM (2015) 080 Final
Firestone J, Kempton W (2007) Public opinion about large offshore wind power: underlying factors. Energy Policy 35(3):1584–1598
Firestone J, Kempton W, Krueger A (2009) Public acceptance of offshore wind power projects in the USA. Wind Energy 12(2):183–202
González JS, Lacal-Arántegui R (2016) A review of regulatory framework for wind energy in European Union countries: current state and expected developments. Renew Sustain Energy Rev 56:588–602
Guarnieri M (2015) The rise of light. In: History of high-technologies and their socio-cultural contexts conference (HISTELCON), 2015 ICOHTEC/IEEE International, pp 1–14
IEA (International Energy Agency) (2015) FAQ: Renewable Energy. http://www.iea.org/aboutus/faqs/renewableenergy/. Accessed 13 June 2015
IPCC (2011) Special report on renewable energy sources and climate change mitigation. Prepared by Working Group III of the Intergovernmental Panel on Climate Change. Cambridge University Press, Cambridge, pp 1075
IPCC (2014) Climate Change 2014: Synthesis Report. http://www.ipcc.ch/report/ar5/syr/. Accessed 17 May 2016
Johnson K (2009) Is nuclear power renewable energy? Wall Street J, 21 May. http://blogs.wsj.com/environmentalcapital/2009/05/21/is-nuclear-power-renewable-energy/. Accessed 17 May 2016
Kaldellis JK, Zafirakis D (2011) The wind energy (r) evolution: a short review of a long history. Renew Energy 36(7):1887–1901
Knill C, Liefferink D (2012) The establishment of EU environmental policy. In: Jordan AJ, Adelle C (eds) Environmental policy in the European Union: contexts, actors and policy dynamics. Earthscan, London
Kopnina H, Blewitt J (2014) Sustainable business: key issues. Routledge, London
Kopnina H, Shoreman-Ouimet E (eds) (2015) Sustainability: key issues. Routledge, New York
Levy DL, Egan D (2003) A Neo-Gramscian approach to corporate political strategy: conflict and accommodation in the climate change negotiations. J Manage Stud 40(4):803–829
Lewis B (2015) EU on track for green energy goal but UK, Dutch lagging. http://uk.reuters.com/article/2015/02/17/eu-renewables-idUKL5N0VQ45R20150217. Accessed 17 May 2016
London J (2012) Of sunflowers and solar plants. https://slice.mit.edu/2012/02/01/of-sunflowers-and-solar-plants/. Accessed 17 May 2016
Manwell JF, McGowan JG, Rogers AL (2010) Wind energy explained: theory, design and application. Wiley, New York
McDonough W, Braungart M (2002) Cradle to cradle: remaking the way we make things. Farrar, Straus and Giroux, New York
Meadows DH, Meadows DL, Randers J, Behrens WW III (1972) The limits to growth. Universe Books, New York
Mendonça M (2009) Feed-in tariffs: accelerating the deployment of renewable energy. Routledge, New York
Michaelowa A (2000) The relative strength of economic interests in shaping EU climate policy: a hypothesis. Energy Environ 11(3):277–292
Nemet GF (2006) Beyond the learning curve: factors influencing cost reductions in photovoltaics. Energy Policy 34(17):3218–3232
Neslen A (2011) Dutch government ordered to cut carbon emissions in landmark ruling. http://www.theguardian.com/environment/2015/jun/24/dutch-government-ordered-cut-carbon-emissions-landmark-ruling. Accessed 17 May 2016
Norwood Z, Nyholm E, Otanicar T, Johnsson F (2014) A geospatial comparison of distributed solar heat and power in Europe and the US. Plos One. http://journals.plos.org/plosone/article?id=10.1371/journal.pone.0112442. Accessed 17 May 2016

Pais A (1982) Subtle is the lord: the science and the life of Albert Einstein. Oxford University Press, USA

Pfenninger S, Gauché P, Lilliestam J, Patt A (2014) Potential for concentrating solar power to provide baseload and dispatchable power. Nature Clim Change 689–692

Randall T (2015) The way humans get electricity is about to change forever. http://www.bloomberg.com/news/articles/2015-06-23/the-way-humans-get-electricity-is-about-to-change-forever. Accessed 17 May 2016

Rhodes CJ (2016) The 2015 Paris Climate Change Conference: Cop21. Sci Prog 99(1):97–104

Ross ML (2013) How the 1973 oil embargo saved the planet. Foreign Affairs. https://www.foreignaffairs.com/articles/north-america/2013-10-15/how-1973-oil-embargo-saved-planet. Accessed 17 May 2016

Sandstede G, Cairns EJ, Bagotsky VS, Wiesener K (2010) History of low temperature fuel cells. Handbook of Fuel Cells. Wiley, New York

Sathyajith M (2006) Wind energy: fundamentals, resource analysis and economics. Springer, Berlin https://www.dolcera.com/wiki/images/Wind_power_energy.pdf. Accessed 17 May 2016

Schelly C (2015) Frameworks for understanding and promoting solar energy technology development. Resources 4:55–69

Seyfang G, Park JJ, Smith A (2013) A thousand flowers blooming? An examination of community energy in the UK. Energy Policy 61:977–989

Steer A, Hanson C (2015) Biofuels are not a green alternative to fossil fuels. The Guardian. http://www.theguardian.com/environment/2015/jan/29/biofuels-are-not-the-green-alternative-to-fossil-fuels-they-are-sold-as. Accessed 17 May 2016

Teleke S, Barat M, Bhattacharya S, Huang A (2010) Optimal control of battery energy storage for wind farm dispatching. IEEE Trans Energy Convers 25(3):787–794

The Economist (2013) Wood: the fuel of the future. Environmental lunacy in Europe. http://www.economist.com/news/business/21575771-environmental-lunacy-europe-fuel-future. Accessed 17 May 2016

Van Renssen S (2016) Biofuels are back on the EU agenda. http://www.energypost.eu/biofuels-back-eu-agenda/. Accessed 17 May 2016

Visser M (2016) Don Quichot op de Katwijkse Boulevard. Master's thesis. Institute of Cultural Anthropology and Sociology, Leiden University

Walker SL (2012) Can the GB feed-in tariff deliver the expected 2% of electricity from renewable sources? Renew Energy 43:383–388

Walsh B (2014) Even advanced biofuels may not be so green. Time. http://time.com/70110/biofuels-advanced-environment-energy/. Accessed 17 May 2016

Wang U (2012) Report: 180 Solar Panel Makers Will Disappear By 2015. Forbes. http://www.forbes.com/sites/uciliawang/2012/10/16/report-180-solar-panel-makers-will-disappear-by-2015/. Accessed 17 May 2016

Washington H (2015) Demystifying sustainability: towards real solutions. Routledge, London

Chapter 11
European Framework Agreements at Company Level and the EU 2020 Strategy

Stefania Marassi

Abstract The European Union (EU) 2020 strategy is one of the current EU mainstream policies. Its aim is to boost Europe's competitiveness by focusing both on economic and employment policies. Particularly, the increase of the employment rate of the population aged 20–64 to 75% is one of the 5 EU headline targets. Several actors (e.g. social partners, civil society) are asked to give their contributions to the achievement of the EU 2020 strategy's goals. This chapter will look into European framework agreements at company level (EFAs) as potential contributors to the attainment of the employment-related objectives laid down by the EU 2020 strategy. As an emerging form of social self-regulation at European level, these agreements are the outcome of the negotiation process between multinational enterprises and workers' representatives (e.g. European trade union confederation, European industry federations, and European works councils). In particular, this chapter will examine the topics covered by the EFAs that have been concluded between the launch of the EU 2020 strategy (March 2010) and April 2015. In doing so, it will analyse whether the topics touched upon by the signatory parties of these agreements align with the EU 2020 strategy's employment-related objectives.

Keywords EU 2020 strategy · Social self-regulation at European level · European · Framework agreements at company level · EU 2020 strategy's flagships · Employability · Youth employment

S. Marassi (✉)
The Hague University of Applied Sciences, The Hague, The Netherlands
e-mail: S.Marassi@hhs.nl

J. de Zwaan et al. (eds.), *Governance and Security Issues of the European Union*, DOI 10.1007/978-94-6265-144-9_11

Contents

11.1 Introduction

Following the Lisbon strategy, in March 2010 the European Union (EU) 2020 strategy was launched in an effort to bring Europe back to the competitiveness necessary to endure in an increasingly globalised market, and to tackle the consequences of the economic crisis of 2008.

The "governance architecture"[1] laid down by this 10-year strategy plan can be said to contribute to the development of social governance at European level. In the EU 2020 strategy the European Commission has set three main priorities to focus on in the following 10 years: smart, sustainable and inclusive growth.[2] Social policies and their strong linkage with economic growth have received in-depth attention. In that respect the European Commission has outlined that "[t]he adoption of the EU 2020 strategy put social policy at the core of the EU economic strategy for the first time".[3] As a result, increasing the employment rate of those aged 20–64 is one of the five EU headline targets that follow from the three main priorities. In order to reach these targets, the European Commission has developed seven flagships containing action points to work on both at European and national level.[4]

The flagships deal with current diverse topics that range from tackling environmental issues (e.g. the use of renewable energy sources), to strengthening research and innovation in Europe and addressing industrial policy as well as promoting a digital agenda for Europe. Two of the seven flagships can be said to address issues that are directly linked with the employment policy field: Flagship 2 "Youth on the move" as representative of the smart growth priority and Flagship 6 "An agenda for new skills and jobs" as representative of the inclusive growth priority.

---

[1] Armstrong 2012, p. 287 (the author refers to the concept of "governance architecture" defined by Borrás and Radaelli).

[2] European Commission 2010a, p. 3.

[3] European Commission 2013, p. 2.

[4] European Commission 2010a, p. 5.

Now that the content of the EU 2020 strategy has been briefly outlined, the question still remains as to which actors participate in the realisation of its objectives. Even though the European Council remains the full owner of the EU 2020 strategy, the European Commission calls upon the effort and the contribution of social partners, stakeholders and civil society for the achievement of the objectives laid down therein.[5] Not only the European Commission but also the European Parliament has stressed the importance of these actors for the realisation of the strategy's goals.[6]

However, by looking in more detail at the flagships on employment and social policies, one can ascertain that civil society has not been explicitly called upon for the realisation of the EU 2020 strategy's objectives. Along the same lines, social partners have rarely been mentioned. For this reason, the exclusion of these actors, and more generally, social dialogue, from the core of the implementation of the EU 2020 strategy has been harshly criticised.[7] Little to no mention is made in Flagships 2 and 7 of the involvement of social partners in reducing the level of youth unemployment and poverty. More attention is paid to national and European social dialogue in Flagship 6, according to which "the Commission will work: […] To strengthen the capacity of social partners and make full use of the problem-solving potential of social dialogue at all levels (EU, national/regional, sectoral, company) […]".[8]

In spite of this, this chapter will take a closer look at whether the activity of civil society, which is said to include not only trade unions but also businesses,[9] can still be considered as a valuable tool for the success of the EU 2020 strategy. More specifically, this chapter will not explore the recognised forms of European collective bargaining as contributors of the EU 2020 strategy (European cross-border and sectoral agreements).[10] Rather, it will focus on a form of social dialogue at company level that is widespread both at European and international level,[11] namely transnational company agreements (hereinafter: TCAs).

These agreements are concluded between multinational enterprises and workers' representatives on a wide variety of topics and have been traditionally divided in two categories on the basis of their scope of application and signatory parties on the employees' side: international framework agreements (hereinafter: IFAs) and European framework agreements at company level (hereinafter: EFAs). Because of its link with one of the core European policies, this chapter will focus only on EFAs. Section 11.4 will provide an in-depth overview of these agreements and

---

5 European Commission 2010a, 4; See also Social Protection Committee 2011, p. 8.

6 European Parliament 2014, paras 8 and 50; See also European Commission 2016, p. 2.

7 Dukes 2014, p. 151; Schömann and Clauwaert 2011, p. 5; Conchon et al. 2011, p. 94.

8 European Commission 2010a, p. 18.

9 European Commission's website 'Europe 2020'. http://ec.europa.eu/europe2020/who-does-what/index_en.htm. Accessed 20 October 2015.

10 Conchon et al. 2011, pp. 87–89.

11 European Commission 2012b, p. 1; See also Senatori 2013, p. 87.

their development in the context of the process of Europeanization of industrial relations.

With this in mind, the chapter intends to examine whether the conclusion of EFAs aligns with, and can be considered as contributing to, the objectives underpinning the EU 2020 strategy in the employment policy field. Flagships 2 "Youth on the move" and 6 "An Agenda for new skills and jobs" will be used as benchmarks. In order to answer this question, the chapter is structured as follows. Section 11.2 will put the EU 2020 strategy into context by examining its link with the new economic governance framework. Section 11.3 will address in more detail this strategy and will delve into the content of Flagships 2 and 6. Section 11.4 will look at EFAs as a developing form of social self-regulation at European level. Section 11.5 will analyse the topics covered by the EFAs concluded between the launch of the EU 2020 strategy in March 2010 and April 2015[12] (e.g. if the agreements deal with issues covered by the strategy such as sustainable development, lifelong learning, etc.). It will then illustrate whether there is a correlation with the employment themes laid down in Flagships 2 and 6. Section 11.6 will draw the conclusions.

11.2 EU 2020 Strategy and New EU Economic Governance Framework

The EU 2020 strategy is "the European Union's ten-year jobs and growth strategy".[13] Its focus on employment and social policies is in line with one of the overall objectives of the EU as laid down in Article 3 of the Treaty on European Union (TEU).[14] According to Article 3(3) TEU, "aiming at full employment and social progress" shall be at the core of the EU's actions.[15] In addition, Article 9 TFEU underlines that raising the employment rate is one of the key factors that shall guide the definition and implementation of the EU's policies.[16]

---

[12] For the purpose of this chapter, the selection of EFAs has been made on the basis of the list of agreements in the European Commission's database on transnational company agreements. To date (1 April 2016), the database is updated in April 2015. For more information on the database, see European Commission 2015b.

[13] See European Commission's website "Europe 2020 in a nutshell". http://ec.europa.eu/europe2020/europe-2020-in-a-nutshell/index_en.htm. Accessed 24 September 2015.

[14] Consolidated Version of the Treaty on European Union, signed on 13 December 2007, OJ C 326 (entered into force on 1 December 2009) as amended on 26 October 2012 (TEU), Article 3; European Commission 2012a, p. 2.

[15] *Ibid.* Article 3.

[16] Consolidated Version of the Treaty on the Functioning of the European Union, signed on 13 December 2007, OJ C 326 (entered into force on 1 December 2009) as amended on 26 October 2012 (TFEU), Article 9; European Commission 2013, p. 2.

From the outset of the economic crisis, the EU has encountered difficulties realising this objective. The EU 2020 strategy attempts to tackle and respond to the social consequences stemming from the crisis. This policy document addresses the high level of unemployment faced by young people by making sure that this segment of the population can (re)gain a space and role in the current European labour market. Also, it intends to secure a more inclusive growth that focuses on the development of different sets of skills amongst the workforce.

The achievement of these goals goes hand in hand with economic growth. This is one of the most important realisations that arose from the economic crisis. Economic objectives can no longer be seen as disconnected from employment growth and social progress. As the European Commission noted in its Communication "Strengthening the social dimension of the economic and monetary union", social policy and economic governance are strictly interrelated.[17] Unemployment, social discontent, segmentation of, and disparities in, the labour market are strictly interrelated with economic growth and ultimately with the achievement of a better European economic integration. A recent statement of Valdis Dombrovskis, the Vice-President for the EU and Social Dialogue, underlines this point:

> While growth is picking up in the EU, there is still a very high number of people out of work and suffering hardship. This is more pronounced in those countries most affected by the crisis. Our response requires a combination of policies that strengthen the economy, while improving social conditions. We are reviewing the way economic policy is coordinated across the EU to better take into account social concerns, while fully involving social partners in shaping reforms. […][18]

The importance, or even the necessity, of integrating these policies led to the creation a strong link between the EU 2020 strategy and EU economic governance, more specifically the European Semester.[19] This yearly cycle of coordination and supervision of national economic and social policies was introduced in 2011 and represents one of the most important features of the new EU economic governance framework.

The inclusion of the EU 2020 strategy in the European Semester is evident throughout the annual cycle. First of all, as the European Commission points out, "[t]he goals of the Europe 2020 strategy […] feed into the choice of the priorities of the Annual Growth Survey",[20] which represents the first step of the annual cycle together with the draft Joint Employment Report, amongst other documents. By looking in more detail at the priorities set in the Annual Growth Surveys from 2011 to 2016, one can realise that these documents focus on the employment rate target laid down in the EU 2020 Strategy and the ways to reach it.

---

[17] European Commission 2013, p. 2.

[18] European Commission Press release 2015a.

[19] European Parliament 2015, para 69; On the role of the European Semester in the EU 2020 Strategy, see also Armstrong 2012, p. 290.

[20] European Commission 2014, p. 18.

In 2011, the first Annual Growth Survey stated its intention to "bring[s] together the different actions which are essential to strengthen the recovery in the short-term, to keep pace with our main competitors and prepare the EU to move towards its Europe 2020 objectives."[21] In an attempt to reach these objectives, this Annual Growth Survey put emphasis on the creation of new jobs as well as the flexibility of the labour market and at the same time the security workers look for in their jobs.

At the end of 2015, the most recent Annual Growth Survey corroborated these key priorities and confirmed the commitment already expressed by the President of the European Commission, Jean-Claude Juncker, to achieve job growth.[22] Specifically, this document highlighted once more the importance of integrating and aligning economic and employment and social policies. In defining the priorities for the next Annual Semester, it also considered the attainment of employment and social targets as key priorities for the EU and Members States. In doing so, it stressed the significant role social partners have in this process.[23] These actors have recently regained importance thanks to the commitment of the European Commission to strengthen social dialogue as a vehicle to boost the creation of new jobs and promote the development of skills and training.[24]

Next to the Annual Growth Surveys, the EU 2020 strategy's objectives play an important role in the later phases of the European Semester. The European Semester is also used as a tool to monitor the progress made by EU Member States towards, amongst other things, the accomplishment of the strategy's targets.[25] By way of example, in a recent Communication, the European Commission outlines that "[o]verall, Europe is on its way to meet part of the Europe 2020 strategy targets."[26] When it comes to the employment target set in the EU 2020 strategy (see Sect. 11.3), the unemployment level has decreased in many Member States. Nevertheless, the progress made is still not enough to ensure that this target will be met by 2020.[27]

To conclude, the integration of the EU 2020 strategy's objectives in the European Semester is in line with the repeated attention European institutions have paid towards the importance of boosting employment and social policies in order to address the consequences of the economic crisis.

---

[21] European Commission 2011, p. 3.

[22] In the Political Guidelines for the next European Commission, 15 July 2014, Jean-Claude Juncker, the President of the European Commission, included "A new boost for Jobs, Growth and Investment" as one of the 10 key priorities of the European Commission. See Political Guidelines for the next European Commission 2014.

[23] See European Commission 2015c, p. 4ff.

[24] European Commission Press release 2015b.

[25] See European Commission's website "Making it happen: the European Semester". http://ec.europa.eu/europe2020/making-it-happen/index_en.htm. Accessed 19 January 2016.

[26] European Commission 2016, p. 4.

[27] European Commission 2016, p. 4.

11.3 An Introduction to the EU 2020 Strategy

Following the Lisbon Strategy, the EU 2020 strategy intends to "turn the EU into a smart, sustainable and inclusive economy delivering high levels of employment, productivity and social cohesion."[28] In order to achieve these objectives, the European Commission has set 3 priorities (smart, sustainable and inclusive growth), 5 headline targets to be achieved by 2020 and 7 flagship initiatives which spell out how to accomplish these targets and ultimately foster the 3 core priorities.

Three headline targets and three flagships can be considered as falling directly or indirectly within the umbrella of employment and social policy. As to the headline targets, the EU 2020 strategy intends to set up measures that help to increase the employment rate of the population aged 20–64 from 69% to at least 75% as well as ensuring the better integration in the labour market of more vulnerable groups (e.g. women). Next to this, it sets a target on the dropout rates in education as well as on the percentage of the European population still living in poverty.[29]

In an effort to achieve these objectives, three flagships are put forward: Flagship 2, "Youth on the move"; Flagship 6, "An Agenda for new skills and jobs"; and Flagship 7 "European platform against poverty". Flagship 2 focuses on how to improve the situation of young people in Europe, from their education opportunities, to their vocational training and entry to the labour market. Flagships 6 and 7 intend to create a more inclusive labour market. More specifically, the first aims at securing a steady development of the necessary skills to enter and remain in the labour market and transfer from one job to another. The second addresses the reduction of the poverty level.

Two years after the launch of the EU 2020 strategy, the European Commission introduced an "Employment Package," 'a set of policy documents'[30] that aims at increasing economic growth whilst ensuring the participation of a diverse spectrum of people within the labour market. This includes more vulnerable groups such as women, the elderly and young people.[31] Out of the 7 flagships, the "Employment Package" addresses mainly Flagship 6 "An Agenda for new skills and jobs". Yet the European Commission has stressed that it "also helps to deliver, through better synergies, on flagship initiatives such as […] "Youth on the move".[32]

In March 2014, the European Commission took an important step in assessing the progress made towards the achievement of the goals laid down by the EU 2020 strategy. In the Communication "Taking stock of the Europe 2020 strategy for

---

28 European Commission 2010a, p. 3.

29 European Commission 2010a, pp. 3 and 5.

30 See European Commission's website "Employment package". http://ec.europa.eu/social/main.jsp?catId=1039&langId=en. Accessed 16 October 2015.

31 For the text of the "Employment Package" see European Commission 2012a.

32 European Commission 2012a, p. 3.

smart, sustainable and inclusive growth", the European institution pointed out that "the EU is on course to meet or come close to its targets on education, climate and energy but not on employment, research and development or on poverty reduction."[33] In fact, the prospective employment rate for 2020 is 71.8%, more than 3% points less than the goal set at 75%.[34] Against this background, the European Commission emphasised anew the importance of labour market policies that foresee the inclusive participation of more vulnerable groups as well as the crucial role of skills development through lifelong learning strategies.[35]

The publication of this Communication was followed by a public consultation held between May and October 2014. The results of the aforementioned consultation are laid down in the Communication "Results of the public consultation on the Europe 2020 strategy for smart, sustainable and inclusive growth". This document stresses what was already expressed by the March 2014 Communication, namely that the employment rate is still increasing at a very slow pace (68.4% in 2013).[36] These data are also confirmed by the latest Communication of the European Commission that was issued in March 2016 in the context of the European Semester. According to this document, 70.5% of the population aged 20–64 was working in the third quarter of 2015. However, in spite of the growing percentage, the 75% employment target will not likely be met by 2020.[37]

11.3.1 Flagship 2 "Youth on the Move"

Young people represent one of the categories of people that have been hit most harshly by the economic crisis. The EU28 unemployment rate of young people aged 15–24 was 15.6% in 2008 and it has dramatically increased in the years which followed, reaching a peak in 2013 (23.7%).[38] The situation has slightly improved since then, even though the percentage is still very high (20.4% in August 2015).[39]

Considering that the overall EU28 unemployment rate was 9.1% in November 2015,[40] one can immediately realise the challenges that young people face not only to enter the labour market but also to stay in it. In 2014, more than one out of

[33] European Commission 2014, p. 21.

[34] European Commission 2014, p. 4.

[35] European Commission 2014, p. 12.

[36] European Commission 2015a, p. 3.

[37] European Commission 2016, pp. 4 and 21.

[38] Eurostat 2016.

[39] European Commission 2015d.

[40] Eurostat 2015.

every two young people in Greece in Spain were unemployed. Croatia and Italy followed with unemployment rates of 45.5 and 42.7%, respectively. Germany and Austria were the EU Member States with the lowest percentage, 7.7 and 10.3%, respectively.[41] Moreover, even though less attention is paid to young people aged 24–29,[42] this group is also suffering from the consequences of the economic recession and an ever more segmented labour market.[43]

A number of initiatives have been undertaken to tackle this situation. In 2012, the European Commission adopted a Youth Employment Package that would help to deal with the problematic situation young people are facing. To that end, this package introduced a number of programmes, such as Youth Guarantee schemes to ensure smooth school-to-work transitions, a Quality Framework for Traineeships and the European Alliance for Apprenticeships.[44] As the European Commission pointed out, "youth employment is a priority for the European Union."[45]

In order to achieve the EU headline target of 75% of the population aged 20–64 employed by 2020, a well-developed strategy to tackle youth unemployment is required. In light of this, the European Commission has put forward flagship 2 "Youth on the Move". This initiative intends to contribute to the attainment of the first of the three priorities of the EU 2020 Strategy, a smart growth, namely "an economy based on knowledge and innovation."[46]

Within this flagship, the European Commission has identified four main lines of action.[47] The first three focus on the first step that can allow young people to enter the labour market. Thus they deal with early school leaving, support of high quality traineeship and of lifelong learning initiatives as well as participation in higher education and mobility across Europe. The fourth line of action addresses young people who are about to enter the labour market or are already working but their employment situation is unstable because of the types of jobs they were able to secure and the connected types of contracts.[48]

One of the objectives pursued by this flagship is to make sure that young people can more easily enter the labour market and stay in it. For this reason, it aims at

[41] Eurostat 2016.

[42] Chung et al. 2012, p. 303 (according to the authors, "in neglecting the labour market status of 25–34 years old, policies fail to take into account the fact that this age group is also affected by the increasing flexibilization of the labour market, further postponing their ability to obtain secure jobs").

[43] The EU28 unemployment rate of young people aged 25–29 was 13.6% in 2014. See Eurostat 2016.

[44] See European Commission's website "Youth employment: Commission proposes package of measures". http://ec.europa.eu/social/main.jsp?langId=en&catId=1036&newsId=1731&furtherNews=yesaccessed. 10 November 2015.

[45] European Commission 2015e.

[46] European Commission 2010a, p. 11.

[47] European Commission 2010b, pp. 4–5.

[48] European Commission 2010b, p. 5.

increasing the level of education and vocational training, enhancing labour mobility throughout Europe, for both study and working purposes, and tackling the segmentation of labour. Education, training and lifelong learning are the core action points in this flagship in order to enhance the employment situation of young people. These topics will be used to select and analyse the content of EFAs in sect. 11.5 of this chapter.

11.3.2 Flagship 6 "An Agenda for New Skills and Jobs"

The mismatch of skills and jobs available on the labour market was not a new topic when the EU 2020 strategy was launched in March 2010. This topic gained momentum as early as in 2008, when the European Commission recognised that the lack of skills suitable for a continually evolving labour market was one of the biggest challenges faced by the European workforce. This had consequences not only for people but also for the competitiveness and productivity of the economy. The deep economic crisis brought light to these weaknesses. As a result, in 2008 the European Commission issued the Communication "New Skills for New Jobs".[49]

This topic gained renewed attention in the EU 2020 strategy. Flagship 6 "An Agenda for new skills and jobs" is devoted to address diverse issues such as to how to make sure that the workforce is able to acquire the skills required to face an ever-changing labour market and hence remain employable in the long term. In order to reach this goal, the European Commission has set four key priorities: (1) better functioning labour markets; (2) more skilled workforce; (3) better job quality and working conditions; and (4) stronger policies to promote job creation and demand for labour.[50]

The first priority emphasises the importance of "flexicurity" policies as a tool to help the workforce adapt to an evolving labour market. Lifelong learning is one of the key aspects in this respect[51] as well as the focus on more vulnerable categories of people who often struggle to (re-) enter and/or remain in the labour market (e.g. young people, women and older people).

The second priority addresses in detail the challenges that the current European workforce faces when it comes to the lack of adequate skills for entering or even remaining employable in the labour market. This is particularly the case when organisational changes take place within a company. This action point focuses on how to provide people with the combination of skills, training, mobility and education that are necessary for their current and future professional career. Emphasis

---

[49] For more information, see European Commission 2008c.

[50] European Commission 2010c, pp. 2–3.

[51] European Commission 2010c, p. 4.

is also placed on the potential partnerships between companies and educational institutions for a better integration of young people in the labour market as soon as they leave school.

Finally, the third and fourth priorities deal with the improvement of working conditions, with particular attention given to health and safety standards and the introduction of measures aimed at supporting job creation (e.g. on a tax level).

In summary, a wide range of topics are then covered in this flagship: "flexicurity", lifelong learning, gender equality, anticipation and management of changes, vocational education and training, development of new skills throughout the working lifecycle, mobility, corporate social responsibility. These topics will be used as a framework to select and examine the number and content of EFAs concluded after the EU 2020 strategy was launched.

11.4 European Social Dialogue, Transnational Company Agreements and European Framework Agreements at Company Level

Only since the mid-1980s has the role of social partners started to gain importance in the European context. Enhancing social integration and harmonising some aspects of employment regulations were then considered as important steps to secure a deeper European integration.

Following the Val Duchesse high-level meetings in 1985, EU level social partners acquired a more important role in the realisation of the single European market.[52] The Social Chapter of the Maastricht Treaty incorporated the outcome of the Val Duchesse dialogue in Articles 3 and 4 of the Social Policy Agreement (now Articles 154 and 155 TFEU), which granted European social partners a prominent position in the decision-making process at European level.[53] In particular, these actors can now conclude EU-wide collective agreements that may then be implemented via Council Decision. A few cross-industry and sectoral agreements have followed this procedure leading to the adoption of European Directives,[54] whereas others have been implemented at national level.

Next to cross-industry and sectoral agreements, multinational corporations and workers' representatives have started concluding TCAs since 1988 at international level and 1996 at European level. Defined in scholarly writings as an emerging

[52] Barnard 2012, pp. 17ff.

[53] Articles 3 and 4 of the Social Policy Agreement (now Articles 154 and 155 TFEU).

[54] For some examples see the Council Directive 96/34/EC on parental leave, the Council Directive 97/81/EC on part-time work.

form of social dialogue,[55] the European Commission has described TCAs as follows:

> agreement(s) comprising reciprocal commitments the scope of which extends to the territory of several States and which has been concluded by one or more representatives of a company or a group of companies, on the one hand, and one or more workers' organisations, on the other hand, and which covers working and employment conditions and/or relations between employers and workers or their representatives.[56]

The rise of transnational collective bargaining at company level and in particular the conclusion of TCAs has been one of the characterising features of the European industrial relations landscape. Despite the fact that many legal issues around the conclusion of these agreements still remain unclear,[57] their number has sharply risen since 1988. The most recent data can be found in the database of the European Commission, which lists 282 TCAs until April 2015.[58]

As specified in the introductory section of this chapter, these agreements have been traditionally classified in two main categories according to their scope of application and signatory parties:[59] European framework agreements at company level (EFAs) and international framework agreements (IFAs). The latter have a global scope of application and have been concluded mainly[60] by global union federations and multinational enterprises. The former, on the contrary, have a European scope of application and have been concluded by multinational enterprises and European industry federations and/or European works councils (and sometimes (co-)signed by national unions). The European Commission has identified a third category of TCAs: mixed agreements, namely agreements with global scope of application but dealing with topics usually addressed in EFAs.[61]

If compared to IFAs, the range of topics dealt with by EFAs is much broader.[62] The focus of the latter is not only on topics such as gender equality and working hours, but also on the social consequences stemming from enterprises' restructuring and management and anticipation of changes.

The conclusion of these agreements can be said to contribute to the process of standardisation of certain employment conditions in all the establishments in which the multinational enterprise operates, be it at global level in the case of IFAs or at European level in the case of EFAs. The latter intend to foster and add to the

---

[55] Leonardi 2015, p. 41.

[56] European Commission 2008b, p. 3.

[57] Lo Faro 2012, p. 154.

[58] European Commission 2015b.

[59] Telljohann et al. 2009, p. 508.

[60] Hammer 2005, p. 523 (according to this scholar, the definition of IFAs has been extended to include also agreements concluded by GFUs [Global Union Federations] together with regional structures, such as EIFs [European Industry Federations]).

[61] European Commission 2008a, pp. 3–4.

[62] Marassi 2015, pp. 99–102.

process of Europeanisation of industrial relations[63] and European Economic integration. Within this broader setting, this chapter will focus on the conclusion of EFAs in the context of one of the EU mainstream policies, the EU 2020 strategy.

11.5 European Framework Agreements at Company Level: A Tool to Achieve the Objectives Underpinning the EU 2020 Strategy?

Even though the EU 2020 strategy does not make reference to TCAs, the European Commission does not seem to have overlooked the importance of these texts in the social governance arena. In the Staff Working Document "Transnational company agreements: realising the potential of social dialogue", it has emphasised the significance of this current development in the European industrial relations scenario. Also, it has underlined the link between TCAs and the EU 2020 strategy's objectives. In doing so, it has outlined that:

> [i]t is also clear that [TCAs] serve a useful purpose—to identify and implement feasible negotiated solutions tailored to the structure and circumstances of each company, particularly in the case of large restructuring processes. *This is consistent with the principles and objectives underpinning the Europe 2020 Strategy*. (emphasis added)[64]

Senatori has also pointed out the possible connection between the development of TCAs and the EU 2020 strategy. According to the scholar, "[i]increasing attention to TCB [transnational collective bargaining] and an active role of the EC in favouring its further development is advocated insofar as it is in line with European policies".[65]

The analysis of EFAs[66] concluded between March 2010 and April 2015 shows the link between TCAs and the EU 2020 strategy. Out of 44 EFAs, more than two

---

[63] Leonardi 2012, p. 5ff.

[64] European Commission 2012b, p. 7. Scholarly writings and the European Trade Union Confederation (ETUC) also refer to what said by the Commission in the Staff Working Document 'Transnational company agreements: realizing the potential of social dialogue, SWD (2012) 264 final. On this point, see, *e.g.*, Leonardi 2015, p. 41; Sciarra et al. 2014, p. 11.

[65] Senatori 2013, p. 95.

[66] For the purpose of this chapter, the following definition of EFAs has been used to identify these agreements: "EFAs are those agreements that: (a) are applicable in the EU/EEA, EU candidate countries and/or Switzerland; and (b) have been concluded between European industry federations (EIFs) and/or European Works Councils (EWCs) (or other forms of workers' participation) and/or national trade unions, on the employees' side, and the management of multinational enterprises, on the employer's side".

thirds of them (35 agreements)[67] were concluded on topics covered in the flagships "Youth on the move" and "An Agenda for new skills and jobs".

One EFA specifically deals with the position of young people in the labour market and their career development. The "European Framework Agreement for professional integration of young people" was concluded by Safran and IndustriALL in March 2013. This agreement does not only focus on the collaboration between the company and universities in the establishment of apprenticeships, traineeships and more in general vocational training at European level. Rather, it also takes a step forward by looking at how to integrate young people in the company and how to offer them the skills required to advance in their professional career.[68]

The majority of EFAs address themes covered in the flagship "Agenda for new skills and jobs". Four categories can be identified if one takes into consideration the four key priorities set by the European Commission in relation to flagship 6 and more generally, the text of the EU 2020 strategy: (1) lifelong learning, internal flexibility and gender equality as part of the first key priority on "flexicurity"; (2) vocational training, lifelong learning and skills development as part of anticipating and managing changes in a company or more broadly in the labour market (second key priority); (3) improvement of the quality of life at work with a specific emphasis on health and safety (third key priority); (4) corporate social responsibility. One must note that the topics of some of these agreements are intertwined. By way of example, lifelong learning has been considered as an important aspect in the development of one's skills next to an important feature of "flexicurity". As a result, some agreements can be regarded as falling into two or more of the outlined categories.

Approximately 10 EFAs deal with the issues covered in the first category. Some of them address gender equality in different stages of one's working life, for example recruitment, advancement to high-level positions but also professional training as a key element for career development.[69] On a similar note, job security and internal flexibility are the focus of other EFAs included in this category. These agreements have mainly been concluded to tackle the phenomenon of restructuring. In order to reduce the impact of these processes, the signatory parties have resorted to different mechanisms. The creation of internal flexibility mechanisms (e.g. flexible working arrangements) is one tool which has been used to reduce the number of redundancies. In this respect, the use of part-time work and leaves is very common amongst these agreements.[70]

---

[67] For the list of agreements, see Annex 1. Lafarge's "Declaration <well-being at work> Appendix to the Health, Safety & Security declaration of June 1st 2011" is not included in the number since it is an appendix to an EFA concluded in 2011 (Lafarge's Joint declaration concerning Health, Safety and Hygiene).

[68] The text of the agreement is available at: http://ec.europa.eu/employment_social/empl_portal/transnational_agreements/Safran_young_EN.pdf (accessed 15 February 2016).

[69] See Annex 1, e.g. Scor SE, 2015; Suez Environment, 2015; BNP Paribas, 2014; Groupama, 2013; GDF Suez 2012, Areva 2010.

[70] *Ibid.* e.g. Air France-KLM, 2013 (B); Air France-KLM, 2013 (C); Alstom, 2012; Air France-KLM, 2011; RWE, 2010.

The topic of employability (second category) has attracted a lot of attention from the signatory parties of EFAs. About 10 EFAs deal with how to ensure that employees are in a position to acquire the skills necessary in the labour market, and how they can more smoothly face phenomena such as downsizing and, more generally, organisational changes within a company. In particular, some agreements set down periodical interviews that employees will go through with the company's managers. This process will help both parties to identify the employees' future career developments and the steps they need to take in order to achieve where they want to be, professionally, in the future.[71] Both functional and geographical mobility is considered an important, if not essential, aspect in employees' career progression. For this purpose, in some EFAs companies agree to set up electronic systems in which employees can easily have access to vacancies within the company or, for example, in one of the companies belonging to the corporate group. This as a way to encourage internal and external mobility.[72] Finally, in an effort to anticipate the evolution of the labour market, two EFAs set out the possibility to map out the types of jobs available in the European market and engage in a study concerning their evolution.[73]

The improvement of the quality of life within the company (third category) is an important theme that is discussed by signatory parties of about seven EFAs.[74] These agreements focus on how to ensure a work-life balance and the implementation of company's policies on the broader issue of health and safety at work. Attention is also paid to situations of stress as well as harassment and violence at work.

Finally, five EFAs reiterate the company's commitment to corporate social responsibility (fourth category).[75] This category is often intertwined with previous ones since the signatory parties have often considered health and safety policies as part of the CSR's strategy of their company.

11.6 Conclusions

This chapter set out to explore whether the conclusion of EFAs between March 2010 and April 2015 aligns with the objectives underpinning the EU 2020 strategy. In doing so, it has brought to light that more than two thirds of the agreements concluded in this timeframe touch upon topics that are covered in the Flagships "Youth on the move" and "An Agenda for new skills and jobs".

---

[71] *Ibid.* e.g. Safran, 2015; BNP Paribas, 2012; Alstom, 2011, DBApparel, 2010.

[72] *Ibid.* e.g. BNP Paribas, 2012; Axa Assistance, 2011; Areva 2011, DBApparel 2010.

[73] *Ibid.* e.g. Axa Assistance, 2011; Axa Group, 2011.

[74] *Ibid.* e.g. GDF Suez, 2014; Air France-KLM, 2013 (A); Veolia, 2012; Rheinmetall, 2012; Lafarge, 2011; Allianz, 2011; Pinault Printemps Redoute, 2010.

[75] *Ibid.* e.g. Pernod Ricard, 2014; Michelin, 2014; Valeo, 2012; Santander, 2011, Etex, 2010. The latter deals with health and safety at work as part of the company CSR's policy.

Against this background, it has been established that all but one of the EFAs have addressed topics related to flagship 6 "An Agenda for new skills and jobs". Signatory parties have paid less attention to youth unemployment and the ways to better integrate young people in the labour market.

To conclude, it is difficult to assess whether the signatory parties have used the EU 2020 strategy as a reference document to set their own priorities and ultimately enter into negotiations for the conclusion of EFAs. This will require an insight into the strategies of multinational enterprises and workers' representatives as well as the driving factors that have led to the conclusion of these agreements. In spite of this, one can argue that the analysis of the content of the EFAs concluded between March 2010 and April 2015 shows an alignment with the employment-related themes and topics of one of the main European mainstream policies. In light of this finding, one may also contend that the realisation of the EU 2020 strategy's objectives relies not only on the work of European institutions and Members States but also on civil society in general. For this reason, its contribution to, and involvement in, the achievement of the strategy's targets should be promoted and, if necessary, formalised.

Acknowledgments The author would like to thank the research assistant Jessica den Outer for her valuable contribution and Gillian Kane for the linguistic review.

Annex 1

Multinational enterprise	EFA	Date	Main topic(S)[a]
Scor SE	European Charter on professional equality between women and men	2015	Gender equality, career development, professional training
Safran	European framework agreements for developing skills and career paths	2015	Anticipation of change, career development, development interviews, training, mobility
Suez Environment	Group agreement on gender equality in the workplace	2015	Gender equality, career development, professional training
Pernod Ricard	Pernod Ricard European agreement on CSR	2014	Respect for environment
Michelin	European framework agreement on social responsibility and sustainable development	2014	Respect for environment, competitiveness
BNP Paribas	European social charter on workplace equality	2014	Workplace equality

(continued)

(continued)

Multinational enterprise	EFA	Date	Main topic(S)[a]
Bayer	Joint declaration by Bayer AG's Board of Management and the Bayer European Forum	2014	Employability
GDF Suez	European agreement on improving quality of life at work	2014	Quality of life at work
Safran	European framework agreement for professional integration of young people	2013	Young people professional integration, vocational training
Air France-KLM	Social rights and ethics charter	2013 (A)	Working conditions (health and safety, working hours, equality)
Air France-KLM	Framework agreement regarding the outstations in Europe	2013 (B)	Restructuring (working arrangements, e.g. part-time and leave)
Air France-KLM	Framework agreement regarding the Air France KLM and Martinair Cargo Organisation in Europe	2013 (C)	Restructuring (working arrangements, e.g. part-time and leave)
Groupama	Joint declaration relative to quality of life at work	2013	Equality, non-discrimination
Alstom	European agreement on social commitments during the transition period of the Joint Venture between Alstom and Shanghai Electric	2012	Social commitments (e.g. relocation)
GDF Suez	European agreement on professional equality between men and women	2012	Equality between men and women
Allianz SE	Agreement on guidelines concerning Lifelong Learning	2012	Skills development, training, lifelong learning
Veolia	Letter of commitment from the General Human Resources Management and the members of the Bureau of Veolia Environnement's European Works Council	2012	Health and safety at work

(continued)

(continued)

Multinational enterprise	EFA	Date	Main topic(S)[a]
BNP Paribas	European social charter employment management	2012	Anticipation of change, career development
Valeo	Agreement on social responsibility	2012	Corporate social responsibility
Rheinmetall	Framework agreement on the management of health Rheinmetall Group	2012	Health and Safety
Alstom	Agreement on the anticipation of change or developments in Alstom	2011	Training, competence planning, career planning
Areva	Group Memorandum of Agreement on Professions and Competences Forecast and Management within the Areva Group in Europe	2011	Employability, training, mobility
Santander	Joint declaration of the European Works Council (EWC) and the Central Management of Santander Group regarding the labour relations framework for the provision of financial services	2011	Corporate social responsibility
Allianz	Agreement on guidelines concerning work-related stress	2011	Stress at work
Lafarge	Joint declaration concerning Health, Safety and Hygiene[b]	2011	Health and safety (in view also of anticipating of changes)
Axa Assistance	European agreement on anticipating changes within Axa Assistance	2011	Anticipation of change, employability mobility (external and internal), jobs mapping
Axa Group	European Agreement on anticipating changes within Axa Assistance	2011	Anticipation of change
Air France-KLM	Framework agreement regarding the Outstations in Europe	2011	Restructuring (working arrangements, e.g. part-time and leave)

(continued)

(continued)

Multinational enterprise	EFA	Date	Main topic(S)[a]
DBApparel	Anticipation task force	2010	Skills development, training, anticipation of changes
Pinault Printemps Redoute	Framework of commitments on quality of life at work and prevention of work-related stress for employees within the PPR group in Europe	2010	Health and safety
Etex	Health, safety and environment on the workplace charter	2010	Corporate social responsibility (health and safety)
Adam Opel AG	Agreement on European Restructuring ("Opel Plan for the Future")[c]	2010	Restructuring
Alstom (& Schneider Electric)	European agreement on social commitments in the framework of the take-over of Areva T&D	2010	Transfer, training
Areva	ODEO Open Dialogue through Equal Opportunities—Amendment of the agreement on equal opportunities within the Areva Group in Europe	2010	Equality of opportunity
RWE	Agreement on the application of minimum standards for restructuring in the RWE Group between the European works council and RWE AG while acting on behalf of the companies represented in the European Works Council	2010	Restructuring (flexible working conditions in order to try to secure job stability)

[a]The text of the agreements and the database of the European Commission on Transnational Company Agreements have been used to identify and analyse the topics of the EFAs
[b]The appendix to this Declaration was concluded in 2013. See Declaration "well-being at work". Appendix to the Health, Safety & Security declaration of June 1 2011
[c]The text of this EFA could not be retrieved. For more information on its content see Da Costa and Rehfeldt 2011, p. 159

References

Armstrong KA (2012) EU social policy and the governance architecture of Europe 2020. Transfer 18(3): 285–300
Barnard C (2012) EU employment law. Oxford University Press, Oxford
Chung H, Bekker S, Houwing H (2012) Young people and the post-recession labour markets in the context of the Europe 2020. Transfer 18(3):301–317
Conchon A, Clauwaert S, Jagodzinski R, Schömann I, Stollt M, Vandaele K, Vitols S (2011) Social dialogue and worker representation in EU2020: underappreciated and underplayed. In: Benchmarking working Europe 2011. ETUI aisbl, Brussels, pp 82–100
Da Costa I, Rehfeldt U (2011) Transnational restructuring agreements: general overview and specific evidence from the european automobile sector. In: Papadakis K (ed) Shaping global industrial relations—the impact of international framework agreements. Palgrave Macmillan, New York, pp 143–163
Dukes R (2014) The labour constitution: the enduring idea of labour law. Oxford University Press, Oxford
European Commission (2008a) Mapping of transnational texts negotiated at corporate level, EMPL F2 EP/bp 2008 (D) 14511
European Commission (2008b) Staff Working Document. The role of transnational company agreements in the context of increasing international integration. SEC (2008) 2155
European Commission (2008c) Communication of 16 December 2008, new skills for new jobs: Anticipating and matching labour market and skills needs, COM (2008) 868/3
European Commission (2010a) Communication of 3 March 2010, EUROPE 2020—a strategy for smart, sustainable and inclusive growth, COM (2010) 2020 final
European Commission (2010b) Communication of 15 September 2010, Youth on the move. An initiative to unleash the potential of young people to achieve smart, sustainable and inclusive growth in the European Union, COM (2010) 477 final
European Commission (2010c) Communication of 23 November 2010, An agenda for new skills and jobs: a European contribution towards full employment, COM (2010) 682final
European Commission (2011) Communication of 12 January 2011, Annual Growth Survey: advancing the EU's comprehensive response to the crisis, COM (2011) 11 final
European Commission (2012a) Communication of 18 April 2012, Towards a job-rich recovery, COM (2012) 173 final
European Commission (2012b) Staff Working Document, transnational company agreements: realising the potential of social dialogue, SWD (2012) 264 final
European Commission (2013) Communication of 2 October 2013, strengthening the social dimension of the Economic and Monetary Union, COM (2013) 690 final
European Commission (2014) Communication of 19 March 2014. Taking stock of the Europe 2020 Strategy for smart, sustainable and inclusive growth. COM (2014) 130 final/2
European Commission (2015a) Communication of 2 March 2015. Results of the public consultation on the Europe 2020 Strategy for smart, sustainable and inclusive growth. COM (2015) 100 final
European Commission (2015b) Database on transnational company agreements. http://ec.europa.eu/social/main.jsp?catId=978. Accessed 20 February 2016
European Commission (2015c) Communication of 26 November 2015, Annual Growth Survey 2016—strengthening the recovery and fostering convergence, COM (2015) 690 final
European Commission (2015d) European Semester Thematic Fiche Youth Employment (26 November 2015). http://ec.europa.eu/europe2020/pdf/themes/2015/youth_employment_20151126.pdf. Accessed 15 December 2015
European Commission (2015e) Fact Sheet: Addressing youth unemployment in the EU. http://ec.europa.eu/social/BlobServlet?docId=13422&langId=en. Accessed 25 Sept 2015
European Commission (2016) Communication of 8 March 2016, 2016 European Semester: Assessment of progress on structural reforms, prevention and correction of macroeconomic

imbalances, and results of in-depth reviews under Regulation (EU) No 1176/2011, COM (2016)95 final

European Commission Press Release (2015a) Commission discusses ways to strengthen EU Social Policy. 09 June 2015. http://europa.eu/rapid/press-release_IP-15-5132_en.htm. Accessed 15 January 2016

European Commission, Press Release (2015b) Social dialogue in Europe: together for a new start 04 March 2015. http://europa.eu/rapid/press-release_IP-15-4542_en.htm. Accessed 23 February 2016

European Parliament (2014) Resolution of 25 November 2014, employment and social aspects of the Europe 2020 Strategy, (2014/2779(RSP))

European Parliament (2015) Motion for a European Parliament Resolution of 5 March 2015, European Semester for economic policy coordination: Employment and social aspects in the Annual Growth Survey 2015, 2014/2222(INI)

Eurostat (2015) Unemployment rates, seasonally adjusted, November 2015. http://ec.europa.eu/eurostat/statistics-explained/index.php/File:Unemployment_rates,_seasonally_adjusted,_November_2015.png. Accessed 30 Dec 2015

Eurostat (2016) Youth unemployment by sex, age and educational attainment level [yth_empl_090] (Last update: 08-01-2016). http://appsso.eurostat.ec.europa.eu/nui/submitViewTableAction.do. Accessed 8 Jan 2016

Hammer N (2005) International framework agreements: global industrial relations between rights and bargaining. Transfer 11(4):511–530

Leonardi S (2012) Transnational company agreements: a stepping stone towards a real internationalization of industrial relations? In: EURACTA, European Action on Transnational Company Agreements: a stepping stone towards a real internationalisation of industrial relations? Final Report, IRES, pp 20–35. http://www.fondazionedivittorio.it/sites/default/files/content-attachment/02_2012_EUROACTA-1_0.pdf. Accessed 25 Sept 2015

Leonardi S (2015) Transnational company agreements: the empirical findings of the EURACTA 2 project. In: EURACTA 2, the transnational company agreements: experiences and prospects. Final Report, IRES, pp 40–69. http://www.fondazionedivittorio.it/sites/default/files/content-attachment/Euracta2_Final%20report_0.pdf. Accessed 20 Sept 2015

Lo Faro A (2012) Bargaining in the shadow of "optional frameworks"? The rise of transnational collective agreements and EU law. Eur J Ind Relat 18(2):255–270

Marassi M (2015) Globalization and Transnational Collective Labour Relations: International and European Framework Agreements at Company Level (Blanpain R, ed). Kluwer Law International, Alphen aan den Rijn

Political Guidelines for the next European Commission (2014) A new start for Europe: my agenda for jobs, growth, fairness and democratic change. https://ec.europa.eu/priorities/sites/beta-political/files/juncker-political-guidelines_en.pdf. Accessed 1 Feb 2016

Schömann I, Clauwaert S (2011) European social dialogue and transnational framework agreements as a response to the crisis? ETUI report

Sciarra S, Fuchs M, Sobczak A (2014) Towards a legal framework for transnational company agreements. Report to the European Trade Union Confederation. https://www.etucorg/sites/www.etuc.org/files/publication/files/brochure_transnational_company_en_low.pdf. Accessed 2 Sept 2015

Senatori I (2013) Transnational company bargaining and the discourse of the European Commission: A critical overview. In: Ales E, Senatori I (eds) The transnational dimension of labour relations. G. Giappichelli Editore, Torino, pp 87–109

Social Protection Committee (2011) The social dimension of the EU 2020 Strategy. Report. http://ec.europa.eu/social/BlobServlet?docId=6895&langId=en. Accessed 13 Nov 2015

Telljohann V et al (2009) European and international framework agreements: new tools of transnational industrial relations. Transfer 15(3–4):505–525

Part IV
European Criminal Law

Chapter 12
A Balanced Package: Fighting Money Laundering with the 4th European Directive

Peter Steenwijk

Abstract Money laundering and its underlying criminal activities pose a serious threat to the countries of the European Union (EU). Before the end of 2017 member states will have to turn the 4th new Anti-Money Laundering (AML) directive into national law. This chapter analyses the expected impact of the new legal framework on the prevention and combat of money laundering within the EU. As might have been expected the new directive does not provide governments with a magic bullet to take money launderers out of business. This chapter argues that a number of relevant issues (such as overregulation, compliance costs, privacy protection, and facilitation of financial institutions and other stakeholders) that seriously limit the effectivity of its predecessor, the third AML-directive, have not been fully remedied in the new directive. Despite its shortcomings the new framework does introduce an important element that may greatly contribute to the improvement of the effectivity of AML-policies; the mandatory application of the risk-based approach. This allows governments to calibrate policies and resources according to the related risk profile. An effective implanted risk-based approach can have a profound impact on both the costs and the results of anti-money laundering policies. As there is as yet not a blueprint for a national money laundering risk model this chapter concludes (Fig. 12.1) with the outline of a flexible, anti-money laundering control framework that can be used by national authorities to map, manage and evaluate their money laundering risks in accordance with the requirements of the 4th AML-directive.

Keywords Money laundering · Terrorist financing · Organised crime · European Union · European law · Behavioural economics

P. Steenwijk (✉)
The Hague University of Applied Sciences, The Hague, The Netherlands
e-mail: p.j.w.steenwijk@hhs.nl

J. de Zwaan et al. (eds.), *Governance and Security Issues of the European Union*, DOI 10.1007/978-94-6265-144-9_12

Contents

12.1 Introduction

Organised crime needs money laundering just like any living organism need oxygen. The fact that criminals are able to launder their dirty money is the main driver behind all kinds of criminal activity.[1] Money laundering and its unruly cousin, terrorist financing, present a serious and complex threat to society at large. It is a driver of all kinds serious crimes like drug trafficking, counterfeiting, slavery, fraud and corruption. Although there are only rough estimates available, the amounts involved seem to be staggering. The United Nations (UN) estimate that the total organised crime income could be over 3 trillion dollars per year.[2] Almost half of that amount, 1.4 trillion dollars, of dirty money is being laundered.[3] The International Monetary Fund (IMF) assesses that between 2 and 5 per cent of global GNP is being laundered every year.[4] This humongous volume of dirty money has serious economic side effects. It discourages foreign investment, distorts prices and economic statistics.[5] Because it induces criminals to invest in sectors that are easily accessible, but not necessarily productive, it has a negative influence on economic growth and corrupts financial institutions and other professions.[6]

The potential harm of money laundering exceeds the sheer numerical amounts involved. Money Laundering is especially relevant for the European Union (EU), as the internal market offers criminals no borders and allows for free movement of goods, capital and people. If we apply the above mentioned rule of thumb of the IMF, the volume of laundered money within the borders of the EU could be somewhere in the range of 338 billion euro. To put it in perspective, this corresponds roughly with the size of the GNP of member state Sweden.[7]

---

[1] Bear 2012, p. 259.

[2] UNODC 2011, p. 7.

[3] *Ibid.*

[4] Camdessus 1998.

[5] UNODC 2005, p. 1.

[6] UNODC 2011, p. 11.

[7] Eurostat 2015.

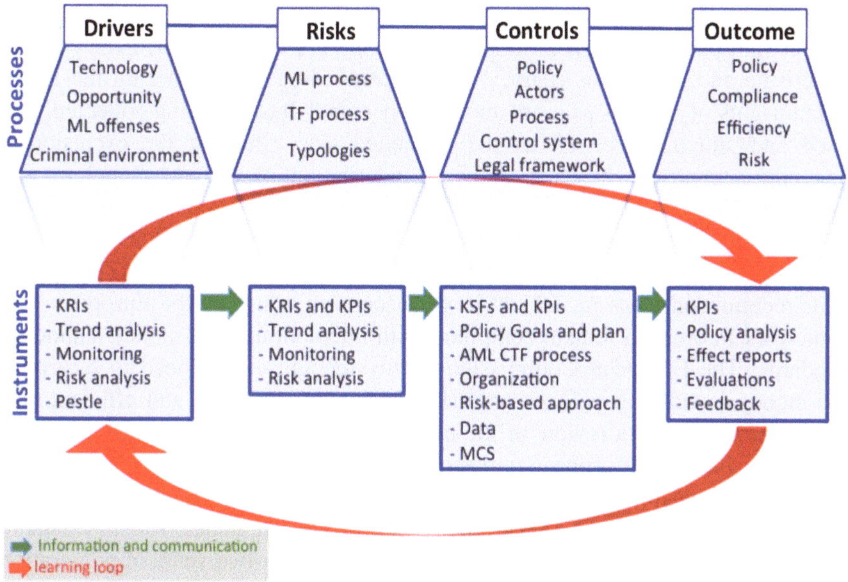

Fig. 12.1 Money laundering risk and control framework. Abbreviation: *ML* money laundering; *TF* terrorist financing; *KRI* key risk indicators; *KPI* key performance indicators; *KSF* key risk indicators; *AML CTF* anti-money laundering and terrorist financing; *MCS* management control system

As money laundering is indeed a serious economic problem that jeopardises the integrity of financial institutions, Europe has found itself struggling since the 1990s to formulate an appropriate answer to the ingenuity of especially organised crime in their efforts to launder their ill-gotten revenues. It has since then invested a great deal to combat money laundering and its related crime, terrorist financing.[8] However, generally speaking, the results are rather poor.[9] This chapter argues that the relative ineffectiveness of the European battle against money laundering can at least partly be explained by the apparent failure to implement a proper risk-based approach, which allows institutions to channel their efforts according to the areas with the highest risk of money laundering. Although the risk-based approach was introduced by the Directive 2005/60/EC of the European Parliament and of the Council and Commission of 26 October 2005 on the prevention of the use of the financial system for the purpose of money laundering and terrorist financing (Third Anti-Money Laundering [AML] Directive) in most member states, the

[8] European Commission 2013.

[9] UNODC 2011, p. 7.

overall approach was one based on compliance.[10] Other detrimental effects of the present European approach to money laundering are: the costs involved for both the private and the public sector,[11] the concerns about the impact on the fundamental rights of citizens as more and more personal data are being collected, analysed and stored,[12] as well as the unwanted side effect of the exclusion of developing countries whose anti money laundering policies are not compliant with the European standards.[13]

Since 1991 the EU has issued three successive directives to address the threat of money laundering. Following the Financial Action Task Forces' (FATF) revision to its recommendations in 2012,[14] it was necessary to update the European legal framework in order to remain compliant with international anti-money laundering standards. The European Commission keenly recognised the need to reform its anti-money laundering policies to make them more effective and efficient. The Commission ordered a review of the present policies and subsequently presented the outline of a new European anti-money laundering directive. In its review the Commission recognised the need to improve the effectiveness and flexibility of the mechanisms that are in place to fight money laundering and terrorism financing within the borders of the Union.[15] In January 2015, after two years of preparation, the European Council and its co-legislator the European Parliament agreed on the text of the new (fourth) AML Directive[16] and a new Wire Transfer Regulation.[17] After endorsement by the full European Parliament, the member states have a two-year window to transpose the new European legislation into their national laws at the latest by May 2017.

This chapter explores the expected impact and the overall effectivity of the European AML policies after its implementation in 2017. As of writing, it is yet unclear how the fourth AML Directive will be implemented by the member states. Therefore, this chapter uses an ex-ante analysis in order to assess to what extent

---

[10] Pellegrina and Mascandiaro 2008, p. 5; See also Takats 2007; Deloitte 2011, p. 5; Directive 2005/60/EC of the European Parliament and of the Council and Commission of 26 October 2005 on the prevention of the use of the financial system for the purpose of money laundering and terrorist financing, L 309/15 (Third AML Directive).

[11] European Commission 2013, p. 42.

[12] European Parliament 2014, pp. 6–7; See also Wesseling 2013, pp. 123–127.

[13] The Economist 2014.

[14] FATF 2012.

[15] European Commission 2012.

[16] Directive 2015/849 of the European Parliament and of the Council of 20 May 2015 on the prevention of the use of the financial system for the purposes of money laundering or terrorist financing, amending Regulation (EU) No 648/2012 of the European Parliament and of the Council, and repealing Directive 2005/60/EC of the European Parliament and of the Council and Commission Directive 2006/70/EC, L 141/73 (Fourth AML Directive).

[17] Regulation (EU) 2015/847 of the European Parliament and of the Council of 20 May 2015 on information accompanying transfers of funds and repealing regulation (EC) No 1781/2006, L 141/1 (Wire Transfer Regulation 2015/8347).

the known issues and bottlenecks of the present Third European AML framework will be effectively addressed by the new directive in terms of effectivity.

As money laundering is an economically significant crime, governments take a great effort and spend a lot of resources to enforce anti-money laundering policies. Notwithstanding, the results are, generally speaking, rather poor. Presently an estimated meagre 0.2 per cent of global criminal money is being intercepted on a yearly basis.[18] Traditionally policy makers and law enforcement officials approach effectiveness from a rather limited, strictly legal, perspective.[19] With the expanding scope and requirements of anti-money laundering legislation and rising compliance costs for the private sector, it is necessary to look into other aspects as well. We will, therefore, distinguish between three aspects of anti-money laundering effectiveness: law, policy, and economy. The first aspect concerns the effectiveness of the way member states transpose and facilitate the requirements of European legislation. Policy effectiveness looks into the actual results of AML and its effect on money laundering, terrorist financing and their predicate crimes. It also takes into account the unwanted side effects of the present legislation. Lately there is growing concern about the impact of AML regulations on the fundamental rights of the EU citizens and data protection. The strict regulation of AML also stimulates risk avoiding behaviour, or de-risking, by financial institutions that may lead to the exclusion from the international financial system of certain groups and countries, mainly in the developing world, that cannot abide by European and international standards.[20]

The economic dimension relates to the proportionality of costs and benefits. The EU spends approximately about two billion euros on anti-money laundering enforcement.[21] It is a legitimate question to ask if this money is well spent. Measuring and calibrating the effectiveness pose a real challenge for member states. Although required to disclose by European laws, there is little to none substantial information about the relative success of national anti-money laundering enforcement.[22] A major obstacle is the lack of relevant data. The success rate of anti-money laundering enforcement is mostly measured by the number of reported suspicious transaction reports. Research indicates that the validity of suspicious transactions action reports as a reliable indicator for money laundering activities is highly questionable.[23]

In order to improve effectiveness, the fourth AML Directive requires member states to design risk-based regulatory frameworks.[24] The risk-based approach cali-

[18] UNODC 2011, p. 7.

[19] Pellegrina and Mascandiaro 2008, p. 5.

[20] The Economist 2014; See also European Parliament 2014, p. 7.

[21] Unger et al. 2014, p. 235.

[22] Eurostat 2010, pp. 15–21.

[23] Pellegrina and Mascandiaro 2008, p. 9; See more on reporting and inefficiency in Takats 2007, p. 6.

[24] Fourth AML Directive, above n. 16, Articles 7–8.

brates policies and resources according to the related risk profile. High-risk situations and sectors call for more resources and attention of the authorities in order to generate better results. Consequently, low-risk situations will get less attention and allocation of resources than high-risk ones. The risk-based approach is not a new phenomenon in European anti-money laundering regulation. It is an element of the third AML Directive but was never fully and consistently implemented by most member states.[25]

This chapter will look into the expected overall effectivity of the fourth AML Directive by analysing the degree to which known gaps, white spots and imperfections of the third AML Directive have been properly fixed by the new regulation. Effectivity includes the extent to which financial institutions and other obliged organisations are being accommodated and facilitated to be able to operate in a way that is compliant with the new directive.

This chapter approaches anti-money laundering from a risk and control perspective and uses the concepts of risk governance and process management. It will focus on the challenges of national authorities to control and measure the outcome of their efforts to prevent and combat money laundering, terrorist financing and its predicate crimes. AML-activities are part of complex production chains and require the smooth co-operation between different (semi) public and private organisations, as well as the transfer of information across a range of organisations. The principal-agent framework will be used to analyse the dynamics and interaction between the different parties of the main mechanism. A money-laundering control framework (Fig. 12.1) will be introduced as a flexible model that can be used by public authorities when implementing a risk-based anti-money laundering approach in order to combat money laundering effectively.

12.2 The European Approach to Money Laundering

Money laundering can be defined as a money transfer with the explicit intention to disguise the illegitimate origin of the funds involved. Money launderers deliberately manipulate the financial system concealing the source of their wealth in order to make it look legal. In the case of terrorism financing, the ultimate goal of the transfers is to camouflage the final purpose of the funds. Both manifestations of money laundering share the same characteristics of being illicit and harmful to society, as they facilitate crime and are instrumental in enabling criminals to enjoy the fruits of their ill-gotten revenues.

Money laundering is a serious economic crime. It is the prime motivator behind all kinds of transnational organised crime such as bribery, prostitution, illegal gambling, slavery and intellectual property piracy. According to the United Nations Office on Drugs and Crime the total amount of organised crime

[25] European Commission 2012, p. 8.

worldwide could be over 3 trillion dollars per year.[26] Fighting money laundering is particularly important for the EU. The liberalised internal market, with its freedom of capital movements and the relatively unrestricted supply of financial services, offers interesting opportunities for money launderers. Illicit flows of money pose a serious threat for both the Union's internal market and its financial system. Since 1991 the EU has issued three directives that closely follow the international standards as formulated by the FATF and are supplemented by other international norms such as the UN Conventions of Vienna against Illicit Traffic in Narcotic Drugs and Psychotropic Substances in 1988 and of Palermo against Transnational Organised Crime in 2000.[27] The European approach is considered to be the strictest regional legislation. It has been transposed in and added to the national legislation of all 28 member states.

The Third present AML Directive dates back to 2005 and aims primarily at the *prevention* of money laundering and terrorism financing.[28] The prohibition of money laundering in Article 1 of the Directive covers different kinds of conduct in relation to the conversion, concealment, or possession of property, while knowing that the property in question has been derived from serious criminal activity. It also forbids the facilitation and counselling of such activities. Serious crimes include fraud, organised crime, terrorism, corruption and drugs trafficking. Intention to launder can be derived from objective, factual circumstances and, therefore, is not required to be proven beyond a reasonable doubt.

In essence the directive imposes certain precautionary measures on financial institutions and other professions (lawyers, traders in goods, notaries, auditors etc.) to prevent money launders and other criminals to manipulate the financial system and channel illicit funds in order to make it look legitimate. Obliged entities need therefore to apply customer due diligence, maintain a solid system of internal controls including proper document management. Suspicious, or unusual, transactions and other relevant information concerning money laundering, associated predicate offences or terrorist financing are to be reported to the national financial intelligence unit. These units are responsible for the analysis and dissemination of money anti-laundering related information.

A key feature of the 2005 Third AML Directive and its corresponding regulation is the explicit requirement for member states to change their approach from rule- to risk-based. Until then, obliged entities used a static set of rules, regardless

[26] UNODC 2011, p. 7.

[27] United Nations Convention Against Illicit Traffic In Narcotic Drugs And Psychotropic Substances, opened for signature on 20 December 1988, UN Treaty Series, vol. 1582, No. 27627 (entered into force 11 November 1990); United Nations Convention against Transnational Organised Crime, opened for signature on 12–15 December 2000, UN Treaty Series, vol. 2225, No. 39574 (entered into force on 29 September 2003).

[28] Directive 2005/60/EC of the European Parliament and of the Council and Commission of 26 October 2005 on the prevention of the use of the financial system for the purpose of money laundering and terrorist financing, L 309/15 (Third Money Laundering Directive), Article 21.

of the context or specifics, to determine whether an activity or transaction should be identified as money laundering. With a complete knowledge of current regulations money launderers were able to comply with those specified rules and make illegal transactions look legitimate. Consequently, the rule-based approached resulted in an overflow of reports of suspicious transactions, with little impact on actual money laundering activities. A risk-based approach is more flexible and allows obliged entities calibrate their resources and measures to those areas where the risk of money laundering is the greatest. It gives focus to anti-money laundering activities and should result in more pinpointed and high quality reporting information.[29]

With the adoption of the Third AML Directive and the introduction of the risk-based approach the responsibility for the implementation of policies shifted from the effect as it was coined by Elodpublic to the private sector. Henceforth private stakeholders had to estimate risks and take proportionate measures. This changed the dynamics between the government and its private stakeholders, as anti-money laundering was to be modelled along the lines of a public-private co-operation. In some countries (e.g. the UK) an essential part of public authority was effectively transferred to the private sector. Other countries like Sweden opted for a more traditional model and retained the dominant position of the government.[30] Irrespective of the actual way the risk-based approach was implemented, the new borderlines between public and private spheres impacted the extent to which the government was in control of its policies. As authority was being delegated to the private sector, the government had to rethink its position and contemplate new mechanisms to control the private agents, in order to remain publicly accountable for the outcome of its policies. These particular issues of public control as a result of the shifting responsibilities can be analysed using the classic principal-agent theory. The principal (*i.e.* the government) needs to motivate the private institutions to show the appropriate behaviour and prevent money laundering. To get assurance about their performance it has delegated the monitoring of their behaviour to a third party, the regulator. Research suggests that the agency-problem creates an incentive for obliged entities to produce large quantities of mainly useless suspicious money laundering reports. This so-called *crying wolf* effect as it was coined by Elod Takats is the consequence of the reporting entities' zealousness to show their regulator that they are compliant.[31] Another stimulus for extensive, non-relevant reporting is the excessive fines that regulators give to entities in case they fail to detect money laundering activities. This stimulates a better- safe-than-sorry attitude and contributes to over-reporting.[32]

[29] Takats 2007, pp. 7–9.

[30] Bergstrom and Svedberg 2011, p. 10.

[31] Takats 2007, p. 15.

[32] Pellegrina and Macandiaro 2008, pp. 7–9.

12.3 Effective Anti-money Laundering Policy

Money laundering is a complex international and dynamic phenomenon. Money launderers are searching for new and innovative ways to clean their dirty money all the time. They take advantage of the global market place and the rise of new financial products and payment methods. Most of the time they are one step ahead of law enforcement, policymakers and regulators. Given the dynamics and hazardous impact on the financial system, it is necessary to have a clear understanding of new money laundering techniques and to measure, analyse and adjust the effectiveness of the current policies on a regular basis.

We assume that effective anti-money laundering policies cover three different aspects: 1. Effectiveness of policies; 2. legal effectiveness and 3. Economic effectiveness.

1. Policy effectiveness is an indicator of the relative success of in reaching the desired outcome, that is either to prevent or to combat money laundering and terrorism financing, or the underlying, predicate crime, that feeds money laundering.
2. Legal effectiveness gives an indication about the effectiveness of the integration and enforcement of the European and international legal elements within a member state's own legal structure. It also relates to the extent to which the execution of those laws and regulations are actually being facilitated within a national context.
3. Economic effectiveness looks into the relation between the costs and the outcome. The third directive is very costly especially for financial institutions. The exact amount is hard to determine as the costs are part of a larger regulatory package, the Financial Services Action Plan (FSAP). The third Directive is a component of the FASP. Total costs involved in the prevention of money laundering are estimated to be more than 2 billion euro's on a yearly basis.[33] Customer due diligence, transaction monitoring, reporting and the retention of massive data are indeed very costly and labour intensive, especially for smaller institutions.[34] A Deloitte survey of the Luxemburg financial industry indicates that about 11% of all bank staff works on compliance.[35]

The sheer amount justifies the question whether this is money well spent. Therefore, it is necessary to have a clear understanding and insight in the costs and benefits of anti-money laundering. Essentially it is about the proportionality between the outcome of anti-money laundering and the corresponding costs. A cost and benefit analysis also looks into the unwanted effects of anti-money laundering, such as the impact on the privacy of customers and the exclusion of bona

[33] Unger et al. 2014, p. 235.

[34] KPMG 2014, pp. 13–17.

[35] Deloitte 2009, p. 15.

fide consumers, businesses and even countries. In order to balance these different objectives both the FATF principles and the European laws put emphasis on the proper use of the risk-based approach as a necessary condition for a successful anti-money laundering policy.

The available research suggests that anti-money laundering outcome is, generally speaking, meagre at best. The introduction of the Third AML Directive induced a rise in the number of suspicious transaction reports, but the impact on money laundering and predicate crime seems to be limited. Measuring, comparing and benchmarking anti-money laundering outcome is very complicated.[36] The third AML Directive pursued minimal harmonisation between member states. This resulted in diverging standards and definitions which make it difficult to compare the anti-money laundering performance within the EU. As there is limited insight in the actual workings of money laundering mechanisms and the impact on the financial system, it is difficult to establish a valid relation between implemented policy and its effect on crime and money laundering. An additional complication is the lack of significant performance data as effectiveness is mostly measured in by the number of reports, convictions, investigations, etc. This administrative output does not necessarily reflect the actual impact on money laundering or the underlying crime. An increase in suspicious transaction reports may be an indicator of increased laundering activities but could have a number of different causes e.g. increased supervisory activities, changes in the legal framework, or simply a cry wolf effect.

Article 33 of the Third AML directive requires member states to look periodically into the effectiveness of their anti-money laundering systems in order to establish whether their systems provide an adequate answer to their national money laundering risks. Most countries, however, give sparse information about the effectiveness of their anti-money laundering systems. Cost-benefit analyses of anti-money laundering have as yet to be carried out and is being qualified by Eurostat as "*terra incognita*".[37]

12.4 Towards a New European AML Directive

After the financial action taskforce evaluated and revised its international standards on combatting money laundering and the financing of terrorism in 2012, the European Commission decided to prepare a revision of the EU legal framework. Deloitte was commissioned with the task to examine the effectiveness of the present directive and identify areas of improvement.[38] Based on the findings of the

---

[36] Unger et al. 2014, pp. 187–205.

[37] Eurostat 2010, p. 9.

[38] Deloitte 2011.

Deloitte study the commission concluded that overall, the third AML Directive seemed to be functioning properly, without any fundamental flaws or defects. Nonetheless it was clear that measures needed to be taken to improve the effectiveness, and a more consistent application by the member states, of the directive. In order to realise this, the European Commission formulated a number of clarifications and improvements. They included the enlarging of the scope of the directive and adopting stricter requirements for the application of the risk-based approach, reporting, customer due diligence and cross border supervision. A number of key technical definitions were clarified and the legal privilege exemption of legal professionals to report suspicious transactions was to be severely curtailed.[39]

The European Commission floated its conclusions and the proposed modifications to its public and private anti-money laundering stakeholders and requested feedback. A total of 77 public and private parties responded positively to the Commissions' request. The European Banking Federation, probably the most important private stakeholder for money laundering detection, formulated three main areas of concern: 1. Alignment with international legislation; 2. sufficient support of the public authorities in order to be able to comply with the directive and 3. Clear commitment to contain administrative rigmarole and operational costs.[40]

International alignment alludes to conformity of the new Directive with the revised international recommendations but also looks into conformity with extraterritorial legislation, such as the United Kingdom Bribery Act and United States Foreign Account Tax Compliant Act. The federation made it clear that the private sector needs more and substantial support from the authorities to be able to comply with the legal framework. The lack of reliable and complete databases makes it costly and time consuming to identify and verify the identity of political exposed persons and ultimate beneficial owners. It therefore suggested that authorities facilitate access to public databases with up-to-date information on political exposed persons and ultimate beneficially owners. In order to identify the ultimate beneficially owner within complex legal constructions it is mandatory that the new directive includes a clear and practical definition of control. Banks would also appreciate timely feedback from the financial intelligence units after reporting suspicious transactions or activities, and the availability of relevant (generic and individual) statistical information. Adequate information enables banks to follow trends and developments concerning money laundering and terrorist financing. The enhancement and broader scope of the risk-based approach is being appreciated but needs to be applied in a flexible way that allows for sector specific differentiation.

Extending the scope of the directive to tax crimes and lowering the threshold for mandatory application of customer due diligence in case of occasional cash transactions induce extra costs and is, therefore, unnecessary. The third country

[39] European Commission 2013, pp. 21–26.

[40] European Banking Federation 2012, p. 5.

equivalence list that identifies non-EU countries with acceptable anti-money laundering frameworks should be maintained as it is an important instrument to reduce compliance costs. Countries with weak regimes should be put on a binding black list. It is also advisable to indicate clearly the different, supervisory responsibilities when dealing with cross-border transactions.[41]

12.5 The Fourth AML Directive, a Balanced Package?

After considering the feedback from stakeholders and the trialogue discussions with the European Parliament, the final text of the Fourth AML Directive was endorsed by the parliament and the European Council in May 2015.[42] In the final stages of the negotiations, the European Parliament and Council agreed to include in the new directive the obligation of member states to keep central registers with information on the ultimate beneficial owner of trusts and other legal entities. The Parliament also succeeded to include several provisions in the text meant to protect personal data. Parliament and council also agreed on a draft "transfer of funds" regulation that will facilitate an improved traceability of payers and payees of money transfers.

In the introduction to the final text of the new directive the commission indicates that the new directive and regulation are a balanced package that create a regulatory environment that will protect the stability and integrity of the Union's financial system, without incurring disproportionate costs for companies.[43] The new directive allows for a more flexible and risk-based approach and ensures a more coordination and coherence within the Union. The modifications will mostly align the European approach with the 2012 revision of the international anti-money laundering recommendations of the FATF. A number of alterations such as the inclusion of gambling services, lower thresholds for cash transactions and the introduction of national registers, even surpass the requirements of that regulatory framework. The new regulation on the traceability transfer of funds, however, does not fully cover the requirements of its seventh recommendation on wire transfers.

The major innovation is unmistakeably the central positioning of the risk-based approach. A truly flexible and risk-based approach is crucial for effective and economic anti-money laundering policy. The new directive allows more clearly for adjusting measures commensurate to the risk that is involved. A strong point is the consistent and encompassing approach of risk between the national authorities, obliged entities and supervisors. All three parties will have to make proper risk assessments and formulate control measures.

[41] *Ibid.*

[42] Fourth AML Directive, above n. 16.

[43] Position Paper of the Council 2015.

It is not quite clear how much room there will be for companies and authorities to calibrate measures to actual risk. It is possible to exempt small entities with low risk from the obligations of the directive. Given the extensive and detailed procedures that need to be followed it is doubtful whether it is a feasible option. This also applies to the option to use less strict customer due diligence in certain low-risk situations. As the combined European Supervisory Authorities will develop guidelines and technical specifications for risk assessment and control it is quite likely that the available room for independent, tailor-made risk-based anti-money laundering policies in the financial sector will be very limited. The strict compliance oriented approach of the fourth AML Directive stimulates a tick-the-box mentality. If simplified due diligence is only allowed in very strictly defined circumstances it is likely that companies will continue to apply the regular due diligence activities. Just to be on the safe side and to prevent from being penalised by their supervisory authority. The new risk approach may also be not fully prepared for the challenges of new, web-based payment methods, as it qualifies situations without face-to-face in principle as risky.

The feedback report indicates quite clearly that private stakeholders need more assistance, clarification and instruments in order to comply with the anti-money laundering regulations.[44] The new directive facilitates them in a number of ways. Ambiguous definitions and the coverage of certain categories (political exposed persons, ultimate beneficial owners, etc.) have been enhanced. The directive contains a more operational definition of control and defines the responsibility in case of cross-border transactions. A true milestone in terms of private facilitation is the last-minute inclusion—against the initial opposition of the Commission, and countries like Germany and the Netherlands—of a mandatory register with information on ultimate beneficially owners.

A number of other clearly articulated suggested improvements, such as a register with political exposed persons and an authorised list of European identification documents to be used for transnational transactions, did not make it in the final version of the directive. Using third party information is essential in containing screening costs in a global market place. Notwithstanding the third country equivalence list was axed in the new directive. Third party reliance is still possible under the explicit condition that the receiving party is ultimately responsible for compliance with the directive. As the directive quite clearly discourages the use of third-party information, it will induce entities to behave more risk averse. In the end this will contribute to the exclusions of institutions and banks mainly in the third world that are not able to comply with the strict demands of the European framework. European financial institutions will continue to reconsider the business relationship with corresponding banks in underdeveloped countries. This will effectively cut them off from the global financial system.

The Commission missed a golden opportunity to tighten the feedback obligations of financial intelligence units. Entities need to get proper feedback on their

[44] *Ibid.*

(suspicious) transaction reports, as it will allow them to adjust their procedures to new money laundering trends. Generally speaking they are too often complacent when it comes to informing their stakeholders.[45] Obliged entities are formally required to report "promptly" to the national unit, which, however, is under no obligation to inform the reporting entity on the relevance, or follow-up of their report.

The European Parliament successfully advocated a stricter approach towards the protection of personal data. The directive contains several references to the charter of fundamental rights of the EU. It is not quite clear if these assurances go beyond mere lip service to the principle of data protection. Obliged entities will have to retain huge data packages with customer due diligence information for a period up to ten years. Proper management of this data, in line with European law, will be an as yet unanswered challenge.

The major question, however, is whether the new directive will indeed substantially contribute to a more effective and efficacious approach to prevent and combat money laundering. The private sector is thoroughly aware of the necessity to prevent money laundering. Sanctions in case of non-compliance are severe and long-term damage to the reputation of transgressors. Notwithstanding the clear improvements a number of relevant bottlenecks (e.g. compliance of sanctions, identification of complex ownership structures, screening of political exposed persons, monitoring of cross-border wire transfers etc.) still have to be taken care of. Overall the new directive reflects a more compliance-oriented approach. The scope and the prescriptive character of the framework have been enhanced, with less attention for the intricacies of the day-to-day challenges of obliged entities. The new focus on a risk-based approach creates opportunities in terms of more result driven and cost conscious policies. These advantages may well be neutralised by the stronger emphasis on compliance. The cost impact of the new directive is unclear. The commission optimistically states that the benefits will always compensate for the related costs. However it is not able to substantiate its statement.[46] Given the extended scope and the limited opportunities for simplified customer due diligence and third party reliance, it is most likely that compliance costs will continue to rise.

All in all, it is unclear and uncertain what kind of impact the new directive will have on both the efficacy and the efficiency of the European anti-money laundering policies. In its impact analysis, the commission concluded that the policy as well as the cost effects are hard to estimate.[47] This includes the impact in terms on fundamental rights and the financial inclusion of institutions in the developing world. The uncertainty of the outcome makes it all the more necessary that results after the implementation of the new directive in 2017 should be closely monitored. Member states will be required to collect meaningful statistical data and assure

---

[45] European Banking Federation 2012, p. 4; See more in Deloitte 2011, p. 8.

[46] European Commission 2013, pp. 2–11.

[47] *Ibid.*

that effective systems are in place. Given the poor track record of most member states in this respect it goes without saying that more stringent regulation would have been appropriate.

12.6 Solutions for a National Risk-Based Money Laundering Approach

Article 7 of the Fourth AML Directive requires member states to take appropriate steps to identify, assess, understand and mitigate the risks of money laundering and terrorist financing.[48] A properly applied risk-based approach, as required by the directive, will positively influence the effectiveness and efficiency of national anti-money laundering-policies, as well as the prevention of the predicate crimes of money laundering. However, as yet there is no consistent approach available to implement the risk-based approach on the national level. The money laundering risk and control framework (MLRCF) as shown in Fig. 12.1 is a flexible concept that contains the key principles and process steps for the implementation and execution of a risk-based anti-money laundering policy, as prescribed by the 4th directive, by the national authorities of a member state. The upper part of the framework contains the overall risk and control process and its sub-processes. Within the model a successful and effective, risk-based anti-money laundering approach is the result of a process that consists out of 4 different process steps or sub-processes.

Step 1 Drivers: identifies relevant developments and phenomena (drivers) that may potentially develop into money laundering risks. It is crucial that these developments are closely monitored and regularly analysed, as they may signal new, emerging money laundering risks. They may also provide useful insight in the deeper (root) causes of existing risks by scanning a country's external environment, including relevant international economic, technological developments, and criminal trends.

Step 2 Risks: identifies, the actual money laundering risk factors. After rating and ranking they will be used to build a national risk money laundering profile. The actual risk exposure can be compared to the desired (risk appetite) or acceptable (risk tolerance) risk levels as per established policy or international commitment. The difference between actual and aspirational risk level will be taken into account in the next step when risk mitigating strategies are discussed.

Step 3 Controls: formulates and selects the appropriate risk strategies (to accept, mitigate, transfer or terminate the risk) and control measures. Controls are measures should fit both the identified risks and the prior determined goals. Mostly the implicit and explicit policies of choice will evolve around the formulated priorities between money laundering proper, or less predicate crime.

[48] Fourth AML Directive, above n. 16.

Step 4 Outcome: In the final step the actual outcome (for example: less inflow of criminal capital, more legal compliance, reduction of predicate crime, better cost-benefit ratio's or a combination of these elements) of the anti-money laundering approach will be analysed and compared to the policy objectives. The comparison between actual and planned can be used to calibrate and adjust policies.

The lower part of Fig. 12.1 contains the framework that supports the actual money laundering risk and control process and fills the model with relevant risk data, transaction reports, analyses, variables, etc. Each element on the lower part is linked to and supports a corresponding step of the money laundering risk and control process on top. An integrated information exchange and communication process (indicated by the red arrows) secure coherence and coordination within the overall process and between the actors (financial institutions, judicial, law enforcement, supervisors etc.) that co-operate in the execution of the process. Proper exchange of information, registration and follow-up of deviations and unforeseen changes constitutes a continuous learning loop (green arrows) between actors and process steps.

The framework (Fig. 12.1) embodies a flexible and easy-view overall approach to managing money laundering risk on a national level. It can be customised to fit specific national requirements and conditions. It provides public authorities with practical risk management process with key principles and a common language that can be used by all national actors, e.g. for planning and reporting that are involved in the battle against money laundering. By filling the, lower part, of the model with the appropriate data member states will be better equipped to manage money laundering risks across organisations and have a firmer grip and better insight in the results and effects of their anti-money laundering strategies. It will also allow member states to weigh more carefully the overall (side) effects (costs, impact on predicate crime, privacy issues, compliance costs, financial exclusion etc.) of their policies in relation to the adopted policy objectives.

The implementation of the fourth AML Directive offers a unique opportunity for member EU states to kill two birds with one stone. They can combine the mandatory implementation of the new legislation with a fundamental reorientation towards a more and risk and control-oriented approach to the prevention and combat of money laundering. The money laundering risk and control framework could be an interesting solution to combine compliance with a true risk-based approach.

References

Bear M (ed) (2012) Encyclopedia of transnational crime and justice. Sage Publications, Thousand Oaks

Bergstrom M, Svedberg H (2011) A new role for non-profit actors? The case of anti-money laundering and risk management. J Money Laundering Control 14/4

Camdessus M (1998) Speech to the Financial Action Task Force. https://www.imf.org/external/np/speeches/1998/021098.htm. Accessed June 15

Deloitte (2009) Report on Compliance Costs. http://www.ebf-fbe.eu/uploads/D1106A%2D2012%20%2D%20Deloitte%20Report%20cost%20of%20compliance%20%2D%20Luxembourg%202009.pdf. Accessed 15 June 2016

Deloitte (2011) Final Study on the Application of the Anti-Money Laundering Directive. http://ec.europa.eu/internal_market/company/docs/.../20110124_study_amld_en.pdf. Accessed 15 June 2016

Economist (The) (2014) International banking, poor correspondents. www.economist.com/news/finance-and-economics/21604183-big-banks-are-cutting-customers-and-retreating-markets-fear. Accessed 15 June 2016

European Banking Federation (2012) EBF position on the Report from the European Commission to the European Parliament and the Council on the Application of Directive 2005/60/Ec on the Prevention of the Use of the Financial System for the Purpose of Money Laundering and Terrorist Financing. D1027C-2012

European Commission (2012) Report from the Commission to the European Parliament and the Council on the Application of Directive 2005/60/EC on the Prevention of the Use of the Financial System for the Purpose of Money Laundering and Terrorist Financing, COM (2012), p 168

European Commission (2013) Commission Staff Working Document Impact Assessment (SWD 2013) http://ec.europa.eu/justice/civil/files/swd_2013_144_en.pdf. Accessed 15 June 2016

European Parliament (2014) Evaluation of EU Measures to Combat Terrorism Financing, in-depth analysis for the LIBE Committee. http://www.europarl.europa.eu/RegData/etudes/note/join/2014/509978/IPOL-LIBE_NT%282014%29509978_EN.pdf. Accessed 15 June 2016

Eurostat (2010) Money laundering in Europe, ISSN 1979-0375. http://ec.europa.eu/eurostat/en/web/products-statistical-working-papers/-/KS-RA-10-003. Accessed 15 June 2016

Eurostat Statistics Explained: File GDP at Current Market Prices, 2003–04 and 2012–14 YB15.png. http://ec.europa.eu/eurostat/statistics-explained/index.php?title=File:GDP_at_current_market_prices,_2003—04_and_2012—14_YB15.png&oldid=237562. Accessed September 2015

Financial Action Taskforce (FATF) (2012) The FATF Recommendations. International Standards on Combatting Money Laundering and the Financing of Terrorism and Proliferation

KPMG Risk Consulting (2014) Global Anti-Money Laundering Survey. https://www.kpmg.com/KY/en/.../global-anti-money-laundering-survey-v3.pdf. Accessed 15 June 2016

Pellegrina da L, Mascandiaro D (2008) The Risk Based Approach in the New European Anti-Money Laundering Legislation: A Law and Economics Review. Universita Commerciale Luigi Bocconi. Paolo Baffi Centre Research Papers, p 22

Position of the Council (2015) First Reading With a View to the Adoption of a Directive of the European Parliament and of the Council on the Prevention of the Use of the Financial System for the Purposes of Money Laundering or Terrorist Financing, amending Regulation (EU) No 648/2012 of the European Parliament and of the Council, and repealing Directive 2005/60/EC of the European Parliament and of the Council and Commission Directive (2015). Interinstitutional File 2013/0025 (COD). 5933/15

Takats E (2007) A theory of "crying wolf": the economics of money laundering enforcement. International Monetary Fund D.C. Working Paper No. 81

Unger B, Ferwerda J, van den Broek M, Deleanu I (2014) The economic and legal effectiveness of the European Union's anti money laundering policy. Edward Elgar Publishing Limited, Cheltenham

United Nations Office on Drugs and Crime (UNODC) (2005) Model Legislation on money laundering and terrorist financing. https://www.unodc.org/unodc/en/money-laundering/Model-Legislation.html. Accessed 15 June 2016

United Nations Office on Drugs and Crime (UNODC) (2011) Estimating illicit financial flows resulting from drug trafficking and other transnational organised crimes. https://www.unodc.org/documents/data%2Dand%2Danalysis/Studies/Illicit_financial_flows_2011_web.pdf. Accessed 15 June 2016

Wesseling M (2013) The European fight against terrorism financing. http://essay.utwente.nl/66704/1/Bachelor%20Thesis%20Inca%20Bloemkolk%20%28s0145807%29.pdf. Accessed 15 June 2016

Chapter 13
Harmonising Criminal Laws and EU's Significant Bankers: First Use of Article 83(2) TFEU, Rights of the Accused and Learning Organisations

Ernst E. van Bemmelen van Gent

Abstract This chapter critically reviews the harmonisation of national criminal laws pertaining to bankers active in the 100-plus significant supervised banks of the European bank union ("Significant Bankers"). It discusses the tension between administrative sanctions as mentioned in the Market Abuse Directive (596/2014) and the criminal sanctions as mentioned in Criminal Sanction Directive (2014/57). The chapter is limited in scope and deals with insider trading and market manipulation as international financial crimes only. It is not argued that harmonisation of criminal laws should not take place on the basis of Article 86(2) TFEU. However, it is argued that compliance by Significant Bankers with these substantive rules will not increase, if and when both sanction arrangements are actively made applicable on them. Reasons for that assertion are certain of their rights in criminal procedure, including the legal concepts of *ne bis in idem* (double jeopardy) and *nemo tenetur* (self-incrimination). The argument is also based on the regulatory science's and organisational science's insight that "learning organisations" improve their performance when mistakes are discussed and reviewed and subsequently transformed to innovations and changed behaviour. Hence the argument to restrict the regulatory arrangement around Significant Bankers to the administrative sanctions, and to instruct public prosecutors not to take action against Significant Bankers on the basis of national laws implementing the Criminal Sanction Directive (2014/17).

Keywords Regulation · Administrative sanctions · Criminal sanctions · Learning organisations · Double jeopardy · Self-incrimination

---

E.E. van Bemmelen van Gent (✉)
The Hague University of Applied Sciences, The Hague, The Netherlands;
Utrecht University, Utrecht, The Netherlands
e-mail: ernst@vanbemmelenvangent.com

J. de Zwaan et al. (eds.), *Governance and Security Issues of the European Union*, DOI 10.1007/978-94-6265-144-9_13

Contents

13.1 Introduction

The (European) economy at large and individual households depend on the functioning of financial institutions like banks and insurers,[1] and especially on those banks that are classified as significant European supervised entities,[2] that is the 100-plus banks that manage 80%-plus of all the savings and financial assets of all European citizens and businesses. This chapter looks at, and limits itself to, those banks and the behaviour of the bankers working in them (hereinafter referred to as Significant Banks or Significant Bankers respectively). Intensified since the financial crisis,[3] and given this dependency and vulnerability for international financial crime, the financial services provided by these Significant Banks are subject to an extensive European Union (EU) based regulatory arrangement.[4] Among others, the Market Abuse Regulation 596/2014[5] provides for substantive rules which are

[1] OECD Report for G20 Leaders 2013.

[2] Regulation 468/2014 of 16 April 2014 of the European Bank Establishing the Framework for Cooperation within the Single Supervisory Mechanism between the European Central Bank and the National Competent Authorities and with National Designated Authorities, OJ L 141, p. 1 (SSM Framework Regulation), Article 49(1).

[3] Buckley 2011, p. 12; Wymeersch et al. 2012, p. 9.

[4] See among others the preambles of the various EU legislative instruments pertaining to the financial market, such as EU Regulation 596/2014. See below n. 6.

[5] Regulation 596/2014 of The European Parliament and of the Council of 16 April 2014 on Market Abuse Repealing Directive 2003/6/EC of the European Parliament and of the Council and Commission Directives 2003/124/EC, 2003/125/EC and 2004/72/EC, OJ L 173/1 (Market Abuse Regulation).

enforced through a European System of Financial Supervision (ESFS), which include three European Supervisory Authorities (ESAs) in collaboration with national competent authorities (NCAs).[6] The substantive rules of the Market Abuse Regulation 596/2014 can be summarised as forbidding the abuse of markets through, among others, insider trading and market manipulation. The enforcement mechanism includes permanent reporting obligations and investigations by the ESAs, which include the London-based European Bank Authority (EBA) and the Paris-based European Securities and Markets Authority (ESMA), as well as the NCAs including the national Central Banks and Financial Services Authorities.[7] When infringements are proven, sanctions can be imposed like fines in the amount of EUR 5 million for individual Significant Bankers or prohibition on the exercise of professional activity ("revocation of work licences"). This regulatory arrangement is regarded as having administrative character within legal scholarship and regulatory science,[8] in which Significant Bankers are labelled as regulatees.

In 2014, in an effort to increase the effectiveness of this regulatory arrangement the EU issued the Criminal Sanction Directive 2014/57 providing for the possibility of criminal sanctions against regulatees, on top of the existing administrative sanctions already in place, to be imposed by 28 national criminal law systems.[9] The criminal sanctions are fines and imprisonment up to four years. Technically, this directive is based on a new competence of the EU enshrined in Article 83(2) TFEU, allowing the EU to harmonise the criminal laws of the member states.[10] This Directive has to be implemented by the 3rd of July 2016. As a consequence, the regulatees will not only have to deal with the aforementioned ESAs and NCAs,[11] but also with national criminal law enforcers, like public prosecutors.[12] The involvement of national public prosecutors in the compliance by Significant Banks, the potential criminal sanctioning of Significant Bankers in light of the overall aim to counter white-collar crime[13] and compliance with aforementioned substantive rules, form the main issues tackled in this chapter.

---

[6] See Cappiello 2015, p. 1.

[7] In The Netherlands "De Nederlandse Bank" (DNB) and "Autoriteit Financiele Markten" (AFM) respectively.

[8] See below Sect. 13.3.

[9] Directive 2014/57/EU of the European Parliament and of the Council of 16 April 2014 on Criminal Sanctions for Market Abuse, OJ L 173/179 (Market Abuse Directive).

[10] Consolidated Version of the Treaty on the Functioning of the European Union, signed on 13 December 2007, OJ C 326 (entered into force on 1 December 2009) as amended on 26 October 2012 (TFEU), Article 83(2).

[11] See above n. 7.

[12] In The Netherlands the "Openbaar Ministerie" (OM).

[13] See, among others, van Erp et al. 2015, p. 14.

Pertaining to these main issues and to the Significant Bankers, this chapter will discuss whether the double layer enforcement, that is both administrative and criminal, is putting the effectiveness of the applicable regulatory arrangement at risk. In other words, it is analysed whether this double layer enforcement negatively affects the willingness of Significant Bankers to contribute to internal mechanisms fostering compliance with the substantive rules. It is argued that the answer to this question is negative. Pertaining to Significant Banks and Significant Bankers, as defined in this chapter, criminal law as an ultimate remedy can hardly be seen as the preferred tool for the EU to foster compliance with substantive rules on insider trading and market manipulation. The criminal procedure to enforce the criminal sanctions is less effective because of the rights of the accused, including among others are the concepts of *ne bis in idem* (double jeopardy) and *nemo tenetur* (self-incrimination). Furthermore, it is argued that regulatees and their compliance departments should be stimulated to operate as learning organisation. Consequently, it is argued that the EU should refrain from further harmonisation of the criminal laws of the member states ex Article 83(2) TFEU in similar regulatory arrangements where an extensive and constant regulatory arrangement is in place as is the case regarding Significant Banks and Significant Bankers.

This chapter continues first with an overview of the aforementioned legal instruments, and the substantive and enforcement aspects of insider trading and market manipulation (Sect. 13.2). The scholarly frameworks used to answer the issue in this chapter are discussed in the subsequent section (Sect. 13.3). The chapter closes with a critical analysis of the issue in this chapter (Sect. 13.4). Lastly, this chapter concludes with some recommendations for the future (Sect. 13.5). The issue tackled in this chapter including the critical analysis and recommendations are relevant for the European legislators, and others that deal with the design of the governance of the financial market.

13.2 The Criminal Sanction Directive 2014/57 in Light of the Market Abuse Regulation 596/2014

This section reviews the background of the Criminal Sanction Directive 2014/57[14] and discusses the competence of the EU[15] to harmonise criminal laws of the Member States on the basis of Article 83(2) TFEU in light of the substantive rules of the Market Abuse Regulation 596/2014.[16] The competence laid down in Article 83(2) TFEU has a long history that is closely connected to the integration process of the European Union.[17] It is currently a pinnacle moment in that integra-

[14] Market Abuse Directive, above n 9.

[15] Miglietti 2014, p. 6.

[16] Market Abuse Regulation, above n. 5.

[17] Vervaele et al. 2014, p. 40.

tion, characterised by debates on the general role of the EU in respect of the state-like function of criminal law.[18] It is the expectation that further developments will follow, to which this chapter aims to contribute.

13.2.1 Preliminary Development

The involvement of the EU with regards to criminal law has two main aspects: first, the criminal law response to wrongful acts within the EU as an organisation; and second, the involvement of the EU with the criminal law of the Member States as support to the realisation of a functioning internal market.

As an organisation, the EU deals with internal budgets and with budgets of the Member States to achieve certain goals through subsidies. To monitor the proper use and react to misuse of these funds, the EU (then European Communities) established task forces like the Anti-Fraud Coordination Unit (UCLAF), which later transformed to the current European Anti-Fraud Office (OLAF, *Office Européen de Lutte Antifraude*),[19] and concluded a convention,[20] among others. This will not be discussed in this chapter.

The other aspect is the competence to be involved in the criminal law of the Member States. This competence was an aim since 1999,[21] and subject to fierce debates.[22] Ultimately, it evolved from rulings from the European Court of Justice. These rulings were based on the initial design of the then "third pillar" of the EU through which framework decisions on criminal law could be developed.[23] The leading case in this respect is Case C-176/03,[24] based on a dispute between the Council (who wished to harmonise criminal sanctions in the area of environmental law through the third pillar) and the Commission (who wished to do the same in the "first pillar"). The Court observed that the functioning of the European Communities should not be undermined by initiatives in the "third pillar," and that

[18] Vervaele 2013a, p. 540.

[19] Regulation (EC) No 1073/1999 of the European Parliament and of the Council of 25 May 1999 Concerning Investigations Conducted by the European Anti-Fraud Office, OJ L 136, 31.5.1999, pp. 1–7, 1999 as amended (OLAF).

[20] Council Act of 26 July 1995 Drawing up the Convention on the Protection of the European Communities' Financial Interests, OJ C 316 (27 November 1995) pp. 48–57.

[21] EU Council of the European Union, Presidency Conclusions—Tampere European Council, 15 and 16 October 1999. http://www.europarl.europa.eu/summits/tam_en.htm conclusion 48. Accessed 29 January 2015.

[22] Bianco 2015, p. 228; Luchtman and Vervaele 2014, p. 201.

[23] Council Framework Decision 2003/80/JHA of 27 January 2003 on the Protection of the Environment through Criminal Law, OJ L 29, 5.2.2003, pp. 55–58, 2003.

[24] EU European Court of Justice, Commission versus Council Case C-176/03, Judgment of the Court (Grand Chamber), 13 September 2005, European Reports of Cases 2005 I-07879-ECLI:EU:C:2005:542.

an annex-competence in the "first pillar" exists to harmonise the criminal law of the Member States when that is functional to the substantive policy ensuring effective enforcement:

ECJ C-176/03: 48. However, the last-mentioned finding [that the Community lacks competence in the area of criminal law, EvB] does not prevent the Community legislature, when the application of effective, proportionate and dissuasive criminal penalties by the competent national authorities is an ***essential measure for*** *combating serious environmental offences, from taking measures which relate to the criminal law of the Member States which it considers* ***necessary*** *in order to* ***ensure*** *that the rules which it lays down on environmental protection are fully* ***effective***.[25] *[Emphasis added]*

Subsequent to this victory of the Commission, various legislative instruments were proposed in the area of environment, intellectual property and transportation. However, the debate concentrated on a second land mark case, Case-440/05,[26] in which the Court decided to allow the Council to also follow the "third pillar" approach in harmonising criminal laws of the Member States. The general effect of both landmark cases was, that only limited legislation is realised containing (binding) harmonisation of criminal sanctions, or administrative sanctions for that matter.[27]

13.2.2 Harmonisation Competence in the Lisbon Treaty

The approach of the first Case-176/03 is followed, however, in the drafting of Article 83(2) TFEU. This Lisbon Treaty addition to the European treaties basically codifies this case law, making use of the key words "essential to ensure" and "effective [implementation]". This repeats the annex character[28] of this competence to the main competence of harmonising substantive rules in the internal market, in the case of this chapter, rules pertaining to the financial market.

Article 83(2) TFEU: If the approximation of criminal laws and regulations of the Member States proves ***essential*** *to* ***ensure*** *the* ***effective*** *implementation of a Union policy in an area which has been subject to harmonisation measures, directives may establish minimum rules with regard to the definition of criminal offences and sanctions in the area concerned.*

After this new competence came into effect in 2009 the EU Commission produced two reports on the matter, one on the general approach to criminal policies

[25] See above n. 24.

[26] EU European Court of Justice, Commission versus Council Case C-440/05, Judgment of the Court (Grand Chamber), 23 October 2007, European Reports of Cases 2007 I-09097-ECLI:EU:C:2007:625.

[27] Directive 2008/99/EC of the European Parliament and of the Council of 19 November 2008 on the Protection of the Environment through Criminal Law, OJ L 328/28; Luchtman en Vervaele 2014, p. 34.

[28] Vervaele et al. 2014, pp. 23, 53.

in the post-Lisbon era,[29] and one on the financial sector in particular.[30] The trend to be cautious in dealing with criminal law seems to be continued, now that only one legislative instrument is developed on the basis of the Article 83(2) TFEU competence: Directive 2014/57.

The first report underlines the importance of criminal law, but is modest in the presentation of the power that the EU has in this respect, now that the results depend on the implementation by the Member States.[31] Furthermore, the distinction is underlined between the existing use of criminal law in respect of offence against the EU and misuse of EU budgets (see above) and the use of criminal law to support policy areas of the EU. Various areas are mentioned in the Report as potential topic of legislation in the near future, including the topics mentioned in Article 83(1) TFEU as money laundering, corruption, counterfeiting and computer crime (so-called Euro-crimes), as well as the potential topics that could lead to harmonisation via Article 83(2) TFEU namely the financial sector, road transport, data protection and the environment.[32] The report also identifies in general terms the principles on the basis of which such legislative instrument may be created, including the test of necessity and the corresponding (scientific) proof that such harmonisation will indeed ensure effective implementation of Union policies.

The second report preludes on the introduction of harmonised criminal laws in Directive 2014/57, in assessing the need for further action now that, back then, the financial crisis had put doubt whether financial market rules were always respected and applied as they should be across the Union.[33] This report refers to the Larosière Report that is also used in the legislative process to create Directive 2014/57.[34] Also this report emphasises the key notions behind harmonising criminal law, as the function of (criminal) sanctions providing a deterrent and catalyst to ensure that EU legislation is complied with, as well as the notion that EU involvement in this area should be necessary.[35] The importance of this report lies in the list of shortcomings of the then current state of the regulatory arrangement of the financial market, as described below.

None of these reports deal explicitly with the question how to assess the evidence that is needed to prove that criminal law is necessary to achieve the policy goals.[36] Neither do they give a solution to the tension between criminal sanctions and administrative sanctions as discussed in this chapter. Hence the need to develop a specific new theory on the matter.

---

[29] European Commission 2011.

[30] European Commission 2010.

[31] European Commission 2010, pp. 2–3.

[32] European Commission 2010, p. 11.

[33] European Commission 2011, p. 2.

[34] Larosière 2009, p. 45.

[35] European Commission 2011, p. 4.

[36] Miglietti 2013, p. 8; Klip 2012, p. 7.

13.2.3 Substantive Rules and Administrative Sanctions in the Market Abuse Regulation

The regulatory arrangements in the European financial markets can be divided in arrangements that foster the entrepreneurial soundness of the financial institutions (prudential supervision) and the arrangements that seek to avoid harmful products and services and market behaviour of the financial institutions (conduct supervision). Both arrangements come with substantive norms, as well as with institutions (authorities or agencies) that actively supervise the financial institutions.

These norms and institutions exist on both EU level and on Member State level. On the EU level, this pertains to the above-mentioned EBA and ESMA.[37] Regarding the specific case studies of this chapter, insider trading and market manipulation, the substantive norms for the regulatees are included in the Market Abuse Directive[38] (MAD) now "upgraded" to the Market Abuse Regulation (MAR),[39] applicable as of 3 July 2016.

The rationale for European rules for market abuse, among others, lies in the presumption that a genuine internal market for financial services is crucial for economic growth and job creation in the EU,[40] wherein market should function smoothly, integrated, efficient and transparent in order to secure public confidence, which on its turn is a prerequisite for economic growth and wealth. Moreover, market abuse harms this integrity of the financial market.

The ultimate substantive norm is laid down in Articles 14 and 15 of the Market Abuse Regulation simply stating, "a person shall not engage (…) in insider dealing, (…) unlawfully disclose inside information, (…) or engage (…) in market manipulation."[41] Subsequently, the norms for the obligatory compliance are laid down in Article 16 Market Abuse Regulation, including the obligation to establish and maintain effective arrangements, systems and procedures aimed at preventing and detecting these market abuses internally, as well as notifications to the competent authority in the Member State. Furthermore, pertaining to the sanctions against any non-compliance, the competent authority is required to have enough powers according to national law to refer an infringement to criminal investigation,[42] impose temporary prohibition on the exercise of professional activity,[43] as well as the power under national law to take appropriate administrative sanctions

---

[37] See above Sect. 13.1.

[38] Directive 2003/6/EC of the European Parliament and the Council of 28 January 2003 on Insider Dealing and Market Manipulation, OJ L 96/16 (Market Abuse Directive).

[39] Market Abuse Regulation, above n. 5.

[40] *Ibid.* Consideration 1.

[41] *Ibid.* p. 33.

[42] Market Abuse Regulation, above n. 5, Article 23(2)(f).

[43] *Ibid.* Article 23(2)(l).

and measures[44] like warning,[45] a permanent ban of a person discharging managerial responsibilities or the natural person responsible for the infringement,[46] and maximum administrative pecuniary sanctions of EUR 5 million for natural persons[47] and EUR 15 million for legal persons.[48]

13.2.4 Some Case Law on Market Abuse Directive

On the basis of the previous version of the regulatory arrangement, the Member States enforce the substantive prudential and conduct rules in line with the Market Abuse Directive, the predecessor of the Market Abuse Regulation. Based on the reporting on national cases by the European Securities and Market Authority[49] the following example cases can be reported in this respect. These examples have the function to illustrate the working of administrative sanctions.

In Greece the Market Abuse Directive is implemented in national administrative law.[50] In a case of the Hellenic Capital Market Commission against Investment Analysis SA an administrative fine is imposed of EUR 60,000.[51] The wrongful act consisted of market manipulation. Details are missing on what the actual *actus reus* was.

In Denmark the Market Abuse Directive is partly implemented in national criminal law.[52] In a case instigated by the Danish financial service authority, the Finanstilsynet, dealing with market manipulation, the Aarhus Court ruled against the Vestjysk Bank AS, and imposed a fine on the bank of 1 million Danish Krone and imposed prison sentences against the directors, varying from 30 days to three months.[53] The wrongful act consisted of trading with the own shares on the stock market, while disseminating wrong information about the value of these shares. It is noted that this criminal sanction is not based on Directive 2014/57, but on the general authority of Member States to implement Market Abuse Directive (and most other Directives) in the way it deems most fit.

---

44 *Ibid.* Article 30(1).

45 *Ibid.* Article 30(2)(c).

46 *Ibid.* Article 30(2)(f).

47 *Ibid.* Article 30(2)(i)(i).

48 *Ibid.* Article 30(2)(j)(i).

49 Dougan 2012, p. 75.

50 Greek Government, Market Abuse Law 3340/2005, 2005 as amended.

51 Greece Court HCMC, Case HCMC v Investment marktmanipulatie, 2015.

52 Denmark Government, Securities Trading Act 2003 (Værdipapirhandelsloven), as amended.

53 Danish Financial Service Authority, Case FSA versus Vestjysk Bank, 2014.

In Spain the Market Abuse Directive is implemented in the national financial service act[54] and used by the Spanish authority, the CNMV, to impose an administrative sanction of EUR 30,000 on Fidendtiis Impose Equity SA, for not notifying the CNMV of the suspicion of market manipulation by a client of this company.[55]

In The Netherlands the Market Abuse Directive is also implemented in the national financial service act[56] and used by the Dutch financial market authority, AFM, to impose administrative sanctions on Fortis Bank NV. This sanction is subsequently challenged by this bank resulting in a ruling in 2014[57] of the highest appeal court in this matter, the CBB. The CBB upholds the sanction of EUR 576,000 for the public statements of the chairman of the Fortis bank that the financial situation of that bank, in the context of the purchase of acquiring ABN AMRO Bank, was "according to plan" and "strong", amounting to market manipulation.

On the level of the Council of Europe, more specifically, in a case (Grande Stevens) before the European Court of Human Rights,[58] the enforcement of the Market Abuse Directive as implemented in Italy was successfully challenged in the light of fair trial (Article 6 of European Convention on Human Rights [ECHR]). In this judgement the court uses the concept of *ne bis in idem* to partly acquit the accused. The facts of the case fall outside the scope of this chapter, now that the accused was not a Significant Banker. Obviously, this judgement is an example that indeed prosecuting an accused within an administrative setting bars the subsequent prosecution within a criminal law setting, the topic of this chapter.

13.2.5 Criminal Sanctions in the Criminal Sanctions Directive

Based on the previous descriptions of the regulatory landscape in Europe pertaining to financial services, and the debate on whether or not the EU may introduce harmonisation of criminal laws of the Member States, the Criminal Sanctions Directive contains no big surprises. This directive is the first European legislation on the basis of the competence of Article 83(2) TFEU, as mentioned above. The directive harmonises the criminal laws of the Member States pertaining

[54] Spanish Government, Act 24, 1988 as amended.

[55] Spanish Court CNMV, Case CNMV versus Impose Corp Buss Monte de Piety 2014.

[56] Netherlands Government, Financial Supervision Act (Wet Op Het Financieel Toezicht), Stb. 2006, 475, as amended.

[57] Netherlands Court CBB, Case Fortis v AFM 2014, ECLI:NL.CBB.2014.6.

[58] European Court of the Human Rights, Judgment Grande Stevens vs Italy Case 18,640/10, 18,647/10, 18,663/10, 18,668/10 and 18,698/10, 4 March 2014, available at http://hudoc.echr.coe.int/sites/eng-press/pages/search.aspx?i=003%2D4687386%2D5686720#{%22itemid%22:[%22003%2D4687386%2D5686720%22]}, accessed 7 July 2014., unreported.

to insider trading and market manipulation and complement the Market Abuse Directive, now Market Abuse Regulation, and adds to its regulatory arrangement certain criminal sanctions.

The Criminal Sanctions Directive consists of four parts. Articles 1 and 2 deal with the scope and the definitions, and link the content of the legislation to the new Market Abuse Regulation which consolidates the Market Abuse Directive. Articles 3, 4 and 5 contain the respective norms pertaining to insider trading, inside information and market manipulation. Articles 7, 8 and 9 contain the actual sanctions for natural persons (four years for insider trading and market manipulation, two years for inside information). These sanctions, as said earlier, have to be enforced by the national criminal law enforcement mechanism. This enforcement consists of the classic criminal procedural phases of investigation, accusation, trial and final adjudication and sentencing by an independent national judge.

The other articles of the directive are of technical nature, including the deadline for implementation in national law of Member States, being 3 July 2016.

In assessing this directive, as discussed above, various questions can be raised. One is whether the proof presented in the preparatory documents and the reasoning of this directive meet the essentiality standard of Article 83(2) TFEU. This would be the topic of subsequent research. In this chapter we look at this legislative instrument in the light of the question[59] whether the criminal sanctions will ultimately help to achieve the goals of—in short—the (now) Market Abuse Regulation, limited and applied to Significant Banks and Significant Bankers.

13.3 Scholarly Frameworks

The leading question is reviewed in the light of regulatory science, particularly the responsive regulation, which, among others, looks at the concept of learning organisations. Furthermore, the leading question is reviewed in light of particular aspects of criminal law, that is the rights of the accused. Both aspects are discussed in this section.

13.3.1 Regulatory Science, Responsive Regulation and Learning Organisations

This section investigates EU substantive rules and enforcement mechanisms pertaining to insider trading and market manipulation committed by Significant Bankers in the context of regulatory science.[60] In line therewith, it regards the

[59] See above Sect. 13.1.

[60] Levi-Faur 2005, p. 13.

question how to make regulatees compliance a governance issue.[61] This means that the end goal is leading, being avoidance of market disturbance and avoidance of insider trading and market manipulation, and that all public-private means may and should be mobilised to achieve such goal.[62] Practical and scholarly traditions of sub-disciplines like administrative law or criminal law should not be solely decisive; or management studies, economics or labour psychology, etc., for that matter.

In this light, the Market Abuse Regulation and Criminal Sanction Directive, as chosen case study, represent (only) one of six possible regulatory tools[63]: a statutory norm backed by a sanction (even two). Another tool is collaboration between the regulatory state[64] and the regulatee, as further elaborated in the doctrine of responsive regulation and made concrete with the concept of learning organisation.[65]

In the same vein, next to administrative and criminal sanctions, private sanctions (remedies) exist: litigation to recover damages based on contractual or non-contractual liability, which will not be discussed in this chapter.

Administrative sanctions are sanctions such as warning letter, fine and revocation of licence imposed by the executive branch (and ultimately reviewed by courts). Criminal sanctions are sanctions such as fines and imprisonment imposed by an independent court on the basis of a criminal charge of a public prosecutor in a public trial. Relevant for the leading question of this chapter, one of the many differences between these two procedures are the enforcers involved. In the case of administrative sanctions, the ESFS regulator that has the "daily" contact with the compliance department is also directly involved in the sanction. In the case of criminal sanctions, the regulatee is confronted, without prior notification, with criminal procedures conducted by or lead by a public prosecutor not known to the regulatee. As a consequence, the former has direct and evolving effect on the behaviour of the regulatee and can play a role in the learning of the organisation. The latter has only limited effect in that respect. This is one of the reasons why it is argued that criminal sanctions should not be used. Obviously, outside the objects of this study, criminal sanctions may well be useful to achieve the goal of the substantive rules set out in the Market Abuse Regulation.

In regulatory science all sanctions are regarded to interrelate with each other and form a pyramid. In the concept of responsive regulation this graphic metaphor of the pyramid is used to situate the non-sanction interventions and the light sanctions at the base of the pyramid,[66] and in contrast, in the apex the most severe

61 Ebner and Beck 2008, p. 3; See Avgouleas 2012, p. 23.

62 Burris et al. 2005, p. 32.

63 Morgan and Yeung 2007, p. 153.

64 Bach and Newman 2007, p. 831.

65 Ayres and Braithwaite 1992, p. 5; Parker 2013, p. 6.

66 Ayres and Braithwaite 1992, p. 21.

sanction of imprisonment,[67] or the legal person equivalent of revocation of licence (dissolution of the entity). This pyramid metaphor corresponds with the psychological effects of sanctions identified in criminology, being retribution, deterrence, incapacitating and rehabilitation, and within these types of justification of punishment the degree of severity.[68] Connected to this distribution of sanctions the acts or the behaviour of the regulatees are similarly divided over this pyramid, from full compliance in the bottom, via unknowingly non-compliant, and incompetent non-compliant, to deliberate non-compliant in the top.[69]

Regulatory science experiments with this model,[70] as do the various regulators on the globe using it in the field.[71] These experiments or further developments integrate for instance viewpoints and concepts that emphasise the risk that non-compliance occurs ("risk management"),[72] or the tools with which regulatees can achieve full compliance, like the concept of learning organisations.[73] A learning organisation systematically fosters the mental models, the personal competences, the shared vision and the team learning to understand the applicable behavioural norms (in our case "do not trade insider information", "do not manipulate the financial market"). Furthermore, it designs the work processes and the services accordingly and avoids any non-compliance in this regard. One of the critical aspects of learning organisations is team learning, consisting of a method of internal communication, be it state-of-the-art "intervision",[74] or equivalent interaction, in which the open discussion of mistakes forms an archetypical aspect.

The internal discussion of mistakes, in whatever conceptual setting, is the linking pin in the assessment of the leading question of this chapter whether criminal sanctions are useful in the regulatory landscape of financial services in Europe. Discussion of mistakes presupposes the existence of events of non-compliance. Making mistakes is part of the learning process, according to most views on learning.[75] In contrast, in the current regulatory arrangement, a mistake as insider trading or market manipulation is regarded as a mistake that constitutes a criminal act or *actus reus*. Moreover, in the same vein, based on the extensive reporting obligations, any irregularity should be reported. In our case, it is the Significant Bankers who share this information with the above-mentioned European and national administrative authorities. On the basis of this information those authorities can

[67] *Ibid.* p. 47.

[68] Apel and Nagin 2014, p. 998.

[69] Braithwaite 2010, p. 475.

[70] Resulting in among others bow-tie models, see Reason 1990, 480.

[71] For instance, the Australian Tax Office, often taken as case study in various scholarly research projects in this regard, see Mascini and Van Wijk 2009, p. 27.

[72] Steenwijk 2015, p. 69.

[73] See in general Senge 1990, p. 1.

[74] Hendriksen 2014, p. 1.

[75] Kolb 1984, p. 1.

undertake action and intervene, including imposing administrative sanctions. The director or manager in charge of the unit in which the mistake takes place is equally responsible[76] for the mistake as the employee who is closest to the act in terms of the causal link or spectrum[77] between the wrong or damage and the acts of humans, resulting in the liability of the legal person. With the implementation of the Criminal Sanction Directive, on top of this mechanism, potential criminal investigations and sanctions may occur.

Learning from mistakes and therewith improving the bank business, on the one hand, and taking the risk to be criminally punished, on the other hand, established the dilemma Significant Bankers face. This dilemma leads potentially to behaviour that consists of mechanisms concealing any mistakes and also frustrating the administrative mechanism, let alone the criminal mechanism. The upcoming double regulatory arrangement created by the European Union has a direct influence on that dilemma and subsequent risk of concealment. This supports the argument that no extensive use should be made of the criminal mechanism, to allow the administrative mechanism to fulfil its compliance furthering role.[78]

13.3.2 The Concepts of "Ne Bis in Idem" and "Nemo Tenetur"

It is, moreover, argued that pertaining to Significant Banks and Significant Bankers adding criminal sanctions to the pyramid of responsive interventions worsens this dilemma. Several arguments support this position.

On the one hand, criminal sanctions are regarded as the most severe intervention the (supranational) state or public sphere can have in the lives of people.[79] Criminal law is the ultimate remedy in the artificial mechanism to channel human behaviour. When looking at the content of the sanction for legal persons, both administrative fines and criminal fines amount to the same punishment in monetary terms.[80] So this is an image issue.

On the other hand, the timing of the sanctions differs between administrative sanctions and criminal sanctions. Given the partly constitutional design of administrative regulators as part of the executive branch, these regulators sanction under

76 Market Abuse Regulation, above n. 5, Article 8(1).

77 *Ibid.* Article 8(2).

78 Including the additional function of the whistleblowing directive of 2015, supporting any person that reports infringements on the Market Abuse Regulation to the competent authorities: Commission Implementing Directive (EU) 2015/2393 on Regulation (EU) No 596/2014 of the European Parliament and of the Council as regards reporting to competent authorities of actual or potential infringements of that Regulation, OJ L 332/126 (18 December 2015).

79 Peršak 2007, p. 36; Husak 2008, p. 99.

80 Wermink et al. 2014, p. 731.

executive competences. Only after such executive order may an independent review by an independent court occur.

Conversely, criminal sanctions have to be imposed by such independent court, involving the (national) public prosecutor, who is not otherwise involved in the regulatory arrangement of the respective sector. So this is an organisational or utilitarian issue. Moreover, in the current regulatory design two organs of the (supranational) state are involved pertaining to the same behaviour or *actus reus* (see below). This is also an organisational or utilitarian issue.

These utilitarian issues can lead to court cases, in which a perpetrator, in this chapter the Significant Banker, defends him or herself with the *ne-bis-in-idem* (double jeopardy) principle against the charge of insider trading.[81] This defence is potentially successful if, and when, the EU[82] or Member State[83] market authorities or agencies (administrative regulator) had previously sanctioned the Significant Banker on the basis of administrative sanctions like revocation of the licence to operate as director in a financial institution or equivalent severe sanction.

Similarly, the bank may refuse to report to and co-operate with the regulator to disclose certain information on the principle of *nemo-tenetur* (self-incrimination), although this disclosure is part of the applicable regulatory arrangement[84] in the domain of administrative law. Such refusal ("defence") is potentially successful if, and when, the design of this administrative regulatory arrangement includes the possibility of criminal prosecution on the basis of for instance above mentioned Criminal Sanction Directive (2014/57).

These two issues pose the questions whether the harmonisation of criminal sanctions on the basis of Article 83(2) TFEU is not frustrating the efforts to combat the act of market manipulation and insider trading by Significant Bankers and whether the EU should not better invest in other types of harmonisation related to the efforts of the EU and Member States market authorities or agencies to ensure a functioning financial market in Europe.

13.4 Analysis and Alternatives

Based on this landscape of substantive rules, and corresponding administrative and criminal sanctions pertaining to insider trading and market manipulation, viewed in the light of the scholarly frameworks on among responsive regulation/learning organisations, and the impact of the procedural defences *ne bis in idem* and *nemo tenetur*, it is now time to draw some conclusions and pose some logical assertions.

---

[81] Vervaele 2013b, p. 211.

[82] Such as the European Bank Authority (EBA) or the European Securities and Markets Authority (ESMA).

[83] Such as The Netherlands Dutch Central Bank (DNB) and Financial Services Supervisor (AFM).

[84] See above n. 5, Article 23(4).

13.4.1 Criminal Sanctions Versus Learning Organisation

In contrasting criminal sanctions with the concept of learning organisations, this chapter suggests that Significant Bankers are less willing to participate in the mechanisms of the organisation aimed at learning when criminal sanctions are potentially imposed.

However, based on logic applied by jurists, this chapter connects this assertion to the following. The primary aim of regulation of financial markets, and more in particular insider trading and market manipulation, is to avoid these international financial crimes to occur. This chapter reviews these crimes in the setting of the Significant Banks of the EU where insider trading and market manipulation may occur. And which banks are all heavily connected to the prudential and conduct supervision mentioned above.

In terms of the theory of responsive regulation these banks are to be classified as "willing and able". In case of any non-compliance, wrongful act or *actus reus*, within the organisation, such bank should be classified as "unknowingly non-compliant". So initially low in the metaphor of the pyramid. Being low in the pyramid, non-compliance calls for "soft" intervention. If the aim of regulation is to avoid crimes to occur, such bank should be empowered to discover the non-compliance itself. Or should receive an instruction to that end without connected sanctions. Let alone criminal sanctions. The best tool for that seems the implementation of mechanisms characteristic for learning organisations.

13.4.2 Criminal Sanction Versus Administrative Sanctions

In contrasting criminal sanctions with administrative sanctions[85] in the light of *ne bis in idem* and *nemo tenetur*, this chapter suggests that criminal sanctions are the less effective instruments to avoid the international financial crimes of insider trading and market manipulation. This assertion can be true within the following context.

In The Netherlands and many other Member States sanctions in the top of the metaphoric pyramid of the theory of responsive regulation are imposed by two different state organs. Administrative sanctions are used and imposed by the executive branch, more in particular the state organ responsible for the conduct supervision, the Dutch *Autoriteit Financiele Markten* (AFM) and equivalent in other Member States. As mentioned above, administrative sanctions are imposed by this regulator after disclosure by the Significant Banker, the regulate, of the relevant information, followed by an eventual (seldom) appeal with the judiciary. Criminal sanctions are imposed by the judiciary, based on a full-fledged criminal

85 See for a similar approach Faure and Svatikova 2012, p. 253.

procedure instigated by the state organ of the public prosecutor. Since the investigation is targeted at a bank that in its position as regulatee (continuously) discloses information about compliance and non-compliance to the regulator (AFM etc.) a *ne bis in idem* defence is very likely to be raised and potentially successful. Furthermore, where such disclosure did not occur, a *nemo tenetur* defence is likely to be raised and potentially successful. Obviously, in such situation both state organs should and actually do[86] coordinate their actions, but given their different nature and given the different orientation of administrative jurists on the one side and criminal law jurists on the other side, coordination seems unable to avoid overlap and thus successful defences of the type *ne bis in idem* and/*or nemo tenetur*.

Next to this aspect of the defence of the accused the aspect of time is relevant in the current assessment. Criminal sanctions are only imposed at the end of the criminal procedure which typically takes more than one year in these cases. From the point of view of responsive regulation that is not a timeframe in which assisting a regulatee in becoming compliant is helpful. Furthermore, several other assumptions of criminal law are not proven to be accurate in these cases, such as the concept of deterrence.[87]

13.4.3 Alternatives

As a third line of reasoning in the critical analysis of the leading question, it is argued that no alternative exists within the current system of both administrative sanctions of the Market Abuse Regulations and the national criminal sanctions on the basis of the Criminal Santionc Directive. To continue with the last argument that when administrative and criminal sanctions are simultaneously used by different state organs, the first alternative could be to fuse these state organs to one organ. Then no problem arises in the theory of responsive regulation, in terms of the severe sanctions in the top of the metaphoric pyramid. No defence can be based on *ne bis in idem* because receiving disclosed information, investigation and sanctioning are then all, on the one hand, of the fused state organ. However, given the current state of affairs in The Netherlands and equivalent Member States, such fusion is unlikely to occur. As part of the decision-making process of new directives on the basis of Article 83(2) TFEU these Member States could in that light even invoke para 3 of that article, allowing Member States to oppose harmonisation of criminal law on the basis of the assertion that such harmonisation would affect this fundamental aspect of its criminal justice system, the separation between Dutch AFM and Dutch public prosecutor (OM), and equivalents in other Member States.

[86] Netherlands Government, Convenant ter voorkoming van ongeoorloofde samenloop van bestuurlijke en strafrechtelijke sancties, Stcrt 15-1-2009, Nr. 665., 2009.

[87] Apel and Nagin 2014, p. 998.

A second alternative would be to change the possibility that the executive branch imposes sanctions, and align administrative law with criminal law, in order to have all sanctions be imposed by the judiciary. That would place administrative and criminal sanctions on a single "level playing field". Such move would, however, make the use of the sanction pyramid in the sense of responsive regulation impossible. Any positive effect of this pyramid on the compliance with rules on insider trading and market manipulation would then be reversed.

A third alternative would be to align all levels of (pecuniary) administrative sanctions with the equivalent (pecuniary) sanction in the realm of criminal law. In most Member States this is already the case, so as alternatives it only works in the other Member States. However, such alignment of the fines does not change the concerns expressed above about the nature of criminal law and its effect on compliance of Significant Banks to regulation in the field of insider trading and market manipulation.

All in all, this chapter does not see alternatives that would take away the concerns in regard of having criminal sanctions being added to the regulatory arrangement to combat the international financial crime of insider trading and market manipulation.

13.5 Summary and Conclusions

The EU has developed as regulatory state in the field of financial services by establishing a rather extensive regulatory arrangement including regulators on EU level, coordination mechanisms for national regulators, as well as substantive norms for among others prudential and conduct aspects of financial institutions and financial products. The latest elements in this landscape are the recodification of market abuse norms in the Market Abuse Regulation (596/2014) and the corresponding criminalisation of these acts with the Criminal Sanctions Directive (2014/57). These elements are described as the pinnacle moment in the increase of competence of the EU in the field of criminal law, codified in Article 83(2) TFEU. Based on the scholarly literature the conclusion is drawn that this annex-competence is a very limited. The Criminal Sanction Directive (2014/57) is the only of its kind. And no indication exists that further use of Article 83(2) TFEU will be made in the near future.

This chapter poses the question whether the addition of criminal sanctions to the possibilities to combat the international financial crime of insider trading and market manipulation by administrative mechanisms is useful. The scope of the analysis is limited to Significant Banks and Significant Bankers in the EU, who are currently subject to daily supervision by the ESFS, which includes three ESAs in collaboration with NCAs. This supervision between regulatee and regulator is placed in the theory of responsive regulation, which theory is the dominant guideline in the design of the regulatory arrangements in the EU. Part of this theory is the presentation of a metaphorical pyramid that represents soft sanctions at the bottom for capable and willing regulatees and severe sanctions in the top of the pyramid for non-willing and non-capable regulatees. The leading question is analysed by looking at the possible effects of criminal sanctions by frustrating Significant Banks to innovate as "learning organisations". Also, the question is analysed in light of potential defences of *ne bis in idem* (double jeopardy) and *nemo tenetur* (self-incrimination) by Significant Banks within a criminal procedure.

Learning organisations are thus these financial institutions, and presented as rational entities that systematically work on compliance programs and risk management strategies, as well as more in the general act as organisations that aim at learning from its mistakes and improving its performance over time based on the lessons learned. In terms of the theory of responsive regulation, these banks should be qualified as capable and willing to comply. Being in the bottom area of the pyramid, soft sanctions and assistance by the regulators are prescribed. Moreover, the assertion is defended that development of a learning organisation is hampered by the existence of criminal sanctions. The argument is that learning involves among other discussions and evaluation of incidents. Persons participating in such learning process would stop sharing meaningful information on mistakes if subsequently the information is disclosed to regulators and therewith available as evidence for public prosecutors, despite eventual facilitation of whistle-blowers. In this sense introducing (more) criminal sanctions is evaluated as not useful to improve compliance with internal market rules in the area of financial services.

This conclusion is, furthermore, supported by the answers found in the second part of the analysis. It is argued that given the existence of two state organs, and limited effective coordination between these organs, administrative and criminal sanctions work against each other when combined. Viewed from administrative sanctions the existence of (subsequent) criminal sanctions potentially limits the willingness of the regulatee to co-operate with the imposing of administrative sanctions. Viewed from the criminal sanctions the existence of (predating) administrative sanctions, or at least investigations or disclosure of information, triggers the use of fundamental rights in the defence of the accused, as *ne bis in idem* and *nemo tenetur*.

This chapter also attempted to explore alternatives to the concerns raised. It failed in finding alternatives to the problems around the effects of criminal sanctions on Significant Banks as learning organisations, or the issues around *ne bis in idem* and *nemo tenetur*.

The final conclusion is therefore that the EU should have refrained from making use of Article 83(2) TFEU pertaining to Significant Banks and Significant Bankers who are subject to the extensive regulatory arrangement of the Market Abuse Regulation and its administrative sanctions. Now that the Criminal Sanction Directive (2014/57) exists, this conclusion could be interpreted as a recommendation to national criminal law enforcers to explicitly restrict its powers to non-Significant Bankers and to align its activities with the European and national competent authorities pertaining to insider trading and market abuse.

References

Apel R, Nagin DS (2014) Deterrence. In: Bruinsma G, Weisburd D (eds) Encyclopedia of criminology and criminal justice. Springer, New York, pp 998–1005

Avgouleas E (2012) Governance of global financial markets: the law, the economics, the politics. Cambridge University Press, Cambridge (UK)

Ayres I, Braithwaite J (1992) Responsive regulation: transcending the deregulation debate. Oxford University Press, New York (USA)

Bach D, Newman AL (2007) The European Regulatory State and Global Public Policy: Micro-Institutions, Macro-Influence. J Eur Public Policy 14:827–846. doi:10.1080/13501760701497659

Bianco SL (2015) Tectonic shifts of European integration: identifying deliberation and change in the everyday practice of decision-making in EU's Justice and Home Affairs. Eleven International Publishing, The Hague

Braithwaite J (2010) The essence of responsive regulation, Fasken Lecture University of British Columbia 2010, In: UBC Law Review, vol 44, pp 475–520, available at http://www.anu.edu.au/fellows/jbraithwaite/_documents/Articles/essence_responsive_regulation.pdf, last accessed 16 Dec 2013

Buckley RP (2011) From crisis to crisis: the global financial system and regulating failure. Kluwer International, Alphen aan den Rijn (NL)

Burris S, Drahos P, Shearing C (2005) Nodal governance, temple law school working papers. SSRN: http://ssrn.com/abstract=760928. Accessed 16 December 2013

Cappiello S (2015) The Interplay Between the EBA and the Banking Union. Social Science Research Network, Rochester, NY. http://papers.ssrn.com/abstract=2682529. Accessed 22 Jan 2015

Dougan M (2012) From the velvet glove to the iron fist: criminal sanctions for the enforcement of union law. In: Cremona M (ed) Compliance and the enforcement of EU law. Oxford University Press, Oxford (UK), pp 74–131

Ebner A, Beck N (2008) The institutions of the market: organizations, social systems, and governance. Oxford University Press, Oxford (UK)

van Erp J, Huisman W, Vande Walle G (2015) The Routledge handbook of white-collar and corporate crime in Europe. Routledge, London (UK)

European Commission (2010) Communication from the Commission to the European Parliament, the Council, the European Economic and Social Committee and the Committee of the Regions; Reinforcing Sanctioning Regimes in the Financial Services Sector, vol. COM (2010) 716, 2010, 4

European Commission (2011) Communication from the Commission to the European Parliament, the Council, the European Economic and Social Committee and the Committee of the Regions, Towards an EU Criminal Policy: Ensuring the Effective Implementation of EU Policies., vol. COM (2011) 573, final, 2011

Faure MG, Svatikova K (2012) Criminal or administrative law to protect the environment? Evidence from Western Europe. J Environ Law 24:253–286. doi:10.1093/jel/eqs005

Hendriksen J (2014) Intervisie bij werkproblemen procesmatig en taakgericht problemen oplossen. Nelissen, Baarn

Husak D (2008) Why criminal law: A question of content? Crim Law Philos 2:99–122. doi:10.1007/s11572-008-9048-3

Klip A (2012) European criminal policy. Eur J Crime Crim Law Crim Justice 20:3–12. doi:10.1163/157181712X614943

Kolb DA (1984) Experiential learning: experience as the source of learning and development. Prentice-Hall, Englewood Cliffs, NJ

Larosière J (2009) Report of the High-Level Group on Financial Supervision in the EU, Brussels (BE), European Commission, 25 Feb 2009

Levi-Faur D (2005) The global diffusion of regulatory capitalism. Ann Am Acad Pol Soc Sci 598:12–32

Luchtman M, Vervaele JAE (2014) Enforcing the market abuse regime: towards an integrated model of criminal and administrative law enforcement in the European Union? New J Eur Crim Law 5:192–220

Mascini P, van Wijk E (2009) Responsive regulation at the Dutch Food and Consumer Product Safety Authority: an empirical assessment of assumptions underlying the theory. Regul Gov 3:27–47

Miglietti M (2013) The new EU criminal law competence in action: the proposal for a Directive on Criminal Sanctions for Insider Dealing and Market Manipulation, Working Paper 5. Institute for European Studies, Brussel (BEL). http://www.ies.be/files/Working%20Paper%20Miglietti.pdf. Accessed 22 Jan 2015

Miglietti M (2014) The first exercise of Article 83(2) TFEU under review: an assessment of the essential need of introducing criminal sanctions. NJECL 5:5–26

Morgan B, Yeung K (2007) An introduction to law and regulation: text and materials. Cambridge University Press, Cambridge (UK)

OECD Report for G20 Leaders (2013) The role of banks, equity markets and institutional investors in long-term financing for growth and development. February 2013. http://www.oecd.org/finance/private-pensions/G20reportLTFinancingForGrowthRussianPresidency2013.pdf. Accessed 29 Jan 2015

Parker C (2013) Twenty years of responsive regulation: an appreciation and appraisal. Regul Gov 7:2–13

Peršak N (2007) Harm principle—a comparative analysis. In: Peršak N (ed) Criminalising harmful conduct. Springer, New York, pp 35–94

Reason J (1990) The contribution of latent human failures to the breakdown of complex systems. Philos Trans R Soc Lond B Biol Sci 327:475–484

Senge PM (1990) The fifth discipline: the art and practice of the learning organization. Doubleday-Currency, New York

Steenwijk P (2015) Het topje van de ijsberg. Het Nederlandse anti-witwasbeleid; effictiviteit, risicogerichtheid en de impact van de 4de Europese AML-Richtlijn; een risk en control perspectief. Applies Res Today—Special Edition, pp 66–155

Vervaele JAE (2013a) Has the European Union a criminal policy for the enforcement of its harmonised policies?. In: Govaere I, Hanf D (eds) Scrutunizing internal and external dimensions of European law, pp 533–548

Vervaele JAE (2013b) Ne Bis In Idem: towards a transnational constitutional principle in the EU? Utrecht Law Rev 9:211–229

Vervaele JAE, Fornasari G, Sartori D (2014) European criminal justice in the post-Lisbon area of freedom, security and justice. Università degli Studi di Trento, Trento

Wermink H, Apel R, Blokland AAJ, Nieuwbeerta P (2014) Crime preventive effects of incapacitation. In: Bruinsma G, Weisburd D (eds) Encyclopedia of criminology and criminal justice. Springer, New York, pp 731–738

Wymeersch E, Hopt KJ, Ferrarini G (2012) Financial regulation and supervision: a post-crisis analysis. Oxford University Press, Oxford (UK)

Chapter 14
Corruption and Security: The Role of Negotiated Settlements

Abiola Makinwa

Abstract Negotiated settlements between alleged wrongdoers and prosecuting authorities is a United States enforcement practice for corruption offences that is spreading globally. The absence of a European Union (EU) dimension on negotiated settlements, coupled with the fact that European multinationals are being "policed" for corruption violations primarily by US authorities, calls for some examination. Should Europe develop a negotiated settlement regime for corruption offences? Can a European dimension on negotiated settlements contribute to the realisation of better security in the form of effective anti-corruption enforcement in the Area of Justice, Freedom and Security for EU citizens? Are negotiated settlements compatible with the fundamental right of EU citizens to a fair trial? This chapter examines these questions and argues that to improve security in the EU and in keeping with global trends, there is sufficient justification and legal scope for a European dimension on negotiated settlements. Such a European dimension on negotiated settlements will give Europe and its Member States a stronger voice in shaping this growing global practice as a strategic tool in the fight against corruption.

Keywords Corruption · Security · Negotiated settlements · Fair trial · Harmonisation EU anti-corruption enforcement

Contents

A. Makinwa (✉)
The Hague University of Applied Sciences, The Hague, The Netherlands
e-mail: a.o.makinwa@hhs.nl

J. de Zwaan et al. (eds.), *Governance and Security Issues of the European Union*, DOI 10.1007/978-94-6265-144-9_14

14.1 Introduction

A fundamental objective of the EU is to provide its citizens with a high level of safety within an Area of Freedom, Security and Justice (AFSJ) by preventing and combating organised crime and corruption.[1] The AFSJ is the benefit expected by peoples of the States that are brought together in the Union. "Women and men in Europe rightly expect to live in a peaceful and prosperous Union confident that their rights are fully respected and their security provided."[2]

Corruption[3] poses a fundamental threat to the ability of the EU to deliver on its mandate for an AFSJ. Corruption is the oil that fuels terrorism,[4] money laundering, illicit human, arms and drug trafficking, counterfeiting of means of payment, computer crime and other forms of organised crime.[5] The international network of organised crime is interwoven and systemic and does not stop at the boundaries of the Europe. In this view, there is no separate internal or external EU dimension to corruption. Internally, fighting corruption to protect EU citizens is synonymous with fighting organised crime. Externally, European corporations that pay bribes to acquire contracts contribute to global instability that ultimately impacts upon the internal security of EU citizens.

A large proportion of anti-corruption enforcement actions against multinational corporations have been resolved by way of negotiated settlements.[6] The Organisation for Economic Co-operation and Development (OECD), in its 2014 Foreign Bribery Report, notes that in 69% of foreign bribery cases, sanctions were imposed by way of settlement procedures.[7] The United States is far in the lead

---

[1] Consolidated Version of the Treaty on European Union, signed on 13 December 2007, OJ C 326 (entered into force on 1 December 2009) as amended on 26 October 2012 (TEU), Article 29.

[2] European Commission 2010, Sect. 1 para 5.

[3] UNODC 2004, p. 23. Grand corruption pervades the highest levels of government, engendering major abuses of power. A broad erosion of the rule of law, economic stability and confidence in good governance quickly follow.' All further references in this chapter, unless otherwise indicated, are with respect to grand corruption.

[4] OECD 2016, p. 1. The OECD, for example, identifies four types of connections between terrorism and corruption stating that (1) corruption hampers a countries' ability to fight terrorism especially when it occurs in the judiciary, the army and defence sector; (2) it facilitates terrorist attacks (3) corruption and terrorism financing share methods to hide the money and (4) corruption helps terrorist funding.

[5] Shelley 2005. Shelley speaks of the globalization of crime, terror, and corruption, describing it as "unholy trinity" that manifests itself all over the world from the poorest countries of Latin America and Africa, but also in the heart of prosperous Europe. She points out that both terrorists and criminal proposer by creating unstable governments and depend on systematic corruption.

[6] World Bank Publication 2013, p. 8.

[7] OECD 2014, p. 9. By way of corporate probation in Canada; Sect. 153 (a) of the Criminal Procedure Code in Germany; Patteggiamento in Italy; penalty notice in Norway; reparation under Article 53 of the Penal Code in Switzerland; and non-prosecution agreements, deferred prosecution agreements and plea agreements in the United States.

regarding negotiated settlements for corruption offences worldwide.[8] As a result, European corporations are now effectively being "policed" by the US for corruption offences.[9] The United States' experience shows that private-public dialogue in the form of negotiated settlements for corruption offences can have a significant effect on the management of corruption by corporations. The OECD for example has observed that while it is difficult to quantify deterrence:

> The companies against which DPAs [Deferred Prosecution Agreements] and NPAs [Non Prosecution Agreements] have been brought have often undergone dramatic changes. For instance, prior to or following the entry of DPAs or NPAs, many companies have terminated personnel, including senior managers, established new codes of conduct and compliance policies and procedures, pledged not to use third-party agents, withdrawn from bids tainted by corruption, provided new and substantial resources to compliance and audit functions within their organisations, and instituted new training regimes. These companies, through their remediation efforts under DPAs and NPAs, have often *fundamentally changed* how they conduct businesses.[10]

Should there be a European dimension on negotiated settlements for corruption offences in view of this spreading *de facto* state of affairs? In an attempt to answer this question, Sect. 2 of this chapter explores the current state of anti-corruption

---

[8] OECD 2014, p. 9. The OECD Foreign Bribery Report points out that "[t]he United States has sanctioned individuals and entities for the foreign bribery offence in connection with 128 separate foreign bribery schemes since the entry into force of the OECD Anti-Bribery Convention. Germany has sanctioned individuals and entities for the foreign bribery offence in connection with 26 separate schemes; Korea in connection with 11; and Italy, Switzerland and the United Kingdom in connection with 6."

[9] The following are some examples of European corporations that have entered into settlements with the US Department of Justice (DOJ) and/or the Securities Exchange Commission (SEC) for allegations of bribery in developing countries; in 2008, German Siemens (Germany) agreed to pay $800 million in settlement of allegations of US Foreign Corrupt Practices Act (FCPA) violations involving its subsidiaries in Argentina, Bangladesh and Venezuela; In 2010, BAE Systems (UK) agreed to pay $400 million in settlement of charges relating to a series of substantial bribery payments to shell companies and third party intermediaries without due diligence or proper corporate controls and the bribery of Saudi Arabian officials for an $80 billion deal for the sale of jet fighters; In 2010, Snamprogetti Netherlands B.V. agreed to pay $365 million in penalties to resolve FCPA-related charges for paying bribes to Nigerian government officials to help win contracts to build Liquefied Natural Gas facilities; In 2010, Technip S.A.(France) resolved FCPA-related charges by agreeing to pay a $240 million criminal penalty and enter into a deferred prosecution agreement and by paying $98 million in disgorgement of profits for bribes paid to Nigerian government officials regarding contracts to build Liquefied Natural Gas facilities in Nigeria; In 2013, Total S.A (France) agreed to pay $398 million to settle SEC and DOJ criminal charges for paying bribes to intermediaries of an Iranian government official to obtain valuable contracts to develop oil and gas fields; In 2014, Alstom (France) paid $772 million in penalties to settle charges of bribing government officials in Indonesia, Saudi Arabia, Egypt, and the Bahamas to win infrastructure contracts; In 2016, VimpelCom entered into a Global Foreign Bribery resolution of more than $795 million with respect to FCPA related charges relating to bribery payments to a government official in Uzbekistan between 2006 and 2012 to enable them to enter and continue operating in the Uzbek telecommunications market. Full details of DOJ FCPA cases are available at the US Department of Justice website at https://www.justice.gov/criminal-fraud/related-enforcement-actions.

[10] OECD 2012, p. 20.

enforcement in Europe. Section 3 examines the *notion* of negotiated settlements from a European perspective while Sect. 4 looks at the compatibility of negotiated settlements with the fundamental rights of EU citizens to fair trial as enshrined in Article 6 of the European Convention on Human Rights (ECHR).[11] Section 5 explores the legal scope for an EU dimension on negotiated settlements and Sect. 6 concludes that an EU Dimension on negotiated settlement regime is compatible with the legal systems and fundamental principles of the EU. It is also warranted in order to provide better security and justice for EU citizens. These conclusions coupled with the *de facto* realities of negotiated settlements on the governance of European corporations' supports the argument for the Europeanisation of anti-corruption enforcement.

14.2 The Current State of Affairs

Bribes to gain business contracts were considered by many European countries to be legitimate tax-deductible expenses until 1996 when the OECD passed a recommendation urging Member Countries that allowed the tax deductibility of bribes to foreign public officials to refrain from doing so.[12] In the last few decades, the permissiveness once associated with grand scale corruption in international business has been replaced with its global criminalisation of corruption in a series of international and European instruments.[13] At the domestic level, the US Foreign

[11] Charter of Fundamental Rights of the European Union, OJ C 326, 26.10.2012, pp. 391–407.

[12] OECD Recommendation on the Tax Deductibility of Bribes to Foreign Public Officials 1996.

[13] In 1996, the Organization of American States adopted the Inter-American Convention against Corruption, 29 March 29 1996, 35 ILM, p. 724, adopted at Caracas, Venezuela, entered into force on 6 March 1997; In 1997, the Organization of Economic Co-operation and Development adopted a Convention on Combating Bribery of Foreign Public Officials in International Business Transactions, Paris, 27 November 1997, in force 15 February 1999, 1998, 37 ILM, p. 1; Also in 1997, the Council of the European Union adopted Convention drawn up on the basis of Article K.3(2)(c) Treaty on European Union on the Fight Against Corruption Involving Officials of the European Communities or Officials of Member States of the European Union, Official Journal C 195, 25 June 1997, p. 2; In 2003, this prohibition was extended to private sector bribery with the Council Framework Decision on combating bribery in the private sector. See European Council (2003) Framework Decision 2003/568/JHA of 22 July 2003 on combating corruption in the private sector, OJ L 192, pp. 0054–0056;

In 1999, the Council of Europe adopted the Criminal Law Convention on Corruption, Strasbourg, 27 January 1999, in force 1 July 2002, 173 CETS as well as the Civil Law Convention on Corruption, Strasbourg, 4 November 1999, in force 1 November 2003,174 CETS; In 2000, the United Nations Convention against Transnational Organised Crime, New York, 15 November, 2000, in force 29 September 2003, 2225 UNTS; (2000), 40 ILM, p. 353; This was followed in 2003 by the adoption of the African Union Convention on Preventing and Combating Corruption, in force 5 August 2006 43 (1) ILM, p. 1; In 2003 the United Nations adopted the United Nations Convention against Corruption, New York, 31 October 2003, in force 14 December 2005, 2349 UNTS, p. 41; (2005), 43 ILM, p. 37. In 2008 the EU adopted a Council Framework Decision on the fight against organized crime. See European Council (2008) Framework Decision 2008/841/JHA of 24 October 2008 on the fight against organized crime, OJ L 300, p. 42; See also Makinwa 2007 on the development of the international criminalization of corruption in international business.

Corrupt Practices Act[14] and the UK Bribery Act[15] have universal application for multinational corporations that gives them a special status in the international framework of rules regulating corruption in international business.

However, despite this impressive global criminalisation of corruption in international business, recent EU statistics show that the majority of EU citizens and companies still believe that corruption is a problem in their countries.[16] The statistics also show that six out of ten companies think it is unlikely that corrupt people or businesses would be caught, fined or imprisoned.[17] Furthermore, 32% of companies that have participated in public tenders/public procurement say corruption prevented them winning a contract.[18]

The sum of €120 billion is cited as the yearly cost of corruption to the EU.[19] The EU Commission notes that this is one percent of the EU GDP and represents only a little less than the annual budget of the EU.[20] This figure is criticised as rather low because it only includes lost tax revenue and investments in its estimations.[21] The figure does not include indirect cost components based on how much countries lose relatively in economic terms by not reaching (a) the corruption level of the seven best performing Member States; or (b) by not reaching the EU average corruption level; or (c) the level of the best performing Member States within their peer group. Using this methodology, Bellegoooij and Zandstra revise the cost of corruption, upwards to between 179 and 990 billion euro in GDP annually.[22] Such systemic grand scale corruption impacts on the integrity of the global market and on global security.

In the EU, the abolition of internal barriers has created a market without internal frontiers in which organised crime and corruption can permeate every corner of economic activity. The European Parliament emphasises the pervasive effects of organised crime on European economic activity stating:

> [organised crime] … is increasingly resembling an economic global player with a strong business orientation, enabling it to supply different kinds of illegal—but also, to an increasing extent, legal—goods and services at the same time, and is having an increasing impact on the European and global economy, significantly affecting tax revenues of the Member States and the EU as a whole, and at a cost to business estimated at more than EUR 670 billion annually.[23]

---

[14] The Foreign Corrupt Practices Act 1977, 15 USC Sect. 78dd-1, et seq.

[15] UK Bribery Act 2010 (C.23).

[16] At the European level, three quarters of respondents (76 %) think that corruption is widespread in their own country. See EU Anti-Corruption Report, 2014 p. 6.

[17] European Commission 2014a, p. 24; European Commission 2014b, p. 7.

[18] European Commission 2014b.

[19] European Commission 2014a, p. 3.

[20] European Commission 2014a, p. 3.

[21] Bellegoooij and Zandstra 2016, p. 11.

[22] Bellegoooij and Zandstra 2016, p. 11.

[23] See European Commission, Report on organized crime, corruption and money laundering 2013c p. 12.

Despite the development of an international and EU *acquis* in the area of corruption, Member States exercising their exclusive competences, have implemented EU anti-corruption rules as matters of internal security and with diverging substantive criminal laws and procedures.[24] This has resulted in a fragmented enforcement environment with "multi-speed" levels of protection and anti-corruption enforcement with the not surprising result that despite extensive anti-corruption rule-making, anti-corruption enforcement is "still not satisfactory."[25] The "declared intentions [of Member States] are still too distant from concrete results."[26]

The answer is not more regulation. The character of the principal actors in this form of grand corruption (the government, on the one hand, and the multinational corporation on the other) as well as the deterritorialized environment in which this corruption occurs, presents a conundrum unresolved by traditional criminal law approaches.[27] Structural conflicts of interests undermine the political will to implement effective reform.[28] Indeed, the EU Commission has concluded that it is "the genuine political will to eradicate corruption [that] often appears to be missing."[29] In 2013, the EU commission noted with regard to enforcement by national judicial authorities of offences against the EU budget that:

> Action by national judicial authorities often remains slow, prosecution rates on the average low and results obtained in the different Member States over the Union as a whole unequal. Based on this track record the judicial action undertaken by Member States against fraud may currently not be considered as effective, equivalent and deterrent as required under the Treaty.[30]

Tackling cross-border fraud cases requires closely coordinated investigations and prosecutions at European level. As the EU Commission admitted in its Explanatory Memorandum regarding a proposal for a European Prosecutor, the current levels of information exchange and coordination are not sufficient to

---

[24] European Commission 2004, p. 7. In this report, the EU Commission concluded that "[g]aps and loopholes in the law which allow offences to go unpunished remain possible" and that "The considerable differences between the Member States as regards criminal penalties shed further doubt as to whether the penalties imposed always meet the Court of Justice criteria of being effective, proportionate and dissuasive". This situation was not much improved in 2008 when the EU Commission concluded that "[d]e facto the current system of protection, based on conventions, creates a multi-speed situation. It results in a mixture of different legal situations in terms of the binding effect of the PFI instruments in the individual Member States" internal legal order. Formally, this situation does not produce the desired effective and dissuasive penal protection.' See European Commission 2008, p. 4.

[25] European Commission 2014a, p. 2.

[26] European Commission 2014a, p. 2.

[27] Makinwa 2013, pp. 4–10.

[28] Makinwa 2013, p. 448.

[29] European Commission 2014a, p. 2.

[30] See European Commission 2013d, p. 2.

achieve this.[31] One can conclude, with regard to the current state of affairs, that effective anti-corruption enforcement in Europe remains a big challenge and that this is clearly a challenge that Member States cannot tackle on their own. To develop a *Europe that protects*, Member States must strengthen its co-operation in law enforcement, as well as judicial co-operation in criminal matters in effective ways. Furthermore, the development of an AFSJ requires the political will of Member States to Europeanise anti-corruption enforcement so as to provide a consistent and coordinated enforcement environment.

14.3 The Notion of Negotiated Settlements from an EU Perspective

The negotiated settlements process can be seen as a pragmatic attempt to move away from the structural gaps of state-centred criminalisation to an environment that is more conducive to compliance by creating business incentives for co-operation and collaboration between prosecuting authorities and multinational corporations.[32]

Central to negotiated settlements is the idea of leniency or reward for co-operation. While the notion of "reward" often associated with the US practice is often couched in terms of non-prosecution agreements or deferred prosecution agreements, a reward could also be viewed as *any resolution* arrived at through a process of co-operation that is an alternative to a full trial or that mitigates penalty. This could be a plea bargain, an arrangement for dismissal or conditional discharge, a reduction of the charge to a less serious offence, or an agreement reached for a penalty reduction in exchange for co-operation.

At a High Level Seminar on *Negotiated Settlements for Corruption Offences: A European Perspective* that took place in The Hague on the 22nd—23rd of May 2014, a *working definition* of negotiated settlements that was broad enough to capture the various types of "negotiations" or "collaborations" that can influence the eventual sanction in different European countries was agreed upon. From this perspective a negotiated settlement was defined as:

> An agreed resolution between law enforcement authorities and alleged wrongdoers regarding alleged violations of anti-corruption laws resulting in sanctions or other legal measures.[33]

[31] European Commission 2013d, p. 2.

[32] Makinwa 2013, p. 404. It is "not the anti-corruption rules per se that influences the choice for or against compliance. The rule creates the standard against which choices are make. It is the environment that influences the choice that is made".

[33] See Makinwa 2015, p. 12. At this OLAF sponsored seminar, country researchers and invited experts from eight European countries addressed the question of how negotiated settlements fits into the framework of their legal systems.

Negotiated settlements in this sense are compromises reached between the public prosecutor and the private corporation in a process of public-private dialogue for corruption-related offences. The Advocate General in the *Joined Cases Hüseyin Gözütok and Klaus Brügge*, has noted that "many of the Member States (41) have procedures, called compromises or given other similar names, in which the Public Prosecutor's Office—subject to legal authorisation and, in some systems, without the intervention of any legal pronouncement—discontinues criminal proceedings against an individual after that person pays a sum of money into public funds or fulfils another condition."[34]

There are no doubt several philosophical and procedural questions that can be raised about negotiated settlements. Some examples would be the ethical condemnation of the idea of negotiating sanctions for acts of a serious criminal nature; the fact that the public function of the criminal trial to assuage the public's demand for "revenge" and for a punishment that expresses "moral" condemnation is inadequately reflected in a negotiated settlement process; again, for the most part it is corporations not individuals who get punished, with the perception that since you cannot jail a corporation the resulting corporate fine is simply passed on to customers and consumers; Furthermore, if not properly managed, negotiations' between prosecutors and offenders with regards to the penalty for alleged violations can become a vehicle for impunity; Prosecutors can "blackmail" corporations that have self-reported; there is also the undesirable prospect of multiple enforcement processes with respect to the same allegedly corrupt transaction as more countries adopt US—style negotiated settlement processes.[35]

However, from the viewpoint of advancing the fight against corruption, there are also clear advantages that deserve serious consideration. For regulatory authorities, negotiated settlements can mitigate the challenge of uncovering, investigating and prosecuting complex multi-jurisdictional crimes by creating the incentive and mechanism for companies to self-police, self-report and engage in proactive compliance schemes. This lessens the information asymmetry faced by prosecutors. The traditional criminal trial is typically slow and costly. Furthermore,

[34] Hüseyin Gözütok and Klaus Brügge, 2002, C–385/01 (C–187/01). http://curia.europa.eu/juris/showPdf.jsf?text=&docid=47686&pageIndex=0&doclang=en&mode=lst&dir=&occ=first&part=1&cid=529789. Accessed 31 May 2016, para 79.

[35] See generally Makinwa 2015, pp. 10–11; In addition to the above reservations about the negotiated settlements process, can be added the fact that corporations are forced become "policemen" and investigators. The 2015 US Attorney General Susan Yates Individual Accountability Memo and new FCPA one Year Pilot Program require that corporations must now provide all the facts about individual conduct relevant to securing convictions of individuals for an anti-bribery violation in order to qualify for any co-operation credit. This may affect due process protections where corporations provide all the evidence necessary to indict individuals. See US Department of Justice Individual Accountability for Corporate Wrongdoing, Memorandum from the Deputy Attorney General Sally Quillian Yates 2015 and the US Department of Justice Fraud Sections Foreign Corrupt Practices Act Enforcement Plan and Guidance 2016.

judgements are subject to appeal making the path of a full trial a lengthy and expensive process.[36]

There are also advantages from the viewpoint of corporations. By taking steps to curb corruption, establishing internal controls and other bribery risk assessment and mitigation processes, a corporation is placed in a better position to negotiate with the authorities if a violation, despite best efforts, does occur. There are also savings to be made for the corporation in terms of reduced costs, both in terms attaining the objectives of the corporation, efficiencies in the resolution of bribery allegations as well as the attraction of reduced penalties and reputational damage.[37]

There are, however, wide differences in European countries with respect to negotiated settlements for corruption offences.[38] There are differences with regards to the legal foundation for a process of negotiating with prosecuting authorities. Some countries abide by the principle of legality and mandatory prosecution. Yet this does not necessarily mean that there is no room for a form of negotiation. In Italy, for example, in line with the principle of legality, there is no prosecutorial discretion on whether or not to institute criminal proceedings. However, an opportunity for negotiation of penalties can arise with the procedure of *patteggiamento*, where the public prosecutor and the defendant come to an agreement, approved by a judge, on a penalty that avoids a full criminal trial.[39]

Similarly, prosecutors in Poland are bound by the principle of legality under Article 10 of the Criminal Procedure Code, which imposes a duty to prosecute, except where the damage to society is negligible, an exception that will not apply in cases of corruption. However, by application of Article 387 of the Code of Penal Procedure there is the possibility for negotiation with respect to a mitigated penalty without full trial for certain offences.[40] In Sweden the principle of legality and the rules on mandatory prosecution have several exceptions which give some power of discretion to the prosecutor.[41] In Germany, another country where prosecutors are also bound by the principle of legality, a narrow legal framework for negotiated settlements has developed that is consistent with German criminal law principles of truth-finding, individual guilt, public and oral trial as well as the prohibition against self-incrimination.[42]

---

[36] Makinwa 2015, p. 9.

[37] Makinwa 2015, pp. 9–10.

[38] See generally Makinwa 2015, for the differences in resolutions between law enforcement authorities and alleged wrongdoers regarding alleged violations of anti-corruption laws in the EU Countries of France, Germany, Poland, Italy, The United Kingdom, and Sweden as well as the non-EU country of Norway.

[39] Mariani 2015, pp. 59–75.

[40] Stawicka and Matusiak 2015, pp. 77–104.

[41] Sandgren 2015, pp. 147–169; see also position in Norway in this regard. Soreide 2015, pp. 125–146.

[42] Oehmichen 2015, pp. 35–58.

Other countries have more freedom on whether or not to prosecute, as in France there is strong prosecutorial independence and discretion accorded with regards to charging.[43] In The Netherlands, Dutch prosecutors have the discretion to dismiss a case on the fulfilment of a condition (*Transactie*) under Section 74 of the Dutch Criminal Procedure Code.[44] In the United Kingdom, prosecutors exercise a fair measure of discretion along specific guidelines.[45]

There are also differences with regard to the process of such negotiations, the absence or presence of judicial oversight, the level of transparency, the types of outcomes, the presence or absence of guidelines, and the level of predictability for a corporation that chooses to engage in the process. These differences notwithstanding, it is clear that the *notion* of negotiated settlements as an agreed *resolution* between law enforcement authorities and alleged wrongdoers does exist in Member States as indicated from the practice as examined in these representative countries. What is also clear, however, is that such a fragmented landscape renders the "stick" that is necessary for an effective system of negotiated unpredictable, uncertain and variable. There is no clarity or certainty about the position of corporations that operate across borders. A negotiated settlement approach to corruption offences is only attractive where the "trade—off" is clear. This trade-off is one that the Member States of the EU should attempt to fashion together in a manner that is consistent with the global normative and business environment that European corporations operate in.

14.4 Negotiated Settlements and the Right to Fair Hearing

A critical aspect of fashioning a European approach to negotiated settlements is the question of whether or not such a process is compatible with the right to a fair trial enshrined in Article 6 of the ECHR.[46] Article 6(1) of the ECHR establishes that everyone is entitled *to a fair and public hearing* within a reasonable time *by an independent and impartial tribunal established by law*. The press and public may only be excluded from all or part of the trial in (a) the interests of morals, public order or national security in a democratic society; or (b) where the interests of juveniles or the protection of the private life of the parties so require; or (c) if in the opinion of the court in special circumstances publicity would prejudice the interests of justice.[47] In all other instances, judgement shall be pronounced pub-

[43] Perdriel-Vaissière 2015, pp 17–34.

[44] Wingerde and Smid 2015, pp. 59–75.

[45] Bacarese 2015, pp. 171–192.

[46] Charter of Fundamental Rights of the European Union, OJ C 326, 26.10.2012, pp. 391–407; Convention for the Protection of Human Rights and Fundamental Freedoms, opened for signature in Rome on 4 November 1950, (entered into force in 1953) European Convention on Human Rights, as amended by Protocols 11 and 14, ETS 5 (ECHR).

[47] *Ibid.*

licly. Can a negotiated settlement process that occurs quasi-privately between prosecuting authorities and alleged wrongdoers meet the public hearing standard?

Furthermore, a negotiated settlement process may infringe on the right guaranteed under Article 6(2) the ECHR that anyone charged with a criminal offence be presumed innocent until proved guilty according to law. In addition, a resolution reached outside of the court may infringe on the right to make an application to the European Court of Human Rights (ECtHR) where there is an alleged violation by the prosecuting authorities of the rights guaranteed under the ECHR.[48] By extension it could also infringe upon the right of appeal in criminal matters that is guaranteed under Article 2 of Protocol No. 7.

The public function of the criminal trial may be inadequately reflected in a negotiated settlement process.[49] Furthermore, the process of negotiated settlements itself may lack transparency, may not sufficiently protect the rights of alleged offenders and may in itself be susceptible to corruption if there is a lack of oversight.[50]

Simply put, the EU is expected to constitute itself as an AFSJ with respect for fundamental rights as well as the different legal systems and traditions of the Member States.[51] Actions taken in the fight against corruption must be centred on guaranteeing security of the citizens of Europe while safeguarding the fundamental rights, freedoms and integrity of the person.[52] As such, a negotiated settlement regime must address the due process concerns listed above to be compatible with the due process provisions of the ECHR.

Fortunately, some guidance has been given by the ECtHR about the compatibility of plea bargaining procedures with the fair trail protections of the ECHR. In the 2014 case of *Natsvlishvili and Togonidze v. Georgia*,[53] the applicants alleged that the plea-bargaining process, as provided for by domestic law at the material time and applied in his case, had been an abuse of process and unfair, in breach of Article 6(1) of the Convention and Article 2 of Protocol No. 7 to the Convention. The applicants also alleged that the publicity given to his arrest had breached his right to be presumed innocent under Article 6(2) of the Convention. Furthermore, it was argued that the State had hindered the exercise of the applicant's right of

48 ECHR, above n 46, Article 34.

49 Makinwa 2015, p. 10.

50 See comments of Eijsbouts in Eijsbouts 2014, p. 218. Eijsbouts remarks, 'Negotiated settlement is not always a negotiation, in many cases it is an imposition.

51 Consolidated Version of the Treaty on the Functioning of the European Union, signed on 13 December 2007, OJ C 326 (entered into force on 1 December 2009) as amended on 26 October 2012 (TFEU), Article 67 (1).

52 European Council Notice 2010, Sect. 1.1.

53 The European Court of Human Rights, Natsvlishvili and Togonidze v. Georgia, 29 April 2014, App No 9043/05. http://hudoc.echr.coe.int/eng?i=001-142672#{"itemid":["001-142672"]}. Accessed 31 May 2016.

individual petition, contrary to Article 34 of the Convention, and that the financial penalties imposed as part of the plea-bargaining process had breached their property rights under Article 1 of Protocol No. 1.[54]

The Court reviewed a broad comparative study of the process of plea bargaining in Member States and concluded that the practice of co-operation with the investigative authority in order to obtaining the lessening of charges or to receive a reduction of sentence in exchange for a plea of guilty or a *nolo contendere* plea in advance of trial can be considered a *common feature* of European criminal justice systems.[55] The court observed that plea bargaining in Council of Europe Member States mostly takes the form of sentence bargaining.[56] Charges bargaining can be found in fewer Member States[57] because the principle of legality that operates in many European Countries provides, "less leeway for the prosecution to amend and drop charges".[58]

The court was of the opinion that there cannot be anything improper in the process of charge or sentence bargaining in itself.[59] The court further added that in addition to the important benefits of speedy adjudication of criminal cases and alleviating the workload of courts, in addition and more importantly, the idea of plea bargaining can also, if applied correctly, "*be a successful tool in combating corruption and organised crime…*'[60]

Co-operation leading to the resolution of the criminal case could lead to the discontinuation of criminal proceedings, to a more lenient sentence or charges dropped where a defendant co-operated with the authorities leading to the resolution of the case. In this regard the court noted that Austria, Belgium, France and Liechtenstein have procedures to present elements of plea bargaining leading to the discontinuation of criminal proceedings, while Bosnia and Herzegovina, Bulgaria, the Czech Republic, Estonia, France, Germany, Hungary, Italy, Malta, Moldova, Montenegro, Poland, Romania, Russia, Serbia, Slovakia, Slovenia, Spain, Switzerland, Ukraine and the United Kingdom (England and Wales) have established plea-bargaining processes resulting in a criminal conviction.[61]

The court also noted that countries like Austria, the Czech Republic, Hungary, Montenegro, Russia and Serbia provide for the opportunity to have a more lenient sentence imposed, charges dropped or criminal proceedings discontinued if a

[54] Natsvlishvili and Togonidze v. Georgia, 29 April 2014, App No 9043/05, (Natsvlishvili case), Para 3.

[55] *Ibid.* Para 90.

[56] *Ibid.* Para 65. This being the case in Bosnia and Herzegovina, Bulgaria, the Czech Republic, Estonia, France, Germany, Hungary, Italy, Malta, Moldova, Montenegro, Romania, Russia, Serbia, Slovakia, Slovenia, Spain, Switzerland, Ukraine and the United Kingdom.

[57] *Ibid.* Para 65. Namely Hungary, Serbia, Slovenia, Spain, Switzerland and the United Kingdom.

[58] *Ibid.*

[59] *Ibid.*

[60] *Ibid.* Para 90.

[61] *Ibid.* Para 63.

defendant co-operates with the authorities and thereby contributes to the resolution of the criminal case.[62]

The Court then analysed the effect of plea bargains. The court considered that where the effect of plea bargaining is that a criminal charge against the accused is determined through an *abridged form of judicial examination*, this amounts, in substance, to the *waiver of a number of procedural rights*.[63] Provided that such a waiver of procedural rights is made voluntarily, such a waiver would not be a problem in itself. The Court noted that "neither the letter nor the spirit of Article 6 prevents a person from waiving these safeguards of his or her own free will".[64] The Court concluded that by striking a bargain with the prosecution authority over the sentence and pleading no contest as regards the charges, the applicant waived his right to have the criminal case against him examined on the merits.[65]

However, for such a waiver to be effective for Convention purposes, the Court emphasised that it is a "cornerstone principle" that any such waiver of procedural rights must, be established in an unequivocal manner, and be attended by minimum safeguards commensurate with its importance and not run counter to any important public interest.[66] In addition, such a waiver must not run counter to any important public interest.[67]

The key element on which this "cornerstone principle" is upheld is the extent to which it can factually be shown that the acceptance of the plea bargain, which entails the waiver of the rights to an ordinary examination of the case on the merits and to ordinary appellate review was an "*undoubtedly conscious and voluntary decision*".[68] The court needs to establish that the waiver could not be said to have resulted from any duress or false promises made by the prosecution, but, on the contrary, was accompanied by sufficient safeguards against possible abuse of process.[69]

To this end, the Court laid down the following two conditions to assess the *validity* of a waiver *i.e.,* a waiver that was the result of an "undoubtedly conscious and voluntary decision."

Firstly, the bargain had to be accepted by the first applicant in full awareness of the facts of the case and the legal consequences and in a genuinely voluntary manner; and,

Secondly, the content of the bargain and the fairness of the manner in which it had been reached between the parties had to be subjected to sufficient judicial review.[70]

---

62 *Ibid.* Para 64.

63 *Ibid.* Para 91.

64 *Ibid.*

65 *Ibid.* Para 92.

66 *Ibid.* Para 91.

67 *Ibid.*

68 *Ibid.* Para 97.

69 *Ibid.*

70 *Ibid.* Para 91.

In determining whether these two conditions were fulfilled the Court took the following factors into consideration.

1. The applicant himself requested the prosecuting authority to arrange for a plea bargain and it was not imposed by the prosecution;
2. The applicant expressed the willingness to repair the damage done to the state;
3. The applicant was granted access to the criminal case materials;
4. The applicant was represented by two qualified lawyers of his choice, one of whom started meeting with the applicant from the very beginning of the criminal proceedings;
5. The lawyers ensured that the first applicant received advice throughout the plea-bargaining negotiations with the prosecution, and one of them also represented the first applicant during the judicial examination of the agreement;
6. The judge who was called upon to examine the lawfulness of the plea bargain enquired with the first applicant and his lawyer as to whether he had been subjected to any kind of undue pressure during the negotiations with the prosecutor;
7. The applicant explicitly confirmed on several occasions, both before the prosecution authority and the judge, that he had fully understood the content of the agreement, had had his procedural rights and the legal consequences of the agreement explained to him, and that his decision to accept it was not the result of any duress or false promises;
8. A written record of the agreement reached between the prosecutor and the first applicant was drawn up, signed by the prosecutor and by both the first applicant and his lawyer, and submitted to the trial judge for consideration. This made it possible to have the exact terms of the agreement, as well as of the preceding negotiations, set out for judicial review in a clear and incontrovertible manner
9. The fact that the trial court was not, according to applicable domestic law, bound by the agreement reached between the first applicant and the prosecutor. The trial court was entitled to reject that agreement depending on its own assessment of the fairness of the terms contained in it and the process by which it had been entered into. Not only did the court have the right to assess the appropriateness of the sentence recommended by the prosecutor in relation to the offences charged, it also had the power to lessen it.
10. The fact that the trial court enquired, for the purposes of effective judicial review of the prosecution authority's role in plea bargaining, whether the accusations against the first applicant were well-founded and supported by *prima facie* evidence.
11. The fact that trial court examined and approved the plea bargain during a public hearing

On this basis the ECtHR was able to hold that there was no violation of the fair trial provisions of the ECHR in the *Natsvlishvili* case.

Clearly, plea bargain processes or any agreed resolution between law enforcement authorities and alleged wrongdoers regarding alleged violations of anti-corruption laws that results in sanctions or other legal measures must arguably meet the threshold established in the Natsvlishvili case in order to constitute a valid waiver of procedural safeguards. Processes that reward collaboration and co-operation by individuals and corporations must be "undoubtedly conscious and voluntary decision[s]." This is the framework within which a European dimension of a best practice that has the potential of addressing some of the institutional misalignments inherent in the traditional methods of enforcement of corruption offences can be developed.

14.5 The Legal Scope for an EU Dimension

Under the now-concluded Stockholm Programme 2010–2014, the EU Commission received the political mandate to develop a comprehensive EU anti-corruption policy in the understanding that in the face of cross-border crime, Member States should take all necessary measures at the national level to improve judicial co-operation.[71] With regards to coordinated prevention, the EU Council expressed the view that "the best way to reduce the level of crime is to take effective measures to *prevent them from ever occurring*, including promoting social inclusion, by using a multidisciplinary approach which also includes taking administrative measures."[72] Co-operation within the area of crime prevention was recognised with a new legal basis.[73]

With particular reference to economic crime and corruption, the Council noted that establishing a Europe that protects meant developing mechanisms that reduce the number of opportunities available to organised crime as a result of a globalised economy.[74] To this end, Member States are called upon to enhance the capacity for financial investigations by combining all available instruments in fiscal, civil and criminal law,[75] improving the prosecution of corruption in the private sector and facilitating *the exchange of best practices in prevention and law enforcement*.[76]

Post-Stockholm, the EU intends to *strengthen trust, mobility and growth*[77] within the Union by consolidating, codifying and complementing what has already

[71] European Council Notice 2010, para 3.1.

[72] European Council Notice 2010, Sect. 4.3.2, para 1.

[73] European Council Notice 2010, Sect. 4.3.2, para 3.

[74] European Council Notice 2010, Sect. 4.4.5.

[75] European Council Notice 2010, Sect. 4.4.5.

[76] European Council Notice 2010, Sect. 4.4.5.

[77] European Commission 2014c, p. 3.

been achieved and, when necessary and appropriate, codifying EU law and practice and complementing the existing framework with *new initiatives*.[78] However, the Council emphasises that when applying any of these methods, the EU should fully take account of the fact that the diversity of legal systems and traditions in the EU has to be preserved.[79]

Under Title V of the Treaty on the Functioning of the European Union (TFEU) Article 67(1) TFEU emphasises the need for Member States to constitute an area of freedom, security and justice with respect for fundamental rights and the different legal systems and traditions of the Member States. This will be achieved by taking (1) measures to prevent and combat crime, (2) taking measures to ensure coordination and co-operation between police and judicial authorities and other competent authorities, as well as (3) through the mutual recognition of judgements in criminal matters and, (4) if necessary, through the approximation of criminal laws.[80] Under the concluded Stockholm program it was noted that in order to improve co-operation based on mutual recognition, there may be a need for a *horizontal approach* regarding certain recurring problems during negotiations on instruments.[81] Where necessary the approximation of substantive and procedural law should facilitate mutual recognition.[82]

Article 83 TFEU also seeks to strengthen judicial co-operation in criminal matters.[83] Article 83(1) TFEU encourages the harmonisation of substantive criminal law in Member States to establish minimum rules concerning the definition of criminal offences, as well as sanctions with respect to serious crimes with a *cross border dimension* because of the "special need to *combat them on a common basis*".[84] The TFEU identifies corruption as one of the particularly serious crimes that meets the cross-border dimension threshold and which needs to be combatted on a common basis.[85]

Co-ordinated EU level administrative sanctions are given a legal basis in the TFEU. While there is no clear definition of what an administrative approach is, it has been described as *the non-traditional approach or non-penal approach to*

---

[78] European Commission 2014c, p. 4.

[79] European Commission 2014c, p. 4.

[80] TFEU, above n 51, Article 67 (3).

[81] European Council Notice 2010, para 3.1.1.

[82] European Council Notice 2010, para 3.1.1.

[83] TFEU, above n 51, Title V Chap. 4. The legal basis for the harmonization of substantive laws of Member States is provided in Article 83 TFEU. Article 83(1) provides the legal base for harmonization of substantive criminal laws in crimes with a cross-border dimension while Article 83(2) allows for directives may to establish minimum rules with regard to the definition of criminal offences *and sanctions* in areas that have already been the subject of harmonization. See generally Vervaele 2013, pp 43–72.

[84] TFEU, above n 51, Article 83 (1).

[85] TFEU, above n 51, Article 83 (1), 2nd paragraph.

fighting organised crime.[86] Article 75 TFEU provides that the European Parliament and the Council may *define a framework for administrative measures where they are necessary achieve the high level of security desired in the AFSJ*,[87] provided that necessary provisions on legal safeguards are taken. Agreed resolutions between law enforcement authorities and alleged wrongdoers regarding alleged violations of anti-corruption laws resulting in sanctions or other legal measures, could fall within such a framework.

It is the responsibility of Member States to organise between themselves and under their responsibility such forms of co-operation and coordination as they deem appropriate between the competent departments of their administrations responsible for safeguarding national security.[88] The TFEU provides the possibility for the Council to adopt measures to ensure administrative co-operation between the relevant departments of the Member States, as well as between those departments and the Commission.[89]

Article 75 elaborates on administrative measures that can be taken with regard to capital movements and payments, such as the freezing of funds, financial assets or economic gains belonging to, or owned or held by, natural or legal persons, groups or non-State entities.[90] This would include economic assets or gains made by a natural person or by a corporation engaged in international trade affecting the internal market of the EU.

A legal basis for an EU level prosecuting function is provided in Article 86(4) that provides for the establishment of a European Public Prosecutors Office from Euro just in cases of crimes affecting the financial interests of the Union[91] and in cases of serious crimes having a cross border dimension.[92] In addition, the European Anti-Fraud Office (OLAF) is actively engaged in improving corruption prevention, detection and investigation techniques of EU authorities and Member States.[93] EU Member States are also called upon to improve the prosecution of corruption in the private sector.[94]

---

[86] Sappens et al. 2015, p. 4.

[87] TFEU, above n 51, Article 75.

[88] TFEU, above n 51, Article 73.

[89] *Ibid.* Article 74.

[90] *Ibid.* Article 75.

[91] *Ibid.* Article 86(1).

[92] *Ibid.* Article 86(4).

[93] OLAF is specifically charged with protecting the financial interests of the European Union and to fight fraud affecting the EU-budget, as well as corruption and any other irregular activity, including misconduct, within the European Institutions. Significantly, OLAF is charged to take part in the activities of international bodies and associations specialized in the fight against fraud and corruption for the purpose, among others, of exchanging best practices. See Article 1(1)(c) Commission Decision of 27 September amending Decision 1999/352/EC, ECSC, Euratom establishing the European Anti-fraud Office 2013b.

[94] See Council Framework Decision 2003/568/JHA of 22 July 2003 on combating corruption in the private sector, OJ L 192, 31/07/2003, pp. 0054–0056.

Beyond co-operation in criminal matters under Title V., in the area of protection of the financial interests of the EU, Article 325 calls on the EU institutions and Member States to counter fraud and any other illegal activities affecting the financial interests of the Union through measures which *shall act as a deterrent.*[95] Article 325 measures should afford effective protection across all the Member States, in all the Union's institutions, bodies, offices and agencies.[96] Furthermore the drafters of the proposal note that "the term fraud must in this context be understood in a broad sense, including also certain fraud-related criminal offences."[97] More recently the EU while addressing money laundering and terrorist financing, reiterated the need to ensure consistency between the EU approach and the international one, to ensure consistency between national rules, as well as flexibility in their implementation; ensuring that the rules are risk-focused and adjusted to address new emerging threats so as to meet the objectives of strengthening the internal market.[98] This reasoning should arguably also apply to the corruption that facilitates such acts of money laundering and terrorist financing.

There is a uniform need for an EU dimension in crimes of a cross-border nature. This is clearly articulated in the TFEU. Corruption is a crime that affects the financial interests of the European Union. It is also a serious crime with a cross border dimension. It is for such crimes that the TFEU provides the legal scope for EU level co-ordinated action. In the absence of a European dimension, Member States acting on their own are not likely to succeed in combatting grand scale corruption to the detriment of achieving security in the AFSJ.

14.6 Conclusion

Tackling cross-border corruption in Europe requires closely coordinated investigations and prosecutions at the European level. It also requires the utilisation of global enforcement mechanisms, such as negotiated settlements, that have a significant impact on the management of corruption by corporations. Negotiated settlements from an EU perspective are "agreed resolution[s] between law enforcement authorities and alleged wrongdoers regarding alleged violations of anti-corruption laws resulting in sanctions or other legal measures". Such settlements can be considered a common feature of European criminal justice systems and can, if applied correctly, "be a successful tool in combating corruption and organised crime."

Effective negotiated settlements require a consistency of approach that is not possible in the fragmented evolution that currently characterises anti-corruption

95 This suggests that the EU has the competence under Article 325, independently of Article 83 of the TFEU to take measures and adopt criminal laws to tackle fraud.

96 TFEU, above n 51, Article 325(1).

97 European Commission 2012, p. 6, para 3.1.

98 European Commission 2013a, p. 2. This proposal is based on Article 114 TFEU.

enforcement in Member states. To fight corruption in the AFSJ Member States must show the political will to Europeanise anti-corruption enforcement so as to provide an appropriate regulatory response to a cross-border crime of international scope.

The EU should develop and promote a consistent EU negotiated settlement regime that guarantees and protects the rights and security of its citizens. Article 6 of the ECHR does not prevent a person from waiving procedural rights of his or her own free will by agreeing to a negotiated settlement. However, it is a "cornerstone principle" that any such waiver of procedural rights must, be factually shown to have been an "undoubtedly conscious and voluntary decision". An EU negotiated settlements regime should be unequivocal and attended by the minimum safeguards of full information, voluntariness, and fairness in the manner in which it is reached with sufficient opportunity for judicial review.

Effective and consistent policy for the realisation of the AFSJ starts with the acknowledgment that traditional criminal processes have, until now, been unable to meet the challenges of effectively fighting corruption. New solutions need to be developed. An anti-corruption policy of co-operation and collaboration, of public/private dialogue, that characterises negotiated settlements, is arguably better suited to the fast-moving, multi-jurisdictional and technologically complex processes that characterise corrupt transactions today. Negotiated settlements can bridge the divide between prevention and punishment in anti-corruption enforcement by making compliance with prescribed conditions to prevent corruption a key determinant of the bargain or settlement that is negotiated with the prosecuting authorities. In this perspective, an EU dimension on negotiated settlements for corruption offences will better correspond to the reality of the international enforcement landscape and an important tool to the EU toolbox in the fight against organised crime.

The lack of an EU dimension on negotiated settlements, along with the fact that those European multinationals are now effectively being "policed" for corruption violations primarily by US authorities is an unsatisfactory state of affairs. This lack of a European dimension is, in effect, an abdication of the regulatory role to the most active regulatory authority, *i.e.,* the US. This leaves European corporations exposed to unilateral US policy and gives the US an extraordinary advantage in shaping global corporate governance. Developing a European dimension on negotiated settlements will give Europe and its Member States a stronger voice in shaping the contours of this growing global practice as a tool in the fight against corruption.

Anti-corruption enforcement in the AFJS remains a big challenge for the EU. There are no easy or perfect answers in the fight against corruption. Corruption always fights back. However, one should not perpetuate a handicap. As a global player, the EU does not operate in isolation of the outside world. In keeping with global trends of anti-corruption enforcement, the EU has an obligation to develop and promote a consistent EU negotiated settlement regime to protect the rights and security of its citizens and corporations.

Fighting corruption is a key aspect of the fight against organised crime. The effective enforcement of anti-corruption rules is a critical step in this regard. EU citizens require effective and consistent policy to provide a real response to the internal and external threats that are closely intertwined with corruption. Terrorism, money laundering, human and drug trafficking benefit from the lack of a co-ordinated EU level action. There can be no justice without security and no security without justice. Therefore, a balance must be struck between both. Ultimately, fighting corruption in an era of growing internal and external threats requires the *political will*[99] to Europeanise anti-corruption enforcement so as to achieve the co-ordination and consistency of implementation that is necessary for effective anti-corruption enforcement in the Union.

References

Bacarese A (2015) Negotiated settlements for corruption offences—position in the UK. In: Makinwa A (ed) Negotiated settlements for corruption offences: a European perspective. Eleven International Publishers, The Hague

Bellegooij W, Zandstra T (2016) Organised Crime and Corruption: Cost of Non-Europe Report. European Parliamentary Research Service. http://www.europarl.europa.eu/RegData/etudes/IDAN/2016/558779/EPRS_IDA(2016)558779_EN.pdf. Accessed 31 May 2016

Eijsbouts J (2014) Transcript of Session 1. In: Makinwa A (ed) Seminar Proceedings, Negotiated Settlements for Corruption Offences. Eleven International Publishers, The Hague, p 218

European Commission (2004) Report on the Implementation by the Member States of the Convention on the Protection of the European Communities' Financial Interests and its Protocols under Article 10, COM (2004) 709 final. http://eur-lex.europa.eu/legal-content/EN/TXT/PDF/?uri=CELEX:52004DC0709&from=EN. Accessed 31 May 2016

European Commission (2008) Second Report on the Implementation by the Member States of the Convention on the Protection of the European Communities' Financial Interests and its Protocols under Article 10, COM (2008) 77 final. http://eur-lex.europa.eu/legal-content/EN/TXT/PDF/?uri=CELEX:52008DC0077&from=EN. Accessed 31 May 2016

European Commission (2010) Communication on Delivering an Area of Freedom, Security and Justice for Europe's Citizens—Action Plan Implementing the Stockholm Programme, COM (2010) 171 final. http://eur-lex.europa.eu/legal-content/EN/TXT/PDF/?uri=CELEX:52010DC0171&from=EN. Accessed 31 May 2016

European Commission (2012) Proposal for a Directive of the European Parliament and of the Council, on the Fight against Fraud to the Union's Financial Interests by Means of the Criminal Law, COM (2012) 363 final. http://db.eurocrim.org/db/en/doc/1784.pdf. Accessed 31 May 2016

European Commission (2013a) Proposal for a Directive of the European Parliament and of the Council on the Prevention of the Use of the Financial System for the Purpose of Money Laundering and Terrorist Financing, COM (2013) 045 final. http://eur-lex.europa.eu/legal-content/EN/TXT/PDF/?uri=CELEX:52013PC0045&from=EN. Accessed 31 May 2016

European Commission (2013b) Decision of 27 September 2013 amending Decision 1999/352/EC, ECSC, Euratom establishing the European Anti-Fraud Office (2013/478/EU). https://

[99] It is instructive that in April 2016, the new French bill for Transparency and Modernisation of Economic Life presented to the Council of Ministers in March 2016 included a plan to introduce the possibility for companies to plead guilty in exchange for a financial settlements that is meant to bypass lengthy legal procedures. Following the advice of France's highest administrative court this plan is still under review. See Hartmann 2016.

ec.europa.eu/anti-fraud/sites/antifraud/files/docs/body/olaf_decision_2013_478_jo_en.pdf. Accessed 31 May 2016
European Commission (2013c) Report on Organised Crime, Corruption and Money Laundering: Recommendations on Action and Initiatives to Be Taken, A7-0307/2013 Final Report. http://www.europarl.europa.eu/sides/getDoc.do?pubRef=-//EP//NONSGML+REPORT+A7-2013-0307+0+DOC+PDF+V0//EN. Accessed 31 May 2016
European Commission (2013d) Proposal for a Council Regulation for the Establishment of the European Public Prosecutors Office, COM (2013) 534 final, para 3 of the Explanatory Memorandum, p 3. http://ec.europa.eu/justice/criminal/files/regulation_eppo_en.pdf. Accessed 31 May 2016
European Commission (2014a) EU Anti-Corruption Report, COM (2014) 38 final/3 Feb 2014. http://ec.europa.eu/dgs/home-affairs/e-library/documents/policies/organised-crime-and-human-trafficking/corruption/docs/acr_2014_en.pdf. Accessed 31 May 2016
European Commission (2014b), Businesses' attitudes towards corruption in the EU Report (2014) Flash Eurobarometer 374—TNS Political and Social. http://ec.europa.eu/public_opinion/flash/fl_374_en.pdf. Accessed 31 May 2016
European Commission (2014c) The EU Justice Agenda for 2020—strengthening trust, mobility and growth within the Union, COM (2014) 0144 final. http://ec.europa.eu/justice/effective-justice/files/future_justice_brochure_en.pdf. Accessed 31 May 2016
European Council Notice (2010) The Stockholm Programme—an open and secure Europe serving and protecting citizens. OJ C 115 of 4.5.2010. http://eur-lex.europa.eu/legal-content/EN/TXT/PDF/?uri=CELEX:52010XG0504(01)&from=EN. Accessed 31 May 2016
Hartmann C (2016) Stung by large U.S. fines, France to tighten anti-corruption laws. Reuters, March 29, 2016. http://www.reuters.com/article/us-france-corruption-idUSKCN0WV1RS. Accessed 31 May 2016
Makinwa A (2007) The rules regulating transnational bribery: achieving a common standard? Int Bus Law J 1:17–39
Makinwa A (2013) Private remedies for corruption: towards an international framework. Eleven International Publishers, The Hague
Makinwa A (ed) (2015) Negotiated settlements for corruption offences: a European perspective. Eleven International Publishers, The Hague
Mariani P (2015) Negotiated settlements for corruption offences—position in Italy. In: Makinwa A (ed) Negotiated settlements for corruption offences: a European perspective. Eleven International Publishers, The Hague
OECD (1996) Recommendation on the Tax Deductibility of Bribes to Foreign Public Officials, (adopted by the Council on 11 April 1996 at its 873rd Session [C/M (96)8/PROV]) C (96)27/FINAL
OECD (2012) United States Follow-Up to Phase 3 Report and Recommendations December 2012. http://www.oecd.org/daf/anti-bribery/UnitedStatesphase3writtenfollowupreportEN.pdf. Accessed 31 May 2016
OECD (2014) Foreign Bribery Report: an analysis of the crime of bribery of foreign public officials. OECD Publishing, Paris. doi:10.1787/9789264226616-en. Accessed 31 May 2016
OECD (2016) Report on terrorism, corruption and the criminal exploitation of natural resources, Feb 2016. http://www.oecd.org/corruption/terrorism-corruption-criminal-exploitation-natural-resources-2016.pdf. Accessed 31 May 2016
Oehmichen A (2015) Negotiated settlements for corruption offences—position in Germany. In: Makinwa A (ed) Negotiated settlements for corruption offences: a European perspective. Eleven International Publishers, The Hague
Perdriel-Vaissière P (2015) Negotiated settlements for corruption offences—position in France. In: Makinwa A (ed) Negotiated settlements for corruption offences: a European perspective. Eleven International Publishers, The Hague

Sappens A, Peters M, Van Dale D (2015) Administrative approaches to crime: administrative measures based on regulatory legislation to prevent and tackle (serious and organised) crime. Legal possibilities and practical applications in 10 EU member states. http://ec.europa.eu/dgs/home-affairs/e-library/documents/policies/organised-crime-and-human-trafficking/crime-prevention/docs/final_report_eu_study_administrative_approaches_to_crime_en.pdf. Accessed 31 May 2016

Sandgren C (2015) Negotiated settlements for corruption offences—position in Sweden. In: Makinwa A (ed) Negotiated settlements for corruption offences: a European perspective. Eleven International Publishers, The Hague

Shelley L (2005) The unholy trinity: transnational crime, corruption, and terrorism. Brown J Int Affairs 11(2):101–111

Stawicka Matusiak A (2015) Negotiated settlements for corruption offences—position in Poland. In: Makinwa A (ed) Negotiated settlements for corruption offences: a European perspective. Eleven International Publishers, The Hague

Soreide T (2015) Negotiated settlements for corruption offences—position in Norway. In: Makinwa A (ed) Negotiated settlements for corruption offences: a European perspective. Eleven International Publishers, The Hague

United Nations Office on Drugs and Crime (UNODC) (2004) Handbook on practical anti-corruption measures for prosecutors and investigators, Vienna. https://www.unodc.org/pdf/crime/corruption/Handbook.pdf. Accessed 31 May 2016

US Department of Justice Individual Accountability for Corporate Wrongdoing, Memorandum from the Deputy Attorney General Sally Quillian Yates (2015). https://www.justice.gov/dag/file/769036/download. Accessed 31 May 2016

US Department of Justice (2016) The fraud sections foreign corrupt practices act enforcement plan and guidance. https://www.justice.gov/opa/file/838386/download. Accessed 31 May 2016

Vervaele J (2013) Harmonized policies and the harmonization of substantive criminal law. In: Galli F, Weyembergh A (eds) Approximation of substantive criminal law in the EU. Université de Bruxelles

Wingerde K, Smid G (2015) Negotiated settlements for corruption offences—position in The Netherlands. In: Makinwa A (ed) Negotiated settlements for corruption offences: a european perspective. Eleven International Publishers, The Hague

World Bank Publication (2013) Left out of the bargain: settlements in foreign bribery cases and implications for asset recovery. http://star.worldbank.org/star/sites/star/files/9781464800863.pdf. Accessed 31 May 2016

Part V
External Relations

Chapter 15
Taking Stock of the "Common" in the European Union's Common Foreign and Security Policy

Moritz Pieper

Abstract This chapter takes stock of "the common" in the European Union's Common Foreign and Security Policy. Doing so, the chapter analyses the Common Foreign and Security Policy (CFSP) both in terms of institutions and substantive policies. Showing how European Union (EU) foreign policies after the adoption of the Lisbon Treaty have partially been crafted without the necessary institutional consolidation, it sheds light on the many policy challenges that EU diplomacy is confronted with. Cases that this chapter analyses by way of illustration are policies in reaction to the so-called "Arab Spring" and the transnational war in Syria, the EU's foreign policy performance at the Iran nuclear talks, and the impact of the "Ukraine crisis" on both the EU's foreign policy manoeuvrability and the perception thereof in other parts of the world. Likewise, the 2015 refugee crisis has become a stress test for common foreign policy responses, and will therefore be assessed in its impact on the perception of EU foreign policy. Finally, the chapter also touches upon the Union's Common Security and Defence Policy (CSDP) and its intricate interplay between the North Atlantic Treaty Organization (NATO) structures and EU autonomous defence instruments. The European Union's credibility as a foreign policy actor, it will be argued, hinges on its ability to both formulate common strategies and policies internally, and to hold such policies up in the face of third parties in order to see such European foreign policies implemented beyond declaratory rhetoric.

Keywords Common Foreign and Security Policy · EU diplomacy · Common Security and Defence Policy · Syria · Iran · Ukraine

M. Pieper (✉)
University of Salford, Manchester, UK
e-mail: m.a.pieper@salford.ac.uk

J. de Zwaan et al. (eds.), *Governance and Security Issues of the European Union*, DOI 10.1007/978-94-6265-144-9_15

Contents

15.1 Introduction

Foreign policy is notoriously difficult to formulate and implement when more than one foreign ministry is involved. The European Union (EU) has articulated an ambition to develop and deepen a common foreign policy that requires policy consultation among its 28 member states. Not only is this an arduous task bureaucratically, it also presupposes the existence of common political visions. This chapter asks to what extent such common visions exist and thereby reflects on the European Union's state of play of its Common Foreign and Security Policy (CFSP). It analyses CFSP both in terms of institutions and substantive policies. Showing how EU foreign policies after the adoption of the Lisbon Treaty have partially been crafted without the necessary institutional consolidation, it sheds light on the many policy challenges that EU diplomacy is confronted with. A first section briefly outlines the most important institutional innovations in the foreign policy sphere brought about by the Lisbon Treaty, followed by a second section that reflects on the perception of EU Governance and the portrayal of EU Foreign Policy on a conceptual level. This section is necessary to provide a "framework of narratives" before the remainder of the chapter proceeds with a discussion of empirical cases that "test" the Union's CFSP in action. The first policy challenge to CFSP that this chapter analyses by way of illustration is the implosion of governance structures in the European neighbourhood in the wake of the so-called "Arab Spring" and the transnational war in Syria. At a time where CFSP was undergoing institutional sea changes, world political events caught EU foreign policy flat-footed to respond to crises unfolding at its doorstep. Such a gloomy finding is contrasted in the fourth section with a brief discussion of the EU's foreign policy performance at the Iran nuclear talks, a case widely considered a "success story" of EU diplomatic engagement. The fifth section discusses the impact of the "Ukraine crisis" on both the EU's foreign policy manoeuvrability and the perception thereof in other parts of the world. The aspect of foreign policy perception will also be assessed in relation to the refugee crisis that erupted in 2015, which has become a stress test for common foreign policy responses and continues to occupy EU diplomacy at the time of writing. Finally, this chapter touches upon the Union's Common Security and Defence Policy (CSDP) and its intricate interplay between NATO structures and EU autonomous defence instruments. The EU "used the entire range of its tools—CFSP and non-CFSP—to respond to [...] challenges", and "coupled diplomacy with new and existing Common Security and Defence Policy (CSDP) missions on the ground", the 2014 Annual Report of the High Representative for Foreign Affairs and Security Policy to the European Parliament stated.[1]

It will be the purpose of this chapter to analyse to what extent such a combination of foreign policy instruments has in fact taken place in a way that enhances the EU's external ability to act and to respond to foreign policy challenges in an appropriate manner. The European Union's credibility as a foreign policy actor, it will be argued, hinges on its ability to both formulate common strategies and policies internally, and to hold such policies up in the face of third parties in order to see such European foreign policies implemented beyond declaratory rhetoric.

15.2 From Treaties to Institutions to More Substantive Impact?

Since its inception with the Maastricht Treaty in 1993, the EU's CFSP had been intergovernmental and incremental in nature. The "common" in CFSP has been attested a sluggish development both by scholars and foreign policy practitioners.[2] Born under the impression of the First Gulf War and at a time where German reunification provided for a renewed push for a united European foreign policy, CFSP replaced the loosely coordinated European Political Cooperation (EPC) of the 1970s.[3] For the following 25 years, EU foreign policy was coordinated in an intergovernmental way as the "second pillar" under the Maastricht Treaty, with some reforms and codifications introduced by the 1997 Amsterdam and the 2000 Nice Treaty (most notably, the appointment of a Higher Representative for CFSP by the Amsterdam Treaty).[4] The Council General Secretariat functioned as the focal point where foreign policy on an EU level was coordinated under the rotating presidencies of the Council—in effect, this had been the case ever since the Single European Act of 1987 had established the first permanent EPC Secretariat inside the Council General Secretariat.[5] The 2009 Lisbon Treaty meant a sea change in EU foreign policy. A new diplomatic machinery, the European External

[1] General Secretariat of the Council 2015.

[2] Keukeleire 2003, pp. 31–56; Bruter 1999, p. 183; Duke 2002.

[3] Nugent 2010, pp. 376–383.

[4] Dinan 1999.

[5] Dijkstra 2007.

Action Service (EEAS), was set up in order to assist the High Representative (HR) of the Union for Foreign Affairs and Security Policy, who at the same time became a Vice-president of the European Commission. The EEAS was to be composed of Commission officials, staff from the Council General Secretariat, and seconded diplomatic staff from the Member States.[6] The Commission's Directorate General for external relations (DG Relex) was absorbed by the newly-created EEAS, external delegations reporting to DG Relex became Union delegations reporting to the EEAS and the High Representative.[7] With the Maastricht pillar structure formally abolished, the Lisbon Treaty now also enshrined a "legal personality" for the EU in its own right, bolstering the Union's capacity to act in the global arena. Article 21 of the Treaty on the Functioning of the European Union (TFEU, hereinafter "Lisbon Treaty") made explicit reference to the EU as a foreign policy maker.[8] Despite the intention to streamline foreign policy competencies and reduce irritation over institutional complexities, the Lisbon Treaty still maintained foreign policy mechanisms shared between the HR and the EEAS, the Commission, and the EU Council presidency. The latter's rotation has not been abolished, although the idea was to see its importance in foreign policy decline. The Council presidency can still promote foreign policy priorities, while the European Parliament (EP), though limited in its foreign policy competence, can influence the EEAS budget.[9] Undoubtedly, Lisbon saw a drive for more foreign policy consolidation and clarification, and a renewed ambition to shape a stronger role for the EU on the global stage, as also testified by efforts to secure an "enhanced observer status" for the EU in the UN General Assembly.[10] Before this chapter proceeds to shed light on the performance of EU foreign policy in responding to concrete policy challenges, a few words on the oft-cited concepts of "coherence" and "consistency" precede at this point, without which the "nature of the beast" of EU foreign policy cannot be fully grasped.

---

[6] Vanhoonacker and Reslow 2010, p. 2.

[7] Vanhoonacker and Reslow 2010, p. 13. Yet to complicate matters, missions deployed under the EU's Common Security and Defence Policy (CSDP) have their own staff and policy agendas that can render coordination between CSDP missions and Union delegations bureaucratically cumbersome.

[8] Consolidated Version of the Treaty on the Functioning of the European Union, signed on 13 December 2007, OJ C 326 (entered into force on 1 December 2009) as amended on 26 October 2012 (TFEU).

[9] The legal basis is enshrined in Arts 223–234 and 314 TFEU (*Ibid*). See also European Parliament, "The European Parliament: Powers", http://www.europarl.europa.eu/ftu/pdf/en/FTU_1.3.2.pdf. Accessed 29 April 2016.

[10] Guimarães 2015.

15.3 The "Coherence" and "Consistency" Narrative in EU Foreign and Security Policy

Article 21 of the Lisbon Treaty calls for the responsibility of Commission, Council and the High Representative to ensure coherence of the EU's external actions. Much has been made of the EU's alleged lack of coherence and consistency in its conduct of foreign policy. The "coherence" and "consistency" debates have since long become a hobby horse in the EU Studies scholarship.[11] While coherence distinguishes between vertical (between the EU, Member States, and sub-national levels) and horizontal (inter-institutional and across policy domains, "cross-pillar" before the Lisbon Treaty) coherence of EU policy, consistency is associated with policies that make sense in long-term policy planning, with a more or less reliably strategic foreign policy, in other words. Inabilities on an EU level to agree on a common foreign policy stance, as the Council divisions among Member States in 2003 over the Iraq war have shown, let CFSP appear inconsistent. By design, "coherent" and "consistent" foreign policy as the output of a hybrid entity like the European Union has to be the outcome of a long and often tortuous policy-making process. Important institutional innovations have taken place since Christopher Hill wrote about a "capabilities-expectations gap" that he detected in EU foreign policy in 1993.[12] In coherence-and-consistency speak, streamlining the Union's foreign policy competences that were divided across pillars and actors in an effort to improve the EU's vertical and horizontal coherence was one of the main foreign policy drivers behind the Lisbon Treaty. Criticisms of the EU's policy incoherence and lack of consistency are relatively easy to utter when the organisation is compared with national foreign ministries. Essentially, these are often labels and narratives that are re-produced, reifying images held and concepts superimposed. The "one voice" narrative is another example of a reality-producing expectation ever since Henry Kissinger made his famous joke about the "one number" to call in Europe about foreign policy.[13] Attempts have also been made to conceptualise the *nature* of EU foreign policy, ranging from "civilian power" Europe[14] to "normative power" Europe[15] to an EU "structural foreign policy".[16] At the bottom of all scholarly and policy debates about the best way to conceptualise EU foreign policy, the EU remains a hybrid entity defined by fluid frictions between intergovernmentalism and supranational mechanisms. "The new mega-narrative of Europe in

---

[11] See Gebhard 2011; Nuttall 2005; Bretherhon and Vogler 2006, pp. 174–177; Mayer 2013; Lequesne 2013; Smith 2015, p. 21.

[12] Hill 1993.

[13] Macaj and Nicolaïdis provide a critique of the "one voice mantra" that equates "EU unity" with "EU influence". See Macaj and Nicolaïdis 2014.

[14] Dûchene 1972.

[15] Manners 2003.

[16] Keukeleire 2003.

a non-European world would abandon simplistic 'one voice' straitjackets", Oxford scholar Hartmut Mayer writes to that effect.[17] And Michael Smith, Jean Monnet Professor at Loughborough University, formulates: "[...] the post-Lisbon EU institutionalises hybridity in its diplomacy".[18] CFSP never was as common as, e.g., the Union's Common Commercial Policy. The issue and policy domain at hand decide which end of the intergovernmental-supranational spectrum will dominate the policy debate. It is an entity whose complexity eschews easy categorisations traditionally employed in state governance. An attempt to assess EU foreign policy governance today has to analyse the application, response, and impact of the institutions of CFSP to events that challenged their consolidation from the outset.

15.4 Testing the "Common" in EU Foreign Policy: The Arab Spring, Libya and Syria

CFSP underwent institutional changes and an experimental testing phase with the set-up of the newly created EEAS at a time where tumultuous political changes in the European neighbourhood demanded a common foreign policy reaction on the part of the EU. The annual CFSP report to the European Parliament nebulously states the wordy common place that CFSP "is set against the backdrop of a fragmented but interdependent global environment which is increasingly complex, ambiguous and unpredictable".[19] The EEAS, still in its learning phase, was unprepared for the crises that soon tested its durability as a foreign policy actor, and of CSDP as a genuine defence-coordination structure. One such crisis was what came to be termed "Arab Spring" in media and government parlance. Surprised by the popular uprisings in North African countries that spread from Tunisia in 2010, and at a time where Europe was bogged down in its most severe financial crisis, including ensuing budget cuts in the defence sector, the EU's policy response was inadequate. Without a consolidation of the policy instruments created by the Lisbon Treaty and with different perceptions and interests among member states, the EU sent lukewarm support for democratic upheavals at best. In contradiction with its normative discourse, and in the face of European long-standing partnerships with authoritarian regimes in the region, the EU's reaction to the "Arab Spring" proved to be dishonest, and was anything but a common policy. The EEAS and the Commission responded primarily by channelling emergency aid through the instruments available as part of the EU's Neighbourhood Policy, and a 'European Endowment for Democracy (EED) was set up.[20] The EU's responses

[17] Mayer 2013, p. 115.

[18] Smith 2015, p. 12.

[19] General Secretariat of the Council 2015, p. 20.

[20] Gillespie 2013, p. 125.

focused on the "3M's": Money, Mobility and Markets.[21] A common foreign policy was also entirely absent when civil war broke out in Libya and Colonel Qaddafi responded with a ruthless suppression of the insurgencies. Member states like Germany and Poland opposed a military intervention in response to the conflict in the EU's Southern neighbourhood, while France initiated a military alliance with like-minded states such as the United Kingdom and Italy in March 2011, relying on NATO and US support logistically. US President Obama's mantra of "leading from behind"—conceived as an "anti-free rider campaign" in military and defence matters, as Obama himself put it (Goldberg 2016)[22]—then exposed the inadequacy of the EU's security and defence capabilities. The Libyan crisis, Jean Monnet Professor Jolyon Howorth succinctly puts it, was "in many ways the archetypical scenario for which the EU, through CSDP, had been planning since the Balkans fiasco 20 years earlier".[23] Yet, with internal divisions, a lack of strategic vision and poor operational planning, in which the European "coalition of the willing" almost ran out of munitions,[24] Libya proved to be a disaster for CSDP.

EU policy documents at the time notably lacked any "self-criticism and political, strategic thinking"[25]—an observation that held true all the more with the outbreak of violence in Syria in the same year. HR Catherine Ashton met with the Syrian National Council and started engaging in mediatory diplomacy. Yet, with no common position among member states as to how to engage in a civil conflict that quickly turned into a transnational war, EU mediation lacked strategic vision and impact. Beyond issuing statements in support of the Arab League initiative, "supporting the efforts" of the UN Special Envoy de Mistura, and "welcom[ing] efforts to establish a united platform […] for a shared vision for the future of Syria",[26] the EU remains a passive bystander to the conflict. The only framework text for peace talks remains the 2012 Geneva communiqué. Airstrikes against the so-called "Islamic State" in 2015 were part of unilateral member state foreign policies, and only testified rather deep divisions among member states as to their Syrian policies. The increased multilateral framing of airstrikes in November 2015 as a reaction to November 13 Paris attacks came as the result of the French invocation of Article 42(7) of the Lisbon Treaty—a mutual defence clause, similar to NATO's Article 5, which was now used for the first time. Short of a joint CFSP act, however, the invocation was a French request for bilateral assistance from other EU member states, and arguably cannot compensate for the lack of EU policy on Syria in the preceding five years.

[21] European Commission 2011.

[22] Goldberg 2016.

[23] Howorth 2013, p. 65.

[24] Howorth 2013, p. 73.

[25] Soler i Lecha and Viilup 2011.

[26] European Commission, 'The EU's response to the 'Arab Spring', Press Release, 16 December 2011, http://europa.eu/rapid/press-release_MEMO-11-918_en.htm. Accessed 20 November 2015.

15.5 The EU's Mediation in the Iran Nuclear Talks and the E3+3 Format

Contrary to the EU's failure to appear as the strong foreign policy actor in the "Arab Spring" that many had expected after the Lisbon Treaty, the Iranian nuclear talks are commonly cited as a success story for a proactive European diplomacy both by scholars and practitioners.[27] With the discovery of Iranian covert nuclear facilities, and in the absence of US-Iranian diplomatic relations, it fell to the EU to negotiate with Iran. This necessity gave birth to the format of the 'E3' (*i.e.,* France, Great Britain and Germany). This extra-CFSP format was joined by the EU High Representative for the Union's Common Foreign and Security Policy, Javier Solana at the time, in late 2003. The EU had a history of engagement with the Islamic Republic of Iran, dating back to the phases of "critical dialogue" and "constructive dialogue" during the Rafsanjani administration. When European diplomacy failed to produce tangible results in the ensuing diplomatic stand-off, the case was referred to the UN Security Council in February 2006. The negotiating format was expanded to the 'E3+3' (the E3+ the US, China, and Russia), or the P5+1 (the five permanent Security Council members plus Germany). EU positions in the Iran nuclear dossier from 2006 onwards oscillated between original European positioning, as in the first phase of diplomacy from 2003–2005, and aligning EU policies with policy preferences formulated in Washington, as the adoption of EU Iran sanctions testified, at a time where also European entities were affected by US unilateral sanctions with extraterritorial applications.[28] With the advent of the EEAS, European diplomacy again became a driving force in nuclear negotiations with Iran. The EEAS nuclear negotiation team was at the helm of policy coordination and used to chair the talks, with the EU High Representative briefing the other 25 member states in the Council afterwards.[29] The negotiation of a nuclear agreement with Iran in July 2015 was to no small extent the result of successful European foreign policy. Russian deputy foreign minister Sergei Ryabkov acknowledged the European contribution in an interview as follows: "The role of the EU and of the European External Action Service is hard to exaggerate; they coordinated the talks, they summarised the outcome of the discussions, and in fact they were the ones

---

[27] Sauer 2015. Another case cited in the CFSP annual report where the EU successfully led international peace negotiations is the dialogue between Belgrade and Priština.

[28] Note that this consensus relates to the governmental level. A private sector representative remarked that the US State Department had been anxious of the European Court of Justice being too interventionist with regard to unilateral sanctions legislation, as a number of cases challenging the legality of targeted sanctions against entities or individuals have been successful before the ECJ. While there is often a lack of evidentiary standards and due process, the US government's position has been that "they like the legal uncertainty because it often leads to over-compliance." EU Sanctions workshop under Chatham House rules, 14 May 2015, London.

[29] Interview with EEAS official, Brussels, 4 June 2013.

essentially drafting the text, together with Iranian representatives."[30] Initially created as an ad-hoc mechanism to quickly respond with crisis diplomacy outside of formal CFSP structures, the E3 format has proved to be a useful tool in EU diplomacy. EU foreign policy in this case may not have been as *common* as the treaty had originally envisaged, but it did manage to raise approving recognition worldwide of the EU as a diplomatic actor.

15.6 EU Foreign Policy at the Crossroads in Its Eastern Neighbourhood

The same cannot be said of EU foreign policy in its immediate neighbourhood. The EU's Eastern Neighbourhood Programme (ENP) that was born in 2004 lumped together the Southern and the Eastern neighbourhood and was quickly criticised for taking a too country-unspecific and generic approach. This programme was then refined with a more differentiated approach that separated "the South" from "the East". The 2008 Eastern Partnership now sought to formulate more integrative approaches to the EU's Eastern neighbours (Armenia, Azerbaijan, Belarus, Georgia, Moldova and Ukraine). The means of achieving gradual regional integration was by way of closer market harmonisation. Interregional trade projects, however, have become the stumbling block in EU-Russian relations, as it had become clear that Russia had its own ideas about market integration in this region. The Eurasian Economic Union that was formally launched in January 2015 to succeed the Eurasian Customs Union of 2010 and the "Single Economic Space" that had come into effect in 2012 (consisting of Belarus, Russia, Kazakhstan) was an explicit counter-model to the EU's Eastern neighbourhood projects. Ukraine happened to become the *casus belli* between these two integration models.

The ensuing "Ukraine crisis" became an "actorness" test for the European Union that catapulted trade talks residing with the Commission into the foreign policy and security realm. European mediation was expected at the outbreak of a crisis in which Ukrainians were prepared to die for a future in Europe. The EU's underperformance in this role as a crisis manager led to disillusion not only in Ukraine, where the initial motivation behind the "Maidan" revolts had been to step up for a closer association with the EU. The EU's inability to find a common language on the crisis triggered by the non-signing of the Association Agreement first, and on Russian policies in Ukraine next were received with scorn and ridicule on the part of Moscow, but also Washington. The leaked remarks by US Assistant Secretary of State for European and Eurasian affairs Victoria Nuland to "fuck the EU" have become emblematic for US puzzlement about the EU's internal divisions about the appropriate approach to the Ukrainian crisis and to

[30] Centre for Energy and Security Studies 2015.

European-Russian relations.[31] Single EU member states sought to mediate, when the foreign ministers of Germany, France, and Poland travelled to Kiev in the format of the so-called "Weimar Triangle", but a *common* European foreign policy was conspicuously absent. HR Catherine Ashton travelled to Kiev to express solidarity with the Maidan protesters, yet a common CFSP position was impossible from the outset due to the stark divisions as to perceptions of the nature and origin of the conflict among member states.[32] The only notable "common" reaction was the adoption of EU sanctions against Russia, aided by the momentum generated by the Russian annexation of Crimea in March 2014. These sanctions targeted Russian capital markets and dual-use goods, and imposed travel bans and asset freezes against Russian and Ukrainian individuals, "including persons providing support to or benefitting Russian decision-makers".[33] In the absence of the full implementation of the Minsk agreement on the regulation of the conflict in Eastern Ukraine, and short of a strategic review of the use and lifting process of EU sanctions on Russia, these restrictive measures have been prolonged, and stand emblematic of the frosty state of relations between the EU and Russia. Meanwhile, EU election observer missions as well as loans and grants to support the Ukrainian reform process constitutes the bulk of EU foreign policy instruments to help Ukraine develop stable institutions—a process which cannot be conceived outside the toolbox of crisis management operations anymore. The "Ukraine crisis" has demonstrated how the EU's conduct of regional relations far exceeds the management of its neighbourhood policy with a narrow focus on a political and economic "approximation" between the EU and its neighbours, but has become a crucial test for the EU's CFSP and, indeed, its appeal to be a global actor mindful of the security implications of its foreign policy.

15.7 The Refugee Crisis and Its Implications for EU Foreign Policy

Another structurally and perhaps more difficult test for the EU's CFSP came with the massive influx of migrants and refugees to the EU in the summer of 2015. As a consequence of five years of war in Syria, disintegrating governance structures in Iraq, and a fanning of Islamic extremism across the region, millions of people have fled—into refugee camps in neighbouring countries first, then towards "fortress Europe". The ensuing policy debate did not confine itself to the domain of migration policy. In the absence of a common EU migration policy and with the

---

[31] BBC 2015.

[32] The Dutch rejection of the EU's Association Agreement with Ukraine in a public referendum on 7 April 2016 has forcefully illustrated diverging (public and governmental) Member State perceptions on approaches to Ukraine.

[33] General Secretariat of the Council 2015, p. 46.

realisation that the conceptualisation of the interplay between EU external borders and the internal Schengen area was never logically thought through, migration challenges spilled over into the foreign policy domain. The inherent contradiction between the free movement of persons as one of the "four freedoms" of the EU internal market and the "Dublin system" for asylum seekers came crashing down at a time where foreign policy responses had to be found to handle the root causes of migration.[34] The "Dublin Regulation"—Dublin II and, since July 2013, Dublin III, established Member State responsibility for the examination of asylum applications. According to the regulation, the Member State where migrants first entered the EU are responsible for examining the application. A voluntary refugee redistribution quota failed to gauge momentum in the Council, with Slovakia being the first member state to formally file a lawsuit at the European Court of Justice, followed by Hungary. At the same time, European heads of state and government pledged to fight poverty, instability and radicalism in North Africa, sub-Saharan Africa and Syria's neighbouring countries to reduce the "push factors" for migrants and refugees.[35] European governments realised the urge to address violence and instability in the Middle East and North Africa as a concrete response to a threat to the stability of EU mechanisms. Crisis diplomacy with Syria, Iraq, and neighbouring countries started to be combined with efforts to modify existing mechanisms that traditionally had belonged to the "third pillar" of Justice and Home Affairs under the Maastricht Treaty. The EU is thus challenged on all policy fronts, forcing responses from the tool box of all institutions and policy instruments (development aid residing with the Commission, coordination of migration policies in the Council, diplomacy and crisis management on the part of the EEAS). More than ever, real-life events do not wait for the EU to consolidate its CFSP. Coherent responses must be found, sometimes creatively, and with the level of political willingness and European solidarity required. It is doubtful whether the EU-Turkey agreement reached in March 2016 can be the sole substantive EU-level response in migration policy.[36] Intended to staunch illegal immigration, it falls short of providing a comprehensive solution based on the parameters outlined above. As such, it remains an example of "opportunistic transactionalism".[37]

[34] Council Regulation (EC) No 343/2003 of 18 February 2003 establishing the criteria and mechanisms for determining the Member State responsible for examining an asylum application lodged in one of the Member States by a third-country national, OJ L 50 of 25.2.2003 (entry into force 17 March 2003). http://eur-lex.europa.eu/legal-content/EN/TXT/HTML/?uri=URISERV:l33153&from=DE. Accessed 29 April 2016.

[35] Youngs and Gutman 2015.

[36] European Commission 2016.

[37] This term was used by Dr. Lisel Hintz, Panel discussion with Lakhdar Brahimi and Alexander Aleinikoff, Cornell University, 24 March 2016. https://www.youtube.com/watch?v=cVlPpe887sU&app=desktop. Accessed 29 April 2016.

15.8 Sanctions, Defence Autonomy, and Credibility

Alongside European solidarity, the EU's credibility as a foreign policy actor hinges on its ability to carve out an autonomous voice on the international diplomatic stage.[38] The factor of "autonomy" is illustrated in this section with the two examples of sanctions and defence capabilities. Sanctions are a CFSP instrument and adopted by Joint Council Decisions. Their application and effectiveness are monitored by Sanctions Divisions within the EEAS. However, absent a strategic policy debate about the use, effectiveness and, importantly, the lifting process of CFSP sanctions, it can safely be questioned whether EU sanctions are always adopted in Europe's interest. Let us take the example of the EU's Iran sanctions. While the EU threatened formal resistance through the World Trade Organisation (WTO) against the extraterritorial application of US Iran sanctions in the 1990s, European governments had come to a tacit *modus vivendi* with the US administration over US secondary sanctions. These sanctions are called "secondary" because they do not only affect a targeted entity (Iran), but seek to punish third country engagements with the target country. The "national interest" waivers granted by US administrations to EU entities, however, were substituted by presidential executive orders in the Obama administration which again sanctioned EU trade with Iran.[39] European entities, as a consequence, were sanctioned because of business interactions with Iranian entities that were on US sanctions lists. The EU response was no formal complaint, but, instead, an "over-compliance" with US provisions that manifested itself in Council-adopted EU sanctions that went well beyond UN, or even the US, Iran sanctions. The EU decision to impose an embargo on Iranian oil has even been likened to an "ice-breaker for the EU", lowering "the resistance to further sanctions decisions."[40] Former Iranian official Seyed Houssein Mousavian writes in his 2014 book: "One of the harshest blows to the Iranian financial system came with the US Congress threatening to place sanctions on the Belgian-based Society for Worldwide International Financial Telecommunication (SWIFT) unless they cut ties with all Iranian banks. […] Unsurprisingly, the EU yielded to US threats and consequently cut off the Iranian Central Bank from the international financial system."[41] While the latter quote sums up the Iranian perception, the relevance of this observation for the EU's foreign policy is this: the EU's over-compliance with the US sanctions preferences accounted for a loss of agencies. The implementation of the "Joint Comprehensive Plan of Action" reached between the E3+3 and Iran on 14 July 2015 foresees the lifting of Iran

---

[38] On a discussion of the challenges and prospects of the EU's global strategy, see also Chap. 16, Geor Hintzen.

[39] Lohmann 2015.

[40] Lehne 2012.

[41] Mousavian and Shahidsaless 2014, p. 38.

sanctions as Iran complies with its respective terms of the agreement. While EU, US and UN nuclear-related sanctions began to be lifted on 16 January 2016, US unilateral Iran sanctions that were imposed because of human rights violations and "sponsorship of terrorism" will remain in place. The issue of the extraterritorial application of these sanctions is one that will continue to bedevil the EU-US dialogue on Iran for some time to come. The Iran sanctions debate demonstrates the intricate nexus between CFSP decisions, US-EU relations, and the credibility of Europe as an autonomous foreign policy actor.

A similar autonomy-credibility nexus is pertinent in CSDP. Militarily, the EU remains a decentralised and fragmented entity. EU police and military missions (as defined by the 1998 "Petersburg tasks") are by and large an instrument to support the EU's civilian presence. Following the 1999 Helsinki European Council, the EU established a European Security and Defence Policy (ESDP) that was renamed CSDP in the Lisbon Treaty. The EU currently oversees 16 CSDP missions to, e.g., help build security capacities in Mali, fight piracy at the Horn of Africa, or train police forces in the Palestinian Territories. The Treaty also foresees a "permanent structured co-operation (PESCO)", which encourages Member States to coordinate military capabilities like joint disarmament operations, humanitarian and rescue tasks, […] conflict prevention and peacekeeping tasks, [and] post-conflict stabilisation's.[42] It is here that ideas of "pooling and sharing" of military capabilities resurface, particularly in a context where EU Member States introduce budget cuts in their respective defence industries. As the Libyan crisis in 2011 demonstrated, however, the EU is no military actor capable of living up to the expectations generated by the post-Lisbon CSDP. The Libyan operation, once again, has called into question the NATO-CSDP relationship—a debate reminiscent of the debate about a "European Security and Defence Identity" in the 1990s. In essence, the debate centres around the autonomy of the EU as a security actor. In view of CSDP's disappointments, commentators therefore call for a merger of CSDP with NATO.[43] This would avoid the operational and logistical duplication that then—Secretary of State Madeleine Albright's referred to as the "Three D's": no duplication, no discrimination (against non-EU NATO allies, e.g. Turkey) and no decoupling (of ESDP from NATO).[44] Former US Ambassador to NATO Nicholas Burns even called ESDP a "wasteful, unnecessary and disruptive competitor".[45] Albright's three D's thus had to be understood in a context where the nascent ESDP looked like a threat to the durability of NATO as a security provider. Dobson and Marsh therefore summarise America's approach to and perception of the EU as a security provider: "It [America, M.P.] wants greater European burden-sharing and military capabilities, an informal US seat at the EU table and

[42] TFEU, above n 8, Article 28B.

[43] Howorth 2013, p. 75.

[44] Toje 2008, p. 105.

[45] Ambos 2004, p. 187.

guaranteed NATO primacy."[46] The point here is that it should not be forgotten that the emergence of the EU as a unified foreign policy actor triggered US resistance to the formulation of its CFSP in the early 1990s. A strong European foreign policy voice, so the understanding in Washington, might undermine US foreign policy priorities and trigger a rebalancing of what was seen as a convenient transatlantic consensus in favour of the United States as a security and defence provider. Initial US-fears of a growing European military power rivalling NATO were soothed when in 2002 both organisations agreed on the "Berlin Plus" arrangements which entailed the assurance of coordinated actions, mutual reinforcement, implementation of common security standards, as well as the EU's access to NATO assets and capabilities.[47]

The cases discussed in this chapter, however, have shown how CSDP became inextricably entangled with the overall credibility of the EU's CFSP. At a time where Europe is surrounded by foreign policy challenges in almost its entire neighbourhood, the EU needs to become the foreign policy actor the US did not want it to be for the last two decades, if it wants to survive as an organisational entity. Howorth thus puts it the following way: "Either the Europeans agree to develop the necessary instruments to underpin their global strategic ambitions; or they agree to become a continental-sized Switzerland."[48] Transnational wars in its neighbourhoods with their ensuing migratory and security consequences provide the EU with nothing less than this choice.

15.9 Conclusion

The EU remains a hybrid foreign policy actor that combines elements of supranational and intergovernmental decision-making structures. While its foreign policy appearance erodes traditional understandings of diplomacy that largely stem from nation-state thinking, its claim and ambition to be an autonomous foreign policy actor in its own right will continue to create expectations that the Union's Common Foreign and Security Policy often cannot meet. The institutional innovations created for CFSP and CSDP by the Lisbon Treaty have raised expectations by many that the EU would now become a more capable, confident, and autonomous foreign policy actor. They have been disappointed.

By way of illustration, this chapter has discussed a range of empirical cases that confronted and challenged CFSP in the years following the Lisbon Treaty's innovations. The negotiations surrounding the Iranian nuclear programme are one of the examples where EU foreign policy made its voice heard and where its impact was positively received in the world. In other cases, the sheer lack of a common

[46] Dobson and Marsh 2006, p. 150.

[47] Larrabee 2004, p. 52.

[48] Howorth 2013, p. 71.

foreign policy drew criticism and outright scorn on the part of other international foreign policy actors. This was notably the case with the EU's late and sluggish response to the "Ukraine crisis", and to the implosion of governance structures in Iraq and Syria. The Libyan crisis of 2011 provided an occasion for the Union's CSDP to meet its "reality check". The latter attested the Union an insufficiency as a military actor without NATO reliance. Unsurprisingly for an organisation consisting of 28 sovereign Member States, internal divisions characterised the EU's reaction to conflict and uprisings in Libya, Syria, or Ukraine. As a result, the EU's foreign and security policy was anything but common.

The refugee crisis of 2015, then, added an additional layer of cross-policy complexity: seen for too long as semi-distant crises that could be dealt with by way of traditional diplomacy, the conflicts in the Middle East and elsewhere have generated a migration flow that hit the EU institutionally and conceptually unprepared. Policy challenges traditionally associated with migration, justice, and home affairs have spilled over to become a stress test for CFSP as well. More than ever, coherent actorness demands the efficient combination of CFSP with non-CFSP instruments (development co-operation, trade and humanitarian aid), the latter of which resides largely within the Commission's capacities, and the combination of EU instruments with those of other international actors. The CFSP annual report acknowledges this necessity to "further improve coordination and complementarity of its external action" in what the EU calls a "comprehensive approach".[49] As a consequence, the tool box of EU foreign policy will have to be expanded inter-institutionally and across policy domains to adjust to a situation that will not only define the perception of the EU as a foreign policy actor, but as a sustainable organisation as such.

Finally, this chapter has shown how EU foreign policy could only ever become a genuinely common European policy if a process of emancipation as an autonomous actor takes place. While the institutional consolidation of EU defence structures remains unlikely, a shift away from a transatlantic automatism when it comes to security policies should be in Europe's interests. While this does not necessarily mean a defence duplication of NATO, it should be a call for a more confident foreign policy actorness.

References

Ambos A (2004) The Institutionalisation of CFSP and ESDP. In: Mahncke D, Ambos A, Reynolds C (eds) European foreign policy—from rhetoric to reality? College of Europe Studies. P.I.E Peter Lang, Brussels, pp 165–194

---

[49] General Secretariat of the Council, "Main aspects and basic choices of the CFSP", *Draft Annual report from the Higher Representative of the European Union for Foreign Affairs and Security Policy to the European Parliament*, endorsed by the Council on 20 July 2015, http://data.consilium.europa.eu/doc/document/ST-11083-2015-INIT/en/pdf. Accessed 12 January 2016, p. 301.

BBC (2015) Ukraine crisis: Transcript of leaked Nuland-Pyatt call. BBC Europe News, 7 Feb 2015. http://www.bbc.com/news/world-europe-26079957. Accessed 29 April 2016
Bretherhon C, Vogler J (2006) The European Union as a global actor. Routledge, Abingdon
Bruter M (1999) Diplomacy without a state: the external delegations of the European Commission. J Eur Public Policy 6:183–205
Center for Energy and Security Studies (2015) The Iran nuclear deal: Russia's interests and prospects for implementation. 14 Aug 2015. Transcript of a meeting with Russian Deputy Foreign Minister Sergey Ryabkov. http://ceness-russia.org/data/page/p1494_1.pdf?mkt_tok=3RkMMJWWfF9wsRogvazKZKXonjHpfsX64u8rUKCg38431UFwdcjKPmjr1YUDScd0aPyQAgobGp5I5FEIQ7XYTLB2t60MWA%3D%3D. Accessed 27 March 2016
Dijkstra H (2007) The Council Secretariat's Role in the Common Foreign and Security Policy. Eur Foreign Affairs Rev 13:149–166
Dinan D (1999) Treaty change in the European Union: the Amsterdam experience. In: Cram L, Nugent N, Dinan D (eds) Developments in the European Union. Palgrave Macmillan, Basingstoke, pp 290–310
Dobson AP, Marsh S (2006) US foreign policy since 1945. Routledge, Abingdon, New York
Dûchene F (1972) Europe's role in world peace. In: Mayne R (ed) Europe tomorrow: sixteen Europeans look ahead. Fontana, London, pp 32–47
Duke S (2002) Preparing for European diplomacy? J Common Market Stud 40:849–870
European Commission (2011) The EU's response to the "Arab Spring". Press Release, 16 Dec 2011. http://europa.eu/rapid/press-release_MEMO-11-918_en.htm. Accessed 12 December 2015
European Commission (2016) EU-Turkey agreement: questions and answers. European Commission Fact Sheet, 19 March 2016. http://europa.eu/rapid/press-release_MEMO-16-963_de.htm. Accessed 29 April 2016
European Parliament (2016) The European Parliament: powers. http://www.europarl.europa.eu/ftu/pdf/en/FTU_1.3.2.pdf. Accessed 29 April 2016
Gebhard C (2011) Coherence. In: Hill C, Smith M (eds) International relations and the European Union, 2nd edn. Oxford University Press, Oxford, pp 101–127
General Secretariat of the Council (2015) Main aspects and basic choices of the CFSP. Draft Annual Report from the Higher Representative of the European Union for Foreign Affairs and Security Policy to the European Parliament, endorsed by the Council on 20 July 2015. http://data.consilium.europa.eu/doc/document/ST-11083-2015-INIT/en/pdf. Accessed 29 April 2016
Gillespie R (2013) The European neighbourhood policy and the challenge of the Mediterranean Southern Rim. In: Telò M, Ponjaert F (eds) The EU's foreign policy. What kind of power and diplomatic action? Ashgate, Farnham, pp 121–133
Goldberg G (2016) The Obama Doctrine. The Atlantic, April Issue 2016. http://www.theatlantic.com/magazine/archive/2016/04/the-obama-doctrine/471525/. Accessed 30 March 2016
Guimarães FA (2015) Speak Up! Getting the EU a voice at the UN General Assembly. In: Koops JA, Macaj G (eds) The European Union as a diplomatic actor. Palgrave Macmillan, Basingstoke, pp 88–102
Hill C (1993) The capability-expectations gap, or conceptualizing Europe's international role. J Common Market Stud 31:305–328
Howorth J (2013) The Lisbon Treaty, CSDP and the EU as a security actor. In: Telò M, Ponjaert F (eds) The EU's foreign policy. What kind of power and diplomatic Action? Ashgate, Farnham, pp 65–76
Keukeleire S (2003) The European union as a diplomatic actor: internal, traditional and structural diplomacy. Diplomacy Statecraft 14:31–56
Larrabee FS (2004) ESDP and NATO: assuring complementarity. Int Spectator 34:51–70
Lehne S (2012) The role of sanctions in EU foreign policy. Carnegie Article 14, Dec 2012. http://carnegieendowment.org/2012/12/14/role-of-sanctions-in-eu-foreign-policy/etnv. Accessed 12 January 2016

Lequesne C (2013) The European external action service: can a new institution improve the coherence of the EU foreign policy? In: Telò M, Ponjaert F (eds) The EU's foreign policy. What kind of power and diplomatic action? Ashgate, Farnham, pp 80–83
Lohmann S (2015) Zwang zur Zusammenarbeit. SWP-Aktuell 54:1–8
Macaj G, Nicolaïdis K (2014) Beyond 'one voice'? Global Europe's engagement with its own diversity. J Eur Public Policy 21:1067–1083
Manners I (2003) Normative power Europe: a contradiction in terms? J Common Market Stud 40:235–258
Mayer H (2013) The challenge of coherence and consistency in EU foreign policy. In: Telò M, Ponjaert F (eds) The EU's foreign policy. What kind of power and diplomatic action? Ashgate, Farnham, pp 105–117
Mousavian SH, Shahidsaless S (2014) Iran and the United States. An insider's view on the failed past and the road to peace. Bloomsbury, New York, London
Nugent N (2010) The politics and government of the European Union. Palgrave Macmillan, Basingstoke
Nuttall S (2005) Coherence and consistency. In: Hill C, Smith M (eds) International relations and the European Union. Oxford University Press, Oxford, pp 91–112
Sauer T (2015) The EU as a coercive diplomatic actor? The EU-3 initiative towards Iran. In: Koops JA, Macaj G (eds) The European Union as a diplomatic actor. Palgrave Macmillan, Basingstoke, pp 103–119
Smith MH (2015) The EU as a Diplomatic Actor in the Post-Lisbon Era: Robust or Rootless Hybrid? In: Koops JA, Macaj G (eds) The European Union as a diplomatic actor. Palgrave Macmillan, Basingstoke, pp 11–30
Soler i Lecha, E, Viilup E (2011) Reviewing the European neighbourhood policy: a weak response to fast changing realities. CIDOB (Barcelona), Notes Internacionals 36, June 2011
Toje A (2008) America, the EU and strategic culture. Renegotiating the transatlantic bargain. Routledge, New York
Vanhoonacker S, Reslow N (2010) The European External Action Service: Living Forwards by Understanding Backwards. Eur Foreign Affairs Rev 15:1–18
Youngs R, Gutman JP (2015) Is the EU Tackling the Root Causes of Middle Eastern Conflict? Carnegie Article 1, Dec 2015. http://carnegieeurope.eu/2015/12/01/is-eu-tackling-root-causes-of-middle-eastern-conflict/imi6?mkt_tok=3RkMMJWWfF9wsRouuK3OZKXonjHpfsX64u8rUKCg38431UFwdcjKPmjr1YsBTsN0aPyQAgobGp5I5FEIQ7XYTLB2t60MWA%3D%3D. Accessed 15 February 2016

Chapter 16
Will Sleeping Beauty Wake up? Proposals for a New EU Global Strategy on CFDP

Geor Hintzen

Abstract In 2015, the European Union (EU) published a strategic Review called *The European Union in a Changing Global Environment. A more connected, contested and complex World* and called for contributions. Since 2003 the EU has not adapted its foreign policy and the world has changed in important ways. This chapter is meant as a wake-up call. It analyses the "Strategic Review" and offers proposals for a legitimate and realistic EU vision on foreign affairs, for ways to organise foreign affairs at the EU level, and how priorities could be set in a truly global and integrated Common Foreign and Defence Policy (CFDP) strategy. Taken together, these provide elements on which a new and effective EU global foreign and defence strategy can be based.

Keywords Common Foreign and Defence Policy · EU global strategy · Strategic review · Foreign policy vision · Foreign policy institutions · Foreign policy priorities

Contents

G. Hintzen (✉)
The Hague University of Applied Sciences, The Hague, The Netherlands
e-mail: G.H.Hintzen@hhs.nl

J. de Zwaan et al. (eds.), *Governance and Security Issues of the European Union*, DOI 10.1007/978-94-6265-144-9_16

16.1 Introduction

In June 2015, the High Representative Federica Mogherini called for a new European Union (EU) Global Strategy on a Common Foreign and Defence Policy. Over the past decade or so, both the EU and the world have changed in important ways. Since 2003 the world's largest trading bloc has not adapted its foreign policy. Outside of NATO, a European defence policy has by and large been absent. As described in some detail by Moritz Pieper in the previous chapter (Chap. 15), the track record of the 2003 foreign policy has, on the whole, been a dismal failure. In spite of lofty words, the EU has been powerless before events in Libya, Ukraine, and Syria (to name but a few tragedies). Its moral proselytising has won it precious few friends in Africa, Asia and South America. It is a clear instance where its values have in fact hurt its interests. Its continued reliance on multilateralism may be questioned in view of developments. Its passivity and lack of an integrated foreign policy have left it and its MSs vulnerable to the vicissitudes of geopolitics. Its institutional shortcomings have and the unwillingness of Member States to formulate a unified and effective foreign policy have rendered it unfit to cope with the challenges of a globalising and more contested world.

Mogherini's call is to be welcomed, although clearly it is long overdue. For too long, the EU has been the world's sleeping beauty in security affairs. As the recent terrorist attacks in Paris and Brussels highlight, the present state of affairs in the world demands an effective global strategy. In the "near-abroad" there is Russia's destabilisation of Ukraine and its, annexation of Crimea, the tragic chaos in the Middle East, international terrorism, and mass migration. Further afield there is the rise of East Asia, and in particular China, the reorientation of U.S. military focus towards that area, the financial crises since 2007, climate change, the need to secure energy and raw materials, and cyber warfare and international crime. And these are only some of the most prominent points that come to mind. At the EU level, the rejection of an EU constitution in 2005, the financial and economic crisis since 2008, and the rise of populist and anti-EU parties have only compounded problems. European politicians have become more nationalist and inward-looking. Do they realise what it means to share so much so profoundly in a European Union? All this time, Europe and its Member States have proved unable to formulate joint priorities or a common foreign voice. The EU it seems, is running out of steam. It is time for an effective global strategy in order to be able to chart a course for the road ahead.

This chapter is meant as a contribution to Mrs Mogherini's call for ideas and input for the coming EU Global Strategy. It is also meant to be complementary to Chap. 15 of this book. Above all, it is meant as a wake-up call to the EU, our Sleeping Beauty.

16.2 A More Connected, Contested and Complex World

In 2015, the EU published a "Strategic Review" called *The European Union in a Changing Global Environment. A more connected, contested and complex world.*[1] Clearly this document is intended to structure and guide the consultations for the new EU global strategy. It is a rather short document and consists of an executive summary and three parts: an overview of the global environment, challenges and opportunities for the EU, and the implications this has for the future strategy. Short as it is, it contains some important indications about how the EU proposes to formulate its new global strategy.

The overall tone is not very heartening. According to the "Strategic Review", the EU lives in a "strategic environment [that] has changed radically." Ominously, an "arc of instability surrounds the Union". Further away, in Africa "we see conflicts" and in Asia security tensions. Climate change and scarce natural resources may lead to even more conflict. After more than a decade, the EU seems to be waking up to a difficult world, although "global growth, interdependence and technological progress" are reducing poverty and offering more people, "longer, healthier and freer lives". Somehow, the world is not as it was before. The document refers to the "need to agree on our priorities, our goals and the means required to achieve them".

In the first part, the EU lays down its view of a changing global environment. The world has become more connected, contested and complex. Globalisation is the general trend in a more connected world, and mainly seems to present problems. It compels policy makers to rethink issues, such as migration, citizenship, development and health. It "favours economic and financial crime, terrorism and trafficking. The Eurozone crisis has shown how interconnected the EU really is and why further economic integration is needed. Events in Asia, such as China's 'Double Belt' strategy and the Trans Pacific Partnership negotiations show that markets are becoming more connected too. The world is also more contested, as the 'arc of instability' that surrounds the Union is spelled out: in the East, the EU's neighbours suffer from 'economic, political and energy supply fragilities', in the Middle East and North Africa "the spread of ungoverned spaces has enabled criminals and terrorists to thrive" and "identity politics fuels old and new cleavages". Worldwide, there are 50 million refugees, ideology and identity create tensions, and demographic trends and growing inequality threaten more conflict amid conflicts fuelled by climate change and resource scarcity. Finally, in Europe and beyond "new narratives challenge the open society model" and internal EU forces "increasingly challenge the European project". This should encourage European policymakers, "to better connect foreign policy with citizens' expectations and inject fresh momentum in the European debate". The world has also become more complex. The "age of dominance by any single country is over". Other powers,

[1] Strategic Review 2015.

such as China, are rising, although it is unlikely they will form “a single and cohesive bloc”. “[G]lobally power is diffusing beyond the nation state towards a network of state, non-state, interstate and transnational actors”, but “[t]raditional multilateralism is losing steam as emerging countries want to reform the post-World War II architecture”. Still, creating new “global governance mechanisms” is proving difficult.

In the second part of the “Strategic Review”, the EU presents the challenges and opportunities in five sets of geographical areas. Reform through integration (Western Balkans and perhaps Turkey) and association policies (Eastern Europe and also perhaps Turkey) will be supported amongst its European neighbours. The EU will have to tackle “immediate challenges” in the Middle East and North Africa by improving its “internal-external security nexus” and “addressing immediate humanitarian crises” and will have to “help address the root causes of resentment”. In Africa, the EU will develop policies on migration and mobility, security, and fair trade and economic integration. The EU “needs to continue investing” in its transatlantic relationship through closer ties with NATO and the Transatlantic Trade and Investment Partnership. At the same time, it will seek to “deepen relations” Latin America and the Caribbean through bilateral partnerships and inter-regional arrangements. In Asia, the EU “can offer consistent but also customised support to regional co-operation efforts”, will “foster a rules-based approach to conflict management” and respond to the opportunities offered by “various developments in Asian connectivity”.

In the third part, there is a call for a “comprehensive approach” which is “more relevant today than a decade ago”. “Vertical and horizontal silos hamper the EU’s potential global role”. In the present-day world “with mounting challenges and opportunities this is a luxury we cannot afford”. A clear “sense of direction” is needed. The result should be a “common, comprehensive and consistent EU global strategy”. Five main topics are addressed to illustrate this: Direction, Flexibility, Leverage, Coordination, and Capabilities. Under “Direction”, seven topics are listed: strategic partnerships, disarmament and arms control, the need for a better European defence system, better humanitarian assistance, enlargement in the Balkans, the tensions in trade policy between trade and non-trade issues, and the balance between cyber and counter-terrorism policies. Under “Flexibility”, more flexibility is needed in development assistance, humanitarian aid, and counter-terrorism. Furthermore, the “EU’s declining economic dynamism” and the “high demands it makes on its trading partners” are reducing its “Leverage”. This is highlighted for the European Neighbourhood Policy (ENP), “particularly when it comes to neighbours that have little interest in endorsing EU standards”. “Coordination” is found wanting between the EU and the Member States and between the public-private divide. Finally, in “Capabilities”, the EU needs to develop its migration and defence policies.

As the “Strategic Review” shows, the world is changing quickly and the EU has lost some of its economic dynamism, but it lacks an overall and comprehensive sense of direction. Importantly, there is a lack of policy coordination between the EU and its Member States on important issues. In fact, the European project is increasingly challenged. The overall picture is one more of challenges than opportunities. Choices need to be made, but little by way of solutions is offered.

Compared to earlier documents,[2] however, a shift may be discerned in the direction, priorities, and means the EU proposes to base its strategy on. For instance, throughout the "Strategic Review" there is an unmistakable change in tone, away from the traditional normative approach with its insistence on global governance and multilateralism. As it is formulated in the "Executive Summary", the EU has "a responsibility to protect [its] citizens while promoting [its] interests and universal values". Decision-makers are also enjoined to "better connect foreign policy with citizens' expectations". Multilateralism is also described as "losing steam". A shift in emphasis is apparent. Many of the issues mentioned, furthermore, force a more realist mindset on the reader. State failure, terrorism, migration, conflict, and challenges towards the way global governance has been structured. The world in this view is not only more complex and contested, it is also more anarchic. Unsurprisingly, the means that are proposed go towards further integration and enlargement of the EU and an increase in defence-related capabilities.

Against this background, what can an ordinary European citizen contribute towards a global strategy for the European Union? Among the many things that may be advanced, three main topics are proposed: what should go into a comprehensive vision for the global strategy, what should be the institutional means of ensuring it is effective, and what could be frameworks for determining its priorities? The thrust of my proposals would be to ensure that the next time the EU wants to adjust its global strategy the awakening would be rather less rude than in 2015.

16.3 Ingredients of a Realistic and Legitimate Vision

The quest for a new direction or for the "need to agree on (…) our goals" that lies at the heart of the "Strategic Review", begs the question of what vision the EU has for its future and that of its citizens. In fact, to all intents and purposes, there already *is* a vision that could infuse the EU's global strategy. There are several sources from which this vision has been drawn. They date back to the aftermath of the Cold War in the early 1990s. The first source is Francis Fukuyama's theory about the "End of History".[3] According to Fukuyama, with the demise of the Soviet Union liberalism had defeated the last of the competing ideologies. The era of power politics had come to an end. Liberalism's culture of abundance and consumerism was pursuing its victorious advance over the world. With it, states and borders had decreased in importance and liberal democracy was spreading. The

[2] EEAS Strategic Planning 2003.

[3] Fukuyama 1992.

world was growing towards a state of "Common Marketisation" in which a universal homogeneous state would be established. In the future, multilateralism and international co-operation would be the dominant forms of international relations. In 2007 Fukuyama praised the EU as "the fullest realisation of his theory".[4] The second source may be what has been termed in a different context, the "Rights Revolution".[5] This refers to the increasing tendency to pursue a value-based policy of rights both in international and national governance. This movement has had a profound influence on the EU. It resulted in its fundamental ideal of a rule-based world based on Western core values, such as the rule of law, democracy, and human rights. In fact, these principles today profoundly structure the existing European treaties and inform its foreign policies. A list of rights is included in stipulations on the overall rules (Article 3(5) Treaty on European Union (TEU)) and the foreign affairs guidelines (Article 21 Treaty on the Functioning of the European Union (TFEU)) which the Union should adhere to. Next to such values as peace, human rights, the rule of law and democracy, these include the strict observance and the development of international law, including the UN Charter. These have been based on theories of global governance through a strict adherence to international law.[6] Finally, both of these sources have converged to spawn a large corpus of literature on the special nature of the EU. As Thomas Diez phrased it:

> There is a widespread belief that the European Union [...] is a novel kind of power not only in its own institutional set-up, but also in its external relations. It is said to rely on civilian rather than military means and to pursue the spread of particular norms, rather than geographical expansion or military superiority.[7]

This belief has given rise to such characterisations of the EU as a "postmodern power", a "civilian power" or a "normative power". At the start of his presidency in 2000, Romano Prodi remarked:

We must aim to become a global civil power at the service of sustainable global development. After all, only by ensuring sustainable global development can Europe guarantee its own strategic security.[8]

Rather than a new superpower based on power politics, the EU was a new kind of international body. It was neither wholly international organisation nor wholly state.

In the past decade, this vision has lost much of its lustre.[9] As the "Strategic Review" clearly reflects, power politics has made a come-back in a more contested world. Russia's involvement in Ukraine and Syria, fundamentalist terrorism, and China's assertiveness in the South China Sea are cases in point. Multilateralism "is

---

[4] Brand 2007.

[5] Ignatieff 2000.

[6] Fassbender 1998, p. 531.

[7] Diez 2005, p. 613.

[8] Prodi 2000.

[9] See for instance Ahtisari 2008.

losing steam". Global arrangements, such as the WTO, are being complemented by regional or bilateral agreements, such as the Trans-Pacific Partnership. The financial crisis of 2008 has delivered a blow to the EU's "abundance and consumerism". Finally, the EU's value-laden human rights policies clearly pose a problem of means or ends. In the past, the European Neighbourhood Policy and association treaties have approached rights as a means. This has repeatedly backfired, as the "Strategic Review" itself makes clear when it refers to "neighbours that have little interest in endorsing EU standards".

An important background to a new vision for a global strategy should be a more optimistic vision. Why the problematic exposition of a contested, complex world? Why refer to an arc of instability that surrounds the EU? Within this setting, the search for direction after many years of silence on strategic matters does not sound well. European culture and values have become the foundation of much of the global order. European politics and economics have set the dominant framework for international governance and the global economy. Europe's soft power stands unrivalled in the world. Could a global strategy not reflect more pride in European identity and European goals?

A second major element in a new vision should address the pivotal reorientation of the United States towards East Asia. Although still the dominant power, the US "unipolar moment" belongs to the past. In a contested world, the absence of the US and the lack of an effective European security policy have created a power vacuum in East Europe and the Middle Eastern and North African area, where Russia and terrorist groups have been quick to step in. The EU badly needs an integrated security and defence policy that offers security and support to its "near-abroad" and a threat to any potential aggressors. US opposition to a European security policy in the 1990s and their "Three D's" should no longer be heeded, that is "no duplication, no discrimination (against non-EU NATO allies, e.g. Turkey) and no decoupling (of ESDP from NATO)".[10] As Moritz Pieper has made clear in Chap. 15, "the EU needs to become the foreign policy actor the US did not want it to be for the last two decades, if it wants to survive as an organisational entity".[11] After all, it is often overlooked that US supremacy has always relied on its European and Japanese alliances. A more effective European defence policy would only serve to make that alliance more durable and balanced. Member States bear an especially heavy responsibility in this respect.

This leads to a third important element of a vision for a global strategy. If the EU is to become a credible foreign policy actor, it will have to formulate a vision that takes the security policies of the Member States fully into account. If the assertion that "[w]e have a responsibility to protect our citizens" is to be taken seriously, politicians in the Member States will have to agree to an integrated and consensual view of what European security exactly is and make decisions accordingly. Admittedly, this is a long shot. Recent events have clearly borne this out.

---

[10] Toje 2008, p. 105.

[11] See Chap. 15 in this volume, Sect. 15.8.

Member States have been (and still are) slow to show their solidarity with countries, such as Italy and Greece, in the face of the ongoing refugee crisis. Solutions have been piece-meal at best. Results could be disastrous for European cohesion. Lack of intelligence co-operation has enabled ISIS to stage a number of killing sprees in Europe's capitals. Feelings of insecurity among Europe's electorates have given rise to extremist parties and Islamophobia. Finally, Bundeskanzler Merkel's open-door policy to refugees was in direct opposition to several Central European countries' security policies, which listed mass migration as a threat.[12] There is a clear lack of solidarity and understanding between Member States. Would it not be sensible to adhere to the premise that since the EU Member States share a common market and integrated societies, it would be natural for them to organise a common security to protect what they hold in common? Should politicians in the Member States not seize their responsibilities?

Such an approach would call for a revision of the strictly values-based approach of the EU towards international relations. The EU foreign policy based on the rule of law, democracy and human rights reflected only one aspect of the double nature of European foreign policy: value-based bureaucratic policies at the Union level and interest-driven political actions of the (larger) Member States at the Member State level. As The Economist put it, "[l]arger countries delegated values-based policy to Brussels while they got on with the hard stuff, such as security or access to oil. For every pious expression of support for international justice or condemnation of capital punishment, there was a shabby energy deal or quiet support for a useful dictator".[13] In uncontested times such an approach might work, but you cannot base joint action on fixed rules alone when you are faced with unforeseen circumstances. Perhaps precisely because of the Union's internal successes, there is a danger that Europeans overestimate the potential of such an approach to work in all contexts and at all times. (…) [S]uch an approach is not a solid preparation for times when—given the anarchy across the Mediterranean in Libya and Syria and violence to Europe's East—the exception risks becoming the rule.[14] Violence is now spreading to the EU as well…

This calls for a vision that accommodates "the return of politics" at the EU level and allows for a flexible response to unforeseen circumstances. Since the 1990s none of the EU Member States has been able to deal effectively with crisis situations in the "near-abroad" and the US is no longer willing or able to always step in. "[I]n a world of mounting challenges and opportunities this is a luxury we cannot afford".[15] Member States should empower the EU to do the job. A global strategy now more than ever calls for a shared political, interest-based vision.

A fourth element of a vision for a new global strategy would be to have a truly *global* vision. All prior EU foreign security strategies have largely focused on

---

12 Lefebvre 2010, p. 361; Minkina 2011, p. 628.

13 Charlemagne 2016.

14 Van Middelaar 2015, p. 5.

15 Strategic Review 2015.

Europe's "near-abroad". The 2003 strategy largely subsumes the world beyond the "near-abroad" under the notion of "multilateralism". The "Strategic Review" does not show any marked improvement on this score. Although the EU's trade has a global reach, its security and defence policies do not. The EU singularly lacks a strategic vision that can rival China's "Double Belt" policy or its engagement with African[16] and Latin American nations. Both can have an important impact on the EU's future security. As a global actor in trade and development, the EU needs to develop its own global vision in security matters.

After a generation of successive foreign strategies, the words of Belgian Foreign Secretary Mark Eysken still ring true: "…to many, the Union remained nothing more than 'an economic giant, but a political dwarf and a military worm'".[17] Each new strategy has necessitated a cumbersome treaty change. Each new strategy has fallen short of expectations. An inward looking and confused EU has been increasingly unsure about the direction its foreign policies should take. Member States have been jealous of their own foreign affairs policies. In part, the shortcomings and limits of the common foreign policies have led to a situation where "the EU (…) is more contested, as internal forces increasingly challenge the European project".[18] It is time for a strategy with a realistic vision both of the world and of what the EU wishes to achieve collectively in it.

16.4 Organizing Foreign Affairs at the EU Level

If a global strategy is to be truly credible, the EU and its Member States will have "to agree on (…) the means required to achieve" it. The EU will need to possess institutions that guarantee its effective implementation. The Lisbon Treaty has in fact created a number of new EU competences and joined organs that are meant to improve the implementation of its foreign policy. A new post of High Representative of the Union for Foreign Affairs and Security Policy was created, which finally merged the post of High Representative for the Common Foreign and Security Policy and the European Commissioner for External Relations and European Neighbourhood Policy. The new High Representative is also a vice-president of the Commission and the Administrator of the European Defence Agency. However, the High Representative is pointedly is not an EU institution.[19] The WEU was merged with the EU. A legal basis was laid for the creation of a European diplomatic corps, the European External Action Service (EEAS), which was subsequently set up by the first High Representative, Lady Catherine Ashton.

[16] Gathii 2012–2013, pp. 664–695.

[17] Rogers 2009, p. 13.

[18] Strategic Review 2015.

[19] Consolidated Version of the Treaty on European Union, signed on 13 December 2007, OJ C 326 (entered into force on 1 December 2009) as amended on 26 October 2012 (TEU), Article 13; Craig and de Burca 2015, p. 49.

For the first time, foreign and security policy was in the hands of one official and the military aspect acquired clearer communitarian content. Some things, however, barely changed. Vagueness in competences predominates in an area where clarity is crucial. In fact, the Lisbon Treaty does not specify which kind of competence applies for CFSP. None of the articles on competences mentions CFSP.[20] Craig and de Burca conclude that CFSP is most likely a shared competence based on—although not mentioned in-Article 4 TFEU. However, if this is the case, "the need for close examination of the respective powers of the EU and Member States, in order to be clear about the power sharing, is of especial significance".[21] The "Strategic Review" apparently refers to this when it states that "[v]ertical and horizontal silos hamper the EU's potential global role". This is hardly a promising situation. Member States naturally retained their national diplomatic services alongside the EEAS. And importantly, no institution was created that would allow the EU to respond in a rapid and flexible way to crises. As the "Strategic Review" mentions about new global governance systems, formulating grand strategies for the EU's foreign affairs has proved easier than creating new governance systems for its CFSP.

EU Member States and politicians should take their charges seriously when it comes to their "responsibility to protect our citizens". Measured by its results in recent years, CFSP has failed in important respects. The list is actually quite long: Ukraine, Libya, Syria, terrorism, and migration. Clearly, "output democracy"[22] has not been delivering and the "EU too is more contested, as internal forces increasingly challenge the European project". The way ahead is a better organisation of the core state power of coercive force and public administration in the field of foreign affairs and defence,[23] clearer division of competences, more political legitimacy and operational thrust at EU level, and a more complete toolbox. When will Sleeping Beauty wake up?

Within existing arrangements there is room for a better organisation of core state powers and a clearer demarcation of competences. For once, perhaps, sterile discussions about sovereignty within Member States should give way to the needs and realities of civilian protection and decent crisis management. Institutions should be more effective. Competences should be put at the level that will get the job done, be it terrorism, migration or Ukraine. The EU Member States and politicians should come together and sort matters out. Clear competences are important for the European electorates to know who to vote for. It will show who exactly is responsible for the EU's foreign and defence affairs. It will bring in interest-based politics.

---

[20] Consolidated Version of the Treaty on the Functioning of the European Union, signed on 13 December 2007, OJ C 326 (entered into force on 1 December 2009) as amended on 26 October 2012 (TFEU), Articles 2(4), 3, 4 and 6.

[21] Craig and de Burca 2015, p. 90.

[22] See on this term Scharpf 2003, and Schmidt 2013, pp. 2–22.

[23] Genschel and Jachtsenfuchs 2016, pp. 47 and 50.

At the same time if the EU is true to its value-based message, it should make democratic control of these clearly defined competences on foreign and defence's affairs possible at every level, including the EU. A larger role either for the European Parliament and/or national legislatures is imperative for a durable and flexible foreign and defence policy. This would ensure the much-needed interest aggregation that would form the basis for a common solidarity in foreign and defence affairs. It would avoid the joint-decision trap that has marred many policies at the EU level. It would do away with a form of crisis management that is "inefficient from a problem-solving perspective".[24] Efficiency and transparency could finally steer CSFP. This is a field that is simply too important, too unpredictable and too dynamic to have to rely on a treaty change each time it is updated.

What then would institutions that guarantee an effective implementation of the global strategy look like? Important questions that need to be answered in this context are to what extent the competences have been clearly demarcated, whether there is a veto (e.g. is there an option to never reach a decision on a certain topic?), the extent to which dissenting Member States are bound, and the extent to which the decisions are subject to democratic control at the EU level. In practical terms, there are three possible options within the existing treaty framework: 1—the EU adheres to the present treaty stipulations (while, perhaps, clarifying them); 2- the EU forms a security council; 3- the High Representative gets broad implementation powers.

This first option is perhaps the most probable one. If the EU adheres to the present treaty stipulations, decisions will be made by the (European) Council presided by the High Representative. Decision-making will continue to be subject to the vetoing powers of the Member States. The global strategy and its policies will be formulated and agreed to by the (European) Council. The European Parliament will be consulted, but will not have any controlling powers. By and large, in spite of the important changes the Lisbon Treaty has brought about there will not be any real progress towards an institution that is capable of gradually revising a global strategy as external and internal events require or of responding in a swift and flexible manner to unforeseen circumstances. Decisions made during a crisis will be largely reactive. Member States will have the option to veto decisions in the (European) Council in order to be able to pursue a national foreign policy on the matter. In spite of the intentions that would be formulated in a global strategy, a "common, comprehensive, and consistent global strategy" would still be hampered by "vertical and horizontal silos".

A second option could consist of the formation of a European Security Council. Initially at least, this body could be an intergovernmental body that can be activated to deal with a (looming) crisis situation. Most Member States would probably opt into take a part in it. The normal course of foreign affairs and defence could be dealt with according to the European Treaties. Article 33 jo. 26(3) TFEU provides for such a possibility. The Security Council could resemble the UN

[24] Scharpf 2006, p. 849.

Security Council in important respects. The High Representative would be its chairperson. Major states would have a permanent seat and small states would rotate. Rules would ensure that all the major European areas would always have at least one state in the council and that the interests of the participating states bordering or closest to the crisis would be heard. The council would have full competences regarding the foreign affairs, defence, and intelligence issues related to the crisis. No states participating in the Security Council would have a veto. The Political and Security Committee could serve in a supporting role. Political control would be ensured through involvement of the European Parliament or a body composed of national parliamentarians of the Member States participating.[25] As soon as the crisis is solved or dealt with, the council would end its activities and hand over its competences. The parliamentary body controlling the Security Council would have the power to recall the competences or stop the activities of the Security Council. Security Council would periodically inform the controlling parliamentary body and present a final report once its activities have been terminated with regard to the defined crisis. The advantages of such a Security Council would be obvious. It would offer the EU a powerful tool to deal with the many security crises that it is faced with both in its near-abroad and further away. Important preconditions for an effective Security Council would be capacity-building in the areas of diplomacy, defence, and intelligence. In many respects, this is not an unrealistic future, although it would require a massive mental and cultural change in many European capitals.

A third possibility is perhaps the least probable for the near future. It would involve a more permanent arrangement whereby the High Representative effectively becomes the Minister of Foreign Affairs of the EU or a group of Member States that decides to transfer their foreign affairs, defence, and intelligence competences to the EU. Conversely, the High Representative could become a de facto minister for a number of clearly defined areas. The European Parliament would have real powers to control the High Representative and propose legislation. Since this would amount to officially transferring core state powers to an EU official, it would amount to a form of federal state. The opposition to such a step seems to be too great for now, although with the exception of the UK there seems to be a widespread support amongst the European electorates for some form of further integration in the area of security and defence.[26]

Whatever institutional arrangements are made, however, it is clear that the EU and the Member States bear a heavy responsibility towards their citizens to ensure their security and their defence. In whatever way that is organised, the result should be a truly effective security and defence strategy.

[25] See for instance Glencross 2014.

[26] Genschel and Jachtsenfuchs 2016, p. 52.

16.5 A Framework for Priorities in a Truly Global and Integrated CFSP Strategy

The "Strategic Review" speaks of "a more connected, contested and complex world". Focusing on its "near-abroad" and insulating such matters as trade and science and technology from its foreign and defence affairs is also a "luxury we cannot afford". Poverty or good governance issues should be part and parcel of a set of priorities that further the interests of the EU, the Member States, and its citizens. This calls for an all-encompassing approach of the EU towards its foreign and defence affairs that lay down clear priorities in its activities.

In the following, a brief outline for frameworks within which these priorities could take shape is offered. The first framework should be the global security of the EU,[27] which could serve as a basis for priorities in the field of development. After all, the EU is a global actor in many domains of a more contested world. This entails a "common, comprehensive, and consistent" set of priorities towards our allies and such areas as Eastern Europe and Russia, the Middle East and North Africa region, sub-Saharan Africa, China, and both South and East Asia. Since "the age of dominance by any single country is over" NATO and its allies could be the framework for a global security strategy, in which the different parties could agree to supplement each other in various parts of the world.[28] This would require more of a defence effort on the part of the Member States, but as so often, the threat of EU military power could be a deterrent and therefore an investment that would enable a more constructive engagement with regions otherwise mired in conflict. Actual or potential conflict regions deserve to be identified and prioritised in the global strategy. Contingency planning should be comprehensive. It could provide for a comprehensive plan that underlies the EU's global strategic partnerships.

Moreover, a framework for a comprehensive global strategy could be to couple economic mobility and trade with a parallel security system. In a more connected world, transport and communications plans should be part of any priority planning. This could also open up new possibilities for multilateral agreements that reinforce global governance and strengthen international law. Wherever the EU trades and invests, there can be threats to its interests. Co-operating with allies and other partners on a global scale to ensure peace and stability is a useful instrument that will focus planners on truly global priorities. International organisations, such as the UN, could also be valuable partners.

Furthermore, the EU's value-based policies would benefit from a strategic framework that is both more respectful of cultural diversity and directed at attaining ends rather than pursuing values in the short term that have little chance of

[27] Blagden 2015, p. 340.

[28] TFEU, above n. 20, Article 42(2).

being realised. This would do more justice to a more complex world. For instance, rather than telling Russia to respect the rule of law and human rights, the EU would be more effective if it promoted a Russian civil society by drastically curbing Russia's intelligence gathering and hybrid warfare. After all, intelligence gathering by Russia is in many ways a means of avoiding the need for a free and innovative civil society.[29] In other cases, supporting development in countries will enable them to "afford" European values later on.[30] Value-based policies need not be overtly pursued, but can also be the result of smart side-effects of other policies. This could provide the EU with the much needed leverage in its Neighbourhood Policies and the relations with the ASEAN and ACP countries.[31] This would not entail a complete change of policy, but would result in policies in which the EU chooses its battles for democracy human rights more carefully.

Another framework could be that of framing comprehensive policies. Helping a major country through massive trade, Science and Technology transfer and investments should be balanced against the potential security threats such a country may pose to its region (partly) as a result of this.[32] Additional measures that will ensure the security of such a region could be an integral part of the EU's value-based policies. Fighting Islamic terrorism abroad could be linked to national strategies that seek integration and emancipation of Islamic minorities in European Member States. Similarly, migration calls for comprehensive approaches in which elements, such as economic development, humanitarian missions, culturally sensitive solutions, countering brain drains, allowing for economic and educational exchanges, and military operations would be present.

Finally, a frankly interest-based view of its priorities could serve to enhance its global authority and rally its citizens. Aren't European citizens who adhere to the EU's values not the best form of soft power the EU can wish for? Regulative instruments and corporate responsibility are some of the means through which such a linkage between values and self-interest could be fruitfully explored.

16.6 Conclusion

After more than a decade of foreign policy dormancy, the "Strategic Review" clearly shows an EU in search of new directions for its global foreign and security strategy. Rather than putting forward a world that is more contested, more connected, and more complex, a more positive and optimistic vision of its goals would be welcome. This would, to be sure, have to be coupled to a dose of realism. In order to lay down a credible global strategy, the EU stands in need of

[29] Van Herpen 2015, p. 183.

[30] Landman 2006, p. 101.

[31] See for instance Dennison and Whitney 2015.

[32] Bräuner 2011.

effective means to implement it. More effective institutions at the EU level are needed that will possess the competences and capabilities to carry into effect what the vision sets out to do. Member States should make this possible. Finally, in laying down its priorities, the EU should develop a number of frameworks that will help to define its priorities. A new security-minded focus, a more result-driven approach towards its values, a comprehensive view of foreign and security matters, and a more frankly interest-based are frameworks within which the EU could identify its priorities. These elements could inform a new and effective EU global foreign and defence strategy which takes the interests of the Member States into account and allows for a gradual development of the EU foreign policies. Perhaps, then, Sleeping Beauty would finally wake up to the potential opportunities that lie waiting for her in this globalised world.

References

Ahtisari M (2008) The EU cannot afford to become a symbol of weakness or decline. European Council on Foreign Relations, 25 June. http://www.ecfr.eu/article/commentary_ecfr_statement_on_future_of_the_eu. Accessed 23 May 2016

Blagden D (2015) Global multipolarity, European security and implications for UK grand strategy: back to the future, once again. Int Aff 91:333–350

Brand S (2007) Francis Fukuyama. The "End of History" revisited. Seminars on Long-Term Thinking, 28 June. http://longnow.org/seminars/02007/jun/28/the-end-of-history-revisited. Accessed 23 May 2016

Bräuner, O (2011) China's Rise as a Global S&T Power and China-EU Cooperation on eScholarship, September. http://escholarship.org/uc/item/0zd563ks. Accessed 23 May 2016

Charlemagne (2016) Value shoppers. Europe promised a principled foreign policy. Now it is desperate for quick deals. The Economist, 30 January. http://www.economist.com/news/europe/21689602-europe-promised-principled-foreign-policy-now-it-desperate-quick-deals-value-shoppers. Accessed 23 May 2016

Craig P, de Burca G (2015) EU law: texts, cases and materials. Oxford University Press, Oxford

Dennison S, Whitney N (2015) Europe's neighbourhood: crisis as the new normal. European Council on Foreign Relations, 23 June. http://www.ecfr.eu/publications/summary/europes_neighbourhood_crisis_as_the_new_normal. Accessed 23 May 2016

Diez T (2005) Constructing the self and changing others. Reconsidering 'Normative Power Europe'. Millennium J Int Stud 33(3):613–636

EEAS Strategic Planning (2003) European Security Strategy—a secure Europe in a better world. http://europa.eu/globalstrategy/en/european security-strategy-secure-europe-better-world. Accessed 23 May 2016

Fassbender B (1998) The United Nations Charter as constitution of the international community. Columbia J Transnational Law 36:529–619

Fukuyama F (1992) The End of History and the Last Man. The Free Press, New York

Gathii JT (2012–2013) Beyond China's human rights exceptionalism in Africa: leveraging science, technology and engineering for long-term growth. Columbia J Transnational Law 51:664–695

Genschel P, Jachtsenfuchs M (2016) More integration, less federation: the European integration of core state powers. J Eur Public Policy 23:42–59

Glencross A (2014) The absence of political constitutionalism in the EU: three models for enhancing constitutional agency. J Eur Public Policy 21:1163–1180

Ignatieff M (2000) The Rights Revolution. The House of Anansi Press, Toronto

Landman T (2006) Studying human rights. Routledge, London and New York
Lefebvre S (2010) The Czech Republic and national security: 1993–1998. The emergence of a strategic culture. J Slavic Mil Stud 23:328–369
Minkina M (2011) Evolution of the perception of threats to the security of the Republic of Poland in Polish strategic documents. J Slavic Mil Stud 24:621–647
Prodi R (2000) 2000–2005: shaping the New Europe. Speech to the European Parliament, Strasbourg, 15 February, Speech/00/41. http://europa.eu/rapid/press-release_SPEECH-00-41_en.htm. Accessed 23 May 2016
Rogers J (2009) From "civilian power" to "global power". Explicating the European Union's "grand strategy" through the articulation of discourse theory. J Common Market Stud 47:831–862
Scharpf F (2003) Problem-solving effectiveness and democratic accountability in the EU. MPIfG Working Paper 03/1, February; via http://www.mpifg.de/pu/workpap/wp03-1/wp03-1.html. Accessed 23 May 2016
Scharpf F (2006) The joint-decision trap revisited. J Common Market Stud 44:845–864
Schmidt V (2013) Democracy and Legitimacy in the European Union Revisited: Input, Output and Throughput. Polit Stud 61:2–22
Strategic Review (2015) The European Union in a changing global environment. A more connected, contested and complex world. http://europa.eu/globalstrategy/en/strategic-review-european-union-changing-global-environment. Accessed 23 May 2016
Toje A (2008) America, the EU and strategic culture. Renegotiating the transatlantic bargain. Routledge, New York
Van Herpen M (2015) Putin's propaganda machine: soft power and Russian foreign policy. Rowman and Littlefield, Lanham
Van Middelaar L (2015) The return of politics—The European Union after the crises in the eurozone and Ukraine. J Common Market Stud, article published online on 14 October. http://onlinelibrary.wiley.com.ezproxy.leidenuniv.nl:2048/doi/10.1111/jcms. 12336/references. Accessed 23 May 2016

Chapter 17
Up Towards a Coherent and Inclusive EU Policy on Natural Resources: Treaty Amendment Proposals

Chris Koppe

Abstract This chapter depicts the European Union's struggle to secure its supply of natural resources. From its establishment, the European Union (EU) has developed into an international organisation adopting measures on, basically, all policy areas of governance. The current threats and challenges regarding natural resources, however, were not solved at the time when the EU was established. As a result, the EU has to deal with these contemporary challenges within the limits of its competences conferred to the EU by its Member States. These competences are now listed in the two European Treaties (TEU and TFEU). It seems that the appropriate response would be for the EU to develop a long-term structural policy on natural resources that is coherent and inclusive. The question is, however, whether or not the EU has the competence to develop such a policy? As this chapter will demonstrate, the EU's competences regarding natural resources lie highly fragmented throughout the two Treaties. This fragmentation of competences also seems to explain why the EU has taken several ad hoc decisions over the years to secure its natural resource supply. The view expressed in this chapter is that the TEU and TFEU do not provide for the proper legal basis to develop a long-term structural policy on natural resources that is inclusive and coherent. For that reason, this chapter concludes by proposing treaty amendments to equip the EU with the legal framework to deal with the current threats and challenges regarding natural resources more effectively.

Keywords Contemporary threats and challenges · Natural resources · EU competences · Fragmentation of competences · Ad hoc EU measures · Coherency · Inclusive · EU policy on natural resources · Solution · Treaty amendment proposals

Chris Koppe LL.M., B.A. has his own consultancy firm providing organisations with independent legal and policy advice with regard to natural resources and privacy. Furthermore, he also lectures in EU law at Utrecht University in The Netherlands.

C. Koppe (✉)
Koppe Consultancy, Rotterdam, The Netherlands
e-mail: info@koppeconsultancy.eu

J. de Zwaan et al. (eds.), *Governance and Security Issues of the European Union*, DOI 10.1007/978-94-6265-144-9_17

Contents

17.1 Introduction

Securing access to natural resources is becoming an increasing concern as the global competition for them has begun. Being the biggest net importer of natural resources in the world, it is, therefore, pivotal for the European Union (EU) to secure its supply of natural resources as a lack of resources will, consequently, have significant adverse effects on the EU's global competitive power, its livelihood and ultimately its internal safety. The question is how the EU should respond to the current threats and challenges regarding natural resources. One way to address this question is by looking at the EU's competences in this field. As will be demonstrated, the EU's competences regarding natural resources lie highly fragmented throughout the European Treaties, rendering the EU's chances to almost none if it wishes to solve this dilemma in an inclusive and coherent manner. As such, the fragmentation of the EU's competences poses a more fundamental question, namely whether there is a need for treaty amendments? The view expressed in this chapter is that treaty amendments are necessary in order to equip the EU with the proper legal framework to formulate an effective response to the current threats and challenges regarding natural resources. Yet, before reaching this conclusion and proposing these treaty amendments, this chapter will start off by explaining the reasons why the security of supply of natural resources has become top priority again for countries and companies all over the world.

17.2 Natural Resources Top Priority Again—What Is New?

The competition over natural resources is as old as mankind. Due to several global developments, natural resources are back high on the agenda of countries and companies all over the world. The first reason concerns the expected growth in the world population. On 13 June 2013, the United Nations published its report on world population growth.[1] According to this United Nations (UN) report the world population is estimated to grow to 8.2 billion people in the next twelve years and reach 9.6 billion people in 2050.[2] In order to feed such vast numbers, the world's food production needs to be doubled.[3]

With the rise of new economic world powers, it is expected that the global consumption patterns will increase as well. Both developments, the rise of the world population and the increase of global consumption patterns, will put enormous pressure on the world's supply of natural resources, like fresh water, energy resources, agricultural products and land.

The third reason concerns the geographical location of natural resources. As is well known, natural resources are not equally divided over the world's crust. For example, there are huge oil and gas reserves in the Middle East and bulky phosphate reserves in China and Morocco. The unequal distribution of resources leads to a distinction among countries that have natural resources (the Haves) and those that have not (the Have Nots). The import dependency of the Have Nots forces these countries to import resources from the Haves, putting the Have Nots in a vulnerable position.

Furthermore, there is the phenomenon of scarcity. Some natural resources will simply cease to exist after these resources have been totally exploited. Examples of scarce resources are oil, natural gas, helium and phosphate rock. The understanding that some of the world's most important natural resources will one day cease to exist, causes significant concern for countries, companies and civil societies all over the world, especially, for the Have Nots. Not having access to the required natural resources has significant adverse effects on a country's competitive power, its international political power, its livelihood and ultimately its internal safety. As such, the global competition for natural resources has begun. This global competition for natural resources has led to an increase of global trade barriers, interstate conflicts, unfair competition and price volatilities in the last few years. Moreover, the exploitation of natural resources has sometimes gone hand in hand with the financing of war, severe corruption, human rights violations and irretrievable damage to the environment.

17.3 The Effects of Global Natural Resource Developments on the EU

In the last ten years, the European Union has experienced at first-hand the adverse effects of these global developments regarding natural resources. Tensions between Europe and Russia, for example, have led on several occasions to Russia threatening

[1] United Nations, Department of Economic and Social Affairs 2013.

[2] United Nations, Department of Economic and Social Affairs 2013.

[3] Tomlinson 2011, p. 1.

to cut off its energy supply to Europe. Another example is China declaring export restrictions on rare earths, causing Europe to start legal procedures before the World Trade Organization (WTO).[4] A third and final example is the EU being confronted with unfair competition in the global gas market. In 2015 the wholesale price of gas for European countries was twice as much as for American companies, giving the latter a significant competitive advantage in the global market.[5]

The effects of these global developments become in particular problematic for the EU as the EU is highly dependent on the import of natural resources. As the European Commission points out in its *Roadmap to a Resource Efficient Europe*: "Europe has the world's highest net imports of resources per person, and its open economy relies heavily on imported raw materials and energy".[6] This statement is based on the 2010 European Environment Agency (EEA) report *Material Resources and Waste*, in which it is stated that the European Union imported in 2008 in total 1798 million tonnes of natural resources, consisting of biomass (193 tonnes), manufactures (221 million tonnes) and fuels/mining products (1384 million tonnes), while the EU exported 536 million tonnes to other parts of the world, biomass (126 million tonnes), manufactures (207 million tonnes and fuels/mining products (203 million tonnes).[7] These numbers demonstrate a huge asymmetry between trade flow of natural resources from and to the European Union, especially regarding fuels and mining products, and, above all, demonstrate Europe's resource dependency, which "increased by 19 % during the period 1999–2011".[8] As such, Europe's resource dependency is not a temporary problem, but "a long-term structural trend".[9]

When assessing the impact of these global developments on natural resources another aspect needs to be taken into account, namely the bilateral agreements closed between EU Member States and resource-rich countries outside the EU. The past has demonstrated how bilateral agreements with these third countries have led to conflicting interests between that of the EU Member States and that of the EU. For example, the 90 gas-crisis illustrates how the bilateral relations between Russia, on the one hand, and Germany and Italy on the other, prevented the EU from making a political stance against Putin.[10] As such, the conflicting interests between the EU and its Member States on gas undermined the possibility for the EU to act as a global actor.

Therefore, in order to have a fighting chance and compete internationally with super world powers, like the US, China and Russia, and upcoming economies like Brazil and India, the EU has to develop its own policy on natural resources that

[4] European Commission 2012.

[5] European Commission 2015a.

[6] European Commission 2011b, p. 6.

[7] European Environment Agency 2010, p. 16.

[8] European Environment Agency 2012 update, p. 17.

[9] European Environment Agency 2012 update, p. 17.

[10] Gerbrandy and Arnon 2014, p. 32.

should not be undermined by bilateral agreements between EU Member States and resource-rich third countries. The question is, subsequently, how this EU policy on natural resources should look like. In order to answer this question, the term natural resources needs to be defined first—yet, as the following section will demonstrate defining the term natural resources on a European level seems to be quite a challenge in itself.

17.4 Defining the Term Natural Resources

Currently, there is no agreement on the EU policy level about how to define the term natural resources. Such a finding is confirmed by Eurostat's Environmental Data Centre on Natural Resources, which states on its website:

> When considering the topic of natural resources it is essential that everybody has the same understanding of what is being discussed. Since no commonly agreed definition is available, various strategies of the European Union were reviewed to develop a working definition of the concept.[11]

Due to a lack of a common definition, Eurostat's data centre developed a *working definition* of the term natural resources, by reviewing various policy strategies of the European Union. This entails the categorisation of eight items: raw materials, energy resources, air, water, soil, spatial resources, biodiversity and other ecosystem resources.[12] Waste, labelled as a natural resource by the European Commission,[13] is implied in each of the eight categories identified by Eurostat.

What can be inferred from this working definition? First of all, Eurostat's data centre has not defined the term natural resources substantively, but rather by means of eight different categories. Secondly, Eurostat's working definition is formulated broadly and is not clearly defined (e.g. what are other ecosystem resources?). Thirdly, Eurostat's definition is formulated from an EU governance-perspective in which it seems that other disciplines, such as an EU law perspective, have not been taken into consideration. This is interesting since the Treaty of Lisbon refers to the term natural resources several times.

Furthermore, Eurostat's working definition of the term natural resources seems to depict a changing view in society on what should be considered as natural resources. For example, twenty years ago not many people would have considered waste to be included in this category. However, due to the advancement in technology and recycling our social perception on waste has gradually evolved from waste being the final stage of a used product, to being the source to create a new product. It is this change of perception that also shines through the relevant policy

[11] Eurostat 2015.

[12] Eurostat 2015.

[13] European Commission 2011b, pp. 7–8.

documents of the European Union. According to the European Commission, Europe should move from a linear economy towards a circular economy so that natural resources remain in the production process as long as possible.[14] The rationale behind this transformation from a linear economy towards a circular economy is that the EU would then become less dependent on its imports of natural resources.

17.5 The European Union's Competences

The lack of a proper definition and common agreement on the term natural resources imposes challenges to the identification of the EU's competences with regard to them. Given the scope of this chapter, the following section aims to provide an initial overview of the EU's competences regarding natural resources. Firstly, the EU's competences in the Treaty on European Union (TEU) will be discussed.[15] Subsequently, the EU's competences in the Treaty on the Functioning of the European Union (TFEU) will be discussed.[16]

17.5.1 Treaty on European Union

Article 3 TEU lists the general aims of the European Union. Newly introduced by the Lisbon Reform Treaty is Article 3 (5) TEU. This provision lists the Union's aims "in its relations with the wider world".[17] When reading these aims, many of them are relevant to natural resources, like "the sustainable development of the Earth", "free and fair trade" and "the protection of human rights", thereby allowing the EU to pursue these aims.[18]

Article 3 TEU is closely linked with Article 21 TEU. Article 21 TEU has also been introduced by the Treaty of Lisbon to enhance the EU's external action. It contains a specific reference to natural resources in Article 21 (2) (f) TEU:

> The Union shall define and pursue common policies and actions, and shall work for a high degree of co-operation in all fields of international relations, in order to:
>
> (f) help develop international measures to preserve and improve the quality of the environment and the sustainable management of global natural resources, in order to ensure sustainable development.[19]

[14] European Commission 2011b, p. 13.

[15] Consolidated Version of the Treaty on European Union, signed on 13 December 2007, OJ C 326 (entered into force on 1 December 2009) as amended on 26 October 2012 (TEU).

[16] *Ibid.*

[17] *Ibid.* Article 3(5).

[18] *Ibid.*

[19] *Ibid.* Article (2)(f).

The reason for including this provision by means of the Lisbon Reform Treaty stems from the need to assist developing countries with the sustainable management of their natural resources.[20] In order to assess the EU's competences, the question needs to be answered as to how to interpret the term global natural resources of Article 21(2)(f) TEU? The term global natural resources is not defined by the Treaty itself, nor does it seem that this term has been defined by the Court of Justice of the European Union's case law. Therefore, the term global natural resources of Article 21(2)(f) TEU can be interpreted grammatically, which means an assessment based on our common understanding of what society considers to be global natural resources.

Another relevant treaty provision is Article 8 TEU. This provision confers competence on the EU to develop a European Neighbourhood Policy (ENP). The ENP plays an important role in securing access to natural resources from neighbouring countries, by means of, for example, preferential trade agreements.[21]

The Preventive Policy in Global Issues is one of the latest proposals to secure the Union's access to natural resources.[22] According to the authors of this proposal, this Preventive Policy in Global Issues, which will be discussed later on, should be developed under the Common Foreign and Security Policy (Article 23 TEU—Article 41 TEU).[23]

Europe's primary strategy to secure its natural resource is formulated in the Europe 2020 strategy.[24] The competences to propose and adopt this strategy stems from the generic competences of the European Commission, stated in Article 17 TEU, and those of the European Council, stated in Article 15 TFEU. The principal aim of Europe's strategy regarding natural resources is the sustainable use of natural resources. To reach its aims, the Europe 2020 strategy states the rolc and tasks of the EU institutions, national authorities, civil society and other stakeholders.[25] Furthermore, it states:

> All EU policies, instruments and legal acts, as well as financial instruments, should be mobilised to pursue the strategy's objectives. The Commission intends to enhance key policies and instruments such as the single market, the budget and the EU's external economic agenda to focus on delivering Europe 2020's objectives.[26]

As such, all relevant stakeholders and all EU policy areas are involved in realising the objectives of the Europe 2020 strategy, such as the sustainable use of natural resources.

---

[20] Geiger et al. 2015, pp. 121–122.

[21] European Commission 2015c.

[22] Rijksoverheid 2013.

[23] Rijksoverheid 2013.

[24] European Commission 2010b.

[25] European Commission 2010b, "Under 5.2. Who does what?".

[26] European Commission 2010b, "Under 3. Missing Links and Bottlenecks".

17.5.2 *Treaty on the Functioning of the European Union*

The Treaty on the Functioning of the European Union contains several treaty provisions regarding natural resources, like Article 349 TFEU.[27] The following sections outline the treaty references on natural resources in accordance with the three separate categories of EU competences, being exclusive, shared or supporting/coordinating/supplementing.

17.5.2.1 Exclusive Competences

Policy areas falling under the exclusive competences of the European Union concern those in which only the EU is allowed to adopt legislative acts.[28] The EU Member States can only adopt measures to implement acts of the European Union, or when the EU has empowered the EU Member States to adopt measures.[29] The exclusive competences of the EU are listed in Article 3 TFEU. This section focuses in particular on the Common Fisheries Policy and the Common Commercial Policy; though, having stated this, that does not mean that other policy areas are not involved in this matter regarding natural resources.[30]

The Common Fisheries Policy, stated in Article 3(1) under (d) TFEU, falls under the exclusive competence of the EU. The objective of this policy area is the "the conservation of marine biological resources".[31] The Treaty does not define the term marine biological resources, nor does it seem that this term has been defined by the case law of the Court of Justice of the European Union. Regulation (EU) No. 1380/2013, on the other hand, provides some inspiration on how this term could be interpreted as the regulation defines the term as: "available and accessible

---

[27] Consolidated Version of the Treaty on the Functioning of the European Union, signed on 13 December 2007, OJ C 326 (entered into force on 1 December 2009) as amended on 26 October 2012 (TFEU), Article 349 deals with the EU's outermost regions. Based on this provision the Council can adopt measures relating to "areas such as customs and trade policies, fiscal policy, free zones, agriculture and fisheries policies, conditions for supply of raw materials and essential consumer goods, State aids and conditions of access to structural funds and to horizontal Union programmes".

[28] *Ibid.* Article 2(1).

[29] *Ibid.*

[30] Other policy areas falling under the exclusive competence of the EU that play a role regarding natural resources are the Customs Union and Competition Rules necessary for the Functioning of the Internal Market. For example, by means of the customs union, the EU can use adopt preferential import tariffs to make the imports of natural resources more appealing. By setting and enforcing rules on competition the EU can prevent distortion of competition, like in the commodity markets.

[31] TFEU, above n 27, Article 3(1)(d).

living marine aquatic species, including anadromous and catadromous species[32] during their marine life".[33] Defining the term marine biological resources as a species-based definition, rather than a resource-based definition, limits the scope of the term marine biological resources. Yet, when looking at the policy practice of the European Commission in this field, the term marine biological resources is interpreted more broadly including not only fish species, but also shellfish, crustaceans and aquatic plants.[34]

Article 3(1)(e) TFEU confers on the EU the exclusive competence to develop a Common Commercial Policy. This policy area is further defined in Articles 206 to 207 TFEU. In the light of the Common Commercial Policy the EU has adopted several international commodity agreements, such as on coffee,[35] rubber,[36] tropical timber,[37] olive oil[38] and cocoa.[39] Moreover, the Common Commercial Policy has also been used by the EU to adopt Regulation (EC) No. 2368/2002 implementing the Kimberly Process certification scheme for the international trade in rough

[32] Anadromous and catadromous species are both fish species. The difference between the two is that the first one is born in fresh water, subsequently heads to sea and returns to fresh water to spawn, while the latter one does exactly the opposite.

[33] Regulation (EU) No. 1380/2013 of 11 December 2013 on the Common Fisheries Policy, amending Council Regulations (EC) No. 1954/2003 and (EC) No. 1224/2009 and repealing Council Regulations (EC) No. 2371/2002 and (EC) No. 639/2004 and Council Decision 2004/585/EC of 11 December 2013, OJ L 354, Article 4(1)(2). The legal basis used for this Regulation is TFEU, see above n 27, Article 43(2). This provision states the legislative powers of the EU regarding the Common Agricultural Policy and the Common Fisheries Policy.

[34] European Commission 2015d.

[35] Council Decision 2008/579/EC of 16 June 2008 on the signing and conclusion on behalf of the European Community of the International Coffee Agreement 2007, OJ L 186. The legal basis used for this agreement is Article 133 in conjunction with Article 300(2) first sub para TEC. These provisions now correspond with Article 207 (Common Commercial Policy) and Article 218 TFEU (Negotiation and conclusion of agreements).

[36] Council Decision 82/253/EEC of 8 April 1982 approving the International Natural Rubber Agreement 1979, OJ L 111. The legal basis used for this agreement is Article 113 EEC Treaty, which corresponds with Article 133 TEC and now with Article 207 TFEU.

[37] Council Decision 96/493/EC of 29 March 1996 concerning the signing and provisional application of the International Tropical Timber Agreement 1994 on behalf of the European Community, OJ L 208. As being stated in the preamble of this agreement, this agreement falls under the scope of the Common Commercial Policy.

[38] Council Decision 2014/664/EU of 15 September 2014 on the position to be adopted on behalf of the European Union within the Council of Members of the International Olive Council concerning the prolongation of the 2005 International Agreement on olive oil and table olives, OJ L 275. The legal basis used for this Council Decision is Article 207 TFEU in conjunction with Article 218(9) TFEU.

[39] Council Decision 2012/189/EU: Council Decision of 26 March 2012 on the conclusion of the International Cocoa Agreement 2010, OJ L 102. The legal basis used for this agreement is Article 207(3) and (4) TFEU in conjunction with Article 218(6) TFEU.

diamonds,[40] and forms the legal basis for the legislative proposal of the European Commission to establish a self-certification scheme for responsible importers of tin, tantalum and tungsten, their ores and gold originating in conflict-affected and high-risk areas.[41] In other words, the Common Commercial Policy is used in matters of trade. However, other objectives, like curtailing the opportunities to finance armed conflicts by means of natural resources, may also be reached through trade.

17.5.2.2 Shared Competences

Shared competences concern policy areas in which both the EU and the Member States can adopt measures. However, Member States can only exercise their power when the European Union has not exercised its power; or when the EU has decided to no longer utilise its power.[42] The shared competences of the EU are listed in Article 4 TFEU. This section focuses in particular on the policy area of Energy and that of the Environment. However, this does not mean that other policy areas falling under the shared competences of the EU do not play a role regarding natural resources as well.[43]

Introduced by the Treaty of Lisbon is Title XXI on Energy, which has been qualified as an area of shared competence.[44] The competences of the EU in this policy area are further defined in Article 194 TFEU. Given the EU's high import dependency of energy resources, this policy area aims to fulfil a vital role in

[40] Council Regulation (EC) No. 2368/2002 implementing the Kimberly Process certification scheme for the international trade in rough diamonds, OJ L 358. The legal basis used for this Council Regulation is Article 133 TEC, which now corresponds with Article 207 TFEU.

[41] European Commission 2014. The legal basis for this legislative proposal is Article 207 TFEU.

[42] TFEU, above n 27, Article 2(2).

[43] For example, The Internal Market, Agriculture and Fisheries, Transport, Trans-European Networks, Consumer Protection and Development Cooperation. For instance, based on the provisions of the Internal Market the EU has adopted the Ecodesign Directive, contributing to the sustainable use of natural resources (Directive 2009/125/EC of 21 October 2009 establishing a framework for the setting of ecodesign requirements for energy-related products, OJ L 285). Other examples are the Union's rules on food safety, which the EU has adopted in the light of the Internal Market and Consumer Protection. For example, Regulation (EU) No. 1169/2011 of 25 October 2011 on the provision of food information to consumers, amending Regulations (EC) No. 1924/2006 and (EC) No. 1925/2006 of the European Parliament and of the Council, and repealing Commission Directive 87/250/EEC, Council Directive 90/496/EEC, Commission Directive 1999/10/EC, Directive 2000/13/EC of the European Parliament and of the Council, Commission Directives 2002/67/EC and 2008/5/EC and Commission Regulation (EC) No. 608/2004, OJ L 304. The legal basis for this Regulation is Article 114 TFEU (Internal Market), including a reference to Consumer Protection (Article 169 TFEU).

[44] TFEU, above n 27, Article 4(2)(i).

securing the EU's supply of energy. Based on Article 194 TFEU, the EU can develop a European energy policy "in a spirit of solidarity between Member States".[45] The scope of this policy area includes all energy resources "ranging from fossil fuels, through nuclear power, to renewable (solar, wind, biomass, geothermal, hydro-electric and tidal)".[46] The aims of the European energy policy are listed in Article 194(1) TFEU:

(a) ensure the functioning of the energy market;

(b) ensure security of energy supply in the Union;

(c) promote energy efficiency and energy saving and the development of new and renewable forms of energy; and

(d) promote the interconnection of energy networks.[47]

To achieve these aims the EU can adopt measures based on the ordinary legislative procedure,[48] or by means of the special legislative procedure in case of measures that "are primarily of a fiscal nature".[49]

Although Article 194 (1) TFEU confers competences on the EU, the second paragraph of Article 194 (2) TFEU contains a safeguard clause:

> Such measures[needed to achieve the objectives of Article 194 (1) TFEU] shall not affect a Member State's right to determine the conditions for exploiting its energy resources, its choice between different energy sources and the general structure of its energy supply; without prejudice to Article 192(2)(c).[50]

This means that although the EU has the competence to develop a European energy policy, the EU cannot adopt measures which affect the rights stated in the second paragraph of Article 194(2) TFEU. Of these three rights, the right to determine the conditions for exploiting energy resources cannot be affected by EU measures at all. With regard to the two latter prerogatives, however, based on Article 192(2)(c) TFEU the Council can adopt environmental measures significantly affecting the "Member State's choice between different energy sources and the general structure of its energy supply".[51] Other measures, unlike those dealing with environmental issues, cannot affect the latter two prerogatives in Article 194 (2), second paragraph, TFEU.

Another domain is the Environmental policy of the EU, which has also been qualified as an area of shared competence.[52] The EU's competences on environ-

---

[45] *Ibid.* Article 194(1). With regard to solidarity between EU Member States, see also Article 122 TFEU.

[46] Europa, Summaries of EU Legislation, Energy.

[47] TFEU, above n 27, Article 194(1).

[48] *Ibid.* Article 194(2).

[49] *Ibid.* Article 194(3).

[50] *Ibid.* Article 194(2), second para.

[51] *Ibid.* Article 192(2)(c).

[52] *Ibid.* Article 4(2)(e).

ment are elaborated in Articles 191 to 193 TFEU. Based on these provisions the EU can develop an EU policy on environment. One of the aims of this policy is the "prudent and rational utilisation of natural resources".[53] As seen with other treaty references to natural resources, the term natural resources in Article 191 (1) TFEU is not defined by the EU treaties. When reading case law of the Court of Justice of the European Union one notes that the Court refers to this term as part of the general aim of the EU's environmental policy, but never actually defines the term natural resources of Article 191(1) TFEU. Yet, the scope of the term natural resources of Article 191(1) TFEU could be inferred by a case-by-case assessment (including opinions rendered by the Court. For example, based on *Opinion 2/00* the term natural resources of Article 191(1) TFEU encompasses biological diversity, as a natural resource.[54] Further inspiration on how the term natural resources of Article 191(1) can be understood is stated in secondary EU law. According to Council Directive 93/76/EEC the term natural resources of Article 130r of the EEC Treaty, now corresponding to Article 191(1) TFEU, includes "oil products, natural gas and solid fuels".[55] Nonetheless, the term natural resources in Article 191(1) TFEU has not currently been strictly defined, allowing it to be interpreted differently. The upside of not having a well-defined term is that the meaning of the term natural resources can adapt itself to developments in society.

The provisions regarding the European environmental policy contain several references to natural resources. According to Article 192(2) TFEU, the Council has the competence to take measures affecting "quantitative management of water resources or affecting, directly or indirectly the availability of those resources,"[56] "land use, with the exception of waste management,"[57] and "measures significantly affecting a Member State's choice between different energy sources and the general structure of its energy supply".[58]

17.5.2.3 Supporting, Coordinating and Supplementing Competences

The third category of EU competences listed in Articles 5 and 6 TFEU deals with policy areas in which the EU has only supporting, coordinating and/or supplementing competences. It is stated in Article 2(5) TFEU that the EU cannot adopt regulation in these policy areas that intend to harmonise national legislation. This

53 *Ibid.* Article 191(1) TFEU.

54 Opinion of 6 December 2001, Opinion 2/00, Court of Justice, [2001] ECR, at p. I-09713, in particular on p. 28.

55 Council Directive 93/76/EEC of 13 September 1993 to limit carbon dioxide emissions by improving energy efficiency (SAVE), OJ L 237. The legal basis for this Council Directive is Article 130s and Article 235 EEC Treaty, which now corresponds with Article 192 and Article 352 TFEU.

56 TFEU, above n 27, Article 192(2)(b).

57 *Ibid.*

58 *Ibid.* Article 192(2)(c).

means that the EU cannot supersede the powers of the EU Member States by means of regulation with regard to these policy areas.

Unlike in the list of the EU's exclusive and shared competences, the list of supporting, coordinating or supplementing competences of the European Union does not contain a reference to natural resources. However, this does not mean that certain policy areas are not relevant in the area of natural resources. The policy area concerning the Protection and Improvement of Human Health[59] is often used in terms of food safety, while raw materials, like cobalt, indium and tungsten, are of vital importance for the European industry.[60] Yet, as explained above, these policy areas fall within the supporting, coordinating and supplementing competences of the EU, meaning that the EU's competences are significantly limited in comparison to the exclusive and shared competences of the EU.

17.6 Ad Hoc Measures Taken by the EU to Secure Its Supply of Natural Resources

Based on the competences conferred to the EU the European Union has taken several initiatives in the last ten years to respond to the increasing threats and challenges regarding natural resources. The following paragraphs discuss the EU's main measures, namely the Europe 2020 strategy,[61] the POLINARES-project,[62] the Energy Union,[63] the Raw Materials Initiative and the European Innovation Partnership-platform;[64] and the proposal to develop a Preventive Policy in Global Issues.[65]

On 3 March 2010 the European Commission published the *Europe 2020 strategy*.[66] The Europe 2020 strategy contains a strategic ten-year plan leading the European Union towards smart, sustainable and inclusive growth. The sustainability agenda of the European Union has three main targets, namely to reduce the emissions of greenhouse by 20%, increase the share of renewables in final energy consumption by 20% and moving towards a 20% increase in energy efficiency. To reach these targets the European has developed two flagships, *A Resource Efficient Europe*[67] and *An*

[59] *Ibid.* Article 6(a).

[60] *Ibid.* Article 6(b).

[61] European Commission 2010b.

[62] POLINARES 2015.

[63] European Commission 2015b.

[64] European Commission 2015e.

[65] Rijksoverheid 2013.

[66] European Commission 2010b.

[67] European Commission 2011a.

Industrial Policy for the Globalisation Era.[68] The flagship *A Resources Efficient Europe* can be perceived to express the EU's *main answer* on how it will solve the challenges regarding natural resources, namely by means of sustainable use of natural resources. The ultimate goal of this flagship is that by 2050 "All resources are sustainable managed, from raw materials to energy, water, air, land and soil."[69] To reach this target the European Union's economy has to transform itself from a linear economy towards a circular economy.[70] In realising the objectives the Europe 2020 strategy, all policies areas of the EU are involved, as already stated above.[71]

2010 was also the year of the POLINARES project being launched.[72] The POLINARES project was a research project funded under Socio-economic Sciences & Humanities of the Seventh Framework Programme. The name of the project, POLINARES, stems from POLIcy on NAtural RESources and was "designed to help identify the main global challenges relating to competition for access to resources, and propose new approaches to collaborative solutions".[73] The projects started in 2010 and ended on 31 December 2012. In February 2013 the summary of the final project results was published.[74] The main message of the POLINARES project is "that the EU's current policy approaches and today's global institutions are poorly suited to addressing the emerging challenges relating to access to oil, gas and minerals."[75] To overcome these challenges the European External Action Service in particular has a pivotal role to play by further integrating "energy and resource issues into its diplomatic strategies."[76]

On 25 February 2015 the European Commission published its strategy on the Energy Union.[77] The need for an Energy Union stems from four major problems: Europe's import dependence of energy products; Europe's fragmented energy-system; energy pollution; and unaffordable energy prices for citizens' households and companies. To address these challenges, the Energy Union's main goals are to ensure the security of supply of energy resources; to create a fully-integrated internal energy market; reduce energy emissions and stimulate energy efficiency. To realise these aims a holistic approach has been chosen, one that "is multidisciplinary, multinational, inclusive and eliminates the silo mentalities".[78] According to

68 European Commission 2010a.

69 European Commission 2011b, p. 3.

70 European Commission 2011b, p. 13.

71 See Sect. 17.5.1.

72 POLINARES 2015.

73 POLINARES 2013, p. 1.

74 POLINARES 2013, p. 1.

75 POLINARES 2013, p. 8.

76 Styles 2012.

77 European Commission 2015b.

78 EurActiv.com 2015.

the European Commission it will use "all available policy instruments" to implement the already "existing energy and related legislation" to create the basis for the Energy Union.[79] In particular, it will use the EU's competences on competition, foreign policy and trade.[80]

Besides energy resources, the European economy relies heavily on the import of raw materials as well. According to the European Commission: "Sectors such as construction, chemicals, automotive, aerospace, machinery and equipment sectors which provide a total value added of €1324 billion and employment for some 30 million people (Annex 1) all depend on access to raw materials."[81] To prevent disruptions in the supply chain of raw materials and ensure affordable prices the European Commission initialised the Raw Materials Initiative and the European Innovation Partnership on Raw Materials.[82] The first initiative concerns the EU's strategy to solve the challenges just mentioned, while the second performs as a platform for the relevant stakeholders to promote innovation. To ensure security of access to raw materials, "better and more effective coordination and coherence among EU external policies (external relations, trade, and development)" is necessary.[83]

In August 2013 the Ministers of Foreign Affairs of Germany, Italy and the Netherlands proposed to the Vice-President and High-Representative of that time, Baroness Catherine Ashton, that a Preventive Policy in Global Issues should be developed under the Common Foreign and Security Policy (CFSP).[84] The authors of this proposal refer to the adverse effects of globalisation, like climate change, trade barriers and scarcity of resource. According to them these adverse effects "are threat multipliers and have the potential to exacerbate conflict situations".[85] To prevent these conflict situations, hence, a Preventive Policy in Global Issues should be developed "through a long-term approach based on diplomacy and development cooperation".[86]

The question is whether or not these measures taken by the EU are enough to deal with the current threats and challenges regarding natural resources. It seems that the appropriate answer to this question is that the EU's development of a policy on natural resources is still in its infancy. As mentioned before, there is currently no common agreement on the EU level about the definition of the term

79 European Commission 2015b.

80 European Commission 2015b.

81 European Commission 2008, p. 2.

82 European Commission 2015e.

83 European Commission 2008, p. 6.

84 Rijksoverheid 2013.

85 Rijksoverheid 2013, p. 2.

86 Rijksoverheid 2013, p. 3.

natural resources. In addition, the recent proposals, like the Energy Union and Preventive Policy in Global Issues, still need to demonstrate their merit. Yet, the challenges around natural resources are increasing and are complex requiring a long-term structural solution that is inclusive and coherent rather than having an *ad hoc* character. The question is whether or not the EU can develop such a policy on natural resources based on its competences listed in the TEU and TFEU.

17.7 Conclusion: The Best Way Forward—Treaty Amendment Proposals

The European Union can only act, when it has the competence to act. The competences of the EU are attributed to the EU by the EU Member States. The division of competences between the EU and its Member States is governed by the principle of conferral.[87] This principle entails that the "Union shall act only within the limits of the competences conferred upon it by the Member States in the Treaties to attain the objectives set out therein."[88] Competences that are "not conferred upon the EU in the Treaties remain with the Member States."[89] The Lisbon Reform Treaty has clarified the policy areas that are conferred upon the EU by categorising them into three separate categories of competences, being exclusive, shared or supporting/coordinating/supplementing, as outlined above.[90] Policy areas that are not listed in the TEU and TFEU remain with the EU Member States. The question whether or not the EU can develop a natural resource policy that is coherent and inclusive thus depends on the question whether or not the EU has the competence to develop such a policy.

As the section of this chapter on EU competences demonstrated, natural resources, as a separate policy area, have not been conferred upon the EU by its Member States.[91] Based on Article 4(1) and 5(2) TEU, this would mean, strictly speaking, that natural resources remain a national competence. Yet, the section on EU competences demonstrated a much more nuanced division of competences on natural resources between the EU and its Member States. It demonstrated how the EU's competences regarding natural resources lie highly fragmented throughout the TEU and TFEU and that many EU policy areas are involved in this subject matter, like the Common Foreign and Security Policy, the Common Fisheries Policy, the Common Commercial Policy, Environment, Energy, Development

[87] TFEU, above n 27, Article 5(1).

[88] *Ibid.* Article 5(2).

[89] *Ibid.* Articles 4(1) and 5(2).

[90] See Sect. 17.5.2.

[91] See Sects. 17.5.1 and 17.5.2.

Cooperation and Industry, falling under the exclusive, shared or supporting/coordinating/supplementing competences of the EU. The involvement of these EU policy areas demonstrate that the solution for the current threats and challenges regarding natural resources cannot come from merely one policy area, but rather, that an integrative approach is necessary.

Although the EU legislator is allowed to use a double or multiple legal bases for its legislation, namely when the objectives are "indissociably linked" with one and another,[92] the case law of the Court of Justice of the European Union has made it clear that there are clear limits to the use of a double legal basis by the EU legislator. One of these limits, developed in the Court's case law is that the EU legislator cannot arbitrarily choose to decide two or more legal bases to adopt legislation, but rather, that this choice of the EU legislator needs to be based on objective factors that are subject to judicial review:

> It must first be observed that in the context of the organization of the powers of the Community the choice of the legal basis for a measure may not depend simply on an institution's conviction as to the objective pursued but must be based on objective factors which are amenable to judicial review (see the judgment in Case 45/86 Commission v Council [1987] ECR 1493, paragraph 11). Those factors include in particular the aim and content of the measure.[93]

Secondly, the Court's case law makes it clear that the use of a double, or multiple, legal bases is prohibited when the procedural rules of each legal basis is not compatible with one another, or when the use of a double legal bases sort the effect of negatively impair the rights of the European Parliament in the legislative procedure:

> recourse to a dual legal basis is not possible where the procedures laid down for each legal basis are incompatible with each other or where the use of two legal bases is liable to undermine the rights of the Parliament.[94]

In other words, choosing the proper legal basis by the EU legislator to develop an inclusive policy on natural resources is not a matter of randomly choosing various legal bases and putting them together. Rather, the EU legislator is compelled to adhere to the double-legal bases doctrine developed in the case law of the Court of Justice of the European Union, when it decides to use a double, or more, legal bases to develop its natural resource policy.

---

[92] European Court of Justice, The Queen v Secretary of State for Health, ex parte British American Tobacco (Investments) Ltd and Imperial Tobacco Ltd (The British Tobacco case), Judgment of 10 December 2002, Case C-491/01, ECR, p. I-11453, Rec. 94.

[93] European Court of Justice, Commission of the European Communities v Council of the European Communities (The titanium dioxide case), Judgment of 11 June 1991, Case C-300/89, ECR, p. I-02867, Rec. 10.

[94] European Court of Justice, Commission of the European Communities v. Council of the European Union, Judgment of 10 January 2006, Case C-94/03, ECR, p. I-1, Rec. 52.

Besides the specific EU policy areas, like Energy and Environment, the EU legislator furthermore has the possibility to invoke Article 114 TFEU and Article 352 TFEU to develop an EU policy on natural resources. However, there are limits to the use of Article 114 TFEU and Article 352 TFEU as well. The Internal Market provision of Article 114 TFEU can only be used to harmonise national law. For that reason, it is difficult to conceive how this provision in itself, or in combination with other legal bases, would serve as a legal basis for the development of an EU policy on natural resources.

Article 352 TFEU, on the other hand, can be invoked by the EU legislator to adopt legislation in unforeseen circumstances. The use of this provision, however, cannot lead to the creation of new EU competences, but can only be used subsidiarily.[95] Secondly, Article 352, para 3, TFEU states that "Measures based on this Article shall not entail harmonisation of Member States' laws or regulations in cases where the Treaties exclude such harmonisation". Thirdly, Article 352, para 4, TFEU states that: "This Article cannot serve as a basis for attaining objectives pertaining to the common foreign and security policy and any acts adopted pursuant to this Article shall respect the limits set out in Article 40, second para, of the Treaty on European Union." The limitation of Article 352, para 4, TFEU is of particular importance with regard to the latest proposal to develop a Preventive Policy in Global Issues under the Common Foreign and Security Policy.

As discussed earlier, based on the current competences of the EU, as listed in the TEU and TFEU, the EU would be able to develop a policy on natural resources under the policy area of Environment. Article 191(1) TFEU in conjunction with Article 192 TFEU provide the EU with the competence to develop an environmental policy with the aim of "prudent and rational utilisation of natural resources", or to put it in more contemporary words, the sustainable use of natural resources.[96] The upside of such an approach would be that the sustainability goal, stated in Article 191(1) TFEU, in conjunction with the legislative power, stated in Article 192 TFEU can be neatly tied into the external sustainability objectives stated in Articles 3(5) TEU, Article 21(2)(f) TEU, and the sustainability goal of Article 11 TFEU, thereby creating a legal framework for a coherent policy with an internal as well as an external dimension. Yet, there are two downsides to this approach. First of all, such an approach is not inclusive as it is based on one policy area, Environment, while the input of other relevant policy areas of the EU is not taken into account. Secondly, this approach can only have as its objective the sustainable use of natural resources, while the biggest problem of the EU is the EU's dependence of natural resources. Therefore, the dimension of security of supply should also be taken into account when developing an EU policy on natural resources.

The lack of a separate policy area on natural resources conferred upon the EU, the fragmentation of competences and the emphasis on the sustainable use

[95] Geiger et al. 2015, p. 1051.

[96] TFEU, above n 27, Article 192.

of natural resources in the Treaties prevent the EU from developing a long-term, coherent and inclusive policy on natural resources to meet the current threats and challenges.

Therefore, this chapter proposes the following treaty amendments allowing the EU to develop the required policy response. The first treaty amendment proposal concerns Article 3 TEU, which states the general objectives of the European Union. In particular, this proposal concerns Article 3(5) TEU. The purpose of this proposal is to lessen the EU's import dependency of natural resources by including the security of supply of natural resources in the objectives of the EU's external action. The wording of that provision could then be as follows:

Article 3

5. In its relations with the wider world, the Union shall uphold and promote its values and interests, *secure its supply of natural resources*, and contribute to the protection of its citizens. It shall contribute to peace, security, the sustainable development of the Earth, solidarity and mutual respect among peoples, free and fair trade, eradication of poverty and the protection of human rights, in particular the rights of the child, as well as to the strict observance and the development of international law, including respect for the principles of the United Nations Charter.

The second treaty amendment proposal is inspired by Article 11 TFEU. Article 11 TFEU falls under Part one, Title II TFEU, concerning treaty provisions having general application. This provision imposes the obligation to integrate environmental objectives, in particular, sustainable development, "into the definition and implementation of the Union policies and activities."[97] The proposal suggests including a separate provision, an Article 11A TFEU-provision. The main purpose of this proposal is to enhance the legal coherency within the Treaties and strengthen the coordination between the various EU's policy areas that are involved with natural resources. Secondly, this proposal intends to broaden the array of dimensions that the EU can pursue with its policy on natural resources, rather than merely the sustainability of natural resources. The wording of that provision could be as follows:

Article 11 A

Conservation requirements of *natural resources* must be integrated into the definition and implementation of the Union policies and activities, in particular with a view to *secure the Union's supply of natural resources and the sustainable use thereof.*

[97] TFEU, above n 27, Article 11.

To conclude, the development of the European Union's policy on natural resources is still at its infancy. To meet the current threats and challenges regarding natural resources, this chapter advocates that the EU should develop a long-term natural resource policy that is coherent and inclusive. Yet, as the current competences of the EU prevent the EU from developing such a policy, this chapter puts forward two treaty amendment proposals. Although one can differ whether these treaty amendment proposals are needed or would be suffice, these proposals are intended to spark the debate on the question which competences does the European Union need to meet the current threats and challenges regarding natural resources, as the current progression of EU measures on natural resources are simply not enough.

References

EurActiv.com (2015) EU Adviser: Energy Union should take 'holistic approach'. http://www.euractiv.com/section/energy/interview/eu-adviser-energy-union-should-take-holistic-approach/. Accessed 7 March 2015

Europa, Summaries of EU Legislation, Energy. http://eur-lex.europa.eu/summary/chapter/energy.html?root_default=SUM_1_CODED%3D18&locale=en. Accessed 25 July 2015

European Commission (2008) Communication, The Raw Materials Initiative—meeting our critical needs for growth and jobs in Europe, COM (2008) 699

European Commission (2010a) Communication, An Integrated Industrial Policy for the Globalisation Era Putting Competitiveness and Sustainability at Centre Stage, COM (2010) 614 final

European Commission (2010b) Communication, Europe 2020: A Strategy for Smart, Sustainable and Inclusive Growth, COM (2010) 2020

European Commission (2011a) Communication, A Resource-Efficient Europe—Flagship Initiative under the Europe 2020 Strategy, COM (2011) 21

European Commission (2011b) Communication, Roadmap to a Resource Efficient Europe, COM (2011) 571

European Commission (2012) Press Release, EU challenges China's export restrictions on rare earths, MEMO/12/182

European Commission (2014) Setting up a Union system for supply chain due diligence self-certification of responsible importers of tin, tantalum and tungsten, their ores, and gold originating in conflict-affected and high-risk areas, COM (2014) 111, 2014/0059 (COD), Brussels, 5.3.2014

European Commission (2015a) Press Release, Energy Union: secure, sustainable, competitive, affordable energy for every European, IP/15/4497

European Commission (2015b) Communication, A Framework Strategy for a Resilient Energy Union with a Forward-Looking Climate Change Policy, COM (2015) 80 final

European Commission (2015c) European Neighbourhood Policy, Under 'Benefits'. Last updated 4 Feb 2015. http://ec.europa.eu/economy_finance/international/neighbourhood_policy/index_en.htm. Accessed 12 Sept 2015

European Commission (2015d) Fisheries, CFP, 'Aquaculture'. Last updated 20 Nov 2015. http://ec.europa.eu/fisheries/cfp/aquaculture/index_en.htm. Accessed 12 Sept 2015

European Commission (2015e) Internal Market, Industry, Entrepreneurship and SMEs, 'Policy and Strategy for Raw Materials'. http://ec.europa.eu/growth/sectors/raw-materials/policy-strategy/index_en.htm. Accessed 13 Sept 2015

European Environment Agency (2010) State and Outlook 2010 (SOER 2010), The European Environment: Material Resources and Waste

European Environment Agency (2012 update) State and Outlook 2010 (SOER 2010). The European Environment: Material Resources and Waste

Eurostat (2015) Environmental Data Centre on Natural Resources, 'Natural Resource Concepts'. http://ec.europa.eu/eurostat/web/environmental-data-centre-on-natural-resources/overview/natural-resource-concepts. Accessed 26 July 2015

Geiger R, Khan D, Kotzur M (2015) European Union Treaties: A Commentary: Treaty on European Union, Treaty on the Functioning of the European Union, Charter of Fundamental Rights of the European Union. C.H. Beck & Hart, North America (US and Canada)

Gerbrandy GJ, Arnon K (2014) Europa moet investeren in grondstoffendiplomatie. Int Spectator 68(1):29–34

POLINARES (2013) Project Results, Summary of Final Project. February 2013. Results. http://www.polinares.eu/news/preview.php?id=44. Accessed 19 Aug 2015

POLINARES (2015) EU Policy on Natural Resources: Competition and Collaboration in Access to Oil, Gas and Mineral Resources. http://www.polinares.eu/. Accessed 20 June 2015

Rijksoverheid (2013) Document, Bijlage bij Kamerbrief over Conflict Vrij Tin Initiatief. http://www.rijksoverheid.nl/documenten-en-publicaties/brieven/2013/08/01/bijlage-bij-kamerbrief-over-conflict-vrij-tin-initiatief.html. Accessed 31 May 2015

Styles P (2012) POLINARES, D5.1—Report on the Proposed Options, Policies and Roles for the EU. Working Paper No. 80. http://www.polinares.eu/docs/d5-1/polinares_wp5_chapter6.pdf. Accessed 29 May 2016

Tomlinson I (2011) Doubling food production to feed the 9 billion: a critical perspective on a key discourse of food security in the UK. doi:10.1016/j.jrurstud.2011.09.001

United Nations, Department of Economic and Social Affairs (2013) UN News, world population projected to reach 9.6. billion by 2050 http://www.un.org/en/development/desa/news/population/un-report-world-population-projected-to-reach-9-6-billion-by-2050.html. Accessed 23 July 2015

Part VI
The Future of EU Co-operation

Chapter 18
Flexibility, Differentiation and Simplification in the European Union: Remedies for the Future?

Jaap de Zwaan

Abstract On the basis of the present state of play regarding European Union (EU) policies and law, this contribution will analyse the future perspectives related to the further development of the EU integration process. An important element in this discussion concerns the principle of flexibility, the idea that—in order to have the overall integration process continued and, where possible, deepened—we have to allow for more differentiation with regard to the development of EU policies and the participation of Member States therein. On the other hand, in order to give sufficient contents to EU membership, all Member States have to respect at least a substantive minimum of treaty obligations. It is, furthermore, argued that possibilities for simplification of the treaty amendment procedure have to be examined. Essential preconditions to make such approaches successful are related to the involvement of the institutional framework and ordinary decision-making procedures of the EU. Finally, the question arises whether the composition of an acquis at "minimum" level should not have implications for applicant countries negotiating about their possible accession to the EU.

Keywords Basic values: Peace and Stability · Future of the EU · Flexibility and Differentiation · Enhanced co-operation · Institutional framework of the EU · Simplification · Enlargement

J. de Zwaan (✉)
The Hague University of Applied Sciences, The Hague, The Netherlands
e-mail: dezwaan@law.eur.nl

J. de Zwaan et al. (eds.), *Governance and Security Issues of the European Union*, DOI 10.1007/978-94-6265-144-9_18

Contents

18.1 Introduction

European Union (EU) co-operation is an integration process. Its objectives and achievements are much more intensive and ambitious compared to what is experienced in the classical frameworks of international co-operation.

In the course of time, the scope of EU policy domains and the number of Member States have increased substantially. It is clearly a gradual, but continuing process. At present, a number of third countries has applied for membership, and negotiations with several of them have already started. That said, the final targets of the overall process have not been identified.

If we want this process to continue effectively, we have to take into account today's serious challenges and obstacles. The economic crisis, the tensions at our common Eastern borders, the massive influx of asylum seekers coming from the Middle-East, Africa and Asia, and terrorism are important examples here. The European Union is also faced with differences with regard to economic development between the Member States and, still more evidently, between the present and candidate Member States. Moreover, Member States have witnessed a growing public Euroscepticism within their borders, whereas EU critical governments have come to power in a relatively high number of Member States. In the United Kingdom a discussion has even started on whether or not to withdraw from the Union.

Therefore, it is fair to assume that not all Member States are able or willing to participate in a further deepening of the co-operation.

In view of these considerations, this contribution will analyse modalities of differentiation and flexibility. Obviously, in applying such new working methods, certain conditions have to be respected.

Some simplification ideas will also be discussed. Finally, some considerations will be dedicated to the question to which extent the application of flexibility instruments within the group of existing Member States should have implications for new Member States of the Union.

18.2 Unity and Uniformity as Leading Principles

European Union co-operation is an intensive process. National economies, policies and societies have been integrated and a new governance system has come into being. The objectives of the European Union and, connected to that, the instruments implementing such objectives are decided upon according to a common set of principles and procedures. Once having adopted primary law objectives or secondary law decisions, their content is binding upon all Member States. Similarly, as to the process of implementation, Member States are generally obliged to reach the same results at the same time.

So, unity and uniformity are vital principles inherent to the EU co-operation process. The EU legal order and EU law and policies in principle apply to all partners in an equal manner.[1]

18.3 Instruments of Flexibility so Far

In view of the increasing number of policy domains in which the EU has become active, and the ever-growing number of Member States, a number of instruments allowing for flexible co-operation has been developed in practice.

They can be categorised as follows:

1. Derogations granted to Member States in an instrument of primary law allowing them not to participate in the development of certain common policies. The reservations granted to the United Kingdom and Denmark in the Maastricht

[1] See also Piris 2014, where it is stated on p. 1: "Respect for the unity dogma …. was justified by the necessity to build a common market. A common playing field had to be established:—the same rules had to apply,—they had to be interpreted in the same way by all,—an independent arbitrator had to check their implementation,—their infringement had to be subject to sanctions by a judge." He adds: "For years, the trend was also that the rule should be as complete as possible targeting total harmonisation of national laws." Furthermore, the principle of uniform interpretation is embedded in the several elements of Article 234 TFEU. The importance of that principle is also expressed in the case law of the Court of Justice, such as the judgment of 18 October 2007 in the Case C-195/06, KommAustria/ÖRF), ECR 2007 I-8817, notably consideration 24; In the context of flexible co-operation, reference is made to the traditional "acquis communautaire" as "the cornerstone of the European legal order". See Chatzistavrou 2014, p. 98.

Treaty regarding the introduction of the Euro are examples.[2] The British, Irish and Danish reservations—included in the Lisbon Treaty—not to participate in the Area of Freedom, Security and Justice co-operation are other examples.[3] That said, the nature of the British and Irish reservations in the last case has to be distinguished from the Danish one. Whereas the Danish reservation is an absolute one, the United Kingdom and Ireland possess the right to "opt in" regarding individual substance matters. Another example is the earlier British reservation to the so-called Protocol on Social Policy, annexed to the Treaty of Maastricht which was subsequently withdrawn when the Amsterdam Treaty entered into force.[4]

2. Conditions set in an instrument of primary law which have to be fulfilled by Member States before being able to participate in the development of a common policy. Here the co-operation in the Third Stage of the Economic and Monetary Union regarding the introduction of the Euro as a single currency is an example.[5]
3. Modalities of decision-making, such as the introduction of transitional periods and norms at minimum level, in primary and secondary law. These modalities reflect traditional legislative technics practised since the start of EU co-operation. For example, accession treaties traditionally contain many variants of transitional arrangements. Examples of norms at minimum level allowing for more far-reaching measures at national level, were several provisions regarding a common asylum and immigration policy introduced by the Amsterdam Treaty.[6] At present, the Treaty on the Functioning of the European Union (TFEU)[7] also contains provisions related to minimum prescriptions, such as Article 83(1) TFEU regarding the establishment of minimum rules concerning the definition of criminal offences, and sanctions in the areas of particularly serious crime with a cross-border dimension.
4. Possibility for a Member State to deviate from adopted common measures in case "grounds of national major needs" are at stake. An example here is the regime of Article 114(4–6) TFEU regarding the approximation of laws in the domain of the internal market.

---

[2] Protocols 15 (On certain provisions relating to the United Kingdom of Great Britain and Northern Ireland) and 16 (On certain provisions relating to Denmark) annexed to the treaties.

[3] Protocols 21(On the position of the United Kingdom and Ireland in respect of the area of freedom, security and justice) and 22 (On the position of Denmark) annexed to the treaties.

[4] Protocol on Social Policy and Agreement on social policy concluded between the Member States of the European Community with the exception of the United Kingdom of Great Britain and Northern Ireland, OJ C 191 of 29 July 1992, p. 90.

[5] See the transitional provisions of Articles 139 and 140 TFEU.

[6] Article 73 k EEC, as amended by the Amsterdam Treaty. The provisions were replaced by new versions in the Treaty of Lisbon: Part Three, Title V, TFEU, notably Chapter 2.

[7] Consolidated Version of the Treaty on the Functioning of the European Union, signed on 13 December 2007, OJ C 326 (entered into force on 1 December 2009) as amended on 26 October 2012 (TFEU), pp. 47–390.

5. Common decisions to be implemented not by all Member States, but by groups of Member States. The examples here are related to the domain of defence co-operation. On the one hand, we refer here to the concept of the coalitions of the willing.[8] On the other hand, the reference is to the concept of structured permanent co-operation.[9]
6. Limitation of the legal effect of the application of an EU instrument in the legal order of certain Member States. Here the British and Polish reservations to the Charter of Fundamental Rights of the EU are examples.[10]
7. The implementation of treaty objectives being performed in a first instance by smaller groups of Member States, as forerunner groups. The obvious example here is the instrument of enhanced co-operation, a principle introduced by the Amsterdam Treaty, the modalities of which have been refined by the Nice and the Lisbon Treaties.[11]
8. The implementation of treaty objectives achieved in a first instance through the conclusion of intergovernmental instruments, agreed upon by a number, but not the totality of Member States, before being transformed into instruments of proper EU co-operation. Here a number of decisions adopted by the group of Eurozone countries,[12] respectively by nearly all Member States has to be referred to.[13] The "Fiscal Compact Treaty" is here the most obvious example in that the text itself refers to transformation of the instrument in ordinary EU law.[14]

---

[8] Consolidated Version of the Treaty on European Union, signed on 13 December 2007, OJ C 326 (entered into force on 1 December 2009) as amended on 26 October 2012 (TEU), Articles 42(5) and 44.

[9] *Ibid.* Articles 42(6) and 46.

[10] Protocol 30 on the Application of the Charter of Fundamental Rights of the European Union to Poland and to the United Kingdom, annexed to the treaties. According to Article 1 of the Protocol the Charter does not extend the ability of the Court of Justice, or any court or tribunal of Poland or of the United Kingdom, to find that the laws, regulations or administrative provisions, practises or action of Poland or of the United Kingdom are inconsistent with the fundamental rights, freedoms and principles that it reaffirms.

[11] See for the most recent version: TEU, above n 8, Article 20 as well as TFEU, above n 7, Article 326–334.

[12] The European Financial Stability Facility Framework Agreement of 2010 (EFSF) and its successor text, the Treaty establishing the European Stability Mechanism (ESM) of 2011. In between the European Council in its decision 2011/199 of 25 March 2011 had amended Article 136 TFEU, by adding to that treaty provision a (third) para enabling the Euro-countries to establish a stability mechanism to be activated if indispensable to safeguard the stability of the euro area as a whole: OJ L 91 of 6 April 2011, p. 1. In its judgment of 27 November 2012 in Case C-370/12, Thomas Pringle/Ireland, the Court confirmed the validity of Decision 2011/199: ECLI:EU:C:2012:756.

[13] The Treaty on Stability, Coordination and Governance in the Economic and Monetary Union of 2012 (Fiscal Compact Treaty) concluded by all Member States with the exception of the Czech Republic and the United Kingdom, and the Agreement on the Transfer and Mutualisation of Contributions to the Single Resolution Fund of 2014 concluded by all Member States with the exception of Sweden and the United Kingdom.

[14] *Ibid.* Article 16 stating, shortly speaking, that within a period of five years necessary steps have to be taken to incorporate the substance of the treaty into the legal framework of the European Union.

9. Safeguard clauses aiming to protect the application and enforcement of obligations entered into by individual Member States before their participation in the EU integration process. A first example relates to the existence and completion of regional unions founded by the three Benelux countries.[15] Another example concerns the obligations of Member States arising from agreements concluded before 1 January 1958 respectively, for new Member States, the date of their accession.[16]

18.4 More Flexibility Is Needed

However, practice shows that more flexibility is needed. The enlargement of the EU from originally six states in the 1950s to now twenty-eight Member States is a great success. And there is still a number of new members to come, foremost among which are the remaining successor states of the former Socialist Yugoslav Republic. However, we must realise that already between the present Member States substantive differences do exist with regard to, for example, their level of economic development. In fact, it has become a more heterogeneous group.

Furthermore, the scope of EU objectives and competences has substantially been enlarged over the last decades. European co-operation started in the economic domain, with the internal market as its core business. Since the entry into force of the Maastricht Treaty, crucial complementary domains such as common foreign and security policy as well as justice and home affairs have been added to the list of responsibilities of the Union. In the economic domain, policies directly related to the working of the internal market such as agriculture, transport and common commercial policy, were already included in the first version of the Treaty establishing the European Economic Community (EEC). At a later stage—for example when the European Single Act entered into force in July 1987—domains such as environmental policy and research were added to the list of EEC competences. The Maastricht Treaty introduced the concept of the Economic and Monetary Union in the treaties as well as other domains of policy, such as education, consumer protection and culture.

When looking at the elements mentioned in conjunction and when thinking about the future of EU co-operation, it is to be expected that not all members will be able to accept, implement and enforce the same obligations exactly at the same time and in a uniform way.

[15] TFEU, above n 7, Article 350.

[16] *Ibid.* Article 351.

Moreover, what has been said about the existing Member States is all the more true if one considers the situation of third states having applied for accession[17] and countries having the ambition to do that at a certain moment in time.[18] For sure, the differences in development between these third countries compared to the group of present Member States are huge.

Another tendency, albeit of a different nature, has to do with discussions taking place in several Member States about the speed and scope of EU co-operation over time. Indeed, an increasing number of citizens believes that the integration process has been developed too fast, that its scope has become too wide, and that time has come to review the appropriateness to hand over more competences to the EU. This tendency has become manifest more specifically after the rejection of the Constitutional Treaty of 2004, following referenda in two Member States[19] in May and June 2005. As a consequence, that treaty, formally called the Treaty establishing a Constitution for Europe, never entered into force.

"Euroscepticism" has been given new dimensions, by the activities of Eurosceptic political parties in Member States and, connected to that tendency, by the emergence even of Eurosceptic governments in a number of Member States.[20] A variant of these "internal" discussions concerns the situation in the United Kingdom, where the conservative government of Prime Minister David Cameron being re-elected as a result of the national elections of 7 May 2015, claims that EU co-operation has to be reformed. In that context, a referendum on the continuation of the British membership has been held on 23 June 2016.[21]

Last but not least, the European Council of 26/27 June 2014 also expressed the opinion that the future development of the European Union allows for different paths of integration for different countries.[22] On 18 November 2015, Commission President Jean-Claude Juncker, speaking at a conference in Brussels, stated that a

---

[17] The reference here is to Turkey, Macedonia, Montenegro, Serbia and Albania which are countries having been granted the status of candidate Member State. The government of Iceland has suspended the negotiations for the accession of that country in June 2013. In March 2015 Iceland's government declared that Iceland should not be regarded as a candidate country for EU membership anymore.

[18] Bosnia-Herzegovina and Kosovo are so-called potential Member States.

[19] Respectively France and The Netherlands.

[20] In the year 2016 the reference is, for example, to the governments of the United Kingdom, Greece, the Slovak Republic, Hungary, Croatia and Poland; See also Von Ondarza 2016.

[21] The European Council of 17/18 December 2015 had a first "political exchange of views on the UK plans for an (in/out) referendum." The European Council meeting of 18/19 February 2016 agreed on a set of arrangements constituting, as it was called, "an appropriate response to the concerns of the United Kingdom": doc. EUCO 1/16 of 19 February 2016, under I.

[22] The precise text reads as follows: ".... the European Council noted that the concept of ever closer union allows for different paths of integration for different countries, allowing those that want to deepen integration to move ahead, while respecting the wish of those who do not want to deepen any further:" EUCO 79/14 of 27 June 2014, p. 11.

Two-Speed Europe is the future of an enlarged EU.[23] And, in its Decision concerning a new settlement for the United Kingdom within the European Union of 18/19 February 2016, the European Council repeated, virtually literarily, its statement of 26/27 June 2014. However, now it did so in a formal context. It was stated that the references, in the treaties, to "an ever closer union among the peoples are … compatible with different paths of integration being available for different Member States and do not compel all Member States to aim for a common destination."[24]

18.5 Options of Flexibility and Differentiation

In this discussion notably three instruments ask for attention.

18.5.1 Minimum Norms and Transitional Periods

In the first place, one can think—again—about the introduction of minimum norms and/or transitional periods to the benefit of individual Member States to implement decisions of primary or secondary law. Indeed, such approaches provide a degree of flexibility for individual Member States: those who prefer to go further than the level agreed upon, and those who need more time for the implementation of adopted common measures.

However, in practice the sole application of these technics will most probably not produce enough effect, at least not in the long term.

18.5.2 Enhanced Co-operation

It may be more challenging to review the conditions for the application of enhanced co-operation.[25] Enhanced co-operation is a principle introduced by the Amsterdam Treaty, the modalities of which have been refined by respectively the

---

[23] Guarascio 2015.

[24] Conclusions of the European Council meeting of 18/19 February 2016, doc. EUCO 1/16 of the same date, under Section C. Sovereignty, para 1, fourth sub-para. It is added—in the fifth sub-para—that the treaties allow "an evolution towards a deeper degree of integration among the Member States that share such a vision of their common future, without this applying to other Member States"; See for a recent contribution to the discussion about differentiated co-operation in the EU: AIV (2015). An earlier contribution is the publication former Director-General of the Legal Service of the Council: Piris 2012a.

[25] Ample literature has been dedicated to this subject matter over the time. See for some recent contributions: Kroll and Leuffen 2015; Piris 2014; Chatzistavrou 2014; Tekin and Wessels 2008.

Nice and the Lisbon Treaties.[26] It allows at least nine Member States to further the objectives of the Union, protect its interests and reinforce the integration process.[27] It is a means of last resort, when it is established that the objectives of such co-operation cannot be attained within a reasonable period of time by the Union as a whole.[28] Whereas the initial group can be considered as a sort of forerunner group, other Member States can join later.[29]

Now, practice shows that the principle is difficult to apply. Numerous conditions have been set in the treaties to prevent, on the one hand, interference with the domains of exclusive competence of the EU[30] and, on the other hand, the undermining of the working of the internal market as well as economic, social and territorial cohesion. Enhanced co-operation must also not constitute a barrier to or discrimination in trade between Member States, nor shall it distort competition between them.[31] These conditions have been made on purpose, in order to avoid that the core business of the EU is negatively affected by unilateral approaches of groups of individual Member States. In that respect, practising enhanced co-operation runs, of course, counter to the principles of unity and uniformity referred to earlier.[32] The aim was also to avoid the impression that within the European Union a group of second-class member states does exist, namely the twelve new Member States of Central and Eastern Europe who were negotiating their accession to the Union parallel to the Amsterdam negotiations. That said, in the first ten years after the entry into force of the relevant treaty provisions, enhanced co-operation has never been applied, and only three times in recent years in the following domains: divorce law as a dimension of European family law,[33] the European patent[34] and the international financial tax.[35]

---

[26] See for the present treaty texts: TEU, above n 8, Article 20 TEU and TFEU, above n 7, Articles 326 to 334.

[27] TEU, above n 8, Article 20(1), second sub-para.

[28] *Ibid.* Article 20(2).

[29] TFEU, above n 7, Article 331(2).

[30] TEU, above n 8, Article 20(1), first sub-para.

[31] TFEU, above n 7, Article 326, second sub-para.

[32] See Sect. 18.2.

[33] Council Regulation 1259/2010 of 20 December 2010 implementing enhanced co-operation in the area of the law applicable to divorce and legal separation, OJ L 343 of 29 December 2010, pp. 10–16.

[34] Council Decision 2011/167 of 10 March 2011 authorising enhanced co-operation in the area of the creation of unitary patent protection, OJ L 76 of 22 March 2011, pp. 53–55. In a judgment of 16 April 2013 in the joined cases C-274/11 and C-295/11, Kingdom of Spain/Council and Italian Republic/Council, the Court of Justice dismissed appeals, made by Spain and Italy, against this decision: ECLI:EU:C:2013:240.

[35] Council Decision 2013/52 of 22 January 2013 authorising enhanced co-operation in the area of financial transaction tax, OJ L 22 of 25 January 2013, pp. 11–12. In a judgment of 30 April 2014 in case C-209/13, United Kingdom/Council, the Court of Justice dismissed an appeal, made by the United Kingdom, against this decision: ECLI:EU:C:2014:283.

The question therefore arises whether the procedural rules on how to apply the principle should not be simplified. For example, the requirement concerning a "positive" mandate of the Council[36] to allow a group of at least nine Member States to proceed,[37] could be replaced by a simple condition that a number of Member States representing a "substantial" part of the EU population is willing to implement the Treaty objectives. In this respect, and taking into account the new arrangements for qualified majority voting in the Council as of application since 1 November 2014,[38] one could think at a level of (at least) 45% of the number of Member States comprising (at least) 50% of the overall population of the European Union. In doing so, a certain "critical mass" of Member States supporting the amendments is ensured.[39]

An important side effect of such a new scenario is that a blocking minority of Member States within the Council[40] will not be able to prevent enhanced co-operation to be applied.

Another issue that has to be amended is related to the fact that, in order to have enhanced co-operation applied, the Commission has to submit a formal proposal to the Council.[41] After all, this is a strange requirement in a situation where the Commission already put a first proposal on the table that, however, could not be adopted within a reasonable period of time because the required majority was lacking in the Council.[42] Therefore, and considering that enhanced co-operation essentially aims to further the objectives of the Union and to reinforce the integration process,[43] a "confirmation" by the Commission of an initiative taken by the (small) group of Member States concerned should suffice. So, the appropriate scenario would be that an initiative coming from such a group of Member States only

---

36 To be decided upon by qualified majority, on a proposal from the Commission and with the consent of the European Parliament.

37 TFEU, above n 7, Article 329(1).

38 TEU, above n 8, Article 16(4): at least 55% of the members of the Council, comprising at least fifteen of them and representing Member States comprising at least 65% of the population of the Union.

39 See also: De Zwaan 2015, notably Chapter 9a, pp. 256–258. See for a similar approach AIV (2015), notably p. 17 respectively pp. 30 and 31.

40 Including at least four Council members, see the elements mentioned in TEU, above n 8, Article 16(4), second sub-para.

41 TEU, above n 8, Article 20(2), to be read in conjunction with TFEU, above n 7, Article 329(1). In the last provision it is said, that in the event the Commission will not submit a proposal, it shall inform the Member States concerned of the reasons for not doing so.

42 TEU, above n 8, Article 20(2).

43 *Ibid.* Article 20(1), second sub-para.

has to be confirmed by the Commission, in view of its general mission to protect the general interest of the European Union.[44]

As prescribed in the text of the Treaty on European Union (TEU) as it stands, acts adopted in the framework of enhanced co-operation shall only bind the participating Member States.[45] Yet, unlike the situation at present,[46] decisions adopted by applying the principle of enhanced co-operation should be regarded as part of the acquis to be accepted by future Member States. The main reason for such an alternative approach is that, as already mentioned, the principle of enhanced co-operation essentially aims to further the objectives of the Union. To that extent, the principle of enhanced co-operation is in harmony with the programme subscribed and agreed to by all Member States.

18.5.3 Primary Law Derogations

It is only in the last instance that derogations granted to individual Member States to exempt them from participation in certain EU policies come to mind. Derogations from the obligation to implement treaty objectives can in principle only be envisaged when such issues have been dealt with during negotiations at primary law level. On the contrary, derogations to secondary law objectives and decisions are not conceivable when not "covered" by a derogation, granted at primary law level, for the policy domain concerned. Indeed, such derogations would run counter to the principles of unity and uniformity, the idea that European co-operation is an integration process, aiming to develop common approaches in policy areas selected and commonly agreed to by all Member States.[47] So, whereas transitional periods provide the Member State(s) concerned (only) with an extra deadline for the implementation of certain measures; and whereas enhanced co-operation is an instrument allowing (small) groups of Member States to act in certain policy domains as "fore runners," derogations granted at primary law level enable Member State(s) not to participate in a certain policy domain, possibly even for an unlimited period of time.

---

[44] Such new arrangements, once applied in practice, would have similar effects compared to some specific procedures in the Area of Freedom, Security and Justice context (Title V, Part Three, TFEU). Indeed, there it is said that, in case of disagreement in the Council and the European Council about certain files—all related to the areas of criminal law and police co-operation—the authorization to start enhance cooperation "shall be deemed to be granted": see TFEU, above n 7, Articles 82(3), 83(3), 86(1) and 87(3).

[45] TEU, above n 8, Article 20(4), first sentence.

[46] *Ibid.* Article 20(4), second sentence.

[47] See Sect. 18.2.

In fact, the granting of such far-reaching derogations is difficult to understand—and to justify—considering that the objectives linked to the policy domain concerned have been explicitly subscribed to by the Member State(s) in question. On the other hand, would the instrument not exist, then the Member State concerned would be able to block the Union to start co-operation in that domain.[48] So, it is a matter of making choices: either the Union cannot proceed, or the Union can do so, however, without all Member States participating.

As already mentioned, primary law derogations have in practice been granted in certain cases.[49] With regard to their justification, essentially political arguments have been put forward. In most cases, the Member State(s) concerned essentially didn't accept the EU to be involved in the policy matter at stake.

Of course, one may argue that at the level of treaty-making, Member States can afford themselves a lot. Indeed, Member States are, as it is called in German, "die Herren der Verträge", so the "owners of the European Union" and the supreme governance authority at European level. Nonetheless, Member States should not be put in such a position that they, as it were, are entitled to not participate in the process regarding the implementation of fundamental treaty objectives. In that respect, for example, the granting of a complete derogation to participate in the Area of Freedom, Security and Justice co-operation to the United Kingdom, Ireland and Denmark is to be criticized. This applies particularly with regard to the visa, asylum and immigration dimensions of the Area, all being domains directly linked to the working of one of the fundamental principles of the internal market, namely free movement of persons. On the other hand, primary law derogations may eventually be considered "acceptable" once there is no linkage, at least not a direct one, with the working of the internal market.

18.6 Context and Pre-conditions

18.6.1 Solidity and Stability of the European Union Structures

In all this we have to keep in mind that the stability of the overall EU construction should not be put in danger by the non-participation of individual Member States in certain policy areas. Indeed, practising differentiated co-operation should not have as a consequence that the quality and coherence of the overall integration process is affected negatively, or will water down. So, in all circumstances, individual Member States should not be allowed to escape from fundamental

---

[48] Treaty amendments require a common accord between Member States: TEU, above n 8, Article 48(4).

[49] See Sect. 18.3 under 1.

obligations. To put it differently, a basic and solid framework of co-operation composed of crucial policies and principles must be respected by all Member States at all times.

In this context, the values of peace and stability we can enjoy now since more than seventy years on (the biggest part of) our European continent, should also not be put in danger. Indeed, political stability and peace in Europe are served by the availability of substantive and disciplinary mechanisms guaranteeing that vital issues having a cross-boundary effect are being discussed and decided upon at the negotiation table, and at European level.

18.6.2 Institutional Framework of the European Union

Another vital element concerns the framework in which differentiated co-operation is practised. Here we should stress that the idea of differentiation cannot be looked at in isolation. In fact it is, and should be, directly related to the application of the ordinary EU rules and procedures, thus the rules of decision-making referred to as the "Community method".[50] In other words, once models of differentiated models are developed, that should be done by making use of the institutional framework of the European Union.

Certainly, such an approach may give rise to questions and problems. As to the *Council*, a first example is provided in Article 20, para 3, TEU. According to that provision regarding enhanced co-operation, all members may participate in the deliberations of the Council. However, only members representing Member States participating in enhanced co-operation shall take part in the vote.[51] As to the *Commission*, it is logical that this institution acts in its ordinary composition, thus including members originating from all Member States. Here, the unique, supranational character of the role of the Commission as caretaker of the interests of the European Union as a whole has to be underlined. The same holds true with regard

[50] In French: «la méthode communautaire». The reference is to the former EEC, the European Economic Community, the predecessor organisation of the European Union in the context of which the so-called "supranational" procedures have been developed. See for the impact the Lisbon Treaty has had on the working of these procedures: De Zwaan 2012. See for another contribution about the impact of recent developments on the "Community" method: Dero-Bugny 2014.

[51] It is added that the voting rules are set out in Article 330 TFEU. According to that treaty provision unanimity shall be constituted by the votes of the representatives of the participating Member States, whereas a qualified majority will be defined in accordance with Article 238(3) TFEU. According to that last provision qualified majority shall be defined as "at least 55% of the members of the Council representing the participating Member States, comprising at least 65% of the population of these States".

to the mission of the *Court of Justice*. Indeed, the Court has a responsibility to ensure a correct and uniform application and interpretation of EU law provisions[52] in the whole territory of the European Union. As to the *European Parliament,* one may think differently. However, the same conclusion has to be drawn in the end. In fact, the European Parliament is composed of members being directly elected by the citizens of all Member States. Although the number of members of the European Parliament has been fixed and a system has been developed to distribute that number over the Member States,[53] members of the European Parliament in practice do not represent "their" Member State, but ordinary citizens of that state. In that capacity, they are entitled to be involved in the policy making regarding all treaty objectives subscribed to by all Member States, so independent of the fact whether or not their "own" Member State does co-operate in a given domain. Having said that, it might be a good idea to create a specialised parliamentary committee within the European Parliament's infrastructure, composed of members of Eurozone countries, where exclusively Eurozone issues are discussed. That committee should then report to the plenary, that is the European Parliament as a whole.[54]

18.7 Acquis at Minimum-Level

Once applying models of differentiated co-operation, we have to keep in mind that at least certain "core" obligations will (remain to) be respected by all Member States.[55]

Reflecting on the content of such an acquis at "minimum"-level, a first reference concerns the basic values of EU co-operation in relation to the minimum requirements of EU membership. In the second instance, all Member States should be involved in the co-operation regarding the core businesses of the Union, notably the internal market which from the outset has been its primary and most fundamental objective. Another criterion refers to the level of competence of the Union in policy areas: the more competences the Union possesses in a given area, the fewer possibilities exist for differentiated co-operation.[56] That means for example that, in those areas where the Union is exclusively competent, no possibilities at

[52] TEU, above n 8, Article 19(1), first sub-para.

[53] See for both elements TEU, above n 8, Article 14(2).

[54] Jean-Claude Piris is of the opinion that, in the context of the Eurozone co-operation, only representatives of Eurozone countries should participate in the decision-making in the Council (as has already been provided for by the treaties) but also in the European Parliament: Piris 2014, p. 3. Of this author also: Piris 2012b.

[55] See for this discussion also: De Zwaan 2014, pp. 30–32.

[56] See for the list of categories of Union competences: TFEU, above n 7, Articles 2 to 6.

all do exist to apply differentiated co-operation.[57] On the contrary, in domains where the Union possesses shared[58] or only marginal[59] competences, models of differentiated co-operation should be easier to practise.

In connection with the foregoing a reference can also be made to the functioning of the subsidiarity principle in areas of competences shared between the European Union and the Member States.[60] Indeed, the application of the subsidiarity principle aims to designate in those areas the most appropriate level where action has to be taken—the European level or the national one.[61] To that extent, the way the subsidiarity principle is applied by the institutions is instrumental in determining the dividing lines and the balance between the responsibilities of the European Union and the Member States in areas where both governance levels are competent. In so doing, the application of subsidiarity can also serve as a tool to indicate the margins for differentiated co-operation, particularly for enhanced co-operation.

Applying the criteria just mentioned,[62] a "hierarchical" order of EU principles and policies can be established. In view of the present stage of EU co-operation, such an order can be presented as follows:

1. Basic values of EU co-operation regarding human dignity, freedom, democracy, equality, the rule of law and the respect for human rights, including minority rights.[63] The so-called Copenhagen criteria of 1993 regarding the accession of new Member States are directly connected to this list. "Copenhagen" refers also to complementary criteria such as the existence of a market economy, as well as the capacity of the European Union to receive more Member States (the so-called "absorption capacity");[64]

[57] TFEU, above n 7, Article 3(1) refers to: customs union; competition rules; monetary policy (for those Member States whose currency is the Euro); conservation of marine biological resources; and common commercial policy.

[58] *Ibid.* Article 4. In this provision important policy domains are listed such as the internal market, agriculture, environment, transport and the area of freedom, security and justice.

[59] *Ibid.* Article 6. The areas are listed where the Union possesses (only) so-called supporting, coordinating or supplementing competences.

[60] TEU, above n 8, Article 5(3).

[61] *Ibid.* The wording of para 3 of Article 5(3) reads: " … the Union shall act only if and in so far as the objectives of the proposed action cannot be sufficiently achieved by the Member States ….. but can rather, by reason of the scale or effects of the proposed action, be better achieved at Union level."

[62] Compare in this context also the pre-conditions, earlier mentioned (see Sect. 18.5.2.), for the application of the principle of enhanced co-operation: as explained, that principle cannot be applied in those areas covered by exclusive competences of the European Union and may not undermine the internal market or economic, social and territorial cohesion.

[63] TEU, above n 8, Article 2.

[64] The Copenhagen criteria are implicitly referred to in Article 49, first sub-para: "The conditions of eligibility agreed upon by the European Council shall be taken into account." For the Copenhagen criteria, see: Conclusions of the European Council of Copenhagen of 21–22 June 1993 (SN180/1/93): http://www.consilium.europa.eu/uedocs/cms_data/docs/pressdata/nl/ec/72923.pdf. The relevant passages are to be found in para 7.A.iii, page 14.

2. Internal market law and policy;[65]
3. Policies where the EU possesses exclusive[66] or close to exclusive competences, such as agriculture and fisheries;[67]
4. Policies directly linked to the working of the internal market, such as transport and trans-European networks;[68]
5. Common foreign and security policy, *i.e.* at least the dimension regarding the *development* of that policy;[69]
6. Aliens policy, *i.e.* the acquis regarding external border controls, visa policy, asylum and immigration, so those dimensions of the Area of Freedom, Security and Justice which in their working are closely related to the internal market;[70]
7. Policies closely linked to the working of the internal market, such as environment and climate change;[71]
8. Police co-operation, the law enforcement dimension of the Area of Freedom, Security and Justice co-operation;[72]
9. *Coordination* of the economic policies of the Member States, which is a component of the broader domain of the Economic and Monetary Union.[73]

On the contrary, variants of flexibility, applied either on a temporary basis or even permanently, can be envisaged in policy domains not being linked to the working of the internal market, and thus, having a more "autonomous" character, or in

---

[65] TFEU, above n 7, Article 4(2) under a. The reason why the internal market is listed under the category "shared" competences of the Union is due to the fact that Member States always retain competences to restrict the working of free movement by virtue of the protection of fundamental interests, such as public policy, public security and policy health: see Articles 36 (goods) respectively 45(3) (persons) TFEU.

[66] See TFEU, above n 7, Article 3. See also above n 57.

[67] Both areas mentioned in TFEU, above n 7, Article 4(2) under d.

[68] Mentioned in TFEU, above n 7, Article 4(2) under g. (transport) respectively h. (networks).

[69] CFSP is referred to in Article 2(4) TFEU. The option mentioned is connected to the "development" of CFSP, not to the "implementation" of CFSP decisions. It also does not relate to defence. On the contrary, these other subject matters are mentioned in the list of policy domains where flexibility may be allowed.

[70] The AFSJ is mentioned in TFEU, above n 7, Article 4(2) under j. See for the topics mentioned: Part Three, Title V, Chapter 2 TFEU.

[71] Environment is mentioned in TFEU, above n 7, Article 4(2) under e. Climate change is referred to in the treaty title on environment, in Article 191(1), fourth indent, TFEU.

[72] Part Three, Title V, Chapter 5 TFEU. Certainly, this domain is essentially a domain characterised by national competences. However, to the extent the Union possesses policy making competences, all Member States should participate.

[73] This subject matter is related to a special part of the EMU arrangements, that is Chapter 1, Economic Policy, Title VIII, Part Tree, TFEU, Article 120 et seq. The obligation of Member States concerns (only) their obligation to participate in the process to coordinate national policies, thus not an obligation to agree on the exact content of such policies. To that extent the Monetary Policy domain, including the arrangements regarding the introduction of the single currency, falls outside the scope of this option. This last domain rather belongs to the areas where flexibility can be allowed.

policy areas where the EU possesses less competences.[74] These areas, again, looked at from the perspective of the present stage of EU co-operation, are the following, although in this case listed in a "hierarchical" order reflecting the "intensity" of EU involvement:

10. Common foreign and security policy, *i.e.* the dimension regarding the *implementation* of that policy, and defence policy;[75]
11. *Monetary* policy, including the acquis regarding the introduction of the Euro as common currency;[76]
12. Civil law and criminal law co-operation, the two final dimensions of the Area of Freedom, Security and Justice co-operation;[77]
13. Policies less closely linked to the working of the internal market, such as social and regional policy, energy and research;[78]
14. Policies where the EU (only) possesses so-called supportive, coordinating and supplementing competences, such as culture, education and public health.[79]

Now, certainly, one may wonder how concepts like "directly linked," "closely linked" and "less closely linked" are related to the working of the internal market. A very precise answer cannot be given here. In fact, the degree of connection of the policy domains mentioned with the internal market co-operation serves primarily to underpin the positioning of those policies in the presented hierarchy of Union policies. When it comes to concrete action, and in order to ascertain to what extent differentiated co-operation in those policy areas is at all possible, ultimately an assessment has to be made to ensure that a measure proposed does not interfere with existing internal market law and policy.

In light of the foregoing, and in order to qualify as a full-fledged "member" of the European Union, a state should at least participate in the co-operation regarding the policy domains mentioned under the points 1–9. These elements compose, as it were, the "core acquis" or the "acquis at minimum level" of EU membership. Indeed, going lower than that level would lead to a relationship hardly to be qualified as "membership", but more as a sort of "partnership". In that respect, and as already been touched upon,[80] the derogations granted to the United Kingdom, Ireland and Denmark regarding to the whole Area of Freedom, Security and Justice co-operation are in fact not compatible with the—assumed—commitment

[74] See for a similar approach AIV (2015), notably pp. 18 and 19 respectively p. 31.

[75] See above n 69.

[76] See above n 73.

[77] TFEU, above n 7, Part Three, Title V, Chapters 3 and 4.

[78] Mentioned in TFEU, above n 7, Article 4 under b. (social), c. (regional) and i. (energy) respectively in Article 4(3) (research).

[79] TFEU, above n 7, Article 6. The topics mentioned are listed under a. (health), c. (culture) and e. (education). See also above n 59.

[80] See Sect. 18.5.3.

of "real" Member States to participate in the co-operation concerning that minimum-acquis. The reason being that, as has been explained, at least the dimensions of the Area regarding border controls, visa, asylum and immigration policy belong to that minimum-acquis. The way the European Union is handling the migration crisis of 2015/2016 demonstrates the merits of this finding. Indeed, the countries mentioned have not been essentially affected by issues like the relocation of migrants coming from Syria and other countries.

18.8 New Steps not Being Approved by All Member States

So far models have been discussed in the context of which individual Member States may be exempted from the obligation to participate, right from the start, in the process of implementation of objectives they themselves have subscribed and agreed to.

However, one may wonder whether time has not come to go further. An alternative, for example, could be a model according to which new objectives in the process of European integration do not necessarily have to be approved by all Member States. In such a model, it would be required that those new horizons are subscribed to only by a (large) majority of Member States, whereas those Member States not willing—or able—to subscribe to the new obligations, would not be bound by them, and therefore also not obliged to implement them.[81] Of course, as a preliminary condition, such new steps in the integration process should not interfere negatively with existing policies, but have a rather autonomous character. Nonetheless, the idea is that such a group of Member States, although not constituting the totality of Member States and willing to agree on such new steps, can still make use of the ordinary EU institutions and procedures as in the normal situation. Equally, the contents of such new measures shall not be regarded as part of the European Union acquis to be respected by future Member States.[82]

The idea may sound revolutionary. But, when it comes to its effects, the model essentially is the reverse side of the one concerning Member States having explicitly agreed to include new policy domains in the treaty, although not being obliged to participate in the process of their implementation.

[81] As is the situation at present once applying enhanced co-operation: TEU, above n 8, Article 20(4), first sentence.

[82] Again, as is the case at present when applying enhanced co-operation: TEU, above n 8, Article 20(4), second sentence. However, in the paragraph regarding enhanced co-operation, see Sect. 18.5.2, it has been proposed to amend this element in such a way that enhanced co-operation measures in future would belong to the acquis to be respected (also) by future Member States.

18.9 Simplification of Treaty Amendment Procedures

Now, of course, in order to have the proposals presented in this article adopted, the treaties have to be amended in several ways. This is in particular true with regard to the new modalities of enhanced co-operation[83] and the principle that not all Member States have to approve new policies and/or objectives of the European Union.[84]

However, treaty change is a complicated process. The present rules and procedures for treaty amendments are embedded in Article 48 of the Treaty on European Union. Inherent to these rules and procedures is that all stages are governed by consensus: the outcome of negotiations has to be accepted by all Member States; the text of an agreement has to be signed by all Member States; and the agreement has to be approved, at national level, by the parliaments of all the Member States. In practice, therefore, each individual Member State possesses a right of veto in all stages mentioned. Therefore, because EU co-operation is a gradual process, practically each substantive new step has to be accompanied by treaty change, an alternative and lighter instrument not being available.

Therefore, the question arises whether possibilities for simplification should not be analysed. Or, to put it differently, to reconsider the principle that each individual Member State can veto new developments in the integration process.[85]

At the present state of EU law, there do already exist two variants of a so-called simplified revision procedure, both of them introduced by the Lisbon Treaty:[86]

- Amendment of all or part of the provisions of Part Three TFEU relating to the internal policies and action of the Union.[87] According to this procedure, it is up to the European Council to take a unanimous decision, after having consulted the European Parliament and the Commission;[88]
- Amendment of the modalities of decision-making in a given area: from unanimity to qualified majority voting, and from the application of the "special" legislative procedure to the "ordinary" one.[89] According to this procedure, the European Council can act by unanimity after having obtained the consent of the European Parliament.

---

[83] See Sect. 18.5.2.

[84] See Sect. 18.8.

[85] For good order it is added here that the procedures regarding treaty amendment have to be distinguished from the application of the so-called "passerelle" provisions of Article 333 TFEU. According to these provisions the Council may—with respect to treaty provisions to be applied in the context of enhanced co-operation—decide unanimously to amend "unanimity" as requirement for Council decisions into "qualified majority" (para 1) respectively to replace the reference to a "special" legislative procedure by the "ordinary" legislative procedure (para 2).

[86] See also De Zwaan 2015, Chapter 9b.

[87] TEU, above n 8, Article 48(6).

[88] Also the European Central Bank will be consulted in case of institutional changes in the monetary area: TEU, above n 8, Article 48(6), second sub-para.

[89] TEU, above n 8, Article 48(7).

Certainly, these options do represent an efficient approach with regard to treaty amendments of a relatively low importance. On the other hand, the application of both procedures still requires a formal approval of all Member States before the amendments concerned can enter into force. Indeed, in case of amendments to Part III TFEU, the first option, *i.e.* an approval by all Member States, has to be provided in accordance with their respective constitutional requirements, which in practice refers to approval by national parliaments.[90] Once applying the second option related to institutional rearrangements, the amending decision has to be notified to national parliaments. In case (only) one national parliament makes known its opposition, the decision concerned shall not be adopted.[91]

Nonetheless, in order to bring Union co-operation forward a more far-reaching formula may be considered.[92]

In that context, one can imagine that groups of Member States—so, again, not necessarily all Member States—may be allowed to respectively start negotiations to amend existing treaty provisions, sign the results of these negotiations, and have them applied in their mutual relations. Let's say, as a point of departure, that treaty amendments thus concluded should become binding for at least three quarters of the Member States, that means in the present situation, 21 out of 28.

Equally—and that also would imply an important deviation of the present requirements—such treaty amendments should no longer be formally approved at national level by all 28 national parliaments. On the contrary, in line with the procedure of Article 48(7) TEU, national parliaments may reject such treaty amendments within a certain period—say, nine months——after the adoption of the texts concerned. However, unlike that last procedure, in such a case the treaty amendments concerned can still enter into force when (at least) 21 national parliaments

[90] TEU, above n 8, Article 48(6), second sub-para.

[91] TEU, above n 8, Article 48(7), third sub-para.

[92] See also De Zwaan 2014, pp. 37–39. Also the former ECSC Treaty contained a formula for a simplified treaty amendment procedure: in Article 95, third and fourth sub-para, ECSC it was stated that when an adaptation of the rules for the Commission's exercise of its powers was felt necessary, appropriate amendments could be proposed jointly by the Commission and the Council- acting by twelve-fifteenth majority of its members. Such proposals had to be submitted to the Court for its opinion. Once the Court had ruled that the proposals were compatible with the conditions set, they were forwarded to the European Parliament and could enter into force if approved by a majority of three quarters of the votes cast and two thirds of the members of the Parliament.

do not object to the amendments.[93] And, of course, the Member State whose national parliament has objected shall not be bound.

An important consequence of this new scenario would be that individual Member States no longer possess a right to veto new developments, as is the situation now. On the other hand, a Member State cannot be bound to such new developments against its will. Therefore, it seems that this new approach is legitimate and democratically justified. Also, as was discussed with regard to new policy decisions not approved by all Member States,[94] the contents of the new amendments shall not be regarded as part of the European Union acquis to be respected by future Member States.

Now, of course, in order to have these changes accepted, they first have to be approved according to the existing procedure for treaty amendment. That means, by going through all stages and steps already mentioned and, more importantly, after being accepted and approved by all Member States.[95]

18.10 Implications for Third Countries and Accession

Earlier, the profile of an EU membership at "minimum"-level, to be respected by all states aiming to be referred to as "true" Member State of the Union, was discussed.[96] At the same time, one can imagine that the design of such a minimum approach of EU membership should have implications as well for third countries having applied, or having the ambition to apply, for membership. Would they be entitled, as it were, to invoke the concept of such a minimum package, and to claim that they, once accepting the package, should be able to formally accede to the European Union?

---

[93] These proposals bear a slight resemblance to the options mentioned in Article 41(1) of the Vienna Convention on the Law of Treaties of 23 May 1969: https://treaties.un.org/doc/Publication/UNTS/Volume%201155/volume-1155-I-18232-English.pdf. According to this provision two or more of the parties to a multilateral treaty may conclude an agreement to modify the treaty as between themselves alone if: (a) the possibility of such a modification is provided for by the treaty; or (b) the modification in question is not prohibited by the treaty and: (i) does not affect the enjoyment by the other parties of their rights under the treaty or the performance of their obligations; respectively (ii) does not relate to a provision, derogation from which is incompatible with the effective execution of the object and purpose of the treaty as a whole. In the study of the Spinelli Group (2013), the possibility of amending the treaties without all Member States agreeing to it has also been dealt with. According to their proposal no Member State is entitled to block a treaty amendment, whereas for the adoption of such an amendment a majority of three quarters of the Member States is required. According to the same proposal a treaty amendment may enter into force once the ratification by four fifths of the number of Member States representing half of the overall population of the Union has been completed: pp. 85 and 89–91.

[94] See Sect. 18.8.

[95] TEU, above n 8, Article 48(2–5).

[96] See Sect. 18.7, more particularly the "nine points" acquis.

By way of preliminary point of reference, it must be recalled, that states aiming to become a Member State of the European Union must, first of all, respect the minimum-requirements for membership as mentioned in Article 2 TEU, to be read in conjunction with Article 49 TEU.[97] Secondly, such states must subscribe to all existing objectives of EU co-operation. That said, there are arguments to support the thesis that third states that fulfil the minimum-requirements of membership and subscribe to all EU objectives, should be able to accede to the EU once they commit themselves to implement (at least) the core acquis of the EU at minimum level, eventually after the expiration of a transitional period.

Now, again, in order to have this new approach accepted, political will is needed with all present Member States. On the other hand, one may argue that the vital interests of security and stability on the European continent require such a more flexible approach. This is all the more so because possible future Member States lag generally far behind with regard to their economic development, for example.[98]

18.11 Final Remarks

Whereas originally the European Union was composed of a homogeneous group of Member States, the EU is nowadays characterised by heterogeneity in several respects.

In order to bring the EU further, and to provide it with a new and long-term perspective, we have to rethink the appropriateness of fundamental existing principles of co-operation, such as unity and uniformity. We have to reflect how to make them more flexible. Flexibility, differentiation and simplification are the guiding principles in this discussion.

In this process we have to be creative. On the other hand, a stable acquis at "minimum" level has to be respected by all Member States.

All in all, one should not shy away from reflecting about proposals requiring an amendment of the existing treaty texts. People, politicians in the first place, might argue that the momentum is not ripe to have such proposals discussed, let alone adopted by all Member States. That may be true. However, that doesn't mean that we should not think, or start to think, about such reforms. Reflecting on forms of flexibility, differentiation and simplification serves the interests of the European Union itself, its Member States and its citizens. Such a new approach can only but contribute to securing the basic values of peace and stability on our European continent, now and in the future.

---

[97] See Sect. 18.7 under 1; see above n 63 and 64.

[98] See Sect. 18.4.

References

AIV (2015) Advisory Council on International Affairs of the Dutch Minister of Foreign Affairs of October 2015, Gedifferentieerde integratie, verschillende routes in de EU-samenwerking (Flexible cooperation: different routes within the EU co-operation), no. 98, October 2015: www.aiv-advies.nl (English version not yet available)

Chatzistavrou F (2014) Is flexible integration harming the prospect of a common acquis? Int Spectator Ital J Int Aff 49(1):98–112

Dero-Bugny D (2014) La dilution de la méthode communautaire et la diversification des pratiques intergouvernementales, Revue de l'OFCE 2014/3, ISBN 9782312008370, no. 134, pp 65–74

De Zwaan J (2012) The Treaty of Lisbon, towards a more supranational legal order of the European Union. In: Foblets M-C, Hildebrandt M, Steenbergen J (eds) Liber Amicorum René Foqué, Larcier. Boom Juridische Uitgevers, pp 301–319

De Zwaan J (2014) De voortgang van de Europese integratie, wisselwerking tussen recht en beleid ("Progress of the European integration process, interaction between law and policy"), Valedictory Lecture of 14 March 2014 at the Erasmus University Rotterdam, Erasmus Law Lectures 35, Boom Juridische Uitgevers

De Zwaan J (2015) European Integration and Democracy: A Gradual Process, with Certain Limits, Contribution to the European Group of Public Law (EGPL). In: Conference of 13–14 Sept 2014 in Spetses, Greece, dedicated to "New challenges of democracy/Nouveaux défis à la démocratie" and organised by the European Public Law Organisation (EPLO) in Athens, Greece, European Public Law Series/Bibliothèque de droit public européen, Volume CXVI, EPLO 2015, pp 219–266

Guarascio F (2015) 'Two-speed Europe is the future of enlarged EU, Juncker says' http://uk.reuters.com/article/uk-britain-eu-juncker-idUKKCN0T72N320151118. Accessed 1 June 2016

Kroll D, Leuffen D (2015), Enhanced co-operation in practice. An analysis of differentiated integration in EU secondary law. J Eur Public Policy 22(3):353–373

Piris J-Cl (2012a) The future of Europe, towards a two-speed EU. Cambridge University Press, Cambridge

Piris J-Cl (2012b) The issue: could rescuing the €-17 fatally weaken the EU? My verdict: no, there are several models for a "two-speed Europe", Europe's World Newsletter of 6 December 2012: www.europesworld.org

Piris J-Cl (2014) The acceleration of differentiated integration and enhanced co-operation, Fondation Robert Schuman/European Issues no. 328 of 13 October 2014, pp 1–5

Spinelli Group (2013) A fundamental law of the European Union, 2013 Verlag Bertelsmann Stiftung, Gütersloh

Tekin F, Wessels W (2008) Flexibility within the Lisbon Treaty, trademark or empty promise. EIPASCOPE 2008(1):25–31

Von Ondarza N (2016) Euro-sceptics in power, Stiftung Wissenschaft und Politik, SWP Comments 17 Apr 2016

MIX
Papier aus verantwortungsvollen Quellen
Paper from responsible sources
FSC® C105338

If you have any concerns about our products,
you can contact us on
ProductSafety@springernature.com

In case Publisher is established outside the EU,
the EU authorized representative is:
Springer Nature Customer Service Center GmbH
Europaplatz 3, 69115 Heidelberg, Germany

Printed by Libri Plureos GmbH
in Hamburg, Germany